PLATO'S LITERARY GARDEN

Plato's Literary Garden

HOW TO READ A PLATONIC DIALOGUE

Kenneth M. Sayre

University of Notre Dame
Notre Dame, Indiana

Copyright © 1995
University of Notre Dame
Notre Dame, Indiana 46556
All Rights Reserved
http://www.undpress.nd.edu
Manufactured in the United States of America

Paperback printed in 2002

Library of Congress Cataloging-in-Publication Data
Sayre, Kenneth, M., 1928–
Plato's literary garden : how to read a Platonic dialogue / by
Kenneth M. Sayre.
p   cm.
Includes bibliographical references and indexes.
ISBN 0-268-03808-2 (hardcover : alk. paper)
ISBN 0-268-03876-7 (paper : alk. paper)
1. Plato.   2. Imaginary conversations.   I. Title.
B395.S28   1995
184—dc20   95-16521
                                                            CIP

TO PATTI

CONTENTS

PREFACE

This book is intended as an introduction to the love of wisdom (i.e., to philosophy) as Plato conceived it. The book is not an introduction to the Platonic corpus as such, inasmuch as there are several commonly read dialogues to which it pays little notice (e.g., the *Euthyphro*, the *Crito* and the *Gorgias*). It is an introduction, rather, to the study of Plato's writings as an exercise in the pursuit of wisdom. This is in keeping with the main contention of the book, namely that Plato's written discourses were intended by their author to serve primarily as teaching instruments, modeled after the live conversations in which Plato himself participated with the historical Socrates, and that the right way to read the dialogues, accordingly, is not as repositories of philosophic doctrine, but rather as interactions with a master philosopher that are carefully shaped to guide the attentive reader in a personal pursuit of philosophic understanding.

It follows from this that the present book should always be read as a supplement to a careful study of the original texts. Although there is nothing to prevent such a study from taking place in the privacy of one's own home or office, the ideal context would be within a class of advanced undergraduate or beginning graduate students dedicated to a thorough investigation of major portions of the Platonic corpus itself. The most effective use of the book in such a context, perhaps, would be to read chapter 2 in conjunction with the *Meno*, chapter 3 in conjunction with the *Phaedo*, chapter 4 in conjunction with the *Symposium*, and so forth. A brief glance at the section headings should indicate which dialogues figure most prominently in the discussions of the various chapters. As an exception to this general pattern, the introduction and chapter 1 could well be used as a prelude to full immersion in almost any of the major dialogues, while the appendix invites being read as a more or less independent analysis of the *Theaetetus* specifically. This approach to the *Theaetetus*, I should think, might be particularly useful in a graduate course, inasmuch as it takes up numerous issues regarding that dialogue that are currently being debated in scholarly journals. In the main body of the book, by contrast, I am generally content merely to point the reader in the direction of current debate on relevant issues and to enter into ongoing debate myself only on rare occasions when this contributes background that is important for what I want to say on a given topic (a case in point is the discussion of the nature of the Good in chapter 6). Adoption of this policy seemed a necessary expedient for keeping the book within tolerable page limits.

With the few exceptions indicated (notably in the appendix), the translations of passages quoted within the text are mine alone. In cases where these translations might be controversial, or might otherwise invite scrutiny by an advanced student or by an instructor, I have included transliterated versions of the original Greek text taken from the Collection des Universités de France (Budé edition). Scholars referring to the Oxford edition of John Burnet instead must be prepared to cope with frequent (albeit minor) differences in Stephanus numbering between these two editions.

While as a matter of course I have profited extensively from publications by and conversations with a large number of colleagues and fellow lovers of Plato, my primary indebtedness is to hundreds of students—undergraduate and graduate—with whom I have shared opportunities to explore and to develop the main themes of this book. Among this latter group, I want to single out for special thanks Mark Moes (who stretched my way of thinking about the *Symposium*), David O'Connor (currently a valued colleague who made many helpful comments on the penultimate draft of the manuscript), and Patti White Sayre (to whom, with love, the book is dedicated). I wish also to express my deep gratitude to Robert Vacca, my primary instructor in the Greek of Plato. Although he shares no blame at all for mistakes that remain in the text, without his help I never would have gained the resources even to begin the present study.

INTRODUCTION

Plato's dialogues are read for many different reasons, reflecting a wide variety of expectations and interests. And no way of reading a dialogue can be entirely wrong if it leads the reader to return for yet another reading.

For scholarly purposes, however—and here I am referring to the interests of college and university readers in particular—the difference between right and wrong approaches to Plato is more distinctly marked. As a beginning approximation, we may say that an approach to the dialogues is right if it puts the reader in touch with the (quite literally) astounding intellectual power and philosophic insight with which they have been endowed and that otherwise the approach is wrong. Something like this, of course, can be said about the writing of any great author. But what this amounts to in Plato's case is far beyond truism. For there are powers to be engaged in Plato's writing that remain unmatched in the world's philosophic literature.

Whitehead once observed, in a remark that has become legendary in its own right, that the entire history of Western philosophy, from Aristotle onward, can be viewed as a series of footnotes to Plato.[1] What Whitehead meant basically is that most of the problems with which subsequent philosophy has been concerned, and most of the answers it has proposed as well, can be found foreshadowed in Plato's writing. Beyond this, Plato initiated general views of the world that remain no less interesting today than when first proposed and was as adept as any philosopher since at subjecting opposing views to critical examination. These qualities by themselves are enough to earn Plato a place of singular importance in our philosophic tradition.

But these are not the qualities alone that make the study of Plato's writings such a unique intellectual adventure. If one reads carefully and

thoughtfully, and has the patience to backtrack frequently, then repeated encounters with one or another of Plato's dialogues can result in a
palpable realignment of one's own philosophic perspectives. The experience might be likened to a sense of increased clarity, or penetration, or
comprehension of vision. Regardless of how one chooses to describe the
experience, however, as a consequence of undergoing it one views the
world differently. One literally comes to see things that one had not seen
previously, with the realization that one's former view was lacking for not
having revealed them. It would be wrong to suggest that Plato is the only
author whose writings are capable of enhancing the way we look at the
world, for clearly he is not. What makes Plato's works unique in this
respect is the seemingly almost perceptible energy with which they work
to brighten our mental vision.

With this much at stake, it is more important than with most
philosophic texts to take care that one's approach to Plato's dialogues is
conducive to making their intellectual resources available. A correct
approach, once again, is one that enables the reader to tap this mental
energy and to use it for the improvement of his or her philosophic
discernment. An approach is defective, on the other hand, to the extent
that it fails to bring the reader to a stance from which this energy can be
tapped and all the more so if it actually blocks the reader's access to the
energy of the dialogues. Given these prospects for loss or gain, the
question behind the subtitle of this book takes on a quite practical
significance: How *should* one read a Platonic dialogue?

As generation after generation of readers have discovered, this question does not admit of an easy answer. For one thing, Plato himself
nowhere leaves explicit instructions about how his dialogues should be
read; nor do any of his associates (like Aristotle) whose works are
currently available. For another, the question of how to read the Platonic
dialogues is intimately bound up with the even more evasive question of
why Plato employed the dialogue format in his philosophic writings.
And this latter question seems to elicit a different answer from every
commentator who addresses it. Given the absence of hard textual
evidence to settle the matter, one response to these questions might
seem as good as any other, and many scholars have been content to go
their merry ways without so much as a second thought about the issues.

There is a document in our possession, nonetheless, that is highly
relevant to these issues, in light of what it says about other aspects of
Plato's literary activity. This document is generally known as the Seventh

Letter, purportedly written by Plato to certain public figures in Syracuse. One reason the Seventh Letter is frequently neglected by Plato scholars has to do with doubts that have been raised about its authenticity. But even if this document was not written by Plato, it contains passages that remain relevant to the issues at hand. Several of these passages, more-over, are backed up by other passages in the dialogues themselves, where problems of authenticity do not arise. We will return to the question of this document's authorship. Let us first consider its relevance to Plato's manner of writing.

The Seventh Letter was addressed to certain friends and associates of Dion, a leading politician of Syracuse whom Plato had come to know in the Academy. Dion had secured Plato's collaboration in an effort to educate the younger Dionysius, a kinsman of Dion and heir apparent to the throne of Syracuse, which provided the occasion of Plato's first visit to Sicily. By the time the letter was written, Plato had returned from the last of three visits to Syracuse, the results of which had bordered on disaster, and Dion himself had recently been assassinated in a political intrigue.

About halfway through the letter, which begins (purportedly) with Plato's own account of the events leading up to the assassination, the author mentions a rumor he had heard about Dionysius' having written a philosophic treatise, and launches into a lengthy discussion of the unsuitability of language as a medium for philosophy. His first blanket statement in this regard is that anyone who undertakes to *write* with a pretense of knowing the subject which Plato assiduously pursues—i.e., philosophy—most certainly does not understand anything about it. But it is what the document says about Plato's own involvement in philoso-phy that is particularly arresting.

After observing that no one who understands philosophy would try to put it in writing, Plato (as purported author) very pointedly goes on to say that there are no written works of *his* on the subject and that there never will be. The reason he gives for this disavowal is that philosophy cannot be expressed *verbally* (*hrēton*: 341C6) like other studies. As he puts it again a page or so later, the realities contemplated by the knowing mind—identified at 342D as including "the Good, the Beauti-ful and the Just"—are beyond the expressive power of language (*logōn*: 343A1) generally. This latter remark comes roughly in the middle of a two-page explanation of what it is about language that makes it unsuit-able for this purpose.

Immediately after his claim that philosophic understanding cannot be expressed in language, the author adds a positive note about how it is acquired. The understanding that Dionysius lacked, he goes on to say, can be generated only "from living day by day with the matter itself, and many conversations" (*ek pollēs sunousias . . . peri to pragma auto kai tou suzēn:* 341C6–D1) in its regard. The term translated 'conversation' here is *sunousia*, which includes among its various meanings forms of social interaction that are not primarily verbal, such as dinner parties and cohabitation. But as Plato uses it, the term often refers expressly to verbal intercourse, of the sort that occurs in dialectical conversations specifically. Since the dialogues depict verbal interactions of just this sort,[2] the apparent implications of the remark quoted above is that philosophic knowledge is generated in conversations of the type exemplified in the Platonic dialogues themselves. Although we must look at these passages more carefully in subsequent chapters, enough has been said already to show the relevance of the Seventh Letter to the issues at hand. By way of tentative response at least, these considerations suggest that Plato wrote in the form of dialogues in order to provide a dialectical context in which philosophic knowledge can take shape in the reader. From this it follows that the right way to read a Platonic dialogue, whatever else it amounts to, must be a manner of reading that allows this dialectical process to get under way.

There is another set of passages dealing with the deficiencies of public language that occur in the closing pages of the *Phaedrus*. These passages are often associated with the criticisms of language in the Seventh Letter and have the advantage of being unchallenged as writings of Plato. The features of these passages that commentators emphasize most frequently have to do with the shortcomings of writing in particular as a medium of philosophic communication. In one memorable passage, for instance, Socrates and Phaedrus agree that written language is a mere "image" (*eidōlon:* 276A9) of a more vital discourse that is "inscribed in the soul" (*graphetai en tē . . . psuchē:* 276A5–6) of a person engaged in learning. But spoken language also comes under criticism in this context, most explicitly at 276D where Socrates calls into question the worth of giving speeches of the sort Phaedrus had recited early in the dialogue. A problem with words (*hoi logoi:* 275D7) generally, Socrates points out, is that once they enter the public domain they cannot defend themselves against misunderstanding.

What commentators who dwell on these passages tend to overlook, however, is that in the passages immediately following the reference to writing as a kind of "image," Socrates goes on to acknowledge a fully legitimate role for written language in the activity of dialectic. Although the dialectician will place a higher value on actively planting and cultivating "words accompanied by knowledge" (*met' epistēmēs logous:* 276E7) in souls capable of learning—a task best pursued in actual conversation—another activity that is "entirely noble" (*Pankalēn:* 276E1) in itself is to sow these seeds of knowledge in a "literary garden" (*grammasi kēpous:* 276D1). The dialectician will engage in such writing as a kind of pastime, hoping thereby to provide a "store of reminders" (*thēsaurizomenos:* 276D3) to aid memory in later years and also to assist others who "follow in the same track" (*tauton ichnos metionti:* 276D4). And when this pastime happens to bear fruit—i.e., when the writing of the dialectician happens to inseminate the mind of a subsequent reader with the vital discourse conducive to learning—then he or she will take pleasure in watching the "tender growths" (*phuomenous hapalous:* 276D5) that result. Regardless of the manner in which they are sown, when these growths reach maturity in the mind of the learner they will count among the dialectians "legitimate sons" (*huieis gnēsious:* 278A6).

Although it is not immediately obvious that Socrates in these passages is speaking for Plato himself, this description of the "literary garden" cultivated by the dialectician lends direct support to the proposal above regarding Plato's reasons for writing in dialogue form. If the "most noble" (*kalliōn:* 276E5) activity of the dialectician is to implant "seeds of knowledge" in personal conversation like that cited in the Seventh Letter, but if it is "entirely noble" nonetheless to undertake insemination of this sort through written discourse as well, then a reasonable tactic on the part of the dialectician involved would be to compose a "literary garden" in the form of written conversations. And this is what Plato appears to have done in writing the dialogues. Even though the subsequent reader cannot converse with Plato on a personal basis, he or she thereby will be able to hold *sunousia* with the author in an indirect manner, by participating in conversations expressly composed for that purpose.

Yet other passages can be found in the dialogues suggesting that Plato thought of conversations of this sort as contexts in which philosophic growth most effectively can take place. One is the discussion of Socratic midwifery in the *Theaetetus*, where Socrates talks about the "many beautiful discoveries" (150D7–8) engendered in the minds of those who have held fruitful *sunousia* (150D4, 151A2) with him. Another is the

avowal of the Eleatic Stranger, in his subsequent conversation with
Young Socrates, that the primary purpose of their discussion together
(i.e., the *Statesman*) is for the participants generally to become "better
dialecticians" (*dialektikōterois:* 285D7). Although reference in both contexts is to oral conversations depicted within the dialogues concerned,
these remarks might plausibly be taken to apply to the conversation
between author and reader enabled by the written text as well. We shall
return to these passages in the discussion that follows. For the moment,
let us pull together what we learn from these various sources by way of
anticipating the structure of the present study.

The central theme of this book is that the Platonic dialogues were
written to provide occasions for conversations between author and
reader of the sort identified in the Seventh Letter as leading to philosophic understanding and that a proper reading of the dialogues is one
that enables this conversation to progress in a fruitful direction. The
primary purpose of the book is to spell out this conception of the
dialogues in detail and to articulate the various stages through which the
growth of philosophic knowledge as Plato conceived it might be expected to develop. I shall take advantage of opportunities along the way
to examine certain topics of interest to Platonic scholarship generally,
such as the status of the so-called "theory of recollection," the contribution of dialectic to philosophic knowledge, and the relation between the
Good and the nonhypothetical first principle. The emphasis throughout, however, will be on what we can learn about such topics when we
approach them from the perspective of the Seventh Letter.

To say it again briefly, the conception underlying the present study is
that the dialogues were written as occasions for conversations in which
the author might lead the reader to philosophic understanding. Chapter
1 begins by canvassing alternative conceptions of the dialogues and by
marshalling evidence for the present conception from several of Plato's
writings. The Seventh Letter figures prominently in this pursuit, along
with the *Phaedrus* and the *Theaetetus*.

The burden of distinguishing and describing the various stages along
the way to philosophic knowledge, as Plato seems to have conceived it, is
distributed among chapters 2 through 6. One aspect of the *sunousia*
leading to knowledge that is stressed in the Seventh Letter is a "well-
disposed cross-examination" (*eumenesin elenchois elenchomena:*[3] 344B6),
described alternatively as "question and answer without indulgence of
ill-will" (344B6-7). In terms of the horticultural model of the dialecti-

cian's activity in the *Phaedrus*, the purpose of this "cross-examination" or elenchus is to clear the tangled growth of false opinion from the soul to be seeded. The discussion of this topic in chapter 2 draws heavily upon the *Meno* and locates "Socratic" elenchus in a tradition tracing back to Zeno.

Once the ground has been made clear, as it were, the next step in the establishment of the dialectician's "literary garden" is the implantation of words infused "with knowledge" (*Phaedrus* 276E7) that might germinate as "living discourse" (*logon . . . zōnta:* 276A8) in the mind of the learner. This process of seeding is the topic of chapter 3, which discusses the relevance in that regard of recollection (*anamnēsis*) and of the use (as in the *Statesman*) of exemplary instances. While nothing is said in the *Phaedrus* about the care these seeds require in order to flourish, one thing surely needed is proper nourishment. Mention of this need occurs in the *Theaetetus*, where Socrates bemoans the "bad nourishment" (*kakōs trephontes:* 150E4–5) provided in conversations with other teachers. Proper nourishment comes with the love of beautiful discourse of which Diotima speaks in the *Symposium*. The nourishing effect of this higher form of Eros is the primary concern of chapter 4.

Another requirement for the proper growth of these tender shoots of discourse, once they begin to form, is that they be encouraged to branch out into healthy configurations. The discipline intended to impart a proper development of this sort is identified in the Seventh Letter as "that mode of daily living" (*trophēs tēs kath' hēmeran:* 340D4) most conducive to sober reasoning. As noted by Souilhé,[4] among others, this discipline corresponds to the training of the Guardians in Book VII of the *Republic*, the guiding role in which is played by the procedures of dialectic. Chapter 5, accordingly, concerns dialectical method, and its role in shaping discourse as it grows into knowledge.

When the discourse planted and nurtured by dialectic finally matures into philosophic understanding, it achieves—in the words of the *Phaedrus*—a kind of "immortality" (277A3) and grants its possessor "well-being" (*eudaimonein:* 277A3) in the highest degree of which "humankind is capable" (*anthrōpō dunaton:* 277A4). This matches a parallel description of the onset of philosophic understanding in the Seventh Letter as a state pressing the limits of "human capacity" (*dunamin anthrōpinēn:* 344B8–C1). There are obvious parallels also with the climax of Diotima's discourse in the *Symposium*, where she assures Socrates that someone who has looked upon Beauty itself will be "dear to the gods" (*theophilei*: 212A6) and will gain immortality insofar as humanly possible. This state of *eudaimonia* is the final fruit of the philosopher's quest and presumably is closely related to the vision of the Good in the *Republic*. Chapter 6 is given over to a discussion of the Good and the Beautiful, and to an effort to pin down how the two are related.

If this conception of why Plato wrote in dialogue form is approximately correct, practical consequences follow about how the dialogues should be read. Rather than attempt to marshall these consequences in a list of "do's and don't's"—which almost surely would be unsuccessful—I have chosen to illustrate what appear to be the lessons at hand by applying them to a reading of a familiar dialogue. While several dialogues would serve well in this regard, the *Theaetetus* seems to be particularly well suited. One reason is that it is likely to be familiar to most of my readers. Another is that it exhibits, to one degree or another, all of the major features of a dialectical conversation distinguished in the earlier chapters. A brief discussion of the *Theaetetus* with these features in view occupies the final chapter of the book. The reader should be aware that this discussion is not intended to address all the issues that have been raised in recent scholarship on this dialogue. Its purpose is merely to show the fecundity of one major "seedbed" in Plato's "garden" of written discourse.

As the above remarks indicate, the views developed in this study do not depend upon the Seventh Letter exclusively. They receive extensive support from several dialogues of unquestioned authenticity as well. Nonetheless, these views inevitably will appear more conjectural to someone dubious about the authenticity of the Seventh Letter than to another person ready to accept it as a genuine writing of Plato. While there is little hope of ever being absolutely sure one way or the other, I want to end these introductory remarks with a brief indication of why I am comfortable with accepting the Seventh Letter as authentic.

Our earliest evidence of the Seventh Letter occurs in the canon of Platonic works drawn up by Thrasyllus during the first century A.D.[5] An earlier record of unspecified epistles appeared in the listing by Aristophanes of Byzantium during the third century, but the compilation of Thrasyllus is the first in which the thirteen letters now in our possession can be positively identified. All thirteen seem generally[6] to have been accepted as genuine up to the end of the fifteenth century, when Ficinus found reason to reject the first and the thirteenth of the set as spurious. In the latter part of the eighteenth century, Meiners ruled out the entire set, followed by Ast and Socher a few decades later.[7] The modern debate over the topic was inaugurated by Karsten (in 1864), who argued that all are forgeries, and Grote (in 1865), who defended all save the first as genuine. This debate has continued up to the present decade and by its nature is likely to continue indefinitely.

It is useful nonetheless to survey the course of the debate over the past several decades, particularly with regard to the status of the Seventh Letter. One thing to note initially is that no substantial study within this century accepts all thirteen letters as genuine.[8] The First Letter by itself has found no defenders,[9] and the twelfth generally has been rejected as well. But the Seventh Letter has fared considerably better. The general pattern seems to be that both the seventh and the eighth are accepted by a given scholar who accepts any at all,[10] and that the seventh is defended more frequently than any other in the set.[11] The upshot is that a strong majority of recent scholars find in favor of the Seventh Letter. Particularly noteworthy for their contribution to this pattern are several book-length studies of the issue that have appeared within the last several decades and that contribute useful overviews of the state of the debate at the times they were written. Two of these—Morrow's *Plato's Epistles* and Brisson's *Platon: Lettres*—conclude in favor of the Seventh Letter's authenticity. The other—Edelstein's *Plato's Seventh Letter*—rejects the seventh along with the other twelve, in the tradition tracing back to Meiners and Karsten.[12] Despite the obvious erudition of Edelstein's arguments, however, they consist largely of pointing out inconsistencies between the Seventh Letter and his own conception of Plato's teachings, based on a selective reading of the dialogues.[13] Inasmuch as this conception depends upon a view of Plato's thought to which few people subscribe today—amounting, in the words of one reviewer,[14] to "a tight and closed system, rigid to the extent of excluding any change"— Edelstein's arguments generally have proved unpersuasive to readers with open minds on the issue.[15]

The fact that recent scholarship tends strongly to favor the authenticity of the Seventh Letter, needless to say, does not by itself put the issue to rest. If a head count had been taken toward the end of the last century, the nod would have gone in the other direction. There are several factors, nonetheless, that lend weight to this recent tendency. One is that scholarly opinion has rejoined the view that prevailed for two millennia before the critical work of Meiners, making the century or so of skepticism that intervened appear somewhat anomalous. The presumption once again may be said to favor authenticity, throwing the burden of proof over to those who claim the Seventh Letter is a forgery.

Another factor to take into account is that most of the relevant considerations have been thoroughly debated by now. And inasmuch as most of the arguments commonly brought against authenticity have been effectively answered, the case for the affirmative appears increasingly persuasive. Let us look briefly at some of the arguments against authenticity, along with counterarguments provided in recent commentary.

The consideration that casts doubt on Plato's authorship of the letters in the first place is that there is no positive record of their existence prior to the flourishing of the great library at Alexandria and that with the founding of this and other major libraries of the period there was a financial inducement to produce forgeries under the names of the great classical authors. Moreover, it was standard practice in schools of rhetoric during the centuries after Plato to compose letters in the style of the classical masters. Inasmuch as we have no way of knowing what safeguards, if any, the librarians of the period enforced for the exclusion of unauthentic documents, it is a safe assumption that the collections of letters that have come down to us from these sources—those attributed to Plato included—may include a number that were not written by the authors in question. On the other hand, not all of these letters are spurious. And in the case of the Seventh Letter of Plato in particular, there are features that tend to shield it from blanket suspicion. One is simply a matter of length. A long composition would be difficult to forge convincingly, making unusual length a factor favoring authenticity. And as Morrow has pointed out,[16] there is no recognized forgery in any of these ancient collections that is comparable in length to Plato's Seventh Letter. Another feature counting in favor of authenticity is the considerable range of emotions the letter expresses at appropriate points in the narration. The author is personally grieved at the death of Dion, frustrated in his hopes for a sound government in Sicily, and outraged at the thought of Dionysius composing a philosophic treatise. If these sentiments were committed to writing by anyone other than Plato, then the author possessed skills of dissimulation far beyond those of an ordinary forger.[17] Among various other considerations supporting authorship by Plato is the fact that the Seventh Letter was recognized as genuine by several authors within a few centuries after his death—including Plutarch in the century before the birth of Christ and Thrasyllus during the following century. If there were circumstances of composition that cast particular doubt on the document's authenticity, then these authors might be presumed to know them as well as anyone today.

Other arguments impugning its authenticity have focused on the contents of the letter itself. One set of problems that have been widely debated focuses on the political views expressed by its author and their alleged inconsistencies with the views of Plato. In the opinion of Edelstein, for example, the author of the *Republic* gives precedence to theory over practice and thinks that a true philosopher would be loath to enter politics.[18] Yet the Seventh Letter represents Plato as someone primarily concerned to put his words into actions (328C–D) and who willingly became involved into the political affairs of Sicily. This apparent discrepancy is largely dissolved by the observation, on the one hand, that the political attitudes one finds in the *Republic* cannot automatically be attributed to Plato himself (the author was practical enough to found an Academy) and, on the other, that Plato's motivation in the Sicilian venture was not personal ambition (e.g., to put his "ideal state" into action) but to respond to a request for help from his close friend Dion.[19] Another issue that has received a surprising amount of attention concerns the favorable attitude toward *isonomia* (roughly, political equality) expressed at Seventh Letter 326D and 336D, in contrast with the largely negative cast of the term in Plato's other writing (*Republic* 561E1, 563B8).[20] In Edelstein's estimation, this constitutes an inconsistency that counts against the genuineness of the Seventh Letter. As discussions by other commentators have made evident, however, the term *isonomia* carried various senses at the time of Plato.[21] There is no conflict between his using it in one context (e.g., the *Republic*) to signify an unhealthy lack of civic order and in another (the Seventh Letter) to advocate freedom in contrast with the tyranny of Dionysius. While these are not the only problems of a political nature raised by the Seventh Letter's detractors, they may give the reader a sense of why such debates are generally viewed as inconclusive.

Another source of arguments against authenticity has to do with the contents of the philosophic excursus itself (340C–345C), which some view as contrary to the dialogues on the topics at hand. A number of commentators have fixed upon the epistemological discussion (342A–344C) in particular, raising questions about its compatibility with Plato's account of the Forms.[22] Edelstein, once again, has suggested that the five-tiered ascent to the "true reality" described at 342A–D yields a view of the Forms as mental entities, lacking the transcendence assigned them in the middle dialogues.[23] This suggestion, properly enough, has been rebutted by several respondents as being based on a misunderstanding of the passage in question.[24] Problems of a more general type sometimes found with this philosophic digression concern its apparent espousal of perspectives on the philosophic enterprise that are wholly disparate from the written dialogues. Some commentators, for example, read the imagery used in describing the onset of philosophic understanding in terms of illumination (341C–D, 344B) as an indication of mystical idealism.[25] And there is the widely discussed difficulty of what to make of the author's claim at 341C never to have written on the topic under discussion, in view of Plato's undoubted authorship of numerous dialogues. These issues are taken up in chapter 1, with results that show a striking correspondence between the contents of this digression and well-known views from the *Phaedrus* and the *Theaetetus*. Far from being in conflict with Plato's other writings, these passages show sufficient harmony with the epistemological dialogues to count in favor of common authorship.

One further factor to take into account in assessing the authenticity of the Seventh Letter falls under the heading of stylometric analysis. Although techniques of stylometry were already being applied to Plato's writings by the time of Karsten's wholesale rejection of the letters in the 1870s,[26] it is interesting to note that stylometric considerations have never played a major role in arguments against Plato's authorship of the Seventh Letter. To the contrary, scholars who feature stylometry among their critical tools tend to favor its authenticity. Constantin Ritter, a pioneer in stylometric analysis, found in favor of the Seventh Letter and as early as 1888 made public his opinion that its style is the same as that of the *Laws*.[27] Hans Raeder reinforced Ritter's views on both counts in 1906; and the stylometric studies of Wilamowitz-Moellendorff reached the same conclusions in 1919.[28] The pattern of general support by stylometric considerations has continued to the present, with the synoptic study of Ledger reported in his *Re-counting Plato: A Computer Analysis of Plato's Style*. Ledger's study concludes as follows:

> Epistle 7 is nowadays accepted by the majority of scholars. . . . It hardly seems necessary to rehearse once more the arguments *pro* and *contra*. The importance of having its authenticity confirmed is that it will now be possible to rely on the long excursus on the nature of reality (342A–344C) with confidence as a guide to Plato's later thought.[29]

This consistent support of authenticity by studies like Ledger's is especially significant, in view of the growing capacity of stylometry to ferret out forgery.

While the question of the Seventh Letter's status is one that by nature will never be settled definitively, the presumption at this point leans strongly in the direction of authenticity. For readers who still harbor doubts, perhaps the present study had best be approached as a conceptual experiment. Let us assume (if need be) that the Seventh Letter was actually written by Plato, and see what light this can throw upon the rest of his writings. If the hypothesis bears fruit in terms of an enhanced access to the dialogues, then we have additional evidence that the Seventh Letter is genuine.

1
WHY PLATO WROTE DIALOGUES

1. Alternative Accounts of Plato's Literary Form

There were other forms that Plato might have chosen for his philosophic writing. He might have written in verse, like Parmenides, or in the form of speeches, like Isocrates (the *Menexenus* comes close). He might even have chosen the form of essays or treatises, like the author of the *Dissoi Logoi*[1] (the *Timaeus* and the *Critias* invite comparison). The form he chose for most of his philosophic writing, however, is closer to drama instead. Plato's chosen form was the dialectical discussion, in which a master philosopher leads a discussion with someone less skilled in philosophy. What accounts for Plato's choice of the dialogue form?

One possible answer flows naturally from an assumption that most readers of Plato probably find tempting at first consideration. This is the assumption that the Socratic dialogues (i.e., the dialogues featuring Socrates as the leading character) are reports of actual conversations with the historical Socrates. Stated more circumspectly, it is the assumption that the dialogues are skillfully edited records of actual Socratic conversations. The general sense of the matter is (1) that Socrates had frequent philosophically rich and provocative conversations with prominent figures in and around Athens, (2) that Plato, as good fortune would have it, was on the scene to record a number of these conversations (relying on reports from onlookers when not present himself), and (3) that our fascination through the centuries with these recorded conversations is due in large part to the skill with which Plato captured the Socratic genius in action. If this view of the matter is approximately correct, then an answer to the question above falls out as a matter of course: Plato wrote in dialogue form simply because that was the form of the conversations he undertook to record.

The sense that Plato's dialogues are transcripts of actual conversations is enhanced by the fact that most of Socrates' respondents, in the early dialogues at least, are persons with known historical identity. They are persons, that is to say, with whom we are likely to have at least minimal acquaintance from sources other than the dialogues themselves. And insofar as we think of the persons conversing with Socrates in a given dialogue as actual people, it seems natural to think of the interchange as an actual conversation. Realizing that Theaetetus and Theodorus, for example, probably were around Athens at about the time they are depicted as having a conversation there with Socrates, we tend almost automatically to think of the interchange of the *Theaetetus* as having actually occurred. But this, of course, is a complete *non sequitur*. The fact that Brutus was an actual contemporary of Julius Caesar does not make Shakespeare's story of a conversation between them a depiction of an actual conversation. No more does it follow that Socrates and Parmenides actually conversed together as portrayed in the *Parmenides*, on the basis of the fact merely that the historical persons in question *might* have met under those circumstances. Not even in the *Apology*, which is the only dialogue in which Plato mentions himself as being present, does he give any explicit indication that the interchange there depicted is historically accurate.[2] Given the absence of any claim to historical accuracy on the part of the author, in brief, the mere fact that the participants in a given dialogue are historical persons is scant evidence for the authenticity of the conversation depicted.

Another factor that tends to enhance the illusion of historicity is the stage setting provided at the beginning of most dialogues (the *Philebus* being a notable exception) that suggests how details of the conversation in question might conceivably have found their way into the public domain. In the case of the *Theaetetus*, once again, the dialogue begins with an "outer" dialogue between Euclides and Terpsion, in which the former mentions a manuscript in his possession of a much earlier conversation involving Socrates and Theaetetus—a manuscript (Euclides says) based originally on Socrates' own recollection and later checked by him for accuracy. The "inner" dialogue proper then is read from this manuscript by one of Euclides' slaves. In the case of a dialogue like the *Gorgias* or the *Meno*, on the other hand, the circumstances of the depicted conversation are sufficiently public as to generate no mys-

tery about how someone might have heard it originally and then committed its content to writing. Setting aside questions about how details
might have been retained for eventual transcription (was everything
memorized, or was there some kind of note-taking?), we should have no
problem in principle about how conversations like these might have
found their way to an audience of readers.

Nonetheless, it is surprisingly difficult in most cases to fabricate plausible stories about how Plato in fact might have heard details of historical
conversations of the sort figuring in his Socratic dialogues. A majority of
these dialogues (the *Republic*, the *Gorgias*, the *Symposium*, etc.) depict
conversations purporting to take place before Plato reached adolescence,
while some (e.g., the *Protagoras*) are dated dramatically before he even was
born.[3] Assuming that these conversations actually occurred in the first
place, we can always imagine that someone present took notes which
Plato subsequently inherited. Such an explanation, however, not only is
blatantly *ad hoc*, but moreover it assumes the mediation of an unknown
person with a genius approaching Plato's for dramatic description. A more
credible explanation by far is that the details of these historically distant
dialogues are Plato's own creation, crafted for purposes more subtle than
keeping records of Socratic utterances.

There is another group of Socratic dialogues, of course, with dramatic
dates falling well within the span of Plato's own literary activity, featuring conversations that Plato himself might conceivably have overheard.
One is the *Apology*, as noted above, in which Plato lists himself among
the audience. Another is the *Meno*, which purports to be a conversation
in a public setting which Plato might have attended as an anonymous
bystander. Also within this group, however, are several dialogues which
Plato almost certainly did not witness personally. Phaedo, in the dialogue which bears his name, explicitly mentions Plato as being absent.
The conversation between Socrates and Phaedrus, for another example,
was pointedly private, which means that Plato was not around to record
the details. Plato likewise was absent from the conversation with Crito.
In these latter two cases, we should note, there was no way Plato could
have learned about the details of the conversations save from the
participants themselves; and it seems farfetched to assume that Socrates
(as allegedly in the *Theaetetus*) would have bothered to provide another
party with fully detailed reports.

As far as detailed access by Plato is concerned, in brief, most of the
dialogues of this latter group pose the same problems as those dated

before Plato's maturity. Even if we assume that the conversations depicted have some historical basis, there is no easy explanation of how
Plato might have come to know their specific details. Instead of viewing
the Socratic dialogues as records of historical conversations, it is distinctly more plausible to think of them as literary creations based on
various Socratic themes.[4] Plato's reputation as one of the foremost
philosophers of our civilization, after all, is not due to his skill merely in
recording the sayings of another (in some ways, inferior) philosopher.
Plato's achievement lies rather in his literary creations, in which other
philosophers (not only Socrates) are made to play central dramatic roles.

If Plato's dialogues cannot rightly be viewed as transcriptions of actual
conversations, however, our first attempt to account for his use of
the dialogue form loses its initial credibility. Plato did not write in the
form of dialectical conversations merely to capture the style of the
historical Socrates.

Another way of coming to terms with Plato's choice of literary form
amounts to little more than acknowledging the dialogue as one among
various formats in which philosophic arguments might be developed. In
one common sense of the term today, a dialogue is nothing more specific
than a verbal interchange between two or more persons. People engage
in dialogue merely by talking with one another, regardless of the subject
or the purpose of the conversation. If a contemporary author elects to air
the arguments pro and con a given philosophic position in the form of
an orderly interchange between two or more characters—fictional or
otherwise—the result would be termed a "philosophic dialogue." In the
view of a sizeable contingent of contemporary commentators, this was
the option elected by Plato. According to this way of thinking, the
conversational format employed by Plato boils down to a quaint way of
presenting the moves in a philosophic argument, serving primarily to
accommodate a nontechnical audience.

This way of dealing with Plato's dramatic form is typified by Cornford's translation of the *Parmenides,* in which Aristoteles' responses to
Parmenides are simply eliminated. Cornford's explanation of this omission is that "nothing is gained by casting the arguments into the form of
question and answer."[5] Cornford's view, in effect, is that the conversational format is incidental to Plato's philosophic purposes, and that these
purposes might have been served equally well by a format similar to our
contemporary philosophic essay. I have referred to this elsewhere as the
"proto-essay" view of the dialogues.[6]

More fully stated, the view in question is (1) that Plato's primary purpose in writing the dialogues was to develop arguments for his own positions, while defending these positions against their opponents, and (2) that Plato's own positions are represented by his main protagonists—most notably by Socrates in the early and middle dialogues.[7] But both (1) and (2) are subject to serious objection. Since (1) requires (2) for its *prima facie* credibility, let us look first at some reasons for rejecting the second thesis.

One problem with the notion that Socrates serves as Plato's spokesman in the early and middle dialogues is that there are significant discrepancies within those dialogues among Socrates' pronouncements on major issues. Prominent examples are (a) the opposition between Socrates' conclusion in the *Meno* (99E) that virtue is not teachable and his conclusion that it is teachable at the end of the *Protagoras* (361B), and (b) the opposition between the doctrine of the incomposite soul he puts forth in the *Phaedo* (e.g., 80B) and the doctrine of the tripartite soul at the heart of the *Republic* (e.g., 441A). There are apparent discrepancies as well between views expressed in the middle and in the later dialogues— e.g., the respective treatments of the Good in the *Republic* and the *Philebus*—but these can plausibly be accounted for in terms of Plato's philosophic development.[8] To find conflicts of this sort between dialogues that most probably were written within a few years of each other (the *Meno* with the *Protagoras*, the *Phaedo* with the *Republic*), however, strongly suggests that the views expressed by the major character are not always those of the author himself.

Another problem with thesis (2) above is that most of the conversations in which the character Socrates participates are elenchic in character, which means that they are aimed at refuting views expressed by other characters with whom Socrates is conversing. By way of directing the interchange to this end, Socrates often is pictured as proposing theses for his interlocutors' acceptance that neither Plato nor the historical Socrates would have been likely to endorse themselves. A striking case occurs at the end of the *Protagoras*, where Socrates maneuvers the master sophist into accepting the identity of the good and the pleasant, thereby setting the trap that ensnares him at the end of the dialogue.[9] To read this passage as an expression of "Socratic hedonism" is a flat-footed mistake one could make only by overlooking the rhetorical dimensions of the dialogue overall. The fact that this mistake is fairly common among recent commentators[10] illustrates the difficulties in segregating views attributable (as it were) to the character Socrates from those fed to his opponents in an attempt to ensnare them.

Even when the character Socrates fairly clearly is speaking in his own behalf, moreover, it is often difficult to be sure he is not speaking ironically. He obviously is speaking ironically at the beginning of the *Meno*, for instance, when he claims to have forgotten his impressions of Gorgias. This artful disavowal of knowledge fits in with similar disavowals in several other dialogues, including the remark in the *Apology* (23B) that his only wisdom is the realization that he lacks wisdom. Given the highly rhetorical cast of Socrates' defense overall, the reader of the *Apology* should be prepared to find many other of his remarks in this context laced with irony as well. To speak ironically, however, is to speak disingenuously, which means, among other things, not to speak the whole truth. Given that the *Meno* and the *Apology* are sources to which scholars typically turn in search of a "Socratic philosophy" that might represent the views of Plato himself, they illustrate the serious problem a "proto-essayist" faces of distinguishing between rhetorical display and remarks the characters conceivably might have "intended" to be taken literally.

Socratic irony will be examined more thoroughly in chapter 2, in conjunction with the topic of elenchus. In the meanwhile, we should be advised to exercise caution in reading any of Socrates' remarks in the early and middle dialogues as expressing theses that Plato himself would have endorsed. To follow this restraint with respect to (2) above, after all, is only to treat Plato's works as on a par with those of other dramatic artists. We should be no more ready to assume that Plato's Socrates is a spokesman for its author than to assume that Thomas à Becket was a spokesman for Eliot (in *Murder in the Cathedral*) or Julius Caesar a spokesman for Shakespeare (in his play by that name).

As we move away from the incautious assumption that Socrates speaks for the author of the dialogues, it already becomes difficult to maintain confidence in the "proto-essayist's" thesis that the primary purpose of the dialogues is to argue Plato's own philosophy. If no one serves as Plato's spokesperson, then no argument counts automatically as Plato's own. But there are other reasons to be suspicious of this view of the dialogues as well. If Plato's primary purpose had been to argue his own philosophic theories, he would have indicated clearly what theories he was defending, and he would have shown concern to provide good arguments in support of those theories. In point of fact, neither happens within any of the Socratic dialogues.

Consider first the matter of theories defended. A typical introduction to the history of philosophy portrays Plato as the author of the "theory of Forms." In learning the content of this theory, however, the typical student relies on secondary sources and very little upon the dialogues themselves. The reason is that there is no single dialogue to which the student can turn to find such a theory explicitly stated. The closest one could come is a series of claims about the Forms attributed to a youthful Socrates in the early pages of the *Parmenides*, which are no sooner stated than vigorously refuted. Whatever one might make of this surprising exercise, it clearly is not the presentation of a theory that Plato wants to defend. There are many passages of the middle dialogues, to be sure, in which one can find discussions of various aspects of the Forms from which a theory of some sort might be pieced together. And these passages are sufficiently informative to enable commentators and historians to put together theories in Plato's behalf, perhaps under the presumption that only carelessness prevented him from doing the job himself. But the fact remains that there is no explicitly stated "theory of Forms" defended by Plato within the dialogues;[11] and the reason for this almost certainly is not inadvertence on Plato's part.

The same may be said for other theories commonly associated with the name of Plato in standard textbooks and histories of philosophy. There is reference to certain vaguely described notions of recollection in the *Meno* and the *Phaedo*, but nothing approaching a well-defined "theory of recollection." There are highly figurative discussions of the Good in the *Symposium* and the *Republic*, but nothing like a "theory of the Good" in either context. And so it goes with what we might think of as a "theory of virtue," or a "theory of knowledge," etc. We will return in due course to the question why Plato saw fit not to introduce explicit theories of this sort within his dialogues. For the moment, it is enough to note that the fact that no such theories are there to be found counts heavily against the "proto-essay" view of the dialogue format.

As yet a further piece of evidence against this view, we should attend briefly to the fact that Plato time and again passed up opportunities to provide his characters with better than half-hearted arguments for the views they represent. One of the more notable examples appears at the end of the *Theaetetus*, where three senses of *logos* are introduced (vocal speech, enumeration of parts, distinguishing mark), none of which proves capable of changing true judgment into knowledge. As anyone familiar with the language of the dialogue would know full well, there are several senses of the term *logos* that are more promising by far than the three considered. Yet rather than bring these into the discussion, Plato chose to end the conversation and to send Socrates off to be indicted. The clear implication is that Plato did not want Socrates and Theaetetus to arrive at a satisfactory definition of knowledge on that occasion. At very least, he did not want to provide the best case available for Theaetetus' third hypothesis identifying knowledge as true judgment accompanied by *logos*.

Add to this the many cases in which Plato provides palpably bad arguments for various views we should think his protagonists would want to defend—in the *Meno* (e.g., 87D–88D), the *Phaedo* (e.g., 70D–72A), the *Euthydemus*,[12] etc.—and it should be reasonably clear that Plato's main purpose in writing dialogues was not to present arguments in "popular" form for theories represented by designated protagonists. Despite its wide-spread acceptance among present-day commentators, this "proto-essay" view of the dialogues is no more promising than the view, examined earlier, that the dialogues are public records of actual conversations.

There is another view of the dialogues to be considered that gives more emphasis to their dramatic form and that relates them to other forms of discourse that were current while Plato was writing. The *Symposium* (173A, 175E) mentions Agathon's victory in the competition for tragedy that provided occasion for the festivities depicted in that dialogue. The *Hippias Minor* (363C–364A, 368C) mentions certain Olympic festivals that included competitions for various forms of poetry. In his intrepid book *Plato's Progress*, Gilbert Ryle has marshalled evidence that there were competitions of similar character for philosophic dialogues.[13] Ryle's conjecture is that several of Plato's dialogues (e.g., the *Phaedo* and the *Symposium*) were composed to be performed on occasions such as these. In the case of later dialogues on more technical topics (e.g., the *Parmenides*), his idea is that they were written for the edification of select groups of students within the Academy. In any case, they were written to be performed before audiences. Ryle's conjecture thus may be characterized as the "performance" view of the dialogues.

Ryle's evidence for the performance of Plato's dialogues in public has not appeared substantial enough to convince many of his readers. Yet the idea that the dialogues were written for use in the Academy has been taken up by some scholars as a fruitful insight. A promising variant on the "performance" view can be found in a recent book on the *Parmenides* by Mitchell Miller.[14] While not taking a stand on whether the dialogues were ever performed orally, Miller maintains that their purpose was to put students in the Academy "on stage" before themselves,[15] and to learn from the performance of the youthful respondents in the dialogues. The typical dialogue, Miller believes, has a four-part structure intended to organize the participation of its Academic audience. First comes an "elicitation" in which the leader of the conversation draws out his respondent's position on the topic at issue, followed by a "refutation" in which the respondent is reduced to *aporia*. These two stages correspond neatly to the opening moves of the *Parmenides*, where Parmenides first extracts details of Socrates' conception of the Forms and then submits that conception to withering criticism. The third stage is what Miller calls the "reorienting insight," in which the master philosopher makes suggestions for resolving the *aporia*. In the *Parmenides* this is the "training exercise" that introduces the second part of the dialogue. The final stage is a "return" to the original issue with this insight in view, in which the interlocutor in the dialogue shows himself at least partially incapable of grasping its full significance. The failure of young Aristoteles to see the full implications of the hypothetical arguments with which the *Parmenides* terminates, Miller believes, should be viewed as Plato's challenge to his Academic listeners to develop the "reorienting insight" for themselves and hence to progress personally along the paths of philosophy.

While there are questions to be raised about how Parmenides' "training exercise" (i.e., tracing consequences from hypotheses both that a relevant entity exists and that it does not exist) is supposed to serve as a "reorienting insight" in thinking about the Forms, and while it is inadequately clear how Aristoteles' lackluster performance in responding to Parmenides' demonstration of that "exercise" would inspire an audience of young Academicians to a higher level of performance themselves, there are several respects in which Miller's view of the dialogue form is preferable to the two views considered previously. Unlike the "public record" view, Miller's approach gives due weight to the fact that the Socrates of the dialogues in substantial part is a character shaped by Plato's dramatic purposes. Unlike the "proto-essay" view, moreover, this approach avoids the stultifying assumption that the philosophic merit of the dialogues rests upon the success of their arguments. The "performance" view, nonetheless, has its own inherent difficulties, even in the highly nuanced version advocated by Miller.

One problem with Ryle's and Miller's views alike is that we have very little evidence regarding Plato's interactions with younger members of the Academy. We have no reason to think that they attended formal classes and no evidence that they were trained specifically in Platonic philosophy. In particular, we have no evidence that the dialogues were ever used for didactic purposes within the Academy, to say nothing of being staged dramatically, as the "performance" view suggests. A related problem is that it seems shortsighted to assume that Plato's dialogues were written primarily for aspiring students as distinct from mature scholars (like Eudoxus and Isocrates, for example) both in and out of the Academy. There are many philosophers of great accomplishment, after all, who have been inspired by Plato's dialogues, and it is not unlikely that this result was part of their author's purpose.

Another difficulty with Miller's version in particular, it might be noted, is that a sizeable number of dialogues lack the dramatic structure that his interpretation requires. Neither the *Apology* nor the *Crito*, for instance, is a conversation involving an aspiring neophyte; neither the *Protagoras* nor the *Meno* contains an obvious candidate for the role of "reorientating insight"; and neither the *Timaeus* nor the *Laws* has dramatic features that would make it suitable for "performance" in any sense whatever. What we need, I suggest, is an account of the Platonic dialogue that allows more leeway than Miller's four-stage structure provides.

My fundamental misgiving with Miller's approach, however, is that it fails to take into account the most direct evidence in our possession regarding Plato's own conception of his written conversations. This evidence appears in his Seventh Letter. Let us conclude our survey of scholarly explanations[16] and return to Plato's own testimony about his literary output.

2. Plato's Disavowal of Having Written Philosophy

The portion of the Seventh Letter that pertains most directly to Plato's conception of the philosophic calling occurs between 341B and 345C. The most arresting statement in this document, as noted previously, is the author's claim at 341C5 that there are no written works of *his* on the matter under discussion—philosophy or, more precisely, philosophic understanding[17]—and that there never will be. The reason given for this startling disavowal is that this matter cannot be expressed verbally (*hrēton*: 341C6) like other studies. Immediately following this disavowal, as already noted, is the remark that philosophic understanding can be generated only "from living day by day with the matter itself" (341C7–D1) and from many conversations in its regard. While such understanding cannot be put into words, it can be generated through *sunousia* with a master philosopher.

Now any reader of the dialogues who has never previously encountered the Seventh Letter, and who is facing for the first time Plato's disavowal of having written philosophy, is likely to react with utter astonishment. For here we find the author of what may be the most important body of written work in the history of philosophy claiming never to have produced a single piece of philosophic writing. Indeed, the very passages in which this disavowal is found themselves constitute a written work on philosophic topics. So how could Plato claim seriously never to have written philosophy without the most blatant sort of inconsistency?

Our sense of tension between this disavowal in the Seventh Letter and the de facto existence of the written corpus is alleviated considerably by a careful consideration of the words in which this disapproval is expressed. One thing Plato is not saying, it should be noted, is that he never put his philosophy in *writing*, allowing that he might have expressed it orally on suitable occasions. Despite an enormous literature on his alleged "unwritten teachings,"[18] there is no support in the Seventh Letter for the view that Plato reserved his mature philosophic thought for oral transmission to members of the Academy.[19] The point stressed again and again (see 343D, along with 341C and 343A) is that language generally, both written *and* spoken, is inadequate for the expression of philosophic understanding. Nor is Plato saying, by way of implication, that he never wrote conversations on philosophic topics. Of course Plato wrote the Platonic dialogues. Whatever else his remarks to the companions of Dion might amount to, they could not have been intended to deny anything as obvious as that.

This denial that he had written on the matters in question, we recall, comes directly after Plato's reference to the treatise supposedly written by Dionysius and his disapproving remark to the effect that anyone who (like Dionysius) undertakes to write on philosophy with a pretense of *knowing* it most surely understands nothing about the topic. What Plato is disavowing in this context is not having written on philosophic subjects. A disavowal of this would have been wholly incredible. What he is disavowing, rather, is ever having attempted to put into writing an *understanding* of philosophy, to which Dionysius and others falsely laid claim. What Plato is repudiating here, in other words, is people who "claim to know" (*phasin eidenai:* 341C2) about philosophy—whether by "their own discovery" (341C3) or from another's instruction—and who then attempt to express what they think they know in language. And it is immediately following this blanket repudiation that Plato denies ever having attempted to do such a thing himself.

What Plato is denying here as far as his own practice is concerned, accordingly, is not that he ever had written or ever would write dialogues on philosophic topics. What he is denying most directly is that he ever would make the mistake of trying to express philosophic knowledge or understanding in linguistic form. And what he is denying by way of implication is that his dialogues, as works of writing, should be thought of as attempts to communicate knowledge or understanding of this sort. The obvious consequence is that Plato's dialogues were not conceived by their author as contexts in which to develop and to display positive arguments for one or another thesis—at least not arguments of a sort that might communicate knowledge. To have attempted to communicate knowledge by discursive argument, in his view at least (341C4), would have been a sure sign of the *lack* of the knowledge in question.

Now it would be very nice to be able to say at the outset exactly what Plato thought philosophic knowledge or understanding amounts to, and how he thought such knowledge *could* be communicated. But these are matters that cannot be disposed of easily and that will occupy us in some form through the remainder of this study. Let us return for the present to the Seventh Letter and consider carefully what the author says next.

What we find next is the remark, previously cited in translation, that philosophic understanding can be generated only "from living day by day with the matter in question," and from "many conversations" (*pollēs sunousias:* 341C7) in its regard. The "matter" in question concerns philosophy and its goal of understanding. But what might it be to "live with" this matter on a day-by-day basis? A prerequisite of this exercise, we should observe immediately, is that the young person undertaking it should have an aptness (*oikeios:* 340C2) for the subject and be worthy (*axios:* 340C3) of it. Essentially the same requirement is repeated a few pages later with the remark that ability to learn by itself is not enough for the task but that the student must have a natural affinity (*suggenē:* 344A3) for the topic as well. Put in other words, the pupil must be philosophic by nature (*ontōs ē philosophos:* 340C2), which is nothing less than being divinely gifted (*theios*: 340C3) in the matter. Presumably the same desideratum is at work in the *Phaedrus*, when the dialectician is said to begin the teaching process by selecting an "appropriate soul" (*psuchēn prosēkousan*: 276E6) to be implanted with words infused with knowledge. This image of a "suitable soil" for philosophic growth also appears in the *Theaetetus*, where it is combined with the imagery of the midwife in Socrates' claims that he has the skill of knowing what sort of seed should be sown in what sort of earth (149E3–4). As made quite clear at Seventh Letter 341E, at any rate, Plato believed that relatively few people have the natural ability to make progress in philosophy, which imposes a burden on the teacher to select suitable pupils.

But how does learning proceed once the proper student has been selected? One thing involved in this exercise, clearly enough, is a "suitably ordered regimen" (*diaita . . . prepousa . . . kosmia*: 340E2), which Plato describes as requiring both hard work (340E1) and dedication (340D3, see also 344B3). Another component is characterized as "well-disposed refutation by cross-examination" (*eumenesin elenchois elencho-mena*: 344B6), and alternatively as "question and answer without indulgence of ill-will" (*aneu phthonōn erōtēsesin kai apokrisesin chrōmenōn*: 344B6–7). This component presumably would be added as part of the "many conversations" that provide the context for the discipline. Inasmuch as interactions naturally describable in such terms are conspicuous factors in most of the Socratic dialogues, we might reasonably read these passages in the Seventh Letter with a growing expectation that they describe features deliberately crafted into Plato's written conversations.

In the case of persons adequately dedicated to this discipline, at any rate, they will persevere until they reach the goal (*telos*: 340C6) of their efforts, or at least until they can carry on without the help of an instructor (340D1). And when the knowledge at which their efforts are aimed is finally achieved, Plato says, "it is suddenly generated in the soul like a torchlight kindled by a leaping flame" (*exaiphnēs, hoion apo puros pēdēsantos exaphthen phōs, en tē psuchē genomenon*: 341D1–2) and "straightway becomes self-sustaining" (*auto heauto ēdē trephei*: 341D2). When the soul of the learner has been made ready, to put it somewhat more prosaically, the knowledge for which the aspiring philosopher has been seeking arrives in a "flash of insight"—like the ignition, we might say, of an electric light bulb. The fruition of the philosophic quest is an incandescent state of mind which, although perhaps torched by a spark from outside itself, is sustained thereafter by its own internal resources.

And it is a state of mind that is arrived at suddenly, rather than discursively through transactions of language.

This image of philosophic knowledge as an incandescent state of mind is repeated a few pages later, where Plato says that "wisdom and intelligence" (344B7–8) of "what is true and false of being overall" (344B2–3) "shines forth" (*exelampse*: 344B7), when it comes, with an intensity "pressing toward the limits of human capacity" (*sunteinōn hoti malist' eis dunamin anthrōpinēn*: 344B8–C1). Although the Greek here could be read as saying that the philosopher in this state exerts all of his or her capacity in achieving the intelligence thus gained, a more likely reading seems to be that the state of knowledge, when achieved, is one that represents the most demanding exercise of human mental powers. The discipline imparted through many "conversations" with a teacher and by daily "living with the matter" itself, that is to say, is necessary not only to make the mind receptive to the "flame of intelligence," but also to marshall the resources required to maintain this elevated state once it is achieved.

We shall return to this depiction of understanding as a state of mind in the following section in connection with similar descriptions in the *Phaedrus* and the *Theaetetus*. The next passage that calls for attention in the Seventh Letter is Plato's account of what it is about language generally that makes it unfit for the communication of philosophic knowledge. This account is based on the differences between the Forms themselves and the various means involved in our attempts to grasp them. These means include, in order of mention, (1) the name (*onoma*: 342B2) of the Form in question, (2) its verbal characterization (*logos*: 342B2), (3) a physical image or likeness (*eidōlon*: 342B2), and (4) the state of mind by which the Form itself is grasped, further divided into (a) true opinion (*alēthēs . . . doxa*: 342C5), (b) knowledge (*epistēmē*: 342C4) and (c) intelligence or understanding (*nous*: 342C5). Of these three, understanding (c) is most akin (*sungeneia*: 342D1) to the Form, which Plato adds as fifth item on the list and describes as "knowable and truly real" (*gnōston te kai alēthōs . . . on*: 342B1). Particular Forms mentioned in this context are the Good, the Beautiful, and the Just (cf. 342D4), which are among the Forms most frequently mentioned in the middle and late dialogues.

One shortcoming shared by the first three factors (names, verbal characterizations, and images) in comparison with the Forms is that they all involve "vocal sounds or material shapes" (342C6)—sensible features that are unavoidable in public language. One respect in which language falls short as a medium for communicating an understanding of the Forms, accordingly, is that the very attributes that make language communicable make it essentially different from the Forms it might purport to represent. Another defect of more direct relevance is that language in every case is made up of symbols with particular features, in contrast with the Forms which are not tied to particular instances. A result of this disparity is that a given linguistic symbol in some way signifies (*dēloun:* 342E4) one or another particular quality (*to poion ti:* 342E4) in addition to the thing it might be intended to symbolize. The sense behind this complaint, I take it, is that a drawing of a circle (Plato's example) in a particular color of ink might be taken as an indication of that particular color as well as a symbol for circularity itself.

The first defect is that linguistic symbols are sensible particulars, the second that they have significance in different respects. A third fault stems from these two together. Plato illustrates this further shortcoming by contrasting Circularity itself, which as a Form completely excludes any opposite feature (343A7–9), with a drawing of a circle each point on which is also a point on a tangential straight line.[20] The general point behind this illustration, it seems, is that the presence in particular symbols (like the drawn circle) of opposing characteristics (the curved and the straight line sharing a common point) makes them available for symbolizing opposing objects. A more telling example (adapted from *Republic* 523C–524B) might be a drawing of three fingers, which could be taken to represent three things (the separate fingers) or one thing (what they have in common), depending on context. The point, in any case, is that sensible symbols by nature are without fixed reference. As Plato puts it, names are "in no way stable" (*oudeni bebaion:* 343B1); and nothing prevents things now called round (as in his illustration) from being called straight at other times and vice versa. Using words in altered senses such as these, he goes on to say, we might find them every bit as stable as in their standard use—which is to say that they should not be considered stable in any use whatever. As far as the Seventh Letter is concerned at least, it is this inherent instability of public language that makes it unsuitable for the communication of philosophic knowledge. The philosopher's knowledge is a grasp of immutable Forms, which cannot be contained in mutable language.

A particular liability stemming from preoccupation with sensible symbols, at the expense of the truth (343C7) residing with the fifth

entity itself, is that this makes a person subject to easy refutation
(343C4). The result is that whenever we attempt to explain (*dēloun:*
343D3) a given Form in speech or writing (343D5), we are subject to
upset by anyone capable of overturning arguments. When this happens,
Plato says, bystanders tend to think that the mind of the speaker or
writer has been shown defective, whereas the defect lies by nature with
the means of expression instead. So pronounced are the defects of public
language, indeed, that they make anyone who relies upon it subject to all
manner of *aporia* and uncertainty (343C5).

There are other aspects of this discourse on philosophy in the Seventh
Letter to which we will return in due course, particularly the distinction
between the eristic refutation by which explanations in language are
overturned and the "well-disposed" refutations that contribute to philosophic understanding. For the moment, however, it is well to summarize
what we learn from the Seventh Letter about Plato's view of the philosophic calling and about how it might be served by written and spoken
conversations. As far as Plato's view of philosophic knowledge is concerned, we have seen first of all that this knowledge cannot be imparted
discursively and in particular that it cannot be imparted by discursive
argument for specific philosophic theses. Philosophic knowledge can
be gained only by a demanding course of discipline, including well-
intended refutation by a master philosopher. When knowledge of this
sort finally arrives, moreover, it appears suddenly (*exaiphnēs*) like a
"flash of insight" within the mind of the learner and can be sustained
only in minds with the requisite capacities. With respect to Plato's use of
the dialogue form, in turn, we have seen reason to believe that his
written conversations may have been deliberately shaped to reproduce
certain features of the verbal interchange (*sunousia*) between neophyte
and master that leads to the onset of philosophic knowledge. In particular, it appears that the refutations built into most of the Socratic
dialogues may correspond to the "well-disposed cross-examination"
Plato describes as a necessary part of the discipline that leads to philosophic understanding.

To put it briefly, we have already seen that Plato himself (as distinct
from a character in one of his dialogues) characterizes knowledge
as a state of mind that cannot be achieved by discursive argument; and
we have seen reason to think that the dialogues themselves may have
been constructed by way of partial reproduction of the conversational
context in which philosophic knowledge can be gained. In order to

develop these initial observations more fully, it will be helpful to compare the account of the Seventh Letter with parallel accounts in the dialogues themselves.

3. Parallel Views in the Theaetetus and the Phaedrus

Although several dialogues contain what might be called "metalevel" descriptions of the procedures of inquiry exemplified within them (e.g., recollection in the Meno, collection and division in the Sophist), there is one such description that is particularly striking for its parallels with the account of the Seventh Letter. This description appears early in the Theaetetus, where Socrates explains to his youthful respondent his function as "midwife of the soul." What is important in this description is not so much the metaphor of birthing itself, which seems to have been invented for the particular occasion (cf. 149A),[21] but rather the dynamics of the interaction—the sunousia—between Socrates and the young people who seek his company in hopes of philosophic advancement.

According to the Seventh Letter, as we have seen, philosophic enlightenment comes only after "repeated conversation" and daily "living with" the subject itself. According to Socrates in the Theaetetus, philosophic progress comes to those who "keep company" (150D2) with him regularly, and engage with him in conversation (sunousias: 150D4). The term sunousia is repeated at 150E4, when Socrates talks about the misfortune of falling into "worthless associations" and again at 151A2, where he talks of young men seeking renewal of their conversations with him. According to the Seventh Letter, furthermore, the conversations in question include "well-disposed refutation by cross-examination," also described as "question and answer without indulgence of ill-will." In the Theaetetus, the youthful beneficiary of the Socratic art does his best to answer the questions that Socrates asks, as out of good will (eunoia: 151C8) the latter examines (skopoumenos: 151C2) the former's statements. In the Seventh Letter, once again, the few people who are able to benefit from this regimen are said finally to become "capable of discovering by themselves the nature of things" (341D8, E2-3), with only a little guidance from the teacher (see also 340C7-D1). And in the Theaetetus, the young persons Socrates engages in regular conversation make surprising progress toward "many beautiful discoveries" (150D7-8) that come entirely from "within themselves" (par' hautōn: 150D7).

This latter feature of the learning process is of utmost importance, not only for understanding the sense in which Plato thought philosophic knowledge cannot be put into language, but also for understanding the nature of Socratic *sunousia* in the *Theaetetus* itself. Persons who have undergone the requisite discipline in the Seventh Letter become capable themselves of discovering truth. And like the offspring of biological mothers, the "beautiful discoveries" that come to the fortunate companions of Socrates also arise entirely within themselves, with Socrates assisting merely in their delivery. The point, of course, is not that these philosophic discoveries are made in isolation; in both contexts it is stressed that verbal interaction with a teacher is essential for anyone who would become capable of making them. The point is that the learner, after adequate preparation, is made capable of arriving at these discoveries without further help from the teacher. Just as the well-trained athlete becomes capable of scoring in a competition without further assistance from his or her trainer, so the well-prepared philosopher becomes capable of discerning the truth with no further contribution from his or her teacher.

In the case of an athlete, the point is sufficiently obvious as not to be worth making. To see why it is worth making in the case of the aspiring philosopher, let us consider the alternatives Plato seems to be ruling out with his emphasis that the fruits of philosophy arise within the mind that is properly prepared. Quite clearly, he is ruling out the kind of transaction in which he so emphatically denies ever having played a part—namely, the attempt to convey philosophic truths to the mind of a learner in the form of written or spoken discourse. One does not achieve access to philosophic knowledge by reading, or by listening to, the pronouncements of someone else who may claim to have achieved it previously. One does not achieve such access even when these pronouncements are accompanied by arguments of one sort or another. Arguments, of course, might produce conviction; but knowledge is not a matter merely of gaining conviction. At best, arguments might present reasons why certain propositions are true, by showing how the truth of a conclusion follows from the truth of certain premises. But once again, philosophic knowledge is not awareness of the truth of propositions. As far as Plato is concerned at least, knowledge comes with the discernment of some aspect of reality (the Forms, "how things are," "the nature of being"), and this discernment cannot be conveyed through the medium of language.

The problem with alleged "philosophic treatises," of which he is so harshly critical in the Seventh Letter, is that they purport to transfer philosophic knowledge, as it were, from the mind of the writer to the mind of the reader. One analogy that might suggest itself in this regard is the well-known aviary, discussed and rejected in the *Theaetetus*, in which learning is likened to "bits of knowledge" being entered into one's mind as birds are entered into an oversized birdcage. Another is that of wisdom flowing like water through yarn from one container to another, used with such humorous effect at *Symposium* 175D.²² But philosophic discernment can no more be accomplished in this passive manner than races can be won merely by the injection of hormones. Hormones might help enhance an athlete's ability to win a race, of course, just as arguments might help a philosopher sharpen his or her perception of reality. But in the last analysis, the fruits of philosophy are the product of an individual's own powers of discernment, and cannot be acquired secondhand from another party.

We will return to the *Theaetetus* and its discussion of knowledge. Another set of passages directly relevant to our present concern occur in the final pages of the *Phaedrus*, where Socrates is discussing the hazards of writing. As noted in the Introduction, these passages are frequently linked in the literature with the critique of language in the Seventh Letter. The text begins with a story of Theuth, the inventor of writing, which warns that this invention would cause memory to atrophy, rather than making it more reliable as Theuth had intended. Socrates then adds his own misgivings. The trouble with words (*hoi logoi*: 275D7) generally, Socrates says, is that they seem to be intelligent—comparable to the portrait of a living person—but when one wants to engage them in conversation they just go on "signifying the same thing forever" (*sēmainei monon tauton aei*: 275D9). Although written words are particularly prone to this problem, Socrates notes, it is a problem that attaches to "spoken and written" (277D2) discourse alike. Once committed to the channels of public discourse, that is to say, written and spoken words alike tend to lose association with the circumstances in which they were issued and thus become incapable of "defending themselves" (*boēthēsai . . . hautō*: 275E5–6) against untoward interpretations.

But there is another form of *logos*, Socrates assures Phaedrus, that knows when to speak and when to remain silent, and that is well-prepared to fend off unintended interpretation. This is the "speech, living and animate" (276A8), that goes "with knowledge" (276A5) when "inscribed within the soul of the learner" (276A5-6). Reference to this discourse as "inscribed within the soul" is repeated a few pages later (278A3), where it is further described as discourse "about Justice and Beauty and Goodness" (278A3-4). There are obvious parallels here with the "beautiful discoveries" that come entirely within the mind of the learner, as Socrates described the learning process to Theaetetus. And the explicit identification of Justice, Beauty, and Goodness as Forms that are discovered in this fashion has obvious associations with the Seventh Letter (342D4), where exactly the same Forms serve as examples of objects that the soul can grasp in its "flash of insight." The relevance of the *Phaedrus* to these other contexts is tied down conclusively when Socrates goes on to say that this discourse "written in the soul" is especially worth pursuing "in teaching and conversations for the sake of learning" (278A2-3).

Socrates' description of this "living language" as *written* in the soul of the learner is only a metaphor, of course, inasmuch as this language has none of the defects of writing proper. And after agreeing with Phaedrus that this makes writing proper only an image (*eidōlon:* 276A9) of the discourse of someone who has knowledge, Socrates abruptly changes his figure of speech and begins comparing the teacher of philosophy with the intelligent horticulturalist. If a farmer is really serious about his business, Socrates says, he will sow his seeds in suitable soil and will not look for fruit after a few days only.[23] And the person who knows Justice, Beauty, and Goodness (276C3, also 278A3-4)—i.e., the dialectician (276E5) or philosopher (278D4)—will proceed no less intelligently than the serious farmer. While such a person will choose to work primarily with souls of an appropriate type (*prosēkousan:* 276E6) in contexts where direct conversation is possible, a dialectician might work also through the medium of written conversations. This latter undertaking is described by Socrates as a kind of pastime (276D2), likening it to the cultivation of a "literary garden" (276D1).

Although tending a "literary garden" in this fashion is only a pastime, observes Socrates facetiously, it is better than the drinking parties other people indulge in. By engaging in this activity, moreover, the dialectician provides a resource for others who follow the same pathway (276D4)—i.e., for the potential philosophers among his or her readership.[24] And when this activity produces fruit within the mind of a reader, then the resulting knowledge counts among the dialectician's own offspring (278A6) and thereby contributes to his or her immortality (277A3).

It is the conception of Plato's written dialogues as constituting his own "literary garden," of course, that provides the organizing theme of the present study. As noted in the introduction, chapter 2 takes up the topic of elenchus, which clears the underbrush of false opinion from the soul to be seeded. Chapter 3 concerns the nature of the seeds to be sown, while chapter 4 explores the manner in which the growing seeds are nourished. Chapter 5, in turn, examines the procedures of dialectic by which the growing plant is trained in the right direction. And chapter 6, which focuses on the Good and the Beautiful, is concerned with the character of the final product. The appendix, finally, puts the sequence together, in an attempt to show how it works in the case of a particular dialogue.

Before getting on with this sequence, however, there are some issues yet to be addressed about the application of this horticultural model to Plato's written dialogues. For one, the model in question is applied in the *Phaedrus* primarily to a *direct* dialectical interchange between teacher and student, as distinct from the indirect literary influence of the dialectician upon those who follow in the same pathway. Since Plato's influence upon his readers obviously is of the indirect variety, we need to look more carefully at how the model applies to this particular interaction. Closely related to this is the unfinished business of pinning down, more or less unambiguously, what Plato was trying to accomplish by writing in dialogue form. These are the topics (in reverse order) of the remaining sections of this chapter.

4. Plato's Dialogues as Surrogates of Dialectical Conversations

In the *Phaedrus*, Plato has his character Socrates describe the "living discourse" engendered in the mind of the learner through conversation with a teacher employing the dialectical method. This description is from the third-person standpoint, with Socrates remaining noncommittal about his own capacities to serve as a teacher.[25] In the *Theaetetus*, however, Socrates is quite explicit in representing himself as a leader of conversations in which young persons can give birth to "many beautiful discoveries" within themselves. Although we have seen reason to reject the notion that either of these dialogues was written as a firsthand report of an actual Socratic conversation, it is entirely reasonable to assume that Plato drew extensively upon his acquaintance with the historical

Socrates for his depictions of this character within his dialogues. It is entirely reasonable, in particular, to assume that Plato's description of the relation between teacher and student in the *Phaedrus* and the *Theaetetus* depends heavily upon his own experiences with Socrates in person.

Given the close parallels between these dialogues and the description in the Seventh Letter of the conversations by which young persons can be brought to a state of philosophic knowledge, moreover, we may take it for granted that what Plato says there in his own behalf reflects his personal experience in conversations with the historical Socrates. This means that Plato's views on the unsuitability of writing as a medium for philosophy, with which the passages we have been considering from the Seventh Letter are largely occupied, were at least to some extent conditioned by Socratic conversations in which he participated personally. It follows that the conversations with the character Socrates that Plato nonetheless put in writing were composed under the influence of actual conversations between Plato and the historical Socrates himself. What can we tell from this about Plato's reasons for casting his writings in dialogue form?

One thing to be noted immediately in this regard is that, despite the prominence given to the "teaching relation" between Socrates and Plato by historians of philosophy, we have very little direct information about the nature of their interaction. The impression we receive from both Plato and Xenophon is that Socrates spent most of his waking hours in conversation. In the *Theaetetus* his namesake character represents himself as having a "fearful passion" (169C1) for argument, and in the *Euthyphro* we find him saying, not only that he converses without pay, but that he would gladly pay other people to listen to him (3D8–9). According to Xenophon, he "was constantly in the view of the public" (*Memorabilia* I.i.10), spending early morning in the gymnasiums and covered walks, seen about the marketplace when it was fullest, and passing the rest of the day wherever the most people were congregated. No matter where he was, "he was generally talking" (ibid.); and anyone who wished, Xenophon adds, was free to listen.

Even with this overwhelming "passion" for conversation, however, it seems unlikely that Socrates would have found occasion for a "personal talk" with most of the citizens of Athens, as the language of the *Apology* seems to suggest (*prattein aei idia hekastō prosionta*: 31B3–4). But it seems credible nonetheless that he may have found time to talk

with many of the poets and politicians and expert craftsmen he mentions having interviewed in response to the oracle's estimation of
his comparative wisdom (*Apology* 21C–22E). If we are to take this
account from the *Apology* at face value, the purpose of these inter-
views was entirely negative. Whatever divine justification he might
claim for his behavior, Socrates' intent in these cross-examinations
seems to have been to prove that the people who enjoyed the highest
reputation for wisdom in fact did not know as much as they thought.
One can well imagine the entertainment such an encounter would
provide for the idle bystander—the effect being that of an uneven
cockfight, save that the victim would be a dignified public figure and the
aggressor a bug-eyed gadabout with torn cloak and no sandals. The
result, as Socrates acknowledges before his judges, was that a number of
idle young men with wealthy fathers made it a habit to follow him about,
out of enjoyment at hearing these cross-examinations, and that they
even tried to imitate him by cross-examining other people themselves
(*Apology* 23C2–5). No wonder Socrates was out of favor with the
politicians of the city and had gained a reputation for corrupting the
youth. These were not "well-disposed cross-examinations" of the sort
mentioned in the Seventh Letter.

But there must have been another kind of conversation in which
Socrates regularly engaged as well. For quite apart from the idle young
men that flocked around Socrates to enjoy the spectacle of his encounters, there were people who sought his company for more serious purposes. Alcibiades comes to mind immediately (cf. *Symposium* 217B),
along with Aristides from the *Theaetetus* (151A1), Hippocrates from the
Protagoras, and the several young men mentioned at 33E of the *Apology*.
Xenophon lists Chaerophon and Chaerecrates, among others, as "associates" (*homilētēs: Memorabilia* I.ii.48) of Socrates who, unlike Alcibiades,
never brought discredit upon their relationship. Then of course there are
the eighteen (including Phaedo) named at the beginning of the *Phaedo*,
some of whom had traveled from Thebes (Simmias) and from Megara
(Cebes, Phaedondas, Euclides, Terpsion). These are the persons who,
with Phaedo, had come to know Socrates as friend and comrade (*hetairos*,
as at *Phaedo* 118A13).

Despite what our sources have to say about these other relationships,
however, we have no comparable information about the interaction
between Socrates and Plato himself. Xenophon mentions Plato only
once (*Memorabilia* III.vi.1), saying that Socrates had taken an interest in

Glaucon because of Plato (his brother) and Charmides (his uncle). This suggests that Socrates thought well of Plato but gives no indication of the nature of their relationship. Plato mentions himself twice in his own dialogues (*Apology* 34A, *Phaedo* 59B), but neither time as interacting directly with Socrates. In short, although the dialogues themselves are ample evidence that the influence of Socrates on Plato was quite extraordinary, we have no specific idea of the manner in which that influence was exercised. We learn something about the character of that interaction from Socrates' mention of Plato at *Apology* 34A as someone who was not corrupted by his company. And Plato probably would not have had himself listed at *Phaedo* 59B as absent on the final day if he had not been generally known as one of Socrates' regular associates, a presumption supported by his reference to Socrates as a "friend" (*philos*) at Seventh Letter 324D9. But this is about all we have to go on, by way of direct evidence, in building up a plausible picture of the personal interaction between Socrates and Plato.

A significant amount of indirect information can be brought to bear for this purpose, however, by means of the assumption introduced above, that Plato's personal interaction with Socrates provided the basis for the account in the Seventh Letter of the genesis of philosophic knowledge. Plato's description at 341D1–2 of the "flash of insight" with which knowledge first appears in the mind of the learner is too vivid to allow much doubt about Plato's confidence that he had gone through this experience himself. Given the intimate linkage in these passages between the onset of knowledge and regular association (*sunousia*) with a teacher, moreover, the clear implication is that Plato himself had submitted to the disciplines such an association provides. And with whom other than Socrates might Plato have associated in this fashion?[26] The upshot is that Plato almost certainly took part in regular conversations with the historical Socrates and that these conversations featured the "well-disposed cross-examination" required by way of preparation for the onset of knowledge.

There is nothing in the Seventh Letter, we should note, that indicates any one specific form these conversations might have taken. In some cases, of course, they might have been entirely private, after the manner depicted in the *Phaedrus* and in a few other dialogues. But there is nothing in our sources to suggest that the actual Socrates spent much time in tête-à-tête of this sort. Many didactic conversations with Socrates probably involved several impressionable young men among the respondents, in the manner of the *Phaedo* and the *Republic*. It is conceivable even that a talented neophyte might benefit from involvement in a Socratic conversation as a mere onlooker, as Socrates the Younger presumably would have benefitted from the conversation depicted in the *Theaetetus*. Whatever the nature of his personal involvement on any particular occasion, at any rate, we can take it as almost certain that Plato participated in conversations like these with Socrates on a regular basis and that he attributed his early progress in philosophy to the influence of these conversations.

One fairly obvious point of relevance between the foregoing observations and Plato's choice to write in dialogue form, at any rate, is that the dialogues are literary reproductions of conversations of the very sort that probably set the stage for his own philosophic accomplishments. As Plato was served by the historical Socrates, so Plato has served his reader in turn. The conversations in which Plato himself participated were exclusively oral, to be sure, while those offered to his reader are written instead. But both sets are conversations involving master philosophers. And both have proven able to communicate the benefits that conversations with master philosophers are capable of providing.

It should be noted that there is no inconsistency between what Plato has Socrates say about the uses of written language in the *Phaedrus* and his own strictures in the Seventh Letter regarding language generally as a medium for the communication of philosophic knowledge. What he says in the Seventh Letter is that neither written nor oral discourse is capable of transferring knowledge intact from one mind to another and that persons who undertake to communicate philosophy in this fashion exhibit a lack of understanding of what they are talking about. Socrates' discussion of language in the *Phaedrus* picks up on the same theme, but goes on to identify a *logos* "written in the soul" of the learner as the only kind of discourse capable of exhibiting a knowledge of philosophy. It is in this latter regard that Socrates makes the point about both oral and written language being capable of sowing the seeds from which this knowledge eventually grows in the mind of the learner. Oral communication, without doubt, is better for this purpose, but when necessary the written word might serve instead.

An answer to the question why Plato wrote in dialogue form has been building throughout this chapter and finally is ready for explicit formulation. Described with regard to their literary form exclusively, Plato's dialogues depict conversations between masters of philosophy and

respondents less advanced in philosophic understanding. Looking beyond literary form itself, we have noted that these conversations are of
the sort explicitly said in both the Seventh Letter and the *Theaetetus* to
be conducive to the generation of knowledge in the minds of respondents. Of particular relevance to our concern is the fact that Plato most
certainly viewed himself as having benefitted from conversations of this
sort with the historical Socrates and that he saw fit in the *Phaedrus* to
describe the role of Socrates in this interaction as one of planting "seeds
of discourse" that might mature to knowledge in the mind of the learner.
What Plato is doing with his dialogues, it now seems evident, is attempting to set up conversations of the sort he shared with Socrates, in hopes
of producing a similar effect in the mind of the reader.

An obvious difference, of course, is that the conversations we share
with Plato are written only, while those he shared with Socrates were
oral discourses. The importance of this difference is diminished, however, by Plato's having employed that form of written discourse that most
closely corresponds to the oral conversation of Socrates himself—i.e.,
the form of a Socratic dialogue. And the difference may be largely
counterbalanced by the fact that the skilled author (Plato) of a written
dialogue has more opportunity to polish his discourse than is enjoyed by
the leader (Socrates) of its oral equivalent. It is not unreasonable to
surmise, indeed, that the more successful among the Platonic dialogues
possess a power to inseminate the minds of their readers that matches the
apparent fecundity of the Socratic conversations in which Plato participated himself.

If this way of viewing the matter is somewhere near correct, then the
master-learner relation upon which we should focus in trying to understand Plato's use of the conversational format is not the relation between
Socrates and the other characters in the dialogues. The key relation to
bear in mind is that between the author and ourselves as readers. By
devoting attention to the conversations that Plato has crafted, we
ourselves become involved in *sunousia* with a master philosopher—one
no less adept than Plato's own teacher at preparing the learner for the
"spark of insight" of which the Seventh Letter speaks.

Plato himself was guided toward philosophic understanding through
conversation with Socrates within the precincts of Athens. He responded by crafting a set of literary conversations empowered to provide
similar guidance to their readers in turn. This is the answer I wish to
propose to the question why Plato wrote in dialogue form.

This answer, it should be noted, is one that places a burden upon the reader to engage the dialogues as conversations with their author in the manner intended. In what manner can one converse in the twentieth century with a master who fell silent over two millennia previously?

5. The Dialogues as Conversations between Author and Reader

There is an ordinary sense of the term 'conversation' in which one might be said to be in conversation with the past masters of one's tradition. Aristotle entered into conversation with the presocratics in addressing their concerns at the beginning of the *Metaphysics*. And Plato entered conversation with the Eleatics and the Pythagoreans in taking a stand on the unity of being in the second part of the *Parmenides*. So the modern reader enters into conversation with Plato in undertaking a careful study of his written dialogues. But in suggesting that Plato's dialogues provide occasion for conversation with their author, this is not primarily what I have in mind.

In what *other* sense might a careful reading of the dialogues constitute a conversation between reader and author? In order to converse actively with another person, it might be objected, one not only must be responsive to what the other is saying but also must have some influence on the conversation oneself. And there is no way we can influence either the words or the author of texts that were written such a long time ago. In one obvious respect, this objection is correct. Of course there is no way we could actually speak to Plato, or influence what might be said by way of response. But in another respect, no less obvious, the objection is mistaken, for we have a good deal of influence over what we find in the text.

As any person beyond the sophomore year in college should know, a serious study of any worthwhile text requires active participation on the part of the reader. One must maintain constant effort to confront the text with relevant questions, to distill from one's reading the best available answers, and all in all to retain a clear view of where the text is heading and of how it gets there from where it was previously. The difficulty of doing this effectively accounts for the common experience of a few hours' serious study being more taxing than a comparable period of physical exercise. When one is seriously engaged with a text of philosophy, moreover, the level of active involvement is likely to be even higher, if for no other reason than the complexity of the material. And the rewards of active involvement should be higher in turn, at least if the text has been competently written.

Although Plato's writings are not the only texts to which one might turn for illustration, needless to say, there probably are no other writings within our philosophic tradition of which the remarks above are more palpably true. That is, there are no other writings we are likely to encounter that are more responsive to an active reading. It is one thing, of course, to hear someone else saying this and to write it off as hyperbole by an overzealous Platonist. But it is quite another thing to have experienced it oneself, as have countless readers throughout the ages. And when one experiences it personally, regardless of partisanship, it is natural to wonder how it comes about.

There are various ways of describing this remarkable capacity of Plato's dialogues to reward one's reading in proportion to effort involved. One is to observe that the interaction among the characters moves on several levels at once. On the most superficial level, the dialogue will contain a series of less than clever opinions, expressed by an expositor who at first is much too confident, which then are countered by a series of refutations which lead their expositor to see that these opinions are mistaken. In the *Euthyphro* for instance, the utter dogmatism of Euthyphro's initial reasons for wanting to bring charges against his father gradually gives way, under Socrates' prodding, to palpable confusion about the nature of piety and to an early exit from the court, leaving the father unindicted. Bizarre interchanges of this sort often are enough to catch the beginning reader's attention and to entice him or her into a more careful reading of the dialogue. On a more substantial level, the typical dialogue will begin to engage the reader's own serious thoughts about the matter under discussion, perhaps leading him or her to think up alternative responses to the master dialectician's questioning. Thus an experienced reader of the first part of the *Parmenides*, for example, might be stimulated to "come to Plato's assistance" with more sophisticated responses to Parmenides' arguments against the Forms than the youthful Socrates is able to muster. Such an exercise might contribute to the reader's logical training and will have the useful result at least of inducing consideration of why Plato did not provide Socrates with more effective responses (which unquestionably he could have done).

Then there is the level on which a person stands to get an inkling of what Plato is getting at in the dialogue and begins to see ramifications not articulated by the individual characters. One of the more exciting moments an experienced reader is likely to have with the *Theaetetus*, for example, comes with the realization that the author has withheld the most promising sense of *logos* from the discussion at the end of the dialogue, and that if the quite common meanings of "explanation" or "account" had been brought into play, the characterization of knowledge as "true judgment in the company of *logos*" would have appeared much nearer to the mark. It is at this point that the reader becomes aware of some of Plato's reasons for ending the dialogue as he did and with this gains insight into the character of knowledge as Plato probably saw it at the time of writing. Through *sunousia* with Plato, occasioned by Socrates' dialogue with Theaetetus, the reader thus is led to see things about knowledge that were never written explicitly into the dialogue.

Another way of describing the ability of a typical dialogue to respond to an active reading is provided by the hierarchy of mental states distinguished in the Divided Line of the *Republic*. Although the Divided Line itself can be grasped on several different levels of significance, and although we will want to look at it much more carefully at a later stage in this discussion, anyone who has read more than a smattering of Plato will recall that the Line symbolizes four different stages of mental awareness. First is the stage of "image thinking" (*eikasia*), which corresponds roughly to the mental state of someone who reads a dialogue exclusively for the spectacles it provides. There undoubtedly is something humorous about the way Socrates pushes Polus around in the early pages of the *Gorgias*, for example, or in the petulant outrage of Thrasymachus in Book I of the *Republic* when his views of justice appear to refute themselves under Socrates' relentless questioning. But while entertainment of this sort is available from the dialogues, the state of mind it engenders by itself is of no particular philosophic worth. Next is the stage of belief or opinion (*pistis*), corresponding to the state of mind of someone who reads a dialogue on the level merely of the argument and counterargument taking place between the master philosopher and his interlocutors. To be sure, there are useful lessons to be learned in tracing through the argument mounted against Simmias in the *Phaedo*, for instance, showing why the soul cannot be merely the atunement of the body, or the reasons developed by the Stranger in the *Sophist* to persuade Theaetetus that what is real cannot be identical with what is changeless. But logical displays of this sort engage the reader on the level of opinion only. And even true opinion, in the context of the Divided Line, is two stages short of philosophic knowledge.

The next-to-last stage on the Divided Line is that of reasoned understanding (dianoia), which corresponds to the mental state of a more
advanced reader who attempts to come to grips with a dialogue in terms
of the demonstrations it might contain of one or another intriguing
thesis. Common examples of this approach can be found in the extensive literature on the "third man arguments" of the Parmenides, as well as
in the many discussions available of the so-called "hedonistic argument"
at the end of the Protagoras and of the final argument for immortality at
the end of the Phaedo. To constitute a "demonstration" worth the title,
however, a given line of argument must not only be valid but must be
based on premises that can be known to be true. And as Socrates himself
is made to point out in the Phaedo (107B), the task of arriving at premises
with the requisite status cannot itself be left to demonstrative reasoning.

It is only with a mental grasp corresponding to the final stage of the
Divided Line, I want to suggest, that a reader may be thought to have
encountered a dialogue in the manner that was intended by its author.
The final stage is that of knowledge (epistēmē, as at 533E5) or intelligence
(noēsis, as at 511E1), described in its context as a mental grasp of the
Forms themselves. If Plato's own account of the matter in the Seventh
Letter is to be taken seriously, this state must be reached by the inquiring
mind itself and will not answer to any thesis put in words by the author.
A possible example, briefly alluded to above, might be one's awareness
after repeated readings of the Theaetetus why the nature of knowledge, as
Plato saw it, precluded ending the dialogue on a more positive note—
precluded, that is to say, a definition of the nature of knowledge from
being written into the conversation itself.

The claim here is not that Plato had these several levels of encounter
with the dialogues in mind while laying out the Divided Line, nor even
that these levels of encounter correspond unambiguously with the four
stages of that much discussed image. The point is just to illustrate
another way of characterizing the striking power of the dialogues to
respond to the probings of an active reader—in this case, a manner of
characterization showing how an encounter with the dialogues can be
extended in stages from lower to higher levels of comprehension.

One could employ a metaphor of penetration to much the same
purpose. While an initial two or three passes through a dialogue might
not move a reader much beyond its surface ornamentation—the baiting
of Thrasymachus, for example, or the numbing of Meno—subsequent
readings will gradually show the inner working of the composition and

will distinguish between the surface and the underlying dialectic. The reader will then see that the basic issue of the *Meno* is not whether virtue can be taught but rather the proper method of inquiry into a thing's essential nature, and will then realize that Socrates' purpose in the *Phaedo* is not to prove immortality but to exhibit the peace of soul that is required for philosophy, and will then begin to understand why Socrates must be retired at the end of the *Theaetetus* to make way for a discussion leader who is more "thoroughly trained" in philosophy. Or if not these things, he or she will see other things like them. And having thus penetrated into the inner core of the dialogue, the reader may presently find himself or herself in the singular position of being able to "think through" the conversation from the author's perspective and of being able to anticipate features that until then had escaped notice. At this point it begins to appear as if Plato had actually anticipated the questions that come to mind in the attentive reader and had planted answers that come to light in appropriate order.

From this point onwards the conversation between author and reader is no less lively than that depicted within the dialogue—with the difference that the former is actual whereas the latter is merely fictional! Thus it is that author engages reader in philosophic conversation—the kind of *sunousia* by which a master leads a fortunate neophyte to the sudden spark that marks the onset of philosophic knowledge.

Among the more interesting of the proposals considered in the first section of this chapter is that the dialogues were written for use in the Academy.[27] Despite the fact, noted previously, that there is no direct evidence regarding their use in this context, it seems natural to suppose that Plato encouraged his associates to read his writings and that some would have done so even if not encouraged. So it seems reasonable to assume, in the case of certain dialogues at least, that they were written in anticipation of their being read in the Academy.[28]

But Plato must have realized, at the same time, that a more remote set of readers would probably be reached by the dialogues as well. Indeed the more remote readership might have seemed even more important. For whereas students within the Academy could converse with Plato directly, those who came later could be reached only through the dialogues.

The most likely story about Plato's intended readership, it seems to me, is something like the following. While the dialogues were written to be read by members of the Academy, they were intended to be read by a much wider audience as well. And while in a broad sense they were written for instructional purposes, they were not intended to be used in the manner of textbooks, and they were never part of a fixed curriculum. Most importantly, they were written for instructional use within the constraints laid down in the Seventh Letter. They were written for readers of any era who might have the temperament and talent to submit to their discipline and whose love of wisdom might be stirred by the conversations within them.

If we can accept this as an approximate account of why Plato wrote dialogues, let us move on to a careful look at the various stages of this discipline.

2

REFUTATION AND IRONY:
PREPARING THE GROUND

1. Refutation in the Sophistic Tradition

The central thesis of the preceding chapter is that Plato composed *written* versions of the *sunousia* that are characterized in the Seventh Letter as fostering philosophic understanding in the mind of a suitably prepared learner. While the Seventh Letter stresses that such understanding can be reached only through hard work and discipline, the only part of this regimen it identifies specifically is "well-disposed refutation by cross-examination." Even if there were no other links between Plato's written dialogues and the *sunousia* of the Seventh Letter, this reference to well-meaning refutation should be enough by itself to remind us of the practice of refutation, or elenchus, so prevalent in his Socratic conversations. The main purpose of the present chapter is to examine how elenchus works within the dialogues, with an eye toward finding out what we can about Plato's own conception of its contribution to philosophic understanding.

There are three separate questions in this regard that should be distinguished from the outset. First in order of concern, to say it again, is how elenchus figures in Plato's own thinking about the discipline leading to philosophic understanding. The more we can find out on this score, the better grasp we should be able to achieve of his conception of the relation between teacher and learner in the Seventh Letter and in the *Phaedrus*. This should lead to a better grasp, in particular, of the role he thought elenchus should play in the "cultivation" of his "literary garden"—i.e., in the interaction he initiates with readers of his dialogues.

Next is the question of how elenchus functions in the conversations Plato sets up between the character Socrates and his interlocutors. One difference between the way elenchus works in the dialogues and the way it is supposed to work in the Seventh Letter is that in the dialogues it is never pursued in the context of an ongoing program of philosophic training on the part of the interlocutor. This may be one reason Socrates is never depicted there as leading his interlocutor to the point of knowledge on the topic at issue. Another difference is that elenchus is sometimes portrayed in the dialogues (e.g., the *Meno*) as an integral part of a process of *anamnēsis* or recollection. In other respects, however, it seems safe to assume that Plato's portrayal of elenchus in the dialogues is a good indication of the role he thought it should play in the pursuit of philosophy generally. With these reservations in mind, accordingly, we may draw freely upon examples of Socratic refutation in the dialogues in our attempt to understand the role it was supposed to play in getting his "literary garden" ready for seeding.

A third question concerns the kind of refutation actually practiced by the historical Socrates, in and about the precinct of Athens. The actual practice of Socratic elenchus must have served, to some extent at least, as a model after which the elenchus of the dialogues was patterned (the topic of the second question). And presumably Plato's own experience with refutation at the hands of Socrates had something to do with his conception of the role of elenchus in philosophic training, as characterized in the Seventh Letter (the topic of the first question). But we have seen reason already to conclude that Plato's portrayal of his character Socrates is not historical in every respect, and this caution should be extended to his portrayal of Socratic elenchus in particular. What this means for present purposes is that we should not be content to rely upon the dialogues *exclusively* for our understanding of the elenchus practiced by the historical Socrates, which presumably is the source of Plato's own conception of elenchus that stands behind the role of refutation in the Seventh Letter.

Fortunately for our purposes, there are several other sources from the fifth and fourth centuries that provide insight into the elenchic practices of the historical Socrates. Before returning to our primary question, let us survey the evidence from these other sources.

Literature about Socrates by authors other than Plato can be conveniently divided into three distinct subgroups. To begin with, there were several other authors who wrote dialogues based on the historical Socrates—so many, in fact, that the so-called "Socratic conversations" became a standard literary genre in their own right.[1] Best known among these is Xenophon, author of a *Symposium*, an *Apology*, and an

Oeconomicus (dealing with matters of estate management), as well as the *Memorabilia*, which recounts the life of Socrates in mixed narrational and conversational form. Two others are known by name from the *Phaedo* as having been present during Socrates' last hours—Antisthenes, from whom apparently no fragments remain, and Aeschines, who wrote an *Alcibiades* which has in part been preserved. Since only the *Memorabilia* shows us a Socrates favoring an elenchic form of argument, these other documents can be set aside for present purposes.

Evidence of a rather different sort is available from a number of comedies in which a burlesqued Socrates plays a prominent role. First to come to mind is Aristophanes' *Clouds*, in which Socrates is portrayed as master of a *phrontistērion* ("think-tank"), offering to teach various forms of fraudulent reasoning for pay. In the *Connus* by Ameipsias, to cite a less well-known example, Socrates was nicknamed *phrontistes*, connoting sophistry, and said to indulge in time-wasting subtleties of dialectic. Socrates also was caricatured in the *Birds* by Aristophanes and at least mentioned in comedies by Eupolis and Telecleides.

Consider how Socrates is portrayed in the *Clouds*. In the opening conversation between Strepsiades and his playboy son, Aristophanes introduces a distinction between a Just (traditional) and an Unjust (sophistic) mode of argument, both of which can be studied in the "think-tank" run by Socrates. In a later passage, these two "logics" engage in a contest, in which the Unjust threatens to destroy the Just by "speaking against" (*antilegōn:* 901) it and scores a win by use of the "weaker argument" (*hēttonas logous:* 1042), employing "novel notions" (*gnōmas kainas:* 896). The fact that both "logics" can be learned for a fee[2] at the "think-tank," combined with the fact that the Unjust handily wins the contest, strongly reinforces the image of Socrates as a professional sophist. Plato has good reason to portray Socrates as rebutting this image with his opening remarks in the *Apology*, where, after explicit reference to this "comedy by Aristophanes" (19C2–3), he denies either being among those who "make the weaker argument prevail" (*ton hētto logon kreittō poiein:* 23D5–6; also 18B10, 19B5–C1) or having replaced the traditional gods with "novel divinities" (*daimonia kaina:* 24C1) of his own invention.

Xenophon joined forces with Plato in attempting to counteract that aspect of Socrates' reputation that made him a target for parody by the comic playwrights. The express purpose of the *Memorabilia* was to show how the youth benefitted from keeping company with Socrates, both by

his "conversations" (*dialegomenos:* 1.iii.1) and by the "actions that revealed his nature" (ibid.). Xenophon goes on to support his case by citing
several instances in which Socrates cross-examined (*ēlenchen:* 1.iv.1)
people who thought they knew everything, presumably for the edification of those who were listening. His response, both to Aristophanes
and to those whose formal charges led to Socrates' execution, was in
effect to admit Socrates' skill in refutation but to insist that he used this
skill only for upright purposes and never to "corrupt the youth."[3]

Yet another perspective is provided by various passages from Aristotle
which mention logical techniques attributed expressly to Socrates.[4] Of
direct relevance is 186b of *On Sophistical Refutations,* having to do with
distinctions drawn at the beginning of that work among four kinds of
argument: didactic, dialectical, examinational, and contentious. The
latter, of course, is the province of the sophist, characterized in 165a as
one who makes money from an apparent but unreal wisdom. Didactic
and examinational arguments, in turn, are deductions from premises
that are "properly known" and in the case of the former are appropriate
to the subject under discussion. Dialectical arguments, on the other
hand, are deductions from premises that are "reputable" only and are
aimed to contradict a given thesis. The technique of dialectic, Aristotle
then remarks at 183b, is similar to that of sophistry, in that the former
also can be used with a show of knowledge when "reputable" premises are
replaced with ones seemingly unknown. It is at this point that he makes
his cryptic reference to Socrates, to the effect that Socrates (apparently
in contrast with the standard sophist) only *asked* questions but did not
attempt to answer them himself, because he explicitly disavowed any
pretence of knowledge. The gist presumably is that Socrates' style of
asking questions was similar to dialectic (in Aristotle's sense) in being
aimed toward the contradiction of given theses but was distinguished
from dialectic and sophistry alike in avoiding premises that were either
"reputable" or speciously known. That is, Socrates would ask questions
tending toward the contradiction of theses but would not introduce
theses of his own into the argument. In brief, he dealt only in refutation,
offering no positive views in lieu of those that were refuted.

Aristotle distinguished Socratic elenchus from sophistic refutation by
reference to Socrates' hallmark claim to have no knowledge. Xenophon
acknowledged Socrates' skill at refutation but stressed that it was in the
service of virtue only. Aristophanes achieved humorous effect by adorn-
ing Socrates with features of sophistry in grotesquely exaggerated form,

which would have been impossible had the real Socrates lacked these features entirely. And Plato himself, as we know, at one point actually referred to Socratic refutation as a form of sophistry, set apart from other forms by its "noble lineage" (*genei gennaia: Sophist* 231B9).

One obvious inference from all this is that Socrates was seen by his literary detractors and admirers alike as being somehow aligned with that group of traveling teachers who specialized in the techniques of manipulative discourse. And this fairly clearly was the perception of many citizens of Athens as well, as gauged both by the reception of the "Socratic comedies" and by the success of the charges brought by Meletus and his associates (*Apology* 23E, 36A). In the eyes of the comedians and their popular audiences, Socrates was a sophist, pure and simple. In the eyes of Plato and Xenophon, by contrast, he was someone well-versed in sophistic techniques but unique in the way he saw fit to employ them. Whichever perspective one might tend to favor, it is apparent that the significance of the Socratic practice of refutation cannot be understood in isolation from the practices of the professional sophists.[5] What aspects of the latter are germane to our concern?

Considerable help in this regard is provided by G. B. Kerford, in his careful study *The Sophistic Movement*.[6] The "key to the problem of understanding the true nature of the sophistic movement," Kerford suggests, is a grasp of the "nature of antilogic."[7] Skill in antilogic, he notes, is often attributed by Plato to the sophists, and in this attribution constitutes a "specific and fairly definite technique"—i.e., that of proceeding from a position adopted by one's opponent to the establishment of an opposing *logos* "in such a way that the opponent must either accept both *logoi*, or at least abandon his first position."[8] By way of example, Kerford points to the method of argument used by Zeno of Elea and refers to a discussion by F. M. Cornford in which Zeno for this reason is described as engaging in *antilogikē*.[9] Kerford then ties *antilogikē* into Socratic elenchus by suggesting the latter as an early stage in the process of dialectic, as practiced by Socrates in the early dialogues, and by observing that this "is clearly an application of antilogic."[10]

This identification of Zeno as an *antilogikos* opens up a number of relevant considerations. For one, it enjoys a high degree of plausibility. Not only does the description of *antilogikē* cited by Cornford fairly obviously pertain to Zeno, but there is a similar reference in Plutarch's *Life of Pericles* (4.3).[11] We know enough about this technique, moreover, to describe it in general as a method of refutation in which an opponent's

thesis is shown unacceptable by showing that it entails some unacceptable consequence. The opponent's thesis is thus "reduced to absurdity"
by showing some intolerable consequence that follows if one accepts it.
This is clearly a matter, as Kerford describes it, of setting one *logos* in
opposition to another—i.e., clearly a matter of "opposing *logoi*," which is
the literal meaning of *antilogikē*.

Furthermore, if Zeno is a credible example of an *antilogikos*, then his
mode of argument provides credible examples of *antilogikē*. And we know
a fair amount in detail about Zeno's mode of argument. Among other
things, we know that the four arguments against motion criticized in
Aristotle's *Physics* (cf. 239b9–240a17) all begin with certain assumptions
about the nature of either space or time and then purport to deduce the
denial of certain theses that would have to be accepted by anyone who
accepts the existence of motion. The argument entitled "the Stadium,"
for instance, assumes that space is continuous, or infinitely divisible, and
purports to show that on that assumption nothing can move from one
place to another. The argument entitled "the Flying Arrow," in turn,
begins with the assumption that space is discrete, i.e., not infinitely
divisible, and leads to the conclusion once again that motion is impos-
ible, since a thing can move neither where it is (not having room in that
exact location) or where it is not at any given moment. Since space
either is or is not infinitely divisible, the combined result of these first
two arguments is the unconditional conclusion that motion is impos-
ible. The remaining two arguments team up in the same way to show
that the same conclusion follows on the basis of two mutually exclusive
but exhaustive assumptions about time. This is the form of argument
that contemporary teachers of logic sometimes call a "destructive dilemma;" either way the opponent is brought to ruin.

Kerford makes his case for associating the *antilogikē* of the sophistic
tradition with the elenchus practiced by the historical Socrates[12] without
a detailed discussion of particular forms of argument that might be
involved. An interesting fact that tends to support Kerford's conclusion
is that Plato on occasion has his character Socrates employ arguments
precisely in the form of a destructive dilemma. One striking instance is
the refutation of the so-called "Dream Theory" at the end of the
Theaetetus.[13] A somewhat different use of this argument form occurs in
connection with the "learner's paradox" at *Meno* 80E, when Socrates is
setting up his account of learning as a form of recollection. While these
passages should not be read as direct attributions of particular arguments

to the historical Socrates, for reasons already discussed, they show at least that Plato had no qualms about associating the Socratic elenchus portrayed in his writings with the *antilogikē* practiced by other sophists of the time. Not only is there an apparent continuity in use of this style of argument from Zeno through the professional sophists to the Socrates of the dialogues, indeed, but we are even given a dramatic portrayal in the *Parmenides* of how Socrates might have been influenced by Zeno in this regard.[14] After submitting the youthful Socrates to a blistering elenchus in the first part of the dialogue, Parmenides commends him for eagerness in argument, but cautions that he must submit to a "severer training" (135D4) in what many call "idle talk" (135D5) or otherwise the truth will escape him. This exercise, says Parmenides, should take the form of Zeno's treatise that Socrates had been listening to earlier (127C–D). No matter what thing he is reasoning about, he should consider the consequences not only of the supposition that this thing exists, but also those of the supposition that it does not exist. Zeno, for example, had traced out the consequences of the hypothesis "if plurality exists" (136A5) and in accord with the pattern of his destructive dilemma should next have considered what follows "if plurality does not exist" (136A7). The prescribed form is illustrated, in brief, by the opposing *logoi* "either plurality exists or plurality does not exist" as the basis of his argument; and this is the pattern for Socrates to follow if he wants to be thoroughly disciplined.

Once we begin to take Plato's depiction of Socratic refutation into account, however, this initially straightforward story about Socrates as a member of the current group of sophists begins to require a considerable amount of adjustment. For one thing, there are numerous passages in which Plato has his Socrates take vigorous exception to sophistic modes of argument. For another, there is the well-known description in the *Sophist* of Socratic elenchus as a "noble form" of sophistry set apart from the rest. If the historical Socrates was in one sense was a member of the sophistic movement, there is another sense in which he stood apart as one of its main critics. Let us consider in further detail the differences between Socrates and the other sophists.

2. The Distinctive Marks of Socratic Elenchus

After his brief description of the method of hypothesis in the *Phaedo*, and his advice that this is the right way for the philosopher to follow, the character Socrates warns against the practice of *antilogikē* that shows no concern for the truth of things (101E). Similar disparagement of this sophistic technique occurs at *Republic* 454A, where Socrates describes *antilogikē* as wrangling or quarreling, in contrast with dialectic which he advocates instead. Other well-known passages in which *antilogikē* is cast in an unfavorable light are *Phaedrus* 261D and *Theaetetus* 197A. If Socratic elenchus itself is a form of *antilogikē*, as we saw reason to conclude above, then why is Plato's character so hostile to this style of argument in the dialogues? An obvious explanation would be that the style of refutation actually practiced by Socrates differed from that of the other sophists in ways Plato considered significant enough to warrant treating Socratic refutation as a distinct class of argument. In what ways did refutation as practiced by Socrates differ from the *antilogikē* of the other sophists?

One distinctive feature of Socratic elenchus, it seems clear, is that it was practiced with unmatchable skill. According to the dialogues, at least, Socrates was well-known abroad for his skills of refutation (*Meno* 80A, *Protagoras* 361E), and had built up such a reputation at home for being able to defeat all comers that a good part of his defense in the *Apology* is taken up with an attempt to justify his contentious behavior. But surely it was not Socrates' superiority in refutation that led Plato to portray Socratic elenchus in such sharp contrast with the techniques of the other sophists. If Protagoras, say, had proven more successful than Socrates in disputatious argument, this would have not induced Plato to write dialogues touting Protagorean refutation as a model for philosophers to follow. It was not because Socrates was the most skilled sophist around, in brief, that Plato singled out Socratic elenchus as a style of argument especially suited to the pursuit of philosophy. The features of Socratic refutation that marked it off as superior to other versions of *antilogikē* in Plato's view, we may safely say, had to do with the purposes behind the Socratic practice rather than the power of the arguments involved.

Our best source of information about the differences Plato found significant between Socratic elenchus and other forms of refutation is the five-page characterization of elenchus in the *Sophist* (226B-231B). The main business of these passages is to identify what is described there as "the sophistry of noble lineage" (231B9)[15] and to distinguish this from other varieties of sophistic *technē*. Those who practice the "noble sophistry," notes the Stranger from Elea, cross-examine (*dierōtōsin:* 230B4) what a person says when that person is speaking nonsense and easily pick out the errors of the opinions expressed, showing how they stand in opposition regarding the same things in the same respects. As far as *technique* of refutation is concerned, there is no difference indicated in this description between Socratic elenchus and other versions of sophistry. All sophists deal in cross-examination in one form or another and try to catch their subjects in contradiction (cf. 268B). What is different about Socratic elenchus is the effect it is intended to have upon the subject—i.e., the purpose for which it is applied. Whereas the techniques of other varieties of sophistry are employed for coercion or personal gain, the method employed by the "noble sophist" is intended not to exploit but to improve the subject.[16]

More specifically, whereas the other sophists *produce* ignorance in the minds of their students, the "noble sophist" seeks to *eradicate* the false opinion produced by the others. Socratic elenchus is a form of purgation (*kathairon*: 227A10), cleansing the mind of conceit however engendered. In the words of the Stranger as he summarizes the discussion, we should say that "elenchus is the greatest and most authoritative of purifications" (230D7–9) which anyone requires to escape mental deformity (*aischron*: 230E2). When a person has undergone this kind of purgation, however, he or she gains the benefits that come with modesty and consequently becomes more gentle toward others.

What is particularly interesting about this discussion of Socratic refutation in the *Sophist* is that Plato makes no distinction between the styles of argument employed by Socrates and by the other sophists. These others might even proceed by question and answer (225B8–9), the form of discourse to which Socrates is given in the written dialogues. What makes the elenchus of Socrates distinctive is that it is applied, not for the benefit of the person applying it, but for the benefit of the person to whom it is applied. It makes its subjects displeased with themselves; it removes opinions that are an impediment to learning (*mathēmasin empodious*: 230D2); and it thereby produces an enduring benefit of a purified soul and of a mind ready for further instruction. In brief, while other sophists practice for their own advantage, the "noble sophist" practices for the good of others.[17]

One notable omission from the Stranger's description is that the "noble sophist" does not charge for his ministrations. That the historical Socrates did not take money for his conversation is adequately attested by *Apology* 31B–C, where the Socrates of the dialogue calls this explicitly to his audience's attention. Plato would not have falsified the Socratic story on an important point like this while there were still people among his readers who knew the real Socrates personally. What are we to make of the fact that nothing is said in the Stranger's account about the "noble sophist" not receiving compensation? One thing we cannot say plausibly is that the matter is irrelevant. In the description of each of the other five sophists, the point is made quite explicitly that what they do is done for profit. The first sophist takes currency in exchange for his goods (223B3), the next three are identified as either merchants or retailers (224C–E), and the fifth makes money from private disputation (225E1–2). If the "noble sophist" also took money, it would be a trait worth mentioning. And given the emphasis on profits where the others are concerned, the fact that nothing is said in this regard about the "noble sophist" certainly suggests that indeed he does not take money. Why did Socrates not charge for his services? And what effect did this have upon the services rendered?

In point of fact, there probably were several reasons why Socrates did not charge his associates for the conversations he held with them, without regard to the elenchic cast of those conversations. Xenophon mentions several in the *Memorabilia*. One is that taking money from another person, in Socrates' opinion, "puts oneself under a master" (I.v.6), in effect making one a slave to the person who pays. A criticism Socrates has of the professional sophists in particular is that by offering their services to all who can afford them, they act in effect "like prostitutes of wisdom" (I.vi.13); while those, on the other hand, who converse without payment are free to choose their conversation partners (I.ii.6). Moreover, says Xenophon in Socrates' behalf, if anyone thinks he is capable of teaching virtue, as Xenophon seemed to think that Socrates was (I.ii.7–8), the friendship and gratitude of those he benefits should be payment enough for the services rendered. While these reasons all seem genuine, however, and are entirely commensurate with the fact that Socrates seemed committed to not taking fees as a matter of principle,[18] they are explanations that seem canted by a touch of rhetoric. They are explanations with the ring of something left unsaid.

One angle to bear in mind as we look for deeper reasons is that the services Socrates offered to the citizens of Athens were not likely to be welcome to many of their recipients. To the extent that his mission actually involved "busying himself with the private affairs" of other people, as *Apology* 31C4–5 puts it, this undoubtedly would cause resentment, and the average citizen would have been no more ready to pay for this attention than to maintain Socrates at state expense, as proposed at *Apology* 37A1. In the more sober description of his calling at *Sophist* 230, the people the "noble sophist" converses with are said to become upset with themselves for having been refuted, to the malicious delight of others in the audience. Once again, this is not the kind of treatment for which one might reasonably request payment.

To be sure, there presumably were a few partners in conversation now and then who realized that they had benefitted from the therapy of Socratic elenchus and who might well have been grateful enough afterwards to pay for the treatment. Crito, Critobulus, and Apollodorus joined Plato in being ready to offer financial support to provide a fine for Socrates after he had been found guilty by the Assembly (*Apology* 38B). Crito, at 45A–B of his namesake dialogue, mentions having given Socrates some money already, in connection with his offer to pay bribes for Socrates' rescue. And there were probably other people of means who would have been willing to exchange money for time spent with Socrates during happier days. But he would not accept outright payment even from these select few. What was it about Socrates' brand of therapy— apart from his desire to be free from servitude—that made payment inappropriate no matter who was conversing with him?

Part of the answer may be tied in with Socrates' persistent profession of ignorance. The conclusion of his quest to find out what the god meant in saying that no one is wiser than Socrates, as reported in the *Apology*, was allegedly the realization that his superior wisdom consists in "knowing that his wisdom is worth nothing" (23B3–4). In the *Meno* he is made to say that he has "absolutely no knowledge about virtue at all" (71B3) and that he is no less numb himself than those numbed by his elenchus— that it is through his own perplexity, so to say, that he "inflicts perplexity on others" (80C8). In the *Theaetetus* he is made to admit that, while skilled in delivering the mental offspring of those who consort with him, he is incapable of giving birth himself because he "possesses no wisdom whatever" (150C6). This portrayal of Socrates as professing to "know only that he knows nothing" is correlated with the fact that his respondents in the early dialogues often end up in genuine perplexity (*aporia*) themselves. If Socrates in real life lacked ability to convey anything more edifying than confusion to his respondents, then we should not expect him to receive a fee for his services. *Aporia* is not a commodity generally considered worth exchanging for money.

Interpretations of "Socratic ignorance" that leave Socrates knowing literally nothing more than that he knows nothing, however, and that make this enough of an intellectual virtue to give substance to the oracle's denial that any other person is wiser, are much too simplistic to do justice to the richness of the Socratic character that Plato has portrayed in the early dialogues. A more adequate understanding of Socrates' profession of ignorance would involve viewing it sometimes as a rhetorical device employed for its effect upon his partners in conversation—i.e., as a thinly veiled exercise of "irony."[19] But it would be a mistake to conclude that this is all there is to it. When Socrates described himself as lacking knowledge, more is involved than a rhetorical ploy. There was a point to be made by professing ignorance in *contrast* with the professions of the other sophists.

Consider Protagoras, who, as noted above, not only was himself a master of *antilogikē*, but also was able to teach its techniques to other people (*Protagoras* 334E). These techniques of disputation, along with the art of flowery discourse, were central among the skills acquired by his pupils on their way allegedly to becoming good citizens (319A). Learning such skills was tantamount, in Protagoras' eyes, to acquiring virtue; and it was for imparting these skills—i.e. for "teaching virtue" (*didakton aretē*: 328C4)—that he charged the fees most of his students seemed so willing to pay (328B). For Protagoras, in brief, the techniques of *antilogikē* were not just ways of winning arguments. They were part of the art of living virtuously. For Protagoras, that is to say, there was a *technē* of virtue. And it was for teaching the skills of this *technē* to others that he received such large payments (*Theaetetus* 161E1). Hippias also purported to teach virtue (*Hippias Major* 284A), for which he also received very ample fees (282D). Prodicus claimed that his teaching provided a cure for ignorance (*Protagoras* 357E), the result of which cure (knowledge) is described in the *Protagoras* as a part of virtue; and for this service Prodicus earned an "astounding amount of money" (*Hippias Major* 282C). While Gorgias, on the other hand, apparently did not purport to teach virtue as such (*Meno* 95C), he considered the techniques of clever speaking, which he taught at great profit (*Hippias Major* 282B–C), to be the best *technē* of all for public persuasion (*Philebus* 58B).

The pattern was the same among the great sophists of the period. They possessed skills of argumentation that they taught for profit. And what they taught was either some manner of civic virtue, or (with Gorgias) some skill with recognized value in public affairs. Not only could virtue be taught, as these people conceived it, but it could be taught in the form of specific techniques. Virtue could be taught in the fashion of flute-playing and wrestling. And since the masters of these other skills received fees for the training they offered (*Meno* 90D–E, 94C–D), it was deemed appropriate by the professional sophists that they also should receive money for their instruction. Socrates apparently was the only exception.

Here we come finally to the basic difference between Socrates and the other major sophists. Like the other sophists, Socrates was a master of *antilogikē*—the art or *technē* of refutation. Like the others, his associations with students took the form of conversations or *sunousia*.[20] Moreover, although Socrates never claims in the dialogues to be a teacher of virtue, it seems fair to say that he thinks of the conversations in which he engages with the people of Athens as occasions for examining their thoughts on virtue (*Apology* 31B5). And there is no doubt that topics of virtue dominate most of the Socratic conversations written by Plato during his early and middle periods. So Socrates shares with many of the other sophists a concern for the moral improvement of the young persons whom they engage in conversation.

But there the similarities end. And the differences that remain are substantial indeed. For one thing, although Socrates himself apparently was unsurpassed in the techniques of *antilogikē*, there is no indication in any of our standard sources (excluding parodies like the *Clouds*) that he was interested in teaching these techniques to other people. It seems quite clear, in particular, that he did not think of skill in refutation as having much to do with the possession of virtue. Whereas Protagoras and various other sophists taught *antilogikē* as an integral part of their instruction in virtue—thinking of it rightly enough as a powerful instrument for swaying opinion in the law courts and public assemblies, which was a mark of civic virtue as they conceived it—Socrates seemed content to practice refutation himself with no concern to pass on the skill to those who conversed with him. While young men of course might pick up some of his techniques just by observing Socrates in action (like the persons described at *Philebus* 15D–E who confuse themselves and other people by "worrying around" statements that are ambiguous with respect to "the one and the many"), he is never portrayed as offering instruction in the elenchus he practiced. Be that as it may, he certainly did not teach it as an instrument of virtue. While he could scarcely disagree that *antilogikē* was useful in the assembly and the law court, ability to sway opinion in public gatherings simply was not part of virtue as Socrates conceived it.

The basic reason Socrates did not accept payment, in short, is that the virtue he hoped to get people to heed (*Apology* 31B5), through conversing with them and asking questions, was not a skill that could be passed on from teacher to student. What Socrates had to teach could not be imparted through lessons, employing *antilogikē* or any other explicit method.[21] In thinking of virtue as a skill they could impart like wrestling or flute-playing, the other sophists thought of it as a commodity fairly exchanged in return for money. As part of his stand against this conception, Socrates refused to treat the virtue he hoped to impart to his audience as a commodity, which entailed his refusal to accept money for the time people spent in his company. Part of his lesson was that this virtue has no monetary measure, which precluded his accepting money in exchange for helping other people achieve it.

These are facts about the Socratic conception of virtue that Plato himself must have come to understand through *sunousia* with the historical Socrates. And while this intercourse almost surely included strong doses of elenchus, he must have come to understand as well that Socrates was employing refutation in a manner radically different from the other sophists. But even this observation goes beyond our meager data regarding any direct interaction between Plato and Socrates. While Plato's personal experience of Socratic elenchus undoubtedly was a major factor in the development of his own conception of how refutation contributes to philosophic understanding, the only reliable access we have to this conception is through the depiction of elenchus in his Socratic conversations. Let us continue our inquiry into Plato's understanding of elenchus by an examination of the instructional role it plays within the dialogues. The dialogue best suited for this particular purpose is the conversation Plato wrote between Socrates and Meno.

3. The Exhibition of Socratic Elenchus in the Meno

The *Meno* is one of relatively few dialogues depicting conversations that conceivably might have occurred in Plato's presence. Although it is wholly implausible to assume that this dialogue was written as an eyewitness report, for reasons already discussed, it may be helpful to set up an imaginary scenario that would account for certain features we find in the dialogue. Let us suppose that Plato actually was present at a public encounter between Meno and Socrates, occurring around the year 401 B.C. when Meno was passing through Athens in the process of gathering up a company of mercenaries which he soon would lead to Persia.[22] And let us suppose that Plato's *Meno* was composed some time after this encounter, on the basis of impressions he had formed of this conversation that seemed best to capture the importance of what had transpired. Working within the context of these suppositions, we may then ask what that conversation must have been like in order to have inspired the treatment we find in the dialogue. What particular features of the conversation might Plato have found memorable that would account for the details he put in writing?

First and foremost, he must have been impressed by Socrates' use of refutation. By this time, of course, Socrates' skill in *antilogikē* was legendary. Meno himself had heard, before arriving in Athens, of his ability "to produce perplexity in other people" (80A2). And Plato must have witnessed the famed elenchus in action many times previously, perhaps even in application to himself. But something about the elenchus on this occasion might have seemed especially noteworthy. For the arguments by which Meno (in the dialogue) was reduced to perplexity seemed aimed, not merely at refutation, but at helping Meno reflect on the nature of his mistakes. Or, to put it more circumspectly, the elenchus seemed directed in such a fashion that it led *Plato* (if not Meno) to think carefully about the nature of Meno's mistakes. And as a result of this reflection on Plato's part, he found himself beginning to understand certain things about learning—the main topic of the dialogue—that otherwise might entirely have passed him by.

Socrates, as we hear from *Metaphysics* XIII, was preoccupied with the ethical virtues, and "in that connection became the first to seek out universal definitions" (1078b18–19). Both concerns are exercised within this dialogue. The question which Meno so abruptly puts to Socrates in his opening words is whether virtue is something that can be taught. And the process of refutation by which Socrates brings Meno to a state of relative docility a few pages later features a number of failed attempts to provide a general definition of virtue. Some of these definitions are supplied by Meno, and others are offered by Socrates ostensibly as illustrations.

After citing particular virtues associated with particular roles in society,[23] which Socrates describes disparagingly as a "swarm of virtues"

(*smēnos . . . aretōn:* 72A7), Meno advances as his first general definition
(taken from Gorgias) that virtue is the capacity to govern men (73C11).
This definition is clearly deficient, as Socrates shows immediately, for it
cannot apply to virtue in a child or in a slave. A second attempt by Meno
fragments virtue in a more interesting way, by mentioning several
general forms that virtue might take—courage, temperance, wisdom,
etc. But what do these have in common that makes them all forms of
virtue? When Meno protests that he cannot understand what Socrates
wants in asking for "a single virtue covering them all" (74B2), Socrates
offers an example of the sort of generality he is looking for. Consider the
definition of shape, he says, as the only thing that always comes with
color (75B10–C1). Now, while this definition has the requisite univer-
sality, it is not difficult to counter (the blue of the sky, for example, does
not have shape), and Socrates may have put it forward as an easy target
for Meno to refute and hence to build up his flagging confidence. But
Meno's criticism employs a different tactic, one he probably had learned
from Gorgias. The definition uses terms, he complains, that are themselves undefined; it would not satisfy someone who professed not to know
what color is.

   More is going on in this interchange than mere elenchic sparring.
Plato has reconstructed the conversation in such a manner as to lead the
reader to reflect upon the nature of definitions—not only with respect to
their universal character (Socrates' concern, according to Aristotle), but
also with regard to the background knowledge that must be in place for
the definition to be effective (Plato's concern, as soon will become
evident). And our surmise, for the present exercise, is that Plato himself
was led to similar reflections as he listened to an actual conversation
between Socrates and Meno. Could it be that coming to know what
anything is (e.g., shape) requires that something else (e.g., what color is)
be known already? If so, then the kind of definition that Socrates is
looking for would seem impossible, and the process of gaining knowledge
in the first place could never get started.

   But Meno is not ready to cooperate in an exploration of such issues.
We find Socrates instead responding to his misgivings with another
definition, one employing only terms that Meno admits he already
understands. Shape, Socrates now proposes, is the limit of a solid
(76A7). This, we might note, not only is an intuitively plausible definition; it is the definition of shape later adopted by Aristotle (*Physics*
211b12–13). But its effect is entirely lost on Meno, whose quite irrelevant

response is to ask for a definition of color. At this point Socrates, as if realizing the rigidity of Meno's mind-set, begins a process of blandishment to make him more flexible. It is easy to tell that Meno is handsome, Socrates cajoles him, because he dominates the conversation with imperious demands. And since Socrates cannot resist such beauty, he will submit to Meno's wishes. His next definition (the fifth in the sequence) is in the style of Gorgias (76C4), expressed in poetic language (76D5) that Meno finds reassuring: color is an effluence from surfaces that is perceptible because commensurate with sight. Although this definition is inferior to that of shape just preceding, Socrates hastens to say, the fact that it pleases Meno so much would convince him to try to find more like it, if only Meno would remain long enough to be initiated into the Mysteries.[24]

Having been made more pliable in this manner by Socrates' ingratiating rhetoric, Meno in turn offers a poetically inspired (77B3) definition of virtue which he now equates with desiring "fine things" (tōn kalōn: 77B4-5) and being able to acquire them. The elenchus then continues, with Socrates pointing out that everyone desires fine things, whether virtuous or not, so that virtue must reside instead in the ability to acquire them. Meno accepts this emended definition (the seventh in the series) and immediately runs afoul of another problem. Since fine things can be acquired either justly or unjustly, virtue cannot be the ability to acquire them by any means whatever. Unjust acquisition cannot be an exercise of virtue. So Meno is induced to accept, as a final definition, that virtue is the ability to acquire fine things justly (78E8–10).

In his criticism of the first definition of shape (as what always accompanies color), Meno had shown himself aware of one type of failure that might afflict a definition. A definition might fail by employing terms which themselves require definition to be understood. But failure of this sort can be avoided by choosing terms that have clear meanings in the appropriate context, as illustrated by Socrates' second definition of shape. The difficulty afflicting Meno's final definition of virtue, however, is not easily remedied. The difficulty is one of circularity. For, as Socrates is quick to remind him, Meno in his second definition had already identified justice as "a part of virtue" (79A3–4), so that his final effort amounts to nothing more than defining virtue in terms of part of itself.

We see the problem here, as readers of the dialogue. And Plato clearly saw it in writing the dialogue, because he has Socrates point it out as the final step in the elenchus. The fact that Meno, however, cannot see it without Socrates' help enables the latter to soften the blow with a touch of irony; Meno, he says, seems to be mocking (79A7) him, by fragmenting virtue yet once again in saying that virtue is part of itself and thus ignoring his request to define virtue as a whole. Only then does Meno realize that he has made a fool of himself instead, which leads to his comparison of Socrates with a torpedo fish (80A6) that torpifies anyone who comes into contact with it.

What is especially interesting about this flaw in Meno's final definition, however, is not the opening it provides for Socrates to complete his elenchus, but rather its relation to the problem posed by the first definition of color. This latter had raised the specter of an infinite regress of definitions, each in turn employing terms that themselves need defining. Regress of this sort would have to be avoided for individual terms in a language to acquire meaning in the first place; and one way of avoiding it would be for the regress, as it were, to turn into a circle, whereby the terms of the language ultimately are defined by each other. This is the effect, in practice, of any complete dictionary of a natural language, in which every term appearing in any given definition itself is defined in alphabetical order. But this way of avoiding the regress seems blocked by the problem of the final definition. Meaningful language thus appears to be held hostage between circularity and regress, and with it the possibility of discursive knowledge that depends upon language for its acquisition. These reflections underscore a significance that might otherwise pass without notice in Meno's last desperate attempt to escape the sting of the elenchus. The attempt in question, of course, is the argument we know as the "paradox of the learner," which takes the form of one of Zeno's "destructive dilemmas." What we seek to learn we either know or do not know already. If we know it already there is nothing new to learn; and if we don't then we can't tell when we have found it—i.e., can't tell when the search has been completed. So in either case the search for knowledge is sure to be fruitless. Socrates' attempt to break that deadlock, of course, occupies the remainder of the dialogue.

The purpose of this detailed review of the argument in the first part of the Meno has been to show that much more is going on here than just a process of refutation. Although the elenchus performed by Socrates is deft and highly effective, the ability to refute one's opponents in argument is a skill shared with many other sophists. What Plato seems to be emphasizing in his recreation of this conversation is not the elenchus itself but what Socrates *accomplishes* with his use of elenchus. And what he accomplishes is not merely the defeat of an opponent—as if that, for Socrates, had any value in itself. As we follow Socrates' elenchus step by step, rather, what happens is that we are led to an appreciation of the kind of knowledge underlying a Socratic definition. Even more importantly, the elenchus brings us face-to-face with a fundamental problem affecting the very possibility of gaining any kind of knowledge whatever by inquiry. In the course of no more than nine pages of artfully contrived conversation, Plato's Socrates has brought the reader to an explicit awareness of a problem that has set the stage for epistemology ever since—how, if coming to know requires knowing something already, is it possible to know anything in the first place? Plato's first attempt to solve the problem, of course, resulted in his so-called "theory of recollection." Later came the hypothetical method of the *Phaedo* and the *Republic*, and the method of collection and division found in several late dialogues. Descartes in turn had his "clear and distinct ideas," Kant his "synthetic a priori judgments," the modern foundationalist his "terminating judgments," (C. I. Lewis), and the generative grammarian his "innate ideas" (Noam Chomsky). The legacy of Socratic elenchus on this particular occasion reaches all the way into the twentieth century.

We shall return for a careful look at the "theory of recollection" in the following chapter. Our primary concern for the present, however, is with the role of elenchus in the dialogues and with what this can tell us about Plato's own views about its contribution to philosophic understanding. What we have noted thus far is that elenchus in the *Meno* achieves an effect far more interesting than merely reducing Socrates' respondent to a state of confusion. While indeed it serves the purpose noted in the *Sophist* of purging Meno's mind of false opinion on the topic at issue, it does so in a manner that seems to focus attention on problems of genuine philosophic importance. More specifically, to follow up on the supposition introduced at the beginning of this section, it does so in a manner that leads an actively engaged onlooker—Plato himself—to an awareness of certain basic problems regarding the origins of knowledge. What we know at very least, apart from this supposition, is that the conversation Plato *wrote* between Socrates and Meno has had this effect upon *us* as actively engaged readers. And the supposition that Plato himself may have been present at a conversation like the one he wrote into the dialogue provides a scenario in which Plato is overhearing an actual conversation with Socrates in much the manner that we "overhear" the conversation in the written dialogue.

The line of surmise we have been following in that regard, at any rate, is that Plato, through exercise of his dramatic art, contrived in his written dialogues to produce effects upon the reader that were inspired by effects Plato experienced himself through involvement in conversations with the actual Socrates. The upshot of this surmise for the present stage of our account is that the elenchic conversation depicted in the dialogue was intended by the author to direct the reader's attention to certain basic epistemological problems of which Plato himself became aware from similar conversations. This in itself tells us quite a bit about Plato's conception of the powers of well-executed elenchus.

There is another prominent feature of the early Socratic dialogues, however, that often goes hand-in-hand with elenchus and that is worth considering in its own right from the present perspective. This is the artful use of dissimulation that is the hallmark of Socrates as Plato portrays him. Before we continue with the topic of elenchus, it will be useful to make some observations about Socratic irony.

4. Elenchic Purification Assisted by Irony

When we speak of "Socratic irony" today,[25] we typically use the term 'irony' in its current sense of speech conveying the opposite of its literal meaning. Since irony in this sense achieves its effect only when the shift in meaning is obvious to speaker and audience alike, speaking ironically involves no intended deception and generally is not viewed as a lapse from probity. In this respect, our term 'irony' differs importantly from the Greek eirōneia, which at the time of Plato conveyed the pejorative sense of trickery and deception. This pejorative sense is indicated in the Sophist, where the Eleatic Stranger distinguishes candid or genuine (haploun) ignorance from the fake (eirōnikon: 268A7) confidence characteristic of the demagogue and the sophist.[26] Consistent with the public image of his historical counterpart as just another sophist, Socrates is accused by Callicles in the Gorgias (489E1) of "speaking ironically," and Thrasymachus alludes to the "usual feigned ignorance" (eiōthuia eirōneia: 337A5) of Socrates in the Republic. There is no place in the dialogues where the term eirōneia or its cognates are applied to Socrates in the sense of our generally commendatory expression "Socratic irony."

One near-exception, however, occurs as part of Alcibiades' uninhibited portrayal of Socrates in the Symposium. As part of his long and detailed complaint about Socrates' spurning his offers of erotic intimacy, Alcibiades accuses him of spending his whole life in a "game of irony" (*Eirōneuomenos . . . paizōn:* 216E5) with his show of public admiration for such things as wealth and good looks. Particularly ironic (*eirōnikōs:* 218D7), declares Alcibiades, was Socrates' suggestion (219A) that the improvements in character that Alcibiades sought through his companionship—in response for physical intimacy, as Alcibiades had planned it—might turn out to be of no value after all. This suggestion was ironic, in Alcibiades' estimation, because he was aware that *Socrates* knew the true value of the moral improvements that might be available to Alcibiades if he had the discipline to acquire them. The reason Alcibiades' charge of *eirōneia* here is not a full-fledged exception to the observation above (about the use of the term in Plato's dialogues) is that Alcibiades—like Callicles and Thrasymachus—regards Socrates' "game of irony" as a show of admiration by which Socrates knowingly *misleads* young beauties like himself, whereas Socratic irony in our current sense is not deceptive. And yet Alcibiades is insightful enough to realize that there are important lessons to be learned from this disingenuousness on Socrates' part, if only he were capable of absorbing them. We shall return to this interplay between Alcibiades and Socrates in a later chapter. Our present concern is to look more closely at Socratic irony in its original instantiation.

According to Gregory Vlastos, in his recent book on Socrates,[27] Socratic irony differs from the *eirōneia* of the Greek tradition before Socrates in the relation between its surface meaning and the sense intended by the user. In *eirōneia* of the earlier sort, which Vlastos labels "simple," an ironic statement in its "ordinary, commonly understood, sense . . . is simply false."[28] As far as Thrasymachus was concerned, for example, Socrates is simply lying when he pretends not to have answers to the questions people ask him. In "complex" irony of the sort we attribute to Socrates, by way of contrast, "what is said both is and isn't what is meant," in the sense that "its surface content is meant to be true in one sense, false in another." The "complex" irony Vlastos finds in Socrates' response to Alcibiades' attempted seduction at *Symposium* 219A, for example, is that on the one hand Socrates in fact has no benefits to offer of the sort Alcibiades is seeking, so in that respect what Socrates says is true, but that on the other hand there are other benefits that Socrates *can* make available, so in another respect what he says is not actually so. Other examples that Vlastos cites include Socrates' disavowal of moral knowledge, which in one sense of 'know' is true and in another false, and his disavowal of the art of teaching virtue,[29] which is true but also false in a similar manner.

Although Vlastos' analysis of Socratic irony is on the right track, it seems to me, there is one crucial respect in which it appears to go wrong. The irony in question, as he sees it, is based in ambiguity. An ironic remark of this sort is "complex" expressly in its admitting two different senses, one of which makes it true and the other false. The problem with this reading of Socratic irony is that there are remarks by Socrates in the dialogues that are quite clearly ironic, but that lack the requisite ambiguity to be true in one sense and false in another. A case in point is Socrates' description of Euthyphro as "well advanced in wisdom" (porrō . . . sophias elaunontos: 4B1–2) in his conversation with that person in the portico of the King-Magistrate. As the continuation of the conversation makes plain, this description of Euthyphro is simply false. While Euthyphro himself may have considered it true—as appears from his response at 4B3—he is simply mistaken in this estimation. His agreement with Socrates' remark, that is to say, is not a matter of picking up some arcane sense in which what Socrates says is true but a matter merely of misjudging his own mental qualities. Socrates' remark indeed is ironic. But its irony does not consist in its being true or false according to the sense taken—for there is no sense available that makes it true. Its irony consists rather in Socrates' awareness that what he said is exactly opposite the truth of the matter.

The fact that what Socrates says to Euthyphro is opposed to the truth, it should be noted, does not make that remark an out-and-out falsehood. To describe irony in terms of truth and falsehood as Vlastos does, indeed, is already to look in the wrong direction. While the point of an ironic comment is not to say something that is unambiguously true, it is not to say something that admits a false interpretation either. Truth and falsehood are features of factual reports, and ironic speech is not a medium by which facts are conveyed. Socrates' comment that Euthyphro is advanced in wisdom is not a locution involving a mistake—is not a lie or misrepresentation that could be corrected by saying the opposite. If Euthyphro is temporarily misled into thinking that Socrates agrees with his self-estimation (i.e., is speaking truly in that regard), this is incidental to Socrates' purpose. For his purpose is not to comment on the facts of the matter, but rather to focus attention on something that needs further consideration.

Sometimes Socrates speaks ironically in saying what in fact is palpably false, as in the case involving Euthyphro. And sometimes what he says ironically appears to be true, as when he suggests at *Symposium* 219A that Alcibiades may be expecting benefits from his company that he is unable to provide. But in neither case is the point of the ironic discourse to make a pronouncement with one or another particular truthvalue. The point of irony is to achieve a particular rhetorical effect, which may include assumed truth-values being called into question. The general characterization of Socratic irony that Vlastos missed, I suggest, is that it is a manner of discourse intended to draw attention to relevant matters that normally would be expressed in opposite terms. One way of accomplishing this, to be sure, might be to speak in terms that are studiously ambiguous and that would strike the audience as right or wrong depending upon interpretation. This presumably is the form of irony that Vlastos was concerned to capture. But Socratic irony, as we have seen, comes in other forms as well. Its typical characteristic, in any case, is its intent to focus attention on issues of particular relevance by use of terms with an opposite sense from what its intended audience would expect.

Another feature of Socratic irony not adequately brought out by Vlastos' analysis is that its intended audience is not always the person or persons with whom Socrates is directly engaged in conversation. The *eirōneia* of which Alcibiades complains in the *Symposium* seems to have been directed toward him as personal respondent, presumably as part of an ill-fated *sunousia* of the sort Socrates describes in the first part of the *Theaetetus*. The *eirōneia* that Thrasymachus found so infuriating in the *Republic*, on the other hand, quite clearly was aimed at the audience of that interchange instead. Whereas Socrates' professions of ignorance struck Thrasymachus as nothing more than glaring falsehoods (hence *eirōneia* in the original sense of the term), they may have been expected (within the setting of the dialogue) to have a more salutary effect upon Glaucon and Adimantus. From the author's point of view, the intended effect may have been similar to the effect upon himself on occasions of actual conversations with Socrates like that dramatized in the *Meno*. Such may have been the case as well with Socrates' description of Euthyphro as "well advanced in wisdom." If this had been intended for Euthyphro himself, it would have constituted sarcasm instead of irony, for the latter's mind was too rigid to grasp the "counter-speech" involved. The irony of the description addresses the audience instead—which in this case means the reader of the dialogue itself rather than other persons conceivably present in the King-Magistrate's waiting area.

For all this, Vlastos seems on target with his observation that, whereas *eirōneia* previously had been understood as a form of dissimulation pure and simple, these deftly shaped verbal "misdirections" of Socrates were so provocative and compelling as to provide the term 'irony' with an entirely new meaning.[30] Irony in the Socratic sense not only was free from deceit but moreover it had powers of an unprecedented sort to influence the perspectives of its intended audience. For an illustration of these powers, let us return to the *Meno*.

We have already observed how the elenchus in the opening pages of the *Meno* is made more tolerable by ample doses of flattery, artfully blended into the phrasing of Socrates' questions. Another tactic supporting elenchus is his characteristic irony. Whereas flattery serves in the manner of a "sugar coating" to make the elenchic "purge" more palatable, however, irony serves more to "soften up" the subject and to make him more pliable in undergoing refutation. This use of irony is copiously illustrated in the opening interchange of the dialogue.

The interchange begins abruptly with a question by Meno, in effect challenging Socrates to a public debate.[31] The cocky young officer has studied eristic with Gorgias and wants to test his skills against Socrates in front of his followers.[32] The question with which Meno opens the encounter, it should be noted, was being widely debated by sophists and other interested parties at this stage of Greek culture[33] and by no means was original with Meno himself. It clearly was a topic on which Meno considered himself well prepared by his tutor, to the point of being capable of standing up to the formidable Socrates. "Can you tell me, Socrates, whether virtue can be taught" (*Echeis moi eipein, ō Sōcrates, ara didakton hē aretē:* 70A1–2), or whether it comes by practice, or by nature, or in some other way? We may assume that Meno has arguments ready for each alternative.

Socrates, quite naturally, was unprepared for this challenge and takes a minute or two to collect his wits. His initial response is a speech that is laden with irony and that displays intimate knowledge his opponent would probably rather be kept secret. Previously the Thessalians (Meno's countrymen) were known as horsemen (equivalent to a university's being known for its football team today), but now they seem to be famous for wisdom as well. This is especially true, Socrates observes knowingly, of your lover (*erastēs:* 70B5) Aristippus, who along with you has been studying with Gorgias. As far as you are concerned personally, Meno, Gorgias has taught you to respond to any question you are asked as if you knew the answer—a talent for which he himself is known throughout the Greek world. But where I live, Meno, there is a drought of wisdom, as if it had migrated from us to you. I, at any rate—protests Socrates—am igno-rant about virtue, and have no idea how it is acquired or even what it is.

At this point, in a startling turnabout, it is Meno who finds himself unprepared, for he had not come ready to debate Socrates' competency. Everyone knows that Socrates is the wisest man in Athens. What could he be up to in pretending otherwise? Is he about to do Meno the ultimate dishonor and refuse even to acknowledge that Meno has challenged him? What Socrates is doing, of course, is taking the initiative away from Meno, which he then uses to challenge the competency of Meno's teacher. Not only does he not know what virtue is himself, Socrates says pointedly to his flustered opponent, but moreover he has never met another person who knew what it is either. What's this, says Meno, have you never met Gorgias? And don't you think that Gorgias knew? I have a poor memory, replies Socrates—piling irony upon irony—and can't recall what I thought about Gorgias. So let us both forget what Gorgias said about virtue and talk about *your* thoughts of virtue instead. By these tactics Meno's attack is deftly diverted, and Socrates has taken control of the direction of the conversation—a direction that leads shortly to Meno's *genuine* confession of ignorance.

Another application of irony occurs in response to Meno's complaint, noted above, that Socrates' first definition of shape leaves color unde-fined. If the complaint had come from an expert in eristic and verbal combat (which Meno considers himself to be), says Socrates, his answer would be, "You have heard my answer; if it is wrong, your job is to take it up and refute it" (75D1–2). But when friendly people like you and I are conversing (which was *not* the intent with which Meno entered the discussion), then the reply should be "milder and more conducive to discussion" (75D4). Socrates then proceeds with the second definition of shape, first making sure that Meno understands the terms involved.

Socrates resorts to irony once again in suggesting that Meno is mocking him in his final definition of virtue as being able to acquire things virtuously, while Meno is still unaware that his definition is circular (79A); and yet again after Meno has compared him to a torpedo fish (80A6), in avowing that it is only because he is perplexed himself that Meno has become perplexed in the course of his questioning. The effect of pretending that Meno is trying to make fun of him at 79A, presumably, is to give the latter a brief moment of gratification, in thinking at first that he had scored a hit without even realizing it. And the effect of pretending to be no less perplexed than Meno at the end of the elenchus is to ease the latter's sense of devastation—allowing Meno to think that the contest might somehow have ended in a draw, since both of them had admitted ignorance.

Other conspicuous instances of irony occur at 86D, when Meno obsessively reverts to the formulaic question about the source of virtue with which the dialogue began, and in the testy interchange with Anytus beginning at 90B.[34] The cross-examination of the slave boy in which Socrates reenacts the elenchus to which Meno has just been subjected, however, is notable for its lack of irony, apparently in keeping with the fact that the boy has been a slave from birth (82B5) and lacks the spirit to resist refutation. Whereas Meno requires large doses of irony to make his mind receptive to the therapeutic effects of elenchus, the boy moves willingly wherever the argument leads him.

Shifting from the therapeutic to the horticultural analogy of the chapter title, we should be prepared now to think of irony as a technique for dispersing matted clumps of weeds to enable their removal by the elenchic sickle. When the subject's mind is overgrown with a thick brush of false opinion, that is to say, these weeds must be undercut before new seeds can germinate, and Socratic irony acts as an effective harrow on the roots of false opinion. In the *Meno* elenchus combines with cajolery and irony to rid the mind of the young officer of its misconceptions about virtue.

If the mind thus cleared were sufficiently fertile, the next step would be to enliven it with seminal discourse from which true conceptions might eventually grow. As Meno's reversion to the original question at 86D seems to indicate, however, his mind lacks the necessary qualities for new growth to take hold, and the dialogue concludes with a number of brash pronouncements that seem directly contrary to what we would have expected Socrates to say about the matters at hand. True opinion as good as knowledge for the guidance of action (98B7–9)?; virtue acquired by divine dispensation (99E6)?—surely not. The incipient irony[35] in these suggestions is tempered by Socrates' own warning in the final speech of the dialogue, that truth in such matters cannot be reached until we inquire (as Meno has refused to do) into the nature of virtue itself.

Meno is not a respondent with whom Socrates can hold fruitful conversation of the sort described in the Seventh Letter. According to our present surmise, however, there were other persons on the scene— notably Plato himself—with whom Socrates was conversing indirectly and who were ready to respond favorably to his philosophic overtures.[36] One probable response on Plato's part that we have noted already is a series of questions about the origins of knowledge inspired by Socrates' probings into the nature of definition. Another line of thought induced by these encounters must have focused on the character of the elenchic arguments by which Socrates was able to work these effects. Among the suppositions setting the stage for the present chapter is the (seemingly obvious) assumption that Plato's own conception of elenchus, and of its role in philosophy, was directly influenced by his personal experience with Socratic refutation. Let us pull together the findings of the previous sections in an attempt to make this conception perspicuous.

5. Elenchus in the Conversation between Author and Reader

This chapter began with a distinction between (1) Plato's own conception of the role of elenchus in the pursuit of philosophic understanding, (2) elenchus as it figures in the Socratic dialogues, and (3) the elenchus practiced by the historical Socrates. Sections 1 and 2 dealt with the latter topic. In section 1 we drew upon evidence from Xenophon and Aristotle, as well from the dialogues themselves, in support of the judgment that Socratic elenchus as a technique of refutation was indistinguishable from the antilogikē practiced by the other sophists, while in section 2 we saw reason to believe that what set it off from sophistic practice generally was its use for the betterment of Socrates' respondents. Sections 3 and 4, in turn, were given over to topic (2). In section 3 we took a careful look at the use of elenchic argument in the first part of the Meno, which we proceeded to flesh out in section 4 with a consideration of the companion technique of Socratic irony.

Rather than taking the Meno at face value as a conversation between two historical persons, however, we adopted a supposition that cast the dialogue in a new perspective. We supposed that Plato had actually been present at a conversation more or less similar to what is depicted in the dialogue and that the Meno itself was written as an artistic embellishment of certain themes of that conversation that Plato, in reflective hindsight, found especially significant. One theme already noted was the origin of knowledge, while another concerned the power of elenchus to stimulate inquiry into philosophic issues. The effect of this supposition was to direct our concern to the (admittedly speculative) question of what Plato apparently was trying to achieve with the dialogue and to encourage an examination of the conversational techniques that Plato employed to accomplish this purpose. Primary among these, of course, were elenchus and irony, but cajolery and suggestion had roles to play as well.

In approaching the dialogue with this supposition in mind, we already have begun to shift our attention toward the first of the three topics distinguished above—that of Plato's own conception of elenchus and of its service to philosophy. Once this initial supposition has been set in place, moreover, another follows in its train that brings us to face topic (1) directly. This is the supposition that one of Plato's purposes in structuring the dialogue the way he did was to induce a series of philosophic responses in his readers similar to those he experienced himself while listening to the conversation between Socrates and Meno. Insofar as elenchus is prominent among the techniques employed for that purpose, we now find ourselves thinking specifically about Plato's view of elenchus and of its contribution to the growth of philosophic understanding.

With this additional assumption, it should be noted, we return full circle to the thesis defended in chapter 1 regarding Plato's reasons for writing in dialogue form. Briefly put, this is the thesis that his dialogues were intended to set up conversations with properly attuned readers that would be parallel—both in structure and in effect—to the conversations that Plato himself shared with the historical Socrates. In the language of the *Phaedrus*, these conversations with his readers yield vital shoots of discourse that spring up in Plato's "literary garden" and that take their place when mature among his "legitimate progeny." In the language of the Seventh Letter, they are instances of the *sunousia* with a master philosopher by which learners may be led eventually to philosophic understanding. A primary feature of this form of intercourse, according to this document, is "well-disposed" refutation, also called "question and answer without indulgence of ill-will." Within the context of the *Meno* itself, this corresponds to the elenchus applied to Meno and the slave boy by way of inducing their admissions of ignorance. Within the interaction between author and reader, this corresponds to the series of arguments by which Plato seals off dead-end paths that the reader initially might find attractive and redirects his or her attention to the epistemological issues that constitute the main concern of the dialogue.

To repeat, Plato has Meno advance several definitions that the reader at first might be expected to take seriously[37] and then has Socrates refute these definitions in a manner—amounting to "well-disposed" elenchus— that has predictable effects upon Meno but that must have been in-tended to have certain effects upon the reader of the dialogue as well. The effects upon Meno include a state of confusion and an admission of ignorance regarding the nature of virtue. The effects upon the reader, in turn, include an awareness of the deficiencies of certain definitions that might initially seem promising but, more importantly, a growing awareness of some basic problems affecting the nature of definition generally. To the extent that the elenchus displayed in this dialogue was intended to contribute to the type of *sunousia* he describes in the Seventh Letter, the effects of primary concern could not have been those upon Meno—who shows no signs of having the philosophic nature required for such *sunousia* to be fruitful—but must have been those upon the reader instead.

Plato writes conversations between Socrates and various respondents in which the views of the latter are subject to withering refutation. But this refutation by itself cannot be the "well-disposed" elenchus of which Plato speaks in the Seventh Letter, if for no other reason than most of Socrates' respondents in the early dialogues were not capable of the kind of understanding for which this elenchus was an early stage of prepara-tion. In the case of the *Meno*, at any rate, the elenchus depicted within the dialogue must have been aimed at Plato's readership as well, among whom he might reasonably have anticipated a number with more philo-sophic promise than Meno himself. It is with this dual use of refutation within the dialogues, I want to argue, that Plato's own conception of elenchus is most clearly exhibited. What can be said by way of making this conception explicit?

One primary characteristic of elenchus had been obvious from the beginning. In any context pertaining to Socrates, its basic purpose is to eradicate false opinion that might be harmful to the subject. This certainly seems to be the case both with the elenchus of the dialogues (topic (2) above) and with the elenchus practiced by Socrates himself (topic(3)). It is reasonable to assume that this is the case with Plato's own conception of elenchus as well. Put in terms of the horticultural meta-phor adopted from the *Phaedrus*, the purpose of elenchus as Plato conceived it is primarily to clear the ground of false opinion. For only a mind relatively free from misconception provides a place where seeds of knowledge can take root and grow.

What was not obvious from the beginning is the way elenchus not only removes the underbrush of false conceptions but also actively pre-pares the mind of its subject to be receptive to these seeds of knowledge. In what sense is this latter so? One thing to note in this regard is that elenchus is never represented by Plato as a technique capable of purg-ing the mind of false opinion without remainder. The ground to be prepared for seeding, as it were, is never entirely razed of its untoward conceptual growth, but is cleared only of those misconceptions that stand in the way of progress on the topic or topics actually being dis-cussed. In the *Meno,* one such topic is the nature of virtue. As it be-comes clear soon after the conversation gets underway, however, the main topic of the dialogue is not virtue as such but rather the conditions under which knowledge of virtue and like matters could be achieved. So we find Socrates applying elenchus in a selective manner, not only to Meno's stunted conceptions of virtue, but also to his mistaken thoughts about definition and inquiry. Although Meno presumably holds opin-ions on other topics that are no less erroneous, any attempt to refute these other opinions would be extraneous to the present conversation.

While there is nothing extraordinary about this selective application of elenchus in itself, in Plato's hand it achieves an effect beyond limit-ing the argument to relevant topics. By having Socrates probe specific aspects of Meno's views on matters at issue and overlook others that might be equally faulty, Plato shapes their conversation around certain key issues. An actual conversation of the sort depicted in the dialogue, needless to say, might develop in any number of different directions. Plato directs the course of his written version by his selection of the mis-conceptions he has Socrates pursue. A case at point occurs with Meno's definition of virtue at 77B4–5 as "desiring beautiful things and being able to procure them." Whereas fault surely could be found with the notion that virtue is a matter of desiring beautiful things without fur-ther discrimination (gold and silver are mentioned at 78D1), Socrates puts an interpretation on that part that he is willing to accept, and fo-cuses on the other part of the definition, having to do with procure-ment. This enables him to develop the point about virtue requiring just rather than unjust procurement and to catch Meno in the circularity of defining virtue in terms of a specific form it might take. Although this selective application of elenchus obviously is not the only device Plato uses to shape the course of his written conversations, it is one that is particularly noteworthy for its effect in directing the reader to key issues in the dialogue.

Given the standard conception of elenchus as merely an instrument of refutation, however, perhaps the most unexpected aspect of its use in dialogues like the Meno is the way it can actually incline the mind of the reader toward particular solutions to the problems that follow in its train. To continue the example above, consider the quandary regarding the requirements of definition induced by the circularity of Meno's final definition. According to this final definition, we recall, virtue is coming to possess good things by just means of procurement. And since justice had already been acknowledged to be part of virtue (79A3–4), this amounts to defining virtue in terms of its parts. In view of the fact that intralinguistic definitions always involve circularity at some level of remove (as in a dictionary), and in view of the difficulties raised earlier (at 75C–D) with definitions in terms that are not themselves understood, this leads to the puzzle of how any definition can escape both circularity and infinite regress. In generalized form, the quandary is how anything new can come to be known (e.g., the definition of virtue) without something else being known already (e.g., the terms in which virtue can be defined). The upshot, of course, is the basic epistemological problem of how anything can come to be known in the first place.

Put in such terms, the problem raised by Socrates' elenchus in the dialogue literally invites resolution with reference to some kind of knowledge that can be acquired independently of something else known already. Innate knowledge of some sort would serve as a likely candidate. Thus when Plato highlights the problem by having Socrates help Meno articulate the "paradox of the learner" and then proceeds to introduce the so-called "theory of recollection" by way of solution, the reader is inclined to some such solution antecedently and is ready to appreciate the insight it brings to the problem.

With this characterization of elenchus as not only a purge of false opinion but also as a means of shaping the discussion and of inclining the reader toward certain resolutions of relevant issues, it is clear that we have moved beyond the practices of the historical Socrates and even beyond the use of elenchus depicted *within* the dialogues themselves. Within the context of the conversation between Socrates and Meno as Plato depicts it, for example, Meno is not nearly nimble enough to anticipate the kind of solution Socrates offers to the "paradox of the learner." And in the interlude with the slave boy, although Socrates leads the boy toward the solution of the geometrical problem by a series of pointed questions, it would be inaccurate to say that the boy is inclined to the solution by the process of elenchus itself. What we are dealing with at this point, rather, is a use of elenchus in the interchange between author and reader, which is to say a use of elenchus in a *sunousia* conducted by Plato himself.

Given the inherent limitations of our resources, this may be about as close as we can get to the nature of the "well-disposed" refutation of which Plato speaks in the Seventh Letter. And our best access to the manner in which it contributes to the development of philosophic understanding may be the effect we observe within ourselves as we pursue our *sunousia* in the direction indicated. The next stage in the *written* conversation between Socrates and Meno is the introduction of the "theory of recollection." Let us take the next step in our *actual* conversation with Plato by looking carefully at recollection as it figures in the dialogues.

3

RECOLLECTION AND EXAMPLE: SOWING THE SEEDS

1. Recollection and Learning in the Meno

The maxim that learning is recollection first appears in the *Meno*, as part of Socrates' response to the "paradox of the learner." Socrates attributes this maxim to certain priests and priestesses who "exercise care in providing explanations" (*memelēke peri hōn metacheirizontai logon*: 81A11) of the services they offer, as well as to Pindar and many other "truly divine" (*hosoi theioi*: 81B2) poets. The idea, in barest outline, is that the soul is immortal, in the sense of being subject to reincarnation, that it gains knowledge by direct access to reality between incarnations—which it promptly "forgets" with the onrush of bodily experience at birth—and that what we call "learning" is a process of recollecting what the mind knew before it entered its current body. By providing a mode of knowing that, being direct, does not require mediation by previous knowledge, this way of thinking about learning purports to circumvent the paradox that marks the end of the first section of the *Meno*.

Meno's ostensive reason for posing this familiar eristic argument[1] was to score a debater's point against Socrates by blocking his proposal to stop talking about the source of virtue and to begin a joint inquiry into its nature. If inquiry could be shown impossible generally—or if Meno at least could get Socrates to agree that it is—then the particular inquiry proposed by Socrates would have been rendered impracticable and Meno would have won his point. To Meno's probable chagrin, however, Socrates adopts the argument for his own purposes and rephrases it more plausibly than Meno had put it. In Socrates' rendition, the argument takes the form of a "destructive dilemma" like those traced back to Zeno in chapter 2. The dilemma begins with the apparent truism that one inquires either into what one knows or into what one does not know.

But one cannot inquire into what one knows, for since one knows it no inquiry is needed (*Oute gar an ho ge oiden zētoi; oiden gar, kai ouden dei tō ge toioutō zēteseōs*: 80E3–5). Nor can one inquire into what is not known, for then one would not know what is being sought (*oute ho mē oiden; oude gar oiden ho ti zētēsei*: 80E5).

The point in the first case is obvious, if we assume that the purpose of inquiry is to gain knowledge of what was previously unknown. The point in the latter case, although less obvious, is fairly straightforward. When engaged in inquiry one always has some goal in mind, so that one always knows what it is one is looking for. It follows that what is in no way known cannot be an object of inquiry. Since one either knows or does not know what one purports to inquire into, the upshot is that no one can learn by inquiry. So if knowledge can be gained only by inquiry, then coming to know appears to be impossible.

Now there are many ways of responding to this dilemma, as the subsequent history of philosophy makes evident. One way is simply to point out that the term 'know' (*oiden*) is being used ambiguously. The sense in which one knows the proof of a mathematical theorem, for example, is not the same as that in which one knows what one is looking for in seeking a proof of the theorem; being able to give a proof is something more than being able to identify a proof when one sees it. The response given in the dialogue is something like this, inasmuch as Socrates is portrayed as distinguishing two different senses of knowing. One sense is that in which we come to know something explicitly as the result of successful inquiry—for example, come to know that the side of a square that is double in area of a given square is the diagonal of that original square. The other sense is that of retaining the capacity to recognize something that once was known explicitly but subsequently has been suppressed—in the manner of being able to recognize the name of an acquaintance when one hears it, after having failed to come up with the name on one's own. As noted in the previous chapter, there are various ways of expanding on a distinction of this sort, by way of fleshing out the character of this once explicit knowledge. One might go the way of innate ideas, as with Descartes, or with certain contemporary linguists of Cartesian persuasion. Or one might develop a distinction between various senses of "having in mind" (e.g., long- and short-term memory), following the lead of the aviary in the *Theaetetus*.[2] But the way Socrates is made to respond in the *Meno* is by enlisting an epistemologically laden version of the "divine" doctrine attributed to the poets and other holy persons at 81A.

There is one sense of knowing, says Socrates in effect, in which we come to know something explicitly as the result of inquiry, like knowing the side of a square double in area of a given square. The "learner's paradox" is correct in pointing out that we cannot meaningfully inquire into something we already know explicitly in this sense. It is also correct in pointing out that we are unable to inquire into something about which we have absolutely no idea in advance—not even to the point of knowing what it is we are looking for. But there is another sense of knowing that falls between these two cases—the sense of having something in mind that is not known explicitly but that can be recovered from its dormant state by the right kind of prompting. Something known in this latter sense, we might say, is known "implicitly;" and part of what it is to know something implicitly is to be able to recognize it—i.e., bring it back to explicit cognition—under the right set of enabling circumstances. Not only is inquiry into something known in this sense perfectly intelligible, according to Socrates' story, but moreover we have in his practice of elenchus a technique for bringing something known in this sense back to a state of explicit cognition.

In the story that Socrates traces back to Pindar and anonymous holy persons, of course, the things into which we inquire were once known by the soul before it entered the body and were forgotten with the onset of bodily experience, but they are capable of being reinstated as explicit knowledge when the misconceptions engendered by this experience are removed through a process of refutation. To finish off the story, this return to explicit cognition is given a special label—"recollection" (*anamnēsis*)—and is identified with the learning (*mathēsis*) that the inquiry in question is supposed to be capable of producing. Socrates' elenchic encounter with the slave boy in the next section of the dialogue purports to be an illustration of this kind of inquiry.

This, in brief description, is how the maxim that learning is recollection figures in the conversation Plato wrote between Socrates and Meno. Concerns of another sort come to the fore when we step aside from the narrative sequence of the dialogue itself and turn to ask where this so-called "theory of recollection" came from originally and why Plato gave it such prominence in this particular setting. These questions bring us back to the general topic of the previous chapter, concerning Plato's own understanding of the philosophic enterprise and his indebtedness in this regard to actual conversations with Socrates.

What Plato has his character Socrates say about the origin of the notion of recollection in the dialogue clearly is not to be taken as factual. Meno has already shown himself partial to Pindar and poetic diction (76D, 77B), so it is a natural rhetorical device for the character Socrates to introduce his maxim identifying learning and recollection with a quotation from that well-known poet. But there is nothing in the fragment from Pindar at 81B–C about the "noble kings" or the "most wise" persons in question *recollecting* previous knowledge in subsequent reincarnations and nothing in particular about this knowledge contributing to a subsequent learning process. What the quotation illustrates plausibly enough is the doctrine of reincarnation or transmigration, which was central to a number of belief-systems current in the fifth century B.C.[3] But reincarnation is not the same as recollection; and there is nothing we know about these early belief-systems that suggests a precedent for the maxim linking recollection to learning.

Given what we know about fifth-century religious thought, that is to say, it appears that Socrates is striking out on his own when he glosses Pindar's verse with the claim that the soul has "acquired knowledge of all things" (81C7) during previous existence, and that it comes into the world capable of recalling (*anamēsthēnai*: 81C9) what it knew previously. But this still does not answer our question of where the maxim originated. For reasons examined in chapter 1, we should not assume as a matter of course that the words and deeds assigned to Socrates in a particular dialogue match things said and done by his historical counterpart. Do we have any reason to ascribe this notion of recollection to the historical Socrates? Or is the maxim an innovation of Plato himself?

There are two other dialogues, we should be reminded, in which Plato has his character Socrates discuss recollection from previous states of existence. One is the *Phaedo*, in which the notion of recollection plays a role in an argument for immortality, and the other is the *Phaedrus*, in which recollection is associated with a phase of the dialectical method. In the context of the *Phaedo*, moreover, there is reference to the saying that learning is recollection as something Socrates is "accustomed to repeating" (72E4–5). If we had reason to accept the *Phaedo* as an accurate record in detail of Socrates' actual conversation on the day of his death, then this passage would count as evidence that the maxim in question originated with the historical Socrates. Inasmuch as the author of this dialogue is expressly cited (59B) as being absent, however, we have even less reason to accept what Socrates says here as historically accurate than in the case of the *Meno*, where the maxim first appears. Although recollection is explicitly mentioned as part of the myth of the charioteer in the *Phaedrus*, on the other hand, there is no connection in that context between recollection and learning. The practical upshot is that Plato's dialogues provide no direct evidence about Socrates' relation to the maxim in question.

As far as I am aware, the only other explicit mention of the thesis that learning is recollection occurs at *Prior Analytics* 67a22, where Aristotle refers to it only as the "argument in the *Meno*," without attributing it to a particular thinker. There are other passages where Aristotle speaks about Socrates, however, which suggest that such a thesis might not have engaged his interests. In the not wholly flattering description at *Metaphysics* 1078b, he notes that while Socrates "was the first to seek out universal definitions" (1078b18–19), he had to make do without the dialectical power that enables someone "innocent of the essence to study contraries" (1078b26) and to tell whether the contraries in question are treated by "the same science" (1078b27). Although Aristotle's reference to an *epistēmē* of contraries has no particular relevance to Socrates' view on learning, this sounds like the description of someone preoccupied with ethics who has neither interest nor skill in matters of epistemology. That Socrates would have been an unlikely source for a thesis tracing knowledge back to a nonbodily state specifically is indicated by Aristotle's subsequent remark that Socrates did not separate the objects of his definitions from their particular instances (1078b30, 1086b4).

Much the same impression is conveyed by Xenophon's *Memorabilia*, which recalls many conversations with Socrates on matters of ethics but shows little involvement with epistemological issues. While there are several passages in the *Memorabilia* where Socrates discusses the importance of learning, moreover, there is not the slightest hint of any association between learning and recollection. Indeed, it would be hard to find a passage in this writing where a discussion of recollection in this connection would even seem relevant. The portrayal of Socrates by Xenophon joins that of Aristotle in suggesting that Socrates was not the source of the maxim equating learning with recollection.

The only plausible alternative left is that Plato himself was the author of the maxim in question. It may have derived in part from previous views about reincarnation, and it may have owed something as well to

Socrates' well-known concern for the soul. But the use of this notion of the soul's existence apart from the body for epistemological purposes specifically must have been due to Plato himself. Let us return to the further question posed above and consider reasons for the prominence given this notion of recollection in connection with issues like those raised in the *Meno*.

In the same section of the *Metaphysics* where Aristotle declares Socrates to be innocent of dialectic, he also expresses the opinion that the theory of Forms arose from a distinct set of epistemological concerns on the part of its author (1078b12–17).[4] On the basis of our conjectures in the previous chapter of the personal relation between Socrates and Plato, we formulated some careful guesses about how these concerns might have originated. Our initial conjecture, briefly restated, is that the *Meno* was composed on the basis of impressions gathered from an actual conversation Plato had witnessed between Socrates and Meno, and that the dialogue was intended to capture the importance of key issues he saw arising out of that conversation. Our line of conjecture continued with the surmise that these issues were concerned largely with the origins of knowledge and with the role played by elenchus in the pursuit of philosophy. We have already seen reason to believe, however, that Socrates himself would not have stressed these issues in his public conversations regarding matters of virtue. If we are correct in surmising that Plato's attention nonetheless was drawn to these issues by his encounters with Socrates, this must have happened through subsequent reflection upon his own reactions to these public conversations. To return to the topic of chapter 1, the suggestion at this point is that Plato found himself responding to actual encounters with Socrates in much the manner that we as readers find ourselves responding to the written dialogues.

The final step in our series of conjectures, in brief, is that Plato found himself puzzled by the power of these conversations to stimulate his inquiry into epistemological issues and started thinking about the means by which this effect was brought about. By listening carefully to Socrates' probings about the nature of definition, he seemed to reach some understanding of the requirements of knowledge. And by pondering Socrates' questions about the nature of virtue, he seemed to gain insight into the manner by which virtue is acquired. Yet Socrates made no show of teaching such topics, renouncing the public lectures for which other sophists were famous and declining to give private instruction in his techniques for winning arguments. One learned things from Socrates that he consistently denied teaching. Socratic cross-examination had consequences beyond mere refutation; in some elusive way, one could learn from it as well. The question Plato began to ponder was: How is this possible?

The answer that occurred to him, if our line of conjecture is approximately correct, is that he had some prior inkling of the things he learned from Socrates already, and the Socratic elenchus moved this implicit knowledge toward explicit awareness. With reincarnation factored in to make this incipient knowledge intelligible, the answer was that he learned these things in conversation with Socrates by recollecting what he knew from a previous state of existence. Perhaps the answer came in terms that were largely figurative, inviting exposition as a story attributed to anonymous religious spokespersons (as at *Meno* 81A10). And certainly it was an answer that was incomplete at best, for reasons that Plato would have been quick to realize. But this at any rate is the account we find Plato experimenting with when he wrote the conversation between Socrates and Meno.

If the lukewarm reception it receives in the dialogue is any indication, however, this is an account in which Plato had little confidence from the beginning. Consider the purported exhibition of recollection in the conversation with the slave boy. Despite its ostensive purpose of legitimizing inquiry as an avenue to knowledge, the boy emerges from the process of recollection in a state of true opinion only. Although Socrates assures Meno (a bit too glibly, one senses) that the boy would arrive at knowledge eventually if similar questions were repeated to him on other occasions (85C10–D1), the fact remains that no one in this dialogue (or in any other, for that matter) is ever portrayed as reaching knowledge by way of recollection. And consider the afterthought expressed by Socrates himself in summing up the exhibition for Meno's benefit. Although Socrates is sure that it is better to inquire into what one does not know than to succumb to arguments like the "learner's paradox," he "would not stand firm on all parts of the story" (86B8). With that remark, the account of recollection is set aside, and Socrates invites Meno to an investigation of the origins of virtue by a method based on the geometers' use of hypothesis.

Having gone to some length in our attempt to understand how Plato might first have hit upon this account of recollection, we find it to be an account in which he never showed much confidence. One problem must have been obvious from the very beginning. How could the understanding incited by elenchus be explained by recollection in his own case, Plato must have asked, when there are other young people—Alcibiades comes to mind—who had shared the same exposure to Socratic conversation but apparently had learned nothing as a result of the experience? If recollection is part of the learning process at all, then more is involved in the recovery of knowledge than refutation of the sort administered by Socrates.[5]

It is not a matter of happenstance, surely, that the discussions of recollection in both the *Phaedo* and the *Phaedrus* offer different accounts from that found in the *Meno* of the circumstances under which recollection might come about. Before dismissing recollection as a failed experiment, let us consider what Plato does with it in these other two dialogues.

2. Recollection and Forms in the Phaedo

The *Phaedo* is the only dialogue apart from the *Meno* containing a detailed discussion of recollection. Although both discussions treat the maxim that learning is recollection, the differences in treatment are more striking than the similarities. One departure from the *Meno* that springs to mind at once is that no attempt is made in the *Phaedo* to *exhibit* recollection as taking place in one of the characters. Socrates himself is reminded by Cebes of the "famous saying" (72E3–4) he is used to repeating as one having relevance to the topic of immortality. Simmias then asks to be reminded (73A4) of how the maxim is demonstrated—as he puts it facetiously, he needs help in recollecting (*anamnēsthēnai*: 73B7) the maxim that learning is recollection. But neither Cebes' reminder to Socrates, nor Socrates' subsequent reminding of Simmias, is an instance of recollection in the sense the maxim concerns, for both are reminders merely of previous conversations.

Neither Socrates nor Simmias, indeed, is portrayed as being in any great *need* of recollection, as both Meno and the slave boy were portrayed in the earlier dialogue. And this brings to the fore another difference between the two treatments. Whereas close to a half of the conversation in the *Meno* is taken up with elenchus at the service of recollection, the treatment of recollection in the context of the *Phaedo* leaves elenchus entirely out of the picture. There are other passages, of course, in which refutation is prominent—notably in Socrates' response to Simmias' objections aimed at his argument for immortality comparing the soul with the Forms (91E–94A). But while the maxim of recollection is involved as a premise in that argument (91E4), there is no use of refutation at any point in the dialogue as a means for inducing recollection. None of the participants in the discussion of recollection beginning at 72E is sub-jected to elenchus in that particular context; yet none has any trouble grasping at once what the other participants are saying about the topic. In sharp contrast with the conversation between Socrates and the slave boy in the *Meno*, where elenchus was an essential prelude to recollec-tion, there is nothing in the conversation with Cebes and Simmias to suggest that elenchus is necessary for recollection to take place.

Another difference in this regard between the *Phaedo* and the *Meno* concerns the type of evidence the two present for the maxim of recollec-tion. In the earlier dialogue, Socrates' demonstration of recollection with the slave boy ostensibly was intended to convince Meno that a process of this sort could actually occur. The evidence offered for the maxim, in effect, was a demonstration of recollection in action. In the *Phaedo*, on the other hand, the recollection under discussion is depicted as having already occurred. Cebes and Simmias are already aware that the instances of equality they sensibly perceive fall short of perfect equality (74D). This seems to involve a comparison between perceived equals and the Form Equality, which in turn implies a prior awareness of the Form itself. Socrates then poses the question of how this is possible. The evidence offered for recollection in the *Phaedo*, accordingly, is an argument intended to show that there is no time the mind might come to know Equality itself other than before birth (75A ff.), from which it seems to follow that one's present awareness that the equals perceived sensibly are not perfectly equal involves a recollection of the Form in question. The demonstration of recollection that Simmias requested thus is rather like a Kantian "transcendental deduction," as distinct from the demonstration in the sense of "exhibition" found in the *Meno*.

Perhaps the most important difference between the two accounts, however, has to do with the nature of the thing recollected. What the slave boy is depicted as recollecting in the *Meno* is a geometrical theorem, or at least a determinate relation between geometrical figures. In Socrates' discussion of this result, the object of recollection is de-scribed generically as "knowledge" (*epistēmēn*: 85D6, 9, passim), with no elaboration of the nature of the knowledge involved. There is no men-tion of the Forms as objects of knowledge and no suggestion that Forms themselves are the entities recalled.[6] But in the *Phaedo*, what allegedly is recollected is the Form Equality itself (following the formula of 73C9) or, alternatively, one's prior knowledge of this absolute Equality (75C1, E5). Although the distinction between recollecting the Form (recalling Equality) and recollecting knowledge of the Form (recalling that one knew Equality) is not one to be dismissed lightly, it is the former that Plato needs for this particular argument.[7] So what is meant by "recovery of knowledge" (*epistēmēn analambanein*: 75E5) through "recollection" (75E6) in this context must be the reinvigoration of that knowledge— i.e., the return to one's awareness of the Form Equality itself. The basic difference between the *Meno* and the *Phaedo* in this respect, to put it briefly, is that recollection in the former is of a mathematical truth, while in the latter what is recollected is a mathematical Form.

This difference in object recollected has further ramifications with regard to the factors said by Socrates to be involved in the process of recollection. In the *Meno* there was nothing more helpful than Socrates' talking vaguely about being "questioned often and in various ways on the same topics" (85C10–D1) and his actually posing a series of leading questions that contained all the information necessary for formulating the geometrical truth in question. In the *Phaedo*, on the other hand, there are some fairly specific statements about the sort of mental exercise involved in the process of recollection. As Socrates puts it at 73C, we agree that recollection occurs when we come to know in a certain way— i.e., when by hearing, or seeing, or otherwise grasping one thing, a person comes to "think not only of that thing but of something else" (73C7–8), which then becomes the object of a "different act of knowl- edge" (73C8). This recollection, moreover, might be caused "either by similar or dissimilar things" (74A2–3). Examples in the text include: a lyre or piece of clothing reminding a lover of its owner, the sight of Simmias reminding someone of Cebes, the picture of an object remind- ing someone of a person associated with it, and a picture of Simmias reminding someone of Simmias himself. In general, recollection occurs when perception of an object "by vision or hearing or any other sense faculty" (76A1) brings to mind (*ennoēsai*: 76A2) another object that has been forgotten, with which it is associated, "being either dissimilar or similar" (76A3).

It is on the basis of such analogies that Simmias is asked to understand what happens when one is reminded of the Form Equality itself. Our present knowledge of perfect Equality comes from "perceiving equal stones and sticks and other such cases of equality" (74B6–7), on which occasions we are reminded of Equality itself and come to realize that the instances of equality we have perceived are defective in comparison with perfect Equality. In such cases the mind must be working on two distinct levels. Sense perception of imperfect equals recalls to mind a Form which cannot itself be grasped by sense, whereupon a higher noetic faculty compares the Form with its sensible instances and judges that the latter fall short of the former.

With this treatment in the *Phaedo* fresh in view, we may return to the question posed in the section above: What might be needed in addition to Socratic elenchus to accomplish the recall to knowledge that Plato termed *anamnēsis*? The context out of which this question arose was an attempt on our part to reconstruct Plato's reaction to conversations with the historical Socrates, in hopes of gaining some understanding of how this notion of recollection originated. In view of the role played by *anamnēsis* in the *Phaedo*, however, this question appears to be frustrated on at least two counts. For one, there is no procedure specified to follow elenchus by way of completing the process of recollection (such as further questioning on the same topics, as in the *Meno*). For another, there is no indication that elenchus itself has a part to play within the process. Not only is nothing said in the *Phaedo* about elenchus being necessary to remove false conceptions based on sensory experience before recollection can take place, to be sure, but in fact nothing is said about false opinion being an impediment to knowledge in the first place. As if to accentuate the differences between the two treatments even more starkly, moreover, sense experience now appears to play a positive role in recollection. For the recollection Socrates discusses with Cebes and Simmias is a matter of being reminded of an absolute Form by the perception of one of its sensible instances. What qualifies a sensible instance for this role, as noted above, is some relation of similarity (or dissimilarity)[8] to the object recalled.

Something happened between the *Meno* and the *Phaedo*[9] to make Plato think that the Forms should play a role in what he wrote about recollection. And with Forms part of the story, the conception of recollection we find Plato describing seems to have undergone some major changes. Not only is elenchus no longer essential by way of preparation, but moreover there appears to have been a shift in emphasis in the way recollection accounts for the possibility of knowledge. In the *Meno*, the possibility of knowledge seems threatened by infinite regress of the sort described generally in the "paradox of the learner." And the solution put forward there was an account of the mind as capable of knowing something first on an unmediated basis and capable of restoring that knowledge later by recollection. The account of recollection we find in the *Meno*, that is to say, stresses certain capacities on the part of the knower, with little concern for the nature of the object known. Elenchus enters this account as a kind of therapy by which the mind's capacity for recollection can be freed for action. In the account of the *Phaedo*, by contrast, emphasis is shifted to the object of knowledge and to the features that make it capable of being known. Above all, the Form Equality is "absolute" or "self-existent" (*auto ho esti*: 75D2), in a manner that makes it knowable prior to sense experience (75A1).[10] It is also an exemplar toward which sensible instances "strive" (*oregetai*: 75A2), approaching it through similarity but remaining faulty by comparison (*phaulotera*: 75B7). While the mind for its own part retains the requisite capacities, these features of the Forms are primarily responsible for the possibility of knowledge.

According to the *Phaedo*, by way of recapitulation, recollection is a process by which the Forms can be known. And it is a process enabled by certain capacities on the part of the things known themselves. First and foremost, the Forms (1) are intelligible, in the sense of being knowable by mind before the onset of sensation. The Forms further (2) are capable of relating to sensible instances by way of similarity, somehow promoting a "willing" (*prothumeitai*: 75B5) in the latter to imitate their essential characters.[11] Finally, the Forms (3) are capable of being recalled to mind on the occasion of its experience of a sensible instance. When this happens, says Socrates to Cebes and Simmias, the mind recollects the Form that it had known previously; and it is in this sense that learning is recollection.

Reading behind the lines, as it were, of Plato's descriptions of recollection in the *Meno* and the *Phaedo*, we have seen the attempt to make sense of his own progress in philosophy proceed through what appear to be two distinct stages. Both stages feature an account of recollection as a means of gaining knowledge, and both rely upon a conception of the individual soul as passing through a state of prenatal existence. The primary differences between the two are that the account in the *Meno* but not that in the *Phaedo* makes elenchus a part of the recollection process and that the latter but not the former account focuses upon the Forms as objects of knowledge.

There is one more dialogue in which recollection figures before vanishing from the text of the dialogues.[12] Further changes appear in Plato's conception of this process as we examine its role in the *Phaedrus*.

3. Recollection and Collection in the Phaedrus

The contexts provided for Socrates' discussions of recollection have endowed it with a mythical dimension from the very outset. In the *Meno* it is attributed to various men and women of inspiration—priests and priestesses and poets like Pindar—who are represented as spokespersons for the religious doctrine of reincarnation. When Socrates says at 86B8 that he is not wholly confident about parts of the story, this might fairly be taken as an indication that not everything said about recollection in the dialogue ought to be taken at face value. In the *Phaedo*, although the notion that learning is recollection is presented in the form of a "famous saying" rather than a myth or story, it has obvious affinities with the myth of judgment and reincarnation with which Socrates ends the conversation before taking the hemlock. Once again, Socrates is made to say that he is not confident (*diischurisasthai*: 114D1—the same verb as at *Meno* 86B8) that things are just the way his story tells them, which again cautions against an entirely literal reading of these discourses about reincarnation.

In its final appearance within the *Phaedrus*, however, recollection is part of a story that is explicitly figurative from start to finish. There is no call for Socrates to express his reservations about its contents, for the story lays no more claim to literal truth than does the allegory of the Cave in the *Republic*. The story in question is the myth of the winged charioteer—the self-proclaimed palinode (*palinōdian*: 243B5) in which Socrates recants his previous speech urging submission to a nonlover.

The only explicit mention of recollection in the dialogue occurs in a set of passages halfway through the palinode, where Socrates (as narrator) remarks that only a soul that has "beheld the truth" (249B6) can enter the form of a human being, inasmuch as a human must be able to understand "according to what we call Forms, going from many perceptions to a unity brought together by reasoning" (*kat' eidos legomenon, ek pollōn ion aisthēseōn eis hen logismō xunairoumenon*: 249B8–C1). And this, he goes on to say, is "a recollection of those things our souls once saw" (*anamnēsis ekeinōn ha pot' eiden hēmōn hē psuchē*: 249C2–3) during

their heavenly journey amongst true being. There is an obvious parallel
here with 98A of the Meno, where anamnēsis is identified with the process
of tying down true belief by "causal reasoning" (aitias logismō: 98A4),
thereby (by that account) producing knowledge. In both contexts anamnēsis is cited as the source of knowledge or understanding and in both is
said to involve some sort of reasoning (logismō). There are also parallels
with the account in the Phaedo. The objects recollected, as in that
dialogue, are Forms or Ideas, which are now depicted as abiding in a place
"beyond the heavens" (huperouranion: 247C3) where they can be "viewed
by mind alone" (247C8). Like the Phaedo again, in contrast with the
Meno, the Phaedrus assigns no role to refutation in the process by which
recollection takes place. What we find instead is an initially puzzling
reference to a logismō that "brings many perceptions together in unity."

Yet there are notable respects in which this account in the Phaedrus
differs from those in both of the other dialogues. One striking difference
is the absence in this context of any connection between recollection
and learning. Recollection enters into the discussion of the Meno
explicitly as a form of learning that can circumvent the "learner's
paradox." And the "famous saying" introduced by Cebes into the conversation of the Phaedo is expressly the maxim that learning is recollection.
Here in the palinode of the Phaedrus, however, neither the possibility of
knowledge nor the means of acquiring it is ever addressed as a matter at
issue. Socrates' concern in the palinode is not with the process of
learning, but rather with the effect upon the soul when it gains a vision
of the Forms.

To be sure, there is a vivid description of how the disembodied soul
may "behold truth" (theōrousa talēthē: 247D4) and "perceive being"
(idousa . . . to on: 247D4) in the course of its heavenly circuits, and may
"look down" (kathora: 247D6) on Justice itself, as well as Temperance and
Knowledge. And there is the reference noted above to the "recollection
of those things our souls once saw" by bringing many perceptions
together in unity. But the only consequence of note that is cited in the
myth is the nourishment and well-being the soul receives from this
vision. The central theme of the palinode is the soul's vision of Beauty,
which is so "resplendent to see" (idein lampron: 250B6), both itself and in
its instances, that the soul is reminded of that vision by the sight of a
beautiful creature. Thus when the lover comes to gaze on the beauty of
the beloved, his soul is stirred with longing for the true Beauty it once
encountered; and if the course of love pursues the interests of honor over

lust, the soul finally is conveyed back to its home among the Forms. In brief, the myth of the charioteer is a story about the love that inspires a return to the Forms, rather than an account of how the mind is capable of achieving knowledge.

Another difference concerns the relation between recollection and immortality. Socrates' remarks on recollection in the *Phaedo* are aimed primarily at showing that the soul can exist apart from the body, and his summary of what has been demonstrated by his conversation with the slave boy in the *Meno* stresses immortality no less than recollection. The two topics are intertwined in these previous dialogues in such a fashion that evidence under one heading pertains to the other as well. An interesting departure in the *Phaedrus* is that Socrates purports to demon-strate the soul's immortality *before* recollection is even mentioned, on grounds to which the latter appears irrelevant. The purported demon-stration is similar to that found in Book X of the *Laws*. In general outline, the argument takes the form of a syllogism to the effect that, since by definition anything self-moving is immortal and since the soul is self-moving in that its motion does not originate outside itself, the soul itself must be immortal. The image of the winged charioteer is then introduced as part of a story to elaborate the character of the soul and its immortality, with recollection playing a minor role within this story. Whereas recollection was portrayed as a consequence of immortality in the *Meno* and was offered as part of a proof for immortality in the *Phaedo*, in the *Phaedrus* it is merely a detail in a figurative characterization of what it is for the soul to be immortal. An intriguing by-product of this shift of roles in the *Phaedrus* is to show that Plato can relinquish the notion that learning is a kind of recollection without giving up the thesis of the soul's immortality.

The most significant divergence in the *Phaedrus* from previous ac-counts, nonetheless, remains Socrates' characterization of recollection at 249C1 as tantamount to a bringing together of a unity from many perceptions. Although the meaning of this characterization is left un-clear within the immediate context, Socrates returns to the topic after the palinode is over, mentioning it as one aspect of that "playful story" (*paidia:* 265C8—i.e., the palinode) worth further elaboration. There are "two ways of proceeding" (265C9) alluded to in that story, he says, that we should try to grasp in a more technical fashion. What Socrates says by way of elaborating these procedures constitutes the first appearance in the Platonic corpus of the method of collection and division.[13]

The first procedure Socrates identifies as "bringing a dispersed plurality to a single Idea by seeing it together" (*Eis mian te idean, sunorōnta,
agein ta pollachē diesparmena*: 265D3-4). Although there is no mention
here of the "dispersed plurality" being perceptions, and although the
process is described as a matter of "seeing together" rather than of
"reasoning" as at 249C1, this fairly clearly is the process equated with
recollection in the earlier context. The companion procedure[14] Socrates
then describes as that of "dividing according to Forms, following the
natural articulation" (*kat' eidē . . . diatemnein kat' arthra he pephuken*:
265E1-2)—a procedure likened to that of a butcher who cleaves at the
proper joints. After a purported illustration of these two procedures with
reference to his two speeches on the "madness" (*aphron*: 265E3) of love—
the palinode and the speech it was intended to recant—Socrates goes on
to say that he himself is a lover (*erastēs*: 266B3) of these "collections and
divisions" (*tōn diaireseōn kai sunagōgōn*: 266B4). The reason he is so fond
of this way of dealing with the Forms, he adds laconically, is that "he
thereby is able to speak and to think" (266B4-5). When he comes across
someone else who is "able to discern a natural unity-over-plurality"
(*dunaton eis hen kai epi polla pephukos horan*: 266B5-6) of this sort, he is
eager to follow in the footsteps of such a person. For people with this
power of discernment, he concludes, are those deserving to be called
"dialecticians" (*dialektikous*: 266C1).

The pair of procedures here labeled "collection and division," as any
experienced reader of Plato will recognize, constitute the dialectical
method followed in the *Sophist* and the *Statesman*—dialogues in which
the character Socrates himself plays only a very minor role. We will
return for a detailed consideration of this method in chapter 5. Our
concern now is with the relevance of this "technical" (*technē*: 265D1)
discussion of method to the remarks about recollection at 249C.

As noted above, the last use of the term *anamnēsis* in this special sense
signifying recollection from a previous existence occurs at *Phaedrus*
249C2, in the highly figurative context of the myth of the charioteer.
Recollection here is described, not at all perspicuously, as a matter of
"bringing many perceptions to a unity by reasoning." The same procedure is redescribed in an avowedly nonfigurative manner at 265D3-4
and is paired with another procedure said to run "backwards" (*palin*:
265E1) from the former. The two procedures together are then labeled
"collection and division" and left to be elaborated further in later
dialogues. In effect, the notion of recollection as a stage in the learning

process—which in the *Meno* and the *Phaedo* has served with indifferent results at best—is being phased out in favor of a procedure which Plato sees fit to identify as part of the dialectical method of philosophy. The figurative explanation of learning based on the various religious myths of reincarnation is being replaced by a procedure based on skill (*technē*), which is destined for success in Plato's later writings. What more can we learn from the present dialogue about the procedure of collection?

In both the palinode and the later more "technical" discussion, this process of "bringing plurality to a unity" is described as something that is accomplished by means of the mind's power of discernment. At 265D the dispersed plurality is brought under a single Idea by some manner of "seeing it together" (*sunorōnta:* 265D3). And at 266B, Socrates expresses his eagerness to follow in the footsteps of anyone who has the "power to discern" (*dunaton . . . horan:* 266B5–6) such a "unity-over-plurality." Within the context of the palinode, similarly, the process in question is described as a recollection of things our souls once saw (*eiden:* 249C2); while in his further characterization of how this recollection takes place, Socrates emphasizes the vision (*eidon:* 250A2, passim) of being every soul has before it enters human form. It is because of the prior vision it has of these Forms or Ideas that the soul is capable of the subsequent discernment Socrates describes as recollection.

Here, roughly, is how recollection is said to take place in the *Phaedrus*. The items termed "perceptions" in the description at 149C1 are sensible instances of the Forms that the mind perceived previously. Such an instance serves as an image (*eikōn,* as at 250B5) or a likeness (*homoiōma,* as at 250A6) of the Form involved. In the case of Forms like Justice and Temperance, Socrates observes, their instances lack sufficient "luster" (*phengos:* 250B3) to be recognizable by most persons for what they are. Only a few (*oligoi:* 250B5), that is to say, know justice when they see it, in the sense of recognizing the characteristics the instance shares with Justice itself. It is no easy matter, in general, for the soul to recall (*Anamimnēskesthai:* 250A1) the Forms on the basis of things perceived here in this world. But things are otherwise, he says, in the case of Beauty. For our original vision of Beauty was sufficiently brilliant (*lampron:* 250B6) that it remains "fully manifest" (*enargestata:* 250D3) in its sensible instances. While Beauty itself Socrates might have added is not subject to sense perception,[15] the sense of sight is sufficiently clear that we are able to grasp (*kateilēphamen:* 250D1) Beauty in its sensible instances.

Abstracting from the special praise due Beauty as a key factor in the palinode, the following picture emerges of the relation between Forms and their instances. First and foremost, Forms and their instances are like (*homoios*) or similar to each other. Because of this likeness, Forms can be revealed through their instances to a properly prepared mind. In the case of some Forms like Beauty (and seemingly Equality in the *Phaedo*), the likeness is clear enough to allow the mind to recognize the instance for what it is—i.e., a thing that is beautiful (or a case of equality, etc.). In cases like Justice and Temperance, on the other hand, the emphasis in the palinode is on the difficulty of grasping the similarity between the Form and the instance. Yet even here, the instance provides the stimulus by which the well-disposed mind might begin to recapture its original vision of the Form. The process by which the mind is enabled to move from a set of sensible instances—the "many perceptions" of 249C1—to the unique Form they resemble is termed recollection. And what makes recollection possible is the mind's prior access to the Form recollected, along with the similarity between the Form and its sensible manifestations.

This at least is how recollection is supposed to work in the *Phaedo* and the *Phaedrus*. Now in none of the dialogues in which recollection is a factor, we should note, is this renewed grasp of the Form something that happens *automatically* with perception of the instance. Even in the case of Equality, as Socrates explains it in the *Phaedo*, a certain amount of reflection is required before Simmias and Cebes begin to think of Equality itself as indicated in its sensible instances. In the *Meno* recollection was supposed to have been assisted by elenchus, although elenchus by itself never appeared to be enough. When the Forms become part of the picture in the *Phaedo* and the *Phaedrus*, however, elenchus seems simply to drop from view, and the characters involved have nothing further to say about any procedures by which recollection might be brought about. The fact that Plato, as author, remained silent on this matter would seem to indicate a dissatisfaction on his part with the whole notion of recollection. What good is an account of the origins of knowledge if no procedures are forthcoming for its actual pursuit?

With this question in mind, we are finally prepared to grasp the significance of the replacement of recollection by the procedure of collection at *Phaedrus* 265D. As part of the full dialectical method of collection and division that is put to such good use in the later dialogues, there is no doubt about the practical applicability of this procedure.

Given the accounts of collection that we find in these later contexts, moreover, the old story of recollection provides most of the ingredients already needed for collection to work. The basic ingredients are a distinction between a Form and its instances, along with a relation of similarity between them that enables the instance to provide a mental access to its corresponding Form. Given that the Forms are already on the scene as part of the account of recollection put forward in the *Phaedo*, Plato can shift to the methodology of collection and division without major changes in his conception of the nature of being.

Whether or not Plato was still actively concerned to understand the power of Socratic conversations as a stimulus to knowledge on his own part by the time he wrote the *Phaedrus* is a matter on which we need not speculate further. More than likely his concerns regarding the origin of knowledge had long since taken on a life of their own, quite apart from old memories of his own conversations with Socrates.[16] Nonetheless, there are aspects of the conversations in his own earlier dialogues that may have paved the way for this new methodology. What I have in mind is the use of well-chosen *examples*. While a full examination of the method of collection and division will have to be reserved for a later chapter, let us look briefly at the use of examples in certain Socratic dialogues and then consider its relevance to collection as a dialectical technique.

4. From Recollection to the Use of Paradigms

The character Socrates, in Plato's early dialogues, relies extensively upon examples in his elenchic conversations. At *Hippias Major* 295C–D, to cite a case in point, he uses such examples as a beautiful horse, a beautiful ship, and a body beautifully made for wrestling, by way of helping Hippias understand the sense in which things that function properly are also beautiful. In the opening conversation of the *Protagoras* he alerts Hippocrates to the dangers of trusting the care of his soul to a sophist by pointing out that the sophist's wares are not like those of a food merchant whose goods can be inspected before they are consumed (314A–B). And later on in the same dialogue, he casts doubt upon the teachability of the art of politics by observing that the state requires credentials for the practice of skills that can be learned and taught—like architecture and ship-designing—while no credentials are required for holders of public office (319B–D). In the *Meno*, Socrates offers a credible definition of shape (as the limit of a solid, 76A) by way of illustrating the sort of definition he would like Meno to give of virtue. And in the *Gorgias*, Callicles is represented as complaining to Socrates that he never stops referring to cobblers and fullers and cooks and doctors (491A), as if these people were what their talk was supposed to be about.

We have good reason to believe that this extensive use of illustrations and examples was typical of the historical Socrates as well. The *Memorabilia* of Xenophon contains page after page of homespun illustrations of points made by Socrates about virtuous living,[17] a pattern evident as well in the *Symposium* of that author. Alcibiades' encomium in the final section of Plato's *Symposium*, in turn, sums it up nicely when he alludes to Socrates' way of seeming always to be saying the same things in the same old way in his talk about pack-asses and blacksmiths and tanners and cobblers (221E4–7).[18] Such use of examples, we may conclude, was no less typical of Socrates than was the use of elenchus examined in the previous chapter.

While many of these examples function as analogies and similes, there is a recognizable subgroup that function more like illustrative instances instead. One such case is found in the *Apology*, where Socrates interprets the oracle as using his name only by way of a public example to illustrate the wisdom of acknowledging one's ignorance (23A8–B4). Another case occurs with the first two speeches of the *Phaedrus* as providing prior illustrations of how such discourses can mislead their audiences (262D1–2). Further cases appear in the *Gorgias*, with reference to the examples made of the politicians and tyrants in the myth of the final judgment with which the dialogue closes (525B–D). When Socrates makes a point of alluding to examples of this sort himself, they often go by the name *paradeigmata*.

A case we have already encountered in the *Meno* is Socrates' definition of shape, which he describes as one of the *paradeigmata* (77B1; also 79A10) provided for Meno to follow in his own attempt to reach a definition of virtue. Socrates' definition, that is to say, is an illustrative instance of the kind of definition he wants Meno to produce. It is the use of example in this particular sense of illustrative instance or *paradeigma* that ties in with collection as described in the *Phaedrus*.

The word *paradeigma* in Plato is an elusive term, with meanings ranging from illustrative instance, noted above, to standard of comparison, as at *Euthyphro* 6E6. But in no case is Plato's use of the term potentially more confusing than in its application in several dialogues to

Forms and to their sensible instances alike. When readers familiar with the *Timaeus* consider the term, they are likely to think first of the *paradeigmata* cited in that dialogue as one of the three primordial principles needed for the "new beginning" at 48E. These three principles are identified as (1) the patterns or paradigms that "are intelligible and always the same" (*noēton kai aei kata tauta on*: 48E6), (2) the "imitations of these patterns" (*mimēma . . . paradeigmatos*: 49A1), and (3) the "receptacle of generation" (*geneseōs hupodochēn*: 49A6) in which the imitations are received and nourished. Later at 52D3 these three principles are referred to (with the order of the latter two reversed) simply as "being and space and generation," continuing the distinction between being and becoming that is typical of the "two world" ontology of the middle dialogues. The paradigms of this passage quite obviously are intended to be equivalent to the Forms or Ideas of the *Phaedo* and the *Republic*, while the imitations that are generated in the Receptacle comprise the objects of sense perception in the realm of becoming. A use of the term *paradeigma* in this sense, to be sure, occurs within the *Republic* itself, where at 540A9 the Form of the Good is described as a pattern or model for the ordering of the state and of the lives of its citizens. Other uses of the term in the sense of Form or Idea can be found in the *Theaetetus* (176E3) and the *Parmenides* (132D2).

On the other hand, there are contexts in which the term *paradeigma* is used unmistakably to designate perceptible instances of these eternal Ideas. One such context occurs within the *Timaeus* itself, where at 28B the speaker distinguishes the "created pattern" (*gennētō paradeigmati*: 28B2) of the world from its eternal counterpart—the *paradeigma* (28A8) that is "always the same" (*kata tauta . . . aei*: 28A7). A related case occurs at *Republic* 529D, where the "variegated blazonry of the heavens" (*ton ouranon poikilia*: 529D7—presumably the visible stars and planets) are referred to as *paradeigmata* to aid in the study of "true number and true figures" (529D3) of the sort that only reason can apprehend. The most extensive use of the term in this sense, however, occurs in connection with the technique of example introduced in the *Statesman* and is employed there in the Stranger's definition of the art of statecraft. Let us briefly recall the circumstances within the dialogue that led to the introduction of this particular technique.

The express purpose of the *Statesman*, like the *Sophist* before it, is to provide a definition of the skill named in its title. It is assumed from the outset, without benefit of collection,[19] that the statesman possesses a kind of knowledge. Then, after a perfunctory division occupying scarcely four pages, a definition of statecraft as the nurture of human flocks is proposed and summarily rejected on the grounds that it divides flocks too hastily between human and animal. After instructing Young Socrates that division must result in Forms rather than mere portions, the Stranger adds several intermediate terms to the definition that are intended to provide a division along more natural lines. But this definition also is found to be inadequate, inasmuch as it fails to distinguish statecraft from other skills involved in human nurture—skills such as farming, trade, and medicine. Acting on his judgment that a new start is needed, the Stranger then begins a story about the reign of Cronos, in which the course of life reverses its temporal order. Further distinctions illustrated in the myth are factored into the definition, and once again Young Socrates expresses satisfaction that the task of the dialogue has been completed. But once again the Stranger demurs and explains his reasons in a discussion of the use of examples.

The problem is that examples (*paradeigmata*: 277B4) of kingly rule like that in the myth of Cronos are too coarsely drawn for the purposes at hand. As the first step of his discussion of the proper use of example, the Stranger observes that "example itself requires an example" (277D9–10) and chooses as his example the learning of the written alphabet.[20] When children can distinguish letters in simple syllables but do not yet recognize them in other combinations, the best way of leading them to the knowledge they lack is to set the former in juxtaposition with the latter syllables and to point out the similarity of the elements in both. Letters in the syllables previously known thus serve as examples (*paradeigmata*: 278B4) by which their counterparts in the harder cases can be identified.

With this example of example at hand, the Stranger suggests, a general statement can be formulated of how *paradeigmata* are useful for dialectical purposes. Examples of this sort come into play, he says (very elliptically):

> whenever two separate cases of the same thing are brought together—one set apart from the other in being rightly thought of (already) (*hopotan on tauton en heterō diespasmenō doxazomenon orthōs kai sunachthen peri hekateron:* 278C5–7)—so that a single true judgment is rendered of each (*hos sunamphō mian alēthē doxan apotelē:* 278C7).[21]

In accord with this terse characterization, we see in retrospect, letters in known syllables serve as examples of those in unknown combinations, and the case of the letters provides an example of the use of examples generally. And by way of prospect, the parties in the dialogue now realize what kind of example is needed to elucidate the art of statecraft. Instead of paradigms on the grand scale like the myth of Cronos, what is needed is a paradigm of modest dimensions that will illustrate the subsidiary arts of which statecraft consists. The paradigm chosen for this purpose is that of weaving woolens, which like statecraft comprises both "the combinative and the separative" (*hē sunkritikē te kai diakritikē*: 282B7–8) arts.

This reference to the arts of combination and separation should recall to mind the techniques of collection and division which Socrates ascribed to the dialectician at *Phaedrus* 266B. Like both the statesman and the weaver who serves as his paradigm, the dialectician practices his own art of combination and separation. The type of separation practiced by the latter is illustrated by the numerous divisions undertaken by the Stranger in the first half of the dialogue as part of his attempt to reach a definition of statecraft. As noted above, however, these early divisions were pursued in the absence of the kind of combination supposed to precede them in the right application of the dialectician's art. The kind of combination needed for dialectic, of course, is the collection (*sunagōgē*) of the *Phaedrus*. What should be apparent at this point in the conversation is that the use of example, illustrated by the case of the child's alphabetical studies at 278B, plays the same role as collection in the dialectical process. Indeed, as the Stranger suggests at 285D, the main purpose served by their attempt to define the statesman is to enable the parties concerned to become better dialecticians (*dialektikōterois*: 285D7) generally. And a major part of dialectic as practiced in this dialogue is the use of examples in the manner the Stranger has been demonstrating.

What are the similarities between collection and the use of example that enable them to play the same role in the dialectical process? Collection is characterized in the *Phaedrus* as a matter of bringing a plurality of cases together by viewing them as instances of a single Idea (a close paraphrase of *Phaedrus* 265D3–4). The use of example, in turn, is characterized in the *Statesman* as a matter of bringing different cases of the same thing together in such a way that a single true judgment can be applied to each (a close paraphrase of *Statesman* 278C5–7). Both procedures start with separate instances, both bring these instances together with reference to some common feature, and both end with a unified grasp of these instances in a single mental perception. The basis for the combining process in both procedures is a set of paradigmatic instances. And while the method of collection focuses upon viewing these diverse instances as exemplars of a single Idea, the use of example recommended by the Stranger focuses upon the similarities (*homoiotēta*: 278B2) that allow the instances to be brought together under the same conception.

The main difference between collection and the use of example, as characterized in their respective contexts, is that collection moves from a set of paradigmatic instances to a single Form or Idea, while the use of example seeks to bring out similarities that allow the instances to be viewed together under a single act of comprehension. For dialectical purposes, however, the effect is the same. Either way of proceeding brings a common feature to view, from which the technique of division can proceed in turn. With this common effect in mind, it should come as no great surprise to find passages in which the terminology of these procedures is interchanged. At *Sophist* 226C1, for instance, the Stranger uses the term *paradeigmata* in reference to the instances from which the collection of the separative arts there underway proceeds. And in the Stranger's reflections on the division of the rearing of land-dwelling herds that precedes the myth of Cronos in the *Statesman*, there is mention of collecting (*sunagagein*: 267B7) under a single name the art of tending herds that do not interbreed.

As part of our examination above of recollection in the *Phaedrus*, we saw how recollection gave way to collection, which joins with division as the dominant method in several late dialogues. With this alternative description of collection in terms of the use of example, the relation between recollection and this new method becomes even more explicit. As characterized at *Phaedrus* 249B8–C1, recollection is a matter of bringing a plurality of perceptions together in a unity through reasoning. Assuming that the perceptions in question are instances sharing the same perceptual property, we have here in recollection a procedure that appears equivalent in every important respect to that characterized at *Statesman* 278C5–7 as bringing different cases of the same thing together within the scope of a single true conception. In effect, the transition that appears to be taking place between the final mention of recollection at *Phaedrus* 250A and the procedure identified as collection at 266B boils down to a shift in the manner in which the philosopher is supposed to move from paradigm instances to a grasp of the Form itself.

In the version of recollection first introduced in the *Meno*, the mind gains knowledge in some prenatal state of existence, which it promptly

forgets upon entering a body. With the help of elenchus to remove the
overlay of false impressions resulting from bodily experience, this knowledge is capable of being recalled to active awareness; and the process of
recall is termed *anamnēsis*. The explanation of the mind's capacity to
gain knowledge, in this manner of thinking, lay in the notion of an
innate state of knowledge that is capable of being regained in explicit
form. Given the conception of the Forms that is available to Plato by the
time of the *Phaedrus*, however, this notion of preexistent knowledge
becomes extra baggage for epistemological purposes. From this time
onward,[22] Plato's approach to epistemological issues is premised on his
conception of Forms as identifiable objects of knowledge that are capable of being manifested in their perceptible instances.

In light of this self-revealing capacity of the Forms, it seems not
inappropriate to think of their exemplary instances—like objects of beauty
in the *Phaedrus* and specific forms of sophistry in the *Sophist*—as opportunities for the mind to mount inquiry into the nature of the Form itself. In
the case of Beauty and its many manifestations, which serve as a primary
illustration in the *Phaedrus* of this capacity, the instances in which Beauty
shows itself present are beautiful faces and bodily forms which attract the
lover through his bodily vision. In every case of successful inquiry in the
Sophist and the *Statesman*, however, the paradigmatic instances are presented through the Stranger's discourse rather than in a form directly
accessible by sense perception. And this seems to pose a bit of a problem.
In various passages discussed in chapter 1, mostly notably in the *Phaedrus*
and the Seventh Letter, Plato berates written and spoken discourse as
unfit for the communication of philosophic knowledge. But here we find
the Stranger relying upon written and spoken discourse (for us and for his
respondents respectively) as an inducement to inquire into the nature of
Sophistry and Statecraft. How can the discourse dismissed elsewhere as
unsuitable for philosophy provide exemplars that incite the mind to
philosophic inquiry? In order to gain insight into how Plato might respond
to this question, we must return to the Seventh Letter for a further look at
language and its use in philosophy.

5. Verbal Paradigms as Seeds of Knowledge

When Plato remarks in the Seventh Letter that philosophy "is not
something that can be put into words like other subjects" (341C6), his

sense is not that philosophy cannot be discussed in language—or that there is something wrong about writing dialogues on the subject. His sense rather is that the philosophic *understanding* that arrives with a "flash of insight" (cf. 341D1–2, 344B7) as a consequence of the discipline he had been describing cannot be communicated to other people through the medium of language. Such are "the inadequacies of language" (343A1), he says, that no person of understanding (*noun:* 343A1) will ever venture to commit to it the things he or she has understood (*nenoēmena:* 343A2). While the symbolism of written language is particularly defective in this regard, the spoken word also is expressly rejected as unsuitable for the communication of philosophic understanding.

Plato's account of what it is about public language generally that makes it unfit for the communication of knowledge, we recall from chapter 1, is based upon the differences between the Forms themselves and the various means involved in our attempts to grasp them. These means include, in order of mention, (1) the name of the Form in question, (2) its verbal characterization or *logos*, (3) its physical images or likenesses, and (4) the state of mind by which the Form itself is grasped, which latter is further divided into (a) true opinion, (b) knowledge, and (c) intelligence or understanding. The basic defect of linguistic symbols noted in this context, to say it again, is that the presence in particular symbols (like the drawn circle in the illustration of the Seventh Letter) of opposing characteristics (the curved line and the straight tangent sharing a common point) makes them available for symbolizing opposing objects. The upshot is that sensible symbols by nature are without fixed reference. As Plato puts it, names are "in no way stable" (343B1); and nothing prevents things now called round (as in his illustration) from being called straight at other times, and vice versa. Using words in altered senses such as these, he goes on to say, we might find them no less stable than in their standard use—which is to say that we should not consider them stable in any use whatever. As far as the Seventh Letter is concerned at least, it is this inherent instability of public language that makes it unsuitable for the communication of philosophic knowledge. The philosopher's knowledge is a grasp of immutable Forms, which cannot be conveyed in mutable language.

One point Plato makes at the start of this critique, however, is that the first three factors on the list—names, verbal descriptions and images— nonetheless are necessary aids in the acquisition of knowledge. Although philosophic understanding cannot be communicated in language, neither can such understanding be reached without it. This already relieves the tension reflected in the query at the end of the previous section—i.e., how Plato can reject language as unfit for the communication of philosophy on the one hand and on the other can use language for the expression of paradigms of the sort that lead the mind to philosophic inquiry. Yet the query nonetheless has a useful purpose. For now we are able both to say more about how those three factors function in the acquisition of knowledge and to relate the topic of collection through paradigmatic instances to the teaching practice of the dialectician described in the final pages of the *Phaedrus*.

Let us first look briefly at the role of (1) names, (2) verbal characterizations, and (3) images in the process of inquiry that yields philosophic knowledge. When Plato says at 342A7–8 of the Seventh Letter that these factors are necessary aids in this process, the point seems to be that one or more are needed to get inquiry underway, not that all three are needed in each and every case. Be this as it may, there are some contexts in the dialogues concerned with problems of knowledge where emphasis is given to the role of names in inquiry and other contexts putting the emphasis on verbal characterizations or images. A notable case of the former is the conversation in the *Cratylus*. In this interchange, Cratylus is represented as defending both the thesis that knowing a name that has been correctly assigned requires knowing the thing it stands for (see 435D5–6) and the thesis that things are discovered only in the process of discovering the names that stand for them (see 436A4–6). While this general position makes sense for someone who learns the "true" names of things from someone else who has known them previously, it involves an obvious paradox for the person supposed to discover these "true" names in the first place.[23] The lesson Socrates draws from this approximation to the "learner's paradox" is that we come to know by learning about things in themselves rather than by inquiring into their names (see 439B6–8).

An epistemological context in which the verbal characterization (*logos*) of a thing is emphasized is the search for a definition of knowledge in the *Theaetetus*. The express purpose of this inquiry is to find the "unique formula" (*heni logō*: 148D7) that applies to many kinds of knowledge, and the inquiry gets under way with an illustrative *logos* (offered by Theaetetus) of square roots not commensurable with the integers. The dialogue ends, however, with an unsuccessful attempt to find a sense of *logos* that will convert true opinion into knowledge. The fact that the inquiries of the *Cratylus* (stressing names) and of the

Theaetetus (stressing *logos*) both fail in the end might be taken to indicate that approaches to knowledge relying primarily on factors (1) and (2) need augmenting by factor (3) (images) to stand a chance of succeeding.[24]

What would count as an inquiry conducted by means of images? In Plato's illustration of the five factors involved in coming to know the Form Circularity, he describes an image as something that can be "drawn and wiped out" (*zōgraphoumenon te kai exaleiphomenon:* 342C1–2), turned on a lathe, etc.—i.e., as some sort of physical object. This accords with the standard use of the term *eidōlon* by Plato in the sense of perceptible likenesses. But in the same context of the Seventh Letter, Plato cites the Good, the Beautiful, and the Just, as Forms that have images as well. And while images of Beauty by and large might be perceptible objects, images of the Good and the Just typically would not be perceptible in the same sense. Indeed, this very point is made at *Phaedrus* 250B–D, where Socrates observes that instances of Beauty are clearly perceptible by sight, while images (*eikonas:* 250B5) of Justice are scarcely perceptible by our "dim sense organs" (*amudrōn organōn:* 250B4). Practical wisdom (*phronēsis:* 250D4) is another Form said to lack a sensible image (*eidōlon:* 250D6). What would count as an image of Justice, for instance, given that a sensible object normally would not serve in that role?

One answer that is obvious (there may be others) is provided by the enterprise of Plato's best-known dialogue—the project undertaken in the *Republic* of studying justice on the level of the state in order to grasp its nature in the individual person. Expecting that justice will be easier to make out in the larger context, Socrates proposes examining it first in the state overall and then looking for its likeness (*homoiotēta:* 369A3) on the personal level. The image of Justice that provides the object of study through most of the subsequent dialogue, we should note, is not an actual state that could be studied by modern techniques of social science. The object studied is a state portrayed in discourse. And the manner of study treats this portrayal as an illustrative example through which the nature of Justice itself might be at least partially revealed. When Socrates looks back upon the proceedings at 533A and remarks with regret that he has been able to provide his companions only with an image (*eikona:* 533A3) of the truth as he sees it, the image in question is a likeness constituted by his previous discourse. And the primary function of this discourse has been to present a paradigm through which the major features of Justice at large could be examined.

The exemplary instances of sophistry that the Stranger gathers to-gether by way of collection in the *Sophist*, similarly, are verbal portrayals of different varieties of sophistic practice.[25] And the paradigm that shapes the inquiry in the final pages of the *Statesman* is a verbal portrayal of weaving rather than actual weaving being practiced before a group of spectators. In every illustration of successful dialectic that the dialogues provide, it seems fair to say, the collection that sets the stage for the division that follows deals with *verbal* exemplars of the Form under study as distinct from its sensible instantiations. Obvious as this may be in itself, what makes the point worth noting is the connection it provides between the method of collection through paradigm instances and the literary activity of the dialectician as described in the *Phaedrus*.

In Socrates' own complaints about writing following the story of Theuth in the *Phaedrus*, we may recall from chapter 1, he refers to written discourse as an image (*eidōlon*: 276A9) of the discourse that goes with knowledge and that is "written," as it were, within the soul of the learner (276A5-6). Later in the same context this discourse in the soul is further described as being associated with instruction regarding Justice, Beauty, and Goodness, and is identified with discourse planted (cf. 276E6) in the soul of an appropriate subject. When these plantings sprout and mature in their new setting, they are capable of inseminating other souls in turn, and the line of progeny thus established renders the original discourse immortal, gaining its possessor well-being of the highest available degree (277A3-4).

Given praise like this for transactions of discourse conducted on a soul-to-soul basis, it is somewhat surprising to find Socrates saying something mildly favorable about the written image of this "ensouled" (278A3) discourse as well. When the dialectician sows his seeds in written form instead—an acceptable form of recreation, Socrates allows (see 276D-E)—the "literary garden" thus established will serve both to refresh his own memory in advanced years of forgetfulness and to provide a "treasure trove" for those who "follow in his footsteps" (276D3). If this pastime happens to bear fruit, Socrates remarks in passing, the dialecti-cian will take pleasure in the "tender shoots" (276D5) that spring up from this source as well.

Viewing these brief remarks about the dialectician's "literary garden" in light of our earlier discussion of collection as successor to recollection, it seems to me not implausible to read what Socrates says here as an expression of the author's thoughts about his own literary activity. If the

Seventh Letter (along with the *Phaedrus*) represents Plato's mature views on the place of writing in philosophy, then his authorship of the dialogues must have been *incidental* to his other philosophic activities— i.e., must have been a "recreation." But *Phaedrus* 276D allows a legitimate philosophic role to writing nonetheless.[26] For one thing, a written version of the dialectician's thoughts can serve as a reminder when memory fades. More to the point, what one writes can serve to inseminate the minds of one's readers, assuming that the seeds themselves are viable and that they fall on fertile ground.

Earlier on in Plato's literary career, if the conjectures being developed in the first part of this chapter are near the mark, he was exploring the idea that knowledge derives from innate sources and that it can be reactivated with the help of Socratic elenchus. During this period he wrote dialogues depicting conversations in which interlocutors with modest intellectual endowment were subjected to elenchus by a quintessential Socrates. If Plato took the notion of recollection at all seriously during that period, perhaps the thought was that the effects of this elenchus might tend to rub off, and thereby stimulate a recall of knowledge in the mind of the reader.

With the replacement of recollection by the procedure of collection around the time of the *Phaedrus*, however, the author's conception of how the dialogues might act upon their readers must have taken a significant turn. As if to make this new conception of dialectical interchange explicit, the *Sophist* inaugurates a series of dialogues in which the reader can share in various procedures of collection and division which are administered by master philosophers to very intelligent respondents. In each case, the process of collection is served by verbal paradigms of the Forms under study. And the respondent is pictured as responding to these paradigms, and to the dialectical procedures they serve, with a growing understanding of the issues involved. It does not seem farfetched to assume that Plato might have anticipated a similar response to these dialectical aids on the part of an attentive reader.

Speculation about Plato's expectations aside, the fact remains that the dialogues often do have effects of this sort upon readers who are properly disposed and who take the time to read them carefully. This is the case, not only with dialogues where the procedure of collection is involved explicitly, but with many of the earlier dialogues as well where verbal examples are liberally employed. When this happens, then one way to describe it—the way of the *Phaedrus*—is to say that the seeds of discourse made available in the form of these paradigms have been transferred to the mind of the reader. If these seeds germinate and grow to maturity, then the discourse now "written in the soul" of that person will count among the progeny that contribute immortality to Plato's own original discourse.

But the seeds implanted in this form, to continue the metaphor, cannot grow on their own to philosophic maturity. Nourishment is needed to encourage their growth, and various forms of cultivation are required as well. The topic of nourishment provides the focus of the following chapter.

4

LOVE AND PHILOSOPHY: NURTURING THE GROWTH

1. Eros in the Interaction between Teacher and Student

The first use of the term *philosophos*—lover of wisdom—apparently was due to Pythagoras,[1] who wanted to be known as someone desirous of wisdom as distinct from someone already wise (*sophos*). Later uses of the term up to the time of Plato tended to conflate the love of wisdom with the reputation of possessing it (i.e., with sophistry). Thus Isocrates bemoans the bad repute that had come over sophistry by complaining that chicanery has become more highly regarded than (*sic*) philosophy.[2] And Xenophon attributes the propensity of Callias to spend large sums of money on sophists like Prodicus and Hippias to his being in love with philosophy.[3] With Plato, however, given his concern to dramatize the differences between genuine philosophy and mere eristics, the emphasis shifts once again to the love of wisdom that marks the calling of philosophy.[4] Although passages in support of this claim can be found throughout the dialogues, the affective dimension of philosophy is nowhere more tellingly portrayed than in the speeches of Socrates and of Alcibiades in the *Symposium*. The main concern of this chapter is with these two speeches and with what they tell us about Plato's conception of the love of wisdom.

Readers already familiar with these two speeches may have noticed several respects in which they appear to be at tension. One respect has to do with the erotic character of Socrates. In the drunken panegyric of Alcibiades, on the one hand, Socrates is compared to the satyr Marsyas, capable of arousing Alcibiades to a frenzy of passion as he listens to the melodious discourse of this captivating person. Several pages of Alcibiades' speech is given over to a candid account of his unsuccessful attempt to seduce Socrates into an act of pederasty. And by the time his encomium is finished, Alcibiades has gone so far as to declare that the erotic charms of Socrates are beyond human comparison. As seen through the eyes of Alcibiades at least, Socrates is a person of irresistible attractiveness.

An entirely different portrayal is contained within the speech attributed to Diotima. Diotima's speech, of course, is recounted by Socrates, and makes up the major portion of his contribution to the proceedings of the evening. Since Diotima does not describe Socrates directly, the self-portrayal contained in Socrates' story can only be seen by way of reflection. Here is the way this self-portrayal is presented. Socrates has just refuted Agathon's description of Eros as beautiful, on the grounds that Love is a desire for beauty and that one does not desire what one possesses already. As if to soften the blow, Socrates admits that he once had held the same opinion as Agathon and had been disabused of that mistake in a series of conversations with Diotima. Rather than think of Eros as a great god with only noble features (as all previous speakers that evening had done), Diotima explained, we should think of him as a kind of spirit (*Diamōn:* 202D9) that serves as an intermediary between the divine and the mortal. Diotima then tells the story of his conception, through the coupling of Need (*Penia:* 203B4) and Resource (*Poros:* 203B3) on the birthday of Aphrodite.

Because of his paternity by Resource, Eros is always seeking the good and the beautiful, and employs many contrivances in his desire for intelligence. He is a lover of wisdom (*philosophōn:* 203D7) throughout his life and has a marvelous skill in the use of clever arguments. Because of his mother, on the other hand, Eros is always poor. And far from being beautiful, as *hoi polloi* (including Agathon) think, he is tough and wrinkled and barefoot and homeless. The composite picture is of a being that is neither mortal nor immortal and that likewise is suspended between wisdom and ignorance. Being more than ignorant, Eros knows the value of wisdom; and falling short of wisdom, he desires it passionately. Because of his father, Eros is a lover of wisdom—i.e., a philosopher—and because of his mother this love remains unfulfilled.

No one who reads this passage carefully should miss the fact that the features brought together in this composite picture of Eros are features characteristic of Socrates himself. Eros is Socrates inflated to mythical proportions, and Socrates in turn is Eros personified. This portrayal, of course, is attributed to Diotima, but the words conveying it are spoken by Socrates. Since Diotima's discourse undoubtedly was intended to be read as a fabrication on Socrates' part, Socrates' speech continues the pattern followed by each of the earlier speakers of modeling Eros according to his own personal circumstances. The effect in Socrates' case, however, is not to glorify the speaker, but rather to dramatize his inherent limitations. Socrates is a lover of wisdom; and since wisdom is extremely beautiful (204B2–3), he is also a lover of beauty. From this it follows that Socrates is neither wise nor beautiful, inasmuch as one does not love (i.e., desire) what one already possesses. Like his mythical counterpart in Diotima's story, Socrates is tough and wrinkled and barefoot, and by nature caught short of either wisdom or beauty. How could such a person be erotically attractive? How could Eros himself be the object of love?

Alcibiades portrays Socrates as erotically irresistible and as the source of great passion among the young men of Athens (222B). According to Diotima, on the other hand, he is neither wise nor beautiful, and lacks all the graces that would make him attractive to others. Which description is to be believed in the context of the *Symposium*? Which best represents the role of Eros in the pursuit of wisdom that Socrates personifies?

Another point of tension between the two speeches has to do with the erotic involvement between teacher and student. One thing Alcibiades makes clear in his speech is that he is erotically attracted to Socrates' person. Although it was Socrates' discourse that set his "heart aleaping" (215E1–2) in the first place, Alcibiades soon felt moved to express a passion for Socrates of a physical nature as well. When he finds Socrates unresponsive, his initial reaction is disbelief and humiliation. Isn't Socrates enamored by beautiful boys, he says, always following them around as if dazed by passion (216D2–3)? And isn't he—Alcibiades—one of the fairest youths around? Why shouldn't Socrates be receptive to one of those cozy "teacher-student" relationships enjoyed by Agathon and his lover Pausanias (the relation described so delicately in the latter's speech)? Hasn't Socrates treated him in the most outrageous fashion (222A8)—leading him on like a potential lover and then leaving him unrequited when he responded in kind?

Someone who has read along carefully up to this point in the dialogue might have a ready explanation for Alcibiades' plight. Alcibiades was one of numerous youths who kept company with Socrates in the public places of Athens. Among others were Charmides and Euthydemus (222B1–2), Simmias and Cebes,[5] and presumably Plato himself. All were attracted by his speech and demeanor, and some obviously were attracted by his physical person as well. Although these latter on occasion may have been misled by his banter about loving beautiful boys,[6] however, there is no evidence whatever that Socrates ever engaged in pederastic intercourse. If one of his young companions—like Alcibiades—were bemused by this banter to the point of approaching Socrates with physical overtures, he would soon find that the love professed by this captivating person was directed toward his mind and not his body. While Socrates was not above using his physical charms as a decoy by which to lure promising young men into his presence, the explanation continues, once in his company they would find his solicitations focused upon their mental improvement exclusively. This at least appears to be the nub of Alcibiades' predicament as described at the end of the *Symposium*. He has responded to what at first he took to be an invitation to a physical interaction with Socrates, only to find that the latter was interested in his mental and moral well-being instead. The fact that we hear nothing more about further intimacies between Alcibiades and Socrates on an intellectual level suggests that their relationship did not flourish after the seduction attempt. Unlike one of those youths said in the *Theaetetus* (150D–151B) to have "given birth to many beautiful thoughts" through the ministrations of Socrates, Alcibiades seems fated to be given over to other men of "inspired wisdom" and to move onward toward a life of moral dissolution.

This way of understanding the relationship between Socrates and Alcibiades is supported by the stagewise progression in matters of Eros described in the discourse of Diotima. At the entry level of the sequence, so to speak, the lover is attracted by bodily beauty, and by acting upon that attraction is led to reproduce either in body (through heterosexual relations) or in soul (through relations like that of Pausanias and Agathon). At the next level of the progression, the lover's attention is transferred to the beauty of souls, which results in discourse that "works for the betterment of youth" (210C2–3). Subsequent in order comes love for beautiful social practices and then love for beauty found in the many kinds of knowledge. At the final stage the lover encounters Beauty itself, which is productive of "true virtue" (212A4–5) and "friendship of the gods" (212A6). Seen in terms of this progression, the relationship between Socrates and Alcibiades appears to have begun in the suggested fashion but then to have become stalled at the first stage of development. Instead of moving on to love of the beauty of souls, and so forth, Alcibiades has been unable to progress beyond love of Socrates' physical person (his audible speech included). To give birth to the "beautiful thoughts" of which Socrates speaks in the *Theaetetus*, Alcibiades would have to pass on to the second stage of the progression at least. Insofar as his love remains fixated at the level of bodily beauty, he is unable to realize the benefits of the higher forms of Eros that intercourse with Socrates presumably could provide.

On the basis of the content of Diotima's discourse, accordingly, it appears natural to assume that an erotic relation between teacher and student is a suitable starting point for the philosophic ascent. The problem with Alcibiades was not his passion for Socrates but the fact that he was unable to move beyond that physical passion to love of beauty in its higher manifestations.

This at least is the sense of the manner indicated by the content of Diotima's discourse. But Diotima's discourse, we recall, is only part of the story that Socrates tells about his interaction with this woman. And when we look carefully at the nature of this interaction as Socrates describes it, an entirely different picture of the teacher-student relationship comes into view. In Socrates' story of his own introduction to philosophy, that is to say, the relationship between teacher and student shows no signs of erotic involvement. We are given no sense of Diotima's appearance, no reason to think that Socrates found her attractive, and no indication that they were involved on an emotional basis. As far as Socrates' account goes, in fact, the interchange between these two persons was about as unerotic as any interaction between two high-minded people could possibly be. And this account, fictional or otherwise, is the only full description we find in the dialogues of Socrates' introduction to the love of wisdom. As Plato chooses to describe it, in brief, Socrates' own introduction to philosophy involved none of the eroticism found between Alcibiades and Socrates, and nothing of the attraction to bodily beauty that marks the initial stage of Diotima's ascent.

This portrayal of an entirely dispassionate relationship between Socrates and Diotima, moreover, is in accord with what we read in the Seventh Letter about the interaction between student and teacher. Although the training by which a young person is led to philosophic understanding is said there to involve "well-disposed refutation," along with other personal disciplines, there is no hint of an erotic relation with the young person's teacher. The same may be said of the account in the *Phaedrus* describing the dialectician's instruction for the "purpose of learning" (278A2). Despite the fact that this description comes within the ambience of the most erotic dialogue overall in the entire Platonic corpus, nothing is said there to suggest that this instruction involves an erotic component.

The second point of tension between the speech of Socrates and that of Alcibiades at the end of the *Symposium*, in short, is that the latter portrays the interaction between teacher and student in a way that makes the relationship explicitly erotic, whereas the interaction with Diotima described by Socrates seems entirely to exclude an erotic dimension. Which understanding of this relationship should guide our thinking as we look further into the affective nature of the pursuit of wisdom?

We shall return to these speeches presently for a more thorough examination. It may be useful in the meanwhile to have a preliminary indication of how the tensions noted above might best be resolved. Regarding the disparity between the erotic relation with Socrates described by Alcibiades and the entirely chaste interaction between Diotima and Socrates, clearly the latter must prevail as a paradigm instance of the interaction between teacher and student supporting the pursuit of wisdom. Not only is the latter in accord with similar depictions in the Seventh Letter and the *Phaedrus*, as already noted, but moreover the emotionally charged interaction between Alcibiades and Socrates is not presented as an explicit instance of the teaching relationship in the first place. It is of course conceivable that an interaction like that depicted in Alcibiades' speech might have taken a turn that would have led the younger person to a genuine love of wisdom. Given the erotic misdirections of Alcibiades, however, he is not likely to be better served by Socrates in this particular set of circumstances than Agathon was served in his involvement with Pausanias. Instead of thinking of the interaction between Alcibiades and Socrates as a normal first stage of a proper teaching relationship, we should view it as an initially promising interchange turned sour by the young man's fixation upon bodily love.

If the erotic arousal of Alcibiades is not to be understood as a normal part of the teacher-student relationship, however, then what is the point of the emphasis in this final speech upon the physical attractiveness of Socrates' person? Part of the point, at least, must lie in the contrast it provides with the speech of Diotima, which puts the emphasis upon his unattractive features instead. This contrast, of course, is the other point of tension noted previously between the two speeches. And since the characterization given by Diotima ultimately amounts to a cold-sober description given by Socrates of himself, this characterization also should be given precedence over the passion-laden description of the drunken Alcibiades. As a lover of wisdom (203D7), Socrates is a lover of beauty as well (204B2–4); and since one lacks those things one desires to obtain, he lacks both wisdom and the beauty that comes with it. Whatever we might make of Socrates' attractiveness in other respects, as a philosopher he is essentially deficient in beauty. By being unable to disengage his attentions from the physical charms he finds in Socrates, Alcibiades signals his incompetency to pursue the paths of philosophy.

As we come to consider Socrates' potential as an instructor of young boys like Alcibiades in the love of wisdom, accordingly, the matter of his physical attractiveness should be set aside as irrelevant. Granted that a lover of the higher beauties might typically begin with the love of beautiful bodies, as Diotima indicates, there is nothing in her discourse to suggest that the bodies in question should include that of the young person's teacher. As far as Socrates himself was concerned, it may well be that many young men were attracted to him initially because of fascination with his physical presence. Judging by the character of the interaction depicted in his story about Diotima, however, we must conclude that Socrates' personal charms are extraneous to the teacher-student relationship.

What Diotima inspired in Socrates was not a love of persons, but rather a love for the pursuit of philosophy. Such is the love inspired also by an attentive reading of Plato's dialogues. Let us dig more deeply into the account of the *Symposium* for a better sense of what makes the object of this pursuit attractive.

2. Portrayals of Eros in the Early Speeches

Like Shakespeare's *Midsummer Night's Dream*, Plato's *Symposium* takes place in a magical world between day and night, between wisdom and ignorance, between historical fact and poetic invention. We overhear the story as told by Apollodorus—self-described as "witless and mad" (173E1–2) at the outset—who heard it in turn from Aristodemus, an eccentric character who attended the party uninvited and who had drifted into sleep before the story was over. The conversation is framed by Socrates' trance at the beginning and at the end by the drunken stupor into which everyone had fallen except Socrates and Aristophanes.

The thematic presence behind the narrative is Eros, described at one point as neither mortal nor immortal, and as "skillful in sorcery, enchantment and clever arguments" (203D8). While most of the main characters (except Diotima) have well-known historical identities, all in all the dialogue has a mysterious quality that invites the reader to probe beneath surface appearances.

Apart from the introductory conversation, the *Symposium* breaks down into three distinct sections. Our primary concern in this chapter is with the last two sections, containing speeches by Socrates and Alcibiades respectively. In order to place these latter two speeches in context, however, something must be said about the speeches of the initial section. This section contains five discourses in praise of Love, where the form of love involved is explicitly homosexual.

First in order is a contribution by Phaedrus, whom we know from the dialogue that bears his name as a declaimer of written speeches. In keeping with the theme of the discourse by Lysias which he recited in that dialogue, urging submission in intercourse to a nonlover, Phaedrus' speech in the *Symposium* features the utility of the homosexual relationship. Given the shame a lover feels in exhibiting cowardice before his beloved and the shame of the beloved in opposite circumstances, Phaedrus urges, an army composed of lovers and their youthful beloveds could conquer the world in field of battle. After rambling on for a while about various legendary figures who had died for love, Phaedrus then yields to a series of even less distinguished speakers whom Aristodemus (the original narrator) could not remember.

The next speech in line of narration is that of Pausanias, who was identified in the *Protagoras* as the lover of Agathon.[7] The main burden of this considerably more thoughtful speech is to distinguish two kinds of Eros, one associated with the "Common" (*Pandēmon:* 180E1) Aphrodite, the other with the "Heavenly" (*Ouranian:* 180D8) Aphrodite sprung from Uranus, the god of heaven.[8] The former, says Pausanias condescendingly, inspires love of women and young boys alike and is behind the kind of lewd behavior that moves good men to be especially protective of their wives and daughters. The Uranian goddess, on the other hand, sponsors love between older men of principle who are eager to make themselves available for the improvement of their beloveds and younger men willing to grant favors in return for such improvement. This arrangement of pederasty as a form of pedagogy[9] seems to have been a recognized way of "introducing" young men into the privileged levels of

Athenian society and was exemplified by the relationship between Pausanias and Agathon itself. It is love of this latter sort alone, at any rate, that Pausanias thinks ought to be sanctioned by an enlightened state, because it contributes to "wisdom and virtue generally" (184D7–E1) on the part of the youths involved.

The accommodation of pederasty to pedagogy advocated by Pausanias plays a larger role in the dialogue than at first might appear. On the surface level, it represents something of a rationalization on Pausanias' part of his involvement with Agathon. Whether he brought any skill at pedagogy to the relationship we have no way of knowing; but it obviously pleased him to think of his love for Agathon as serving a lofty ("Uranian") purpose. High-minded as it may have been in his own conception, however, Pausanias' involvement with Agathon basically was a commercial transaction. On the part of Agathon, it amounted to paying for his "instruction" by sexual favors in place of a more standard currency. On the part of Pausanias, in turn, it amounted to buying sexual gratification by services rendered, in place of the fee charged by common prostitutes upon whom he might have relied otherwise. Any actual affection the two men felt for each other, of course, would fall outside the terms of the bargain and would account for their willingness to enter into a relationship of this sort in the first place. It was because of his physical attraction to Socrates, to be sure, that Alcibiades wanted to work out an arrangement of this sort for himself, hoping thereby to exchange his own sexual favors for the help he could receive from Socrates in becoming a "better person" (*ameinōn*: 218E2). Socrates' blunt response to this solicitation, we recall, was that Alcibiades was offering copper in return for gold (219A1). Pausanias' accommodation between pederasty and pedagogy thus takes on significance at a deeper level with the contrast it provides to Socrates' manner of teaching. Not only does the instruction offered by Socrates proceed without involvement of physical sexuality, but moreover it is a service that is not available on a commercial basis at all. For various reasons discussed at length in chapter 1, what Socrates teaches cannot be had for money. Nor can it be had for sex, or for other services rendered. Pedagogy, in brief, is not a commercial transaction; and Pausanias' speech is flawed for suggesting otherwise.

The next major speech is by the physician, Eryximachus,[10] who approves the distinction between two forms of Eros and undertakes to extend it to other domains of human concern. Medicine, for example, is the science capable of replacing desires of a discordant sort with other

desires that show the influence of the noble Eros and that produce con-
cord and mutual love among the opposing elements of the body. The
effects of the Uranian Eros are also manifest in music and in successful divination, extending even to the harmony of the seasons which
encourage good harvests[11] and healthful living generally. All in all, says
Eryximachus, the beneficient form of Eros is responsible for human
happiness, for cohesive social intercourse (*homilein*: 188D8), and for
friendship between the gods and men.

Fourth in line comes Aristophanes' tale about the spherical creatures
with two complete sets of arms, legs, and genitalia, which both provides
comic relief from the pedantry of the preceding speech and offers a
commentary on the role of love in human society.[12] The creatures originally came in three sorts, one combining both male and female parts,
and the others combining two male and two female genitalia respectively. Because of the strength and speed of these naturally combined
beings (they ran by spinning around in cartwheels on their eight arms
and legs; cf. 190A), however, they posed a threat to the gods, to which
Zeus responded by cutting them in half and changing their means of
procreation. Initially they had reproduced out of the earth, "like ci-
cadas" (191C2). But now, to insure continuity of the species, Zeus
moved the genitals from back to front so that an embrace between individual members of the original pairs could result in sexual union. The
male of an originally male-female (*androgunon*: 191D8) pair thus could
inseminate his female counterpart, and produce offspring, while members of the originally male-male and female-female combinations would
remain infertile in their embraces. In deference to the sexual orientations of other guests at the banquet, Aristophanes is quick to identify
adulterers and promiscuous women as deriving from male-female originals, and to praise males who seek union with other males as "bold and
manly and masculine" (192A5) and as the only persons who "turn out
to be politicians" (192A7). But there is an implicit warning here that
this might not be good for the state, inasmuch as the gods' concern in
arranging human sexuality was to insure continuity of the race. Aristophanes' final remarks, at any rate, stress that the source of happiness
of the human race is to respect the gods and "bring love to its perfect
conclusion" (193C4), and that this lesson applies to "everyone, men
and women alike" (193C2–3).

Two things we should note about the speech of Agathon that follows
are that it shifts attention from the advantages gained from love to the

character of love itself and that it makes explicit mention of the relation between Eros and Ares, the god of war. In the former, it sets the stage for Socrates' story about his instruction by Diotima in the nature of love and in the love of wisdom. By the latter, it turns the thoughts of the reader to the military decline of Athens that began with the attack on Syracuse (for which see section 5 below) shortly after Agathon's victory in the tragic competition. Agathon's description of love features what were generally perceived to be ideal characteristics of a beloved youth in a pederastic relationship and was probably modeled after the speaker's conception of his own attractions—a nuance that would not be over-looked by his lover Pausanias. Eros is the youngest of the gods, as well as the most beautiful and the best; he has the biggest share of justice, moderation, bravery, and so forth. It is due to his "manliness" (*andreian*: 196D1) in particular that Eros is able "to stand up against" (*anthistatai*: 196D1) and to prevent war, rather than Ares prevailing over Eros. Although this reference to Eros as an antidote to Ares might have been included primarily for its poetic effect, there is the intimation nonethe-less that Athens' recent fortunes in war might have had something to do with the practice of love within the polis.[13]

A limitation shared by these initial portrayals of love is that each is based on the speaker's conception of his own erotic circumstances. Phaedrus focuses on the sentiments of a lover with no higher motivation in his civic life than the desire to avoid disgrace in the presence of his beloved. Pausanias takes pains to single out the relationship he shares with Agathon and to show reason why such relationships should be valued in the state. Eryximachus in turn is concerned to locate love within the natural order generally, in keeping with his calling as a medical theorist. Aristophanes treats love as a source of amusement (one might recall the treatment of Agathon in the *Thesmophoriazusae*) but at the same time manages to relate human love to the interests of the gods. And Agathon relies upon his own self-image to paint a glowing portrait of Eros himself—twice working his own name (grammatically altered, 196E4 and 197D5) into the description of that god's virtues.

Another limitation of these initial portrayals as a group, not uncon-nected with their focus on the self-interests of the speakers, is that each depicts love as a relation primarily between human persons. Although there is a brief mention in Agathon's speech of Eros' attending to beautiful things instead of ugly (197B6, 9), the beautiful things in question are other people and not objects of beauty in some more general sense. Each of the beginning speeches, that is to say, labors under a conception of love that is directed toward beauty in its physical manifestations exclusively. One of the primary functions of the discourse by Diotima that follows is to show how love can be directed toward beauty in various other manifestations and ultimately can be directed toward Beauty itself.

Despite these limitations, however, the first five speeches in sequence serve to raise the level of the discussion from a crass pragmatic view of homosexuality in a civic setting, to an adept (if mistaken) view of the nature of Eros himself. With the close of Agathon's encomium and the general applause that greets it, the stage is now set for the remarkable story of Socrates' introduction to philosophy by Diotima ("honor of god") from Mantinea (resembling *mantis*—"prophet"—in name).[14]

3. Socrates' Instruction by Diotima in the Ways of Love

Socrates begins his speech with a seemingly effortless refutation of Agathon.[15] The refutation is based on two premises, both of which Agathon readily accepts. The first is that love is desire for an object, the second that what is desired is not presently possessed. But if Eros is already beautiful, as Agathon had said, then he would not desire the beauty he already has. Yet Agathon has agreed (210A8–9) that Eros has a desire for beauty. Agathon agrees furthermore (201C3) that all good things are beautiful, so that if Eros lacks beauty he lacks other good things as well.[16] Thus Eros lacks all the fine qualities with which Agathon had invested him. The problem with Agathon's account of Eros, as Diotima remarks presently (204C), is that it portrays Eros with respect to the object loved (in accord with Agathon's self-image as an ideal beloved), rather than with respect to the desiring lover. This is an error that Diotima purports to remedy.

Before moving into a discussion of Diotima's discourse itself, there are several matters we should consider regarding the character herself. These may be grouped under two convenient headings: (1) Plato's choice of Diotima as a contributor to the dialogue, and (2) the relation between Diotima and Socrates as Plato portrayed it.

Although some weighty voices have spoken otherwise,[17] scholars today tend to agree that the Diotima whom Socrates cites does not represent a historical person. She is introduced auspiciously, but cryptically, as a woman from Mantinea who was wise (*sophē*: 201D3) in love and in many other things, and who delayed the plague for ten years by telling the Athenians of appropriate sacrifices. The plague in question presumably was the famous pestilence of 430 B.C. that claimed the lives of many Athenians, which would date Diotima's alleged benefit to Athens at about 440. The description of Diotima's action in these terms is suspicious in itself—how could a natural event be "postponed" from a decade earlier?—and in fact there is no historical record of such a "postponement." Another indication that the character is fictional is her reference at 205D10–E1 to Aristophanes' tale of the halved spherical creatures. The point of the specific reference to the plague may have been merely to distance Diotima from current Athenian concerns, and hence to make her invention less distracting to other members of the banquet.[18]

Given that Diotima most likely was not a historical person, the question inevitably arises of why Plato chose a woman for this role in the dialogue. Why was a woman given the last word in a set of formal speeches delivered to a group of male homosexuals? Why, moreover, is Socrates—from whom Plato presumably learned philosophy—represented as having learned philosophy himself through conversation with a female sage?[19] While there are several aspects of the issue that would have to be explored before the significance of Diotima's gender could be brought into full view,[20] the following points in this regard are enough for our purposes. For one, Diotima stands as a forceful counterexample to the prevailing prejudice that only males are capable of vigorous intellectual pursuits (evidenced in the speech by Pausanias, 181C), and that males alone are capable of leadership in civic affairs (as urged in the speech of Aristophanes, 192A).[21] For another, Plato's making the teacher of Socrates a woman effectively neutralizes the presumption that he had learned philosophy in the pederastic manner championed by Pausanias.[22] A parallel dramatic effect would be to counteract the expectations of his audience that Socrates' speech, like the others preceding it, would address the merits of homosexual love specifically. Although Diotima acknowledges the interest of the audience in her reference at one point to "loving boys correctly" (211B6), her account emphasizes the function of generation that is served only by love in heterosexual relationships. This ties in directly with the oblique allusion in Aristophanes' speech (190C, 191C) to the fact that homosexual love contributes nothing to the propagation of the race. Perhaps the main reason on Plato's part for making Diotima a woman, accordingly, has to do with the fruitfulness represented by her gender. Given that the teachings about love into which Diotima is about to introduce Socrates concern the products of love as well as its objects—given, that is to say, that the love she is about to talk about is essentially *fertile*—it is simply a matter of fittingness that the teacher be someone who is naturally capable of bearing offspring.

Strictly speaking, of course, Diotima is not a *character* in the dialogue at all. If we take the main dialogue to be the conversation shared by the persons at the banquet, then Diotima is not a participant in that primary conversation. She is a participant rather in an alleged previous conversation with Socrates, which he recounts as part of his contribution to the main set of speeches. In placing Diotima within the dialogue overall, we should remain aware that the main conversation comes to us as readers (or audience) by way of Apollodorus' narration—to an unnamed friend—of what he had heard from Aristodemus about the speeches on love made at Agathon's party. Diotima's teachings about love occur at the innermost layer of this multilayered structure of conversations.[23] As far as the main conversation is concerned, at any rate, Diotima is a character internal to Socrates' story, rather than a participant in that discussion itself. It is perhaps not irrelevant to think of Diotima as one of the "godlike" figures said to be found within Socrates, when Alcibiades compares him to a Silenus-statue at 216D–E.

The role played by Diotima in the main conversation, in brief, is nothing more nor less than what Socrates makes of her—or more accurately, what Plato has Socrates make of her. This means that the context in which this role must be understood is the relation between Diotima and Socrates, as Plato portrays it. And the primary relation between these two figures is that of master philosopher to willing student. But this is also the relation Plato described (without dramatic artifice) in the Seventh Letter, while discussing the rigors of the philosophic discipline. It is the relation as well, we have surmised, between the historical Socrates and Plato himself. And it is the relation that Plato shares with us as readers of the dialogues, save that in our case it involves written rather than spoken discourse. Let us look more carefully at this relation between Diotima and Socrates, with an eye toward these other interactions in turn.

We have already noted an obvious departure of the relation between Socrates and his teacher from the pederastic model put forth by

Pausanias. Not only is the relation between Socrates and Diotima quite explicitly not pederastic; it is not based on an overtly sexual accommodation of any sort whatever. Although Diotima has quite a bit to say about sexuality in her speech, there is no physical eroticism about her person as Socrates describes it. The Eros working in Diotima is directed toward beauty in nonphysical forms; and this is the Eros she wants to share with Socrates.

Even more basic than this departure from the pederastic model in terms of sexual involvement, however, is the fact that there is nothing *commercial* in the relation between Diotima and Socrates. There is no payment for her instruction in the form of cash, as was typical for instruction by the professional sophists. And there is no payment in the form of services rendered, as in the arrangement advocated in the speech of Pausanias. This representation of instruction in philosophy as an inherently noncommercial transaction surely has something to do with the fact, observed above, that the historical Socrates himself—unlike the other sophists—refused to accept fees. And it obviously has to do with the fact that Socrates is represented, in the final section of the present dialogue (218E), as refusing to barter whatever improvements Alcibiades might receive from his company for the sexual favors the latter has urged upon him. In putting together this story of Socrates' introduction to philosophy, Plato clearly is drawing upon a view of philosophic instruction exemplified in the practice of the historical Socrates. What might not come to mind quite so readily is the fact that the instruction Plato offers to the serious reader of his dialogues also comes without payment by way of return. The gift of philosophy, it would appear, is freely offered, whether from Diotima to Socrates, or from Socrates to Plato, or from Plato in turn to the properly prepared reader.

Another aspect of the transaction between Diotima and Socrates that has manifest relevance to the current reader of the dialogues is that *hard work* was required for a grasp of her teachings. As if echoing Plato's own admonishment in the Seventh Letter that the pursuit of philosophy requires both work and dedication, Diotima urges Socrates to follow "to the fullest extent possible" (210E1–2—see also 210A4) that he might understand the reason for "all his earlier labors" (210E6). Unlike the typically passive role of the *erōmenos* in the pederastic approach to learning,[24] Diotima calls for effort on the part of her student. In terms of the Seventh Letter, there is the matter of a "suitably ordered regimen" (340E2), which leads, if one is fortunate, to a moment of enlightenment in which human power is taken to its limit (344B8–C1). Thus Diotima expresses doubts whether Socrates "is capable" (*hoios t' an eiēs*: 210A2) of the final mysteries. And thus the reader in turn might have misgivings about whether he or she is up to the task that is undertaken with a serious study of the dialogues. But something that must have been as clear to Plato then, as it is clear to us now, is that the path set by Socrates—and Diotima—is one that goes nowhere without exertion.

There is one respect, nonetheless, in which Socrates' portrayal of Eros, through the speech of Diotima, follows the pattern of the earlier treatments, including that of Pausanias. Each of the first round of speakers, as noted previously, endows the god of Love with features taken from his own self-image. And so does Socrates in the description he attributes to Diotima. Put more accurately—since we are dealing here with Plato's dramatic character—Socrates, speaking through Diotima, endows Eros with features that are unmistakenly Socratic, given the image of Socrates that prevailed among his friends and fellow citizens. The result is that Socrates, on the one hand, is Eros personified, and that Eros, on the other, is Socrates mythologized. The details by which this effect is accomplished are provided in Diotima's story of Eros' conception, which we have discussed already in the first section of this chapter. It is this "oversized" Socrates that prevails in the final part of the dialogue, given over to Alcibiades' intemperate praise of his erstwhile companion.

The Socrates that figures in the remainder of Diotima's speech, by contrast, seems strangely diminished, as he listens patiently to her story of how love functions in the aspirations of mortal creatures. This story divides naturally into two portions. The featured portion is her description of the lover's progression, leading from bodily beauty to the Form of Beauty itself. Preliminary to this is an account of love's action in nature, dealing first with the impulse that sets loves in motion (204D–206A), second with love's involvement in procreation (206B–207A), and third with the immortality toward which procreation is directed (207B–209E). The overall effect of this preliminary account is to locate love in its biological setting as a natural urge for immortality. A brief consideration of these topics will set the stage for Diotima's ascent.

LOVE'S IMPULSE. Noting that Socrates has already agreed (see 202D) that love desires beautiful things, Diotima asks what this amounts to specifically. Socrates answers that, in loving beautiful things, one desires that they "become one's own" (204D6). In pursuit of the further question why one should desire that, Diotima suggests that they substitute "good" for "beautiful,"[25] and ask why a lover of good things would desire to make them his own.[26] Socrates responds immediately that one desires good things in order to be happy (*eudaimōn*: 205A1), and agrees with Diotima that this desire requires no further explanation.[27]

Diotima goes on to observe that the term 'love' itself is generally used only in cases where desire is directed toward goods of some specific sort— as the term 'poetry,' which literally means anything created by art, is generally used only for verse created in meter. But when people love one or another particular good, she adds, they not only want that good for themselves; they want it further to be theirs forever (*aei*: 206A6). This basic desire to possess good things forever is the wellspring of love in its many manifestations.

THE OPERATION OF LOVE THROUGH PROCREATION. The way love operates, Diotima continues, is a matter of "producing offspring in the presence of the beautiful" (*tokos en kalō*: 206B7). Although her subsequent description of this process is artfully ambiguous between the conception and the delivery of offspring,[28] it is clear that the procreation she has in mind is not exclusively biological. The procreation that love seeks to accomplish with beauty might produce offspring "either of body or soul" (206B7), and so might be achieved by lovers of either sex.

What love really wants, says Diotima accordingly, is not just the possession of beauty, but the "generation and birth" (206E3–4) enabled by beauty's presence. And the reason love seeks procreation, she concludes, is that reproduction provides a form of immortality that is accessible to mortal creatures.

IMMORTALITY AS THE GOAL OF LOVE. The final part of Diotima's preliminary account concerns various ways in which humans can approach immortality, now identified as the goal toward which love aims. First is the process of replenishment through nutrition, by which the body replaces its fluids and parts of its bones and tissues, leaving new components behind as the old pass away. It is in this manner, she observes, that all living creatures are preserved from death (208A8), "sharing in immortality" (*athanasias metechei*: 208B3–4) while their vital functions continue. Biological reproduction extends this process of new replacing old to the level of the individual organism, so that in a sense the parent lives on in the child. It is for this reason, Diotima suggests, that animals are driven to reproduce and are ready to battle to the death for the safety of their offspring.

Whereas procreation inspired by beauty in bodily form produces progeny of the body, procreation with beautiful souls produces offspring of various nonphysical sorts. One form such offspring might take is that of "discourses about virtue" (209B8), produced by a lover (like Pausanias) dedicated to the education of a beloved youth. With such offspring, Diotima suggests deferentially, the pair has more to share than do biological parents, inasmuch as their children are "lovelier and more immortal" (kallionōn kai athanatōterōn: 209C7) than physical offspring. Another variety of offspring is exemplified by the laws of Lycurgus and Solon, which are said to be engendered by the "most beautiful aspect of practical wisdom" (209A6) dealing with the regulation of states and households. Yet other types of offspring are identified in subsequent pages, in connection with the various stages of Diotima's ascent.

Let us recapitulate the results of this preliminary account. Love is empowered by a desire to possess good and beautiful things forever. Love proceeds by the procreation of offspring in the presence of the beautiful. The aim of this procreation is immortality (athanatos, deathlessness), insofar as this is available to mortal creatures. Several ways of forestalling death have been mentioned thus far. One is biological procreation, accomplished by the action of love in the presence of bodily beauty, which results in the production of physical offspring. Another is the production of discourses about virtue, the product of love in the presence of spiritual beauty, which live on in the memory of those who hear them. Yet another is the institution of lasting laws and ordinances, inspired by the love of civic order. Bodily offspring, memorable discourse, enduring legislation—each provides a form of relative immortality. Other forms that are more enduring come into view as Diotima continues.

The featured part of Diotima's discourse is her account of the lover's ascent. This ascent begins with the love of beautiful bodies and ends with the love of Beauty itself, with a number of intermediate stages to be gone through in sequence. This in itself invites comparison with the Divided Line of the Republic, which symbolizes four distinct stages on the way to an apprehension of the Good. The fact that the Form of the Good and the Form of the Beautiful are closely associated in both dialogues further reinforces the sense that these two progressions are to be understood as parallel sequences. In keeping with this parallelism in general, we might expect to find four stages in Diotima's ascent as well. Although it is obviously possible to subdivide her progression in other ways, this division in terms of four distinct stages seems plausible even apart from its relation to the Divided Line.

In the following discussion of Diotima's ascent to the Form of Beauty, there is a distinction at each level between (a) the beautiful object toward which love is attracted as an inducement to procreation, and (b) the offspring produced by that procreation. It should be noted at the outset, however, that the ascent is primarily from lower to higher forms of love rather than a progression with respect to offspring. It is also a progression of forms of immortality. Diotima's overarching point is that the erotic component of the soul can be educated to respond to beauty in increasingly worthy manifestations, providing release from death in forms that are progressively more enduring.

STAGE 1. In order to set about this business properly, says Diotima, a youth must "be attentive toward beautiful bodies" (210A6), typically beginning with love of (1a) an "individual body" (henos . . . sōmatos: 210A7–8). Although this is the level on which heterosexual love produces (1b) physical offspring, even homosexual love, if "rightly guided" (210A7), can get a jump on the next stage and start begetting "beautiful discourse" (210A8) of one sort or another. Diotima might have added that this discourse, because of its bodily origin, is not likely to contribute much to the immortality of its author.

A transitional step is to realize that the beauty of any given body "is closely akin with that of any other" (210B1). Thus realizing that "the beauty of all bodies is one and the same" (210B2–3), the lover's attention then will be directed toward "all beautiful bodies" (210B4). Although it obviously would be possible to make love of bodies generally an additional stage in the sequence, Diotima identifies no specific product of this generalized form of corporeal love that would make a different contribution to the lover's immortality than does love of a single body, which suggests that bodily love of all forms should be grouped together at this initial stage. The relevance of this shift of erotic attention from one to many bodies, in the context of the ascent overall, may be little more than the awareness it provides of "the beauty of form" (to ep' eidei kalon: 210B1–2) generally, as distinct from the beauty of a particular form. In this manner the lover might gain advance notice of the Form of Beauty that stands at the end of the journey, without yet being prepared to join this Beauty in procreation.

STAGE 2. The lover next must be led to realize that there is beauty to be found in souls which is more valuable (*timiōteron*: 210B7) than bodily beauty. Directing his or her attention now to (2a) "beauty of souls" (210B6–7), without regard to imperfections of the body, the lover "seeks to generate such discourse as might make young people better" (210C1–3). Discourse contributing to virtue in this fashion is (2b) the product of the love of beautiful souls said at 209C to contribute more to the immortality of the lover than physical offspring.

The phrasing above allowing that the lover might be either male or female, it should be noted, is directly relevant to the fact that Diotima must be presumed to have gone this path herself if she is to be competent to guide Socrates to an awareness of pure Beauty. As noted previously, one reason for making Socrates' teacher a woman was probably that Plato wanted to emphasize, as in the *Republic,* that the path of philosophy is not restricted to persons of one sex only. Once the initial stage of physical attraction has been transcended, Diotima's ascent has nothing to do with the gender of the initiate.

STAGE 3. With this prelude the lover then will be constrained "to contemplate the beauty of practices and customs" (*theasasthai to en tois epitēdeumasi kai tois nomois kalon*: 210C3–4). It is because of their love of (3a) social order that such practices and customs represent, presumably, that legislators like Lycurgus and Solon were inspired to produce (3b) the laws and ordinances for which they became famous. Although the jump from love of the beauty of souls to love of the beauty of social practices and customs at first may seem abrupt, we should bear in mind the interdependency, explored in the *Republic,* between a well-ordered state and the well-ordered souls of its leading citizens. Someone who has progressed far enough up the "ladder of love" to find beautiful souls more attractive than beautiful bodies might naturally be disposed, Diotima seems to be saying, to find even greater beauty in the social structures upon which the development of moral virtue depends. As she remarks at 209E, the fame of Lycurgus and Solon rests on the "many fine deeds" (209E2) and "manifold virtues" (209E3) that their contributions to social order have produced. When someone has become aware the role of a city's *nomoi* in the production of virtue among its citizens, the progression from love of beautiful souls to love of beautiful *nomoi* may not be such a large step after all.

STAGE 4. After becoming attracted to beautiful social practices (*epi-tēdeumata*: 210C6), Diotima continues, the lover should move on next to "the beauty of knowledge" (*epistēmōn kallos*: 210C7). Inasmuch as knowledge can take many forms (210C7), the lover's attention will not be limited to the beauty of one or another individual instance, but rather will "be directed toward a vast sea of beauty" (*epi to polu pelagos tetrammenos tou kalou*: 210D4–5) present with knowledge in its many appearances. The object of love at this penultimate stage, accordingly, is (4a) knowledge as manifested in many beautiful forms. And in the presence of this "bounteous love of wisdom" (210D6), love gives birth to (4b) "many beautiful discourses and magnificent thoughts" (210D5–6).

One thing to note in this regard is that procreation on this level has effects beyond the production of offspring.[29] For one thing, it adds to the store of beautiful things in the world, as indeed does procreation on each of the lower levels. As love of beautiful bodies and love of beautiful souls alike produce beautiful *logoi* (210A8; 209B8, C7) of a fitting sort, that is to say, and as the laws engendered by a love of social order produce beautiful deeds in turn (209E2), so does love of beauty in knowledge produce beautiful discourse (210D5) of its own appropriate kind. Of more particular interest at this point, however, is the suggestion that the process of producing this beautiful discourse has the additional effect of increasing the philosopher's powers of mental vision. Under the inspiration of the vast sea of beauty present in knowledge, the philosopher produces this bounty of discourse and thought, until—"having then gained strength and grown" (210D7)—he or she "catches sight of that singular knowledge" (*katidē tina epistēmēn mian*: 210D7–8) the object of which will presently be identified as Beauty itself. The sense here quite clearly is that the process of engendering beautiful discourse and thought somehow increases the philosopher's powers of mental discernment, to the point of finally enabling vision of the pure Form of Beauty.

What Diotima seems to be indicating here is that the ascent to love of Beauty itself is not merely a matter of taking the proper steps in the proper sequence. In the upper reaches at least, there are certain exercises to be undertaken, certain disciplines to be mastered, before one is able to pass on to yet higher levels. As the Seventh Letter stresses time and again, the lover of wisdom at some point must submit to a regimen that can produce the wit needed for the final revelation. Perhaps it is because of this, if for no other reason, that Diotima is made to express reservations at 210A about Socrates' ability to make his way to the "final mystery."

STAGE 5. These reservations surface again at 210E, when Diotima warns Socrates to pay the most careful attention as they approach the final stage. For the person who has been educated thus far in matters of love, she says, and who "has beheld beautiful objects in the proper sequence" (210E3), now comes to the goal (*telos*: 210E4) toward which all this loving has been directed. The initiated "suddenly will catch sight of something marvelously beautiful in nature" (*exaiphnēs katopsetai ti thaumaston tēn phusin kalon*: 210E4–5),[30] which provides the reason for all these previous labors.

Diotima's description of the Form Beauty that follows constitutes the most succinct characterization of the Forms to be found in the middle dialogues. Like other Forms, Beauty itself is (a) *real*, in the sense of being wholly what it is and in no way other. Beauty, that is to say, is in no way opposed to itself—is "not beautiful in this respect and ugly in that, nor beautiful at one time and not at another" (211A2–3), etc. Beauty moreover is (b) *directly knowable* "in itself and by itself" (*kath' auto meth' auto*: 211B1-2), not appearing under the guise of "some face or pair of hands or any other thing pertaining to a body" (211A6–7). Furthermore, (c) all other beautiful things "participate" (*metechonta*: 211B3) in Beauty, whereby it is the *cause* of their being beautiful. This relation of participation also is such that Beauty is (d) *absolute*, in the sense that when "these other beautiful things come to be or pass away" (211B3–4), Beauty itself "becomes neither smaller nor larger, nor suffers change in any degree" (211B4–5).

The only feature missing from the description thus far that makes it incomplete as a characterization of the Forms in the middle dialogues[31] is (e) the role the Form plays as a standard for the naming of its sensible instances. And even this feature seems to come into play at 211D, where Diotima remarks that once Socrates has contemplated "Beauty itself" (*auto to kalon*: 211D3), he will no longer be inclined to judge beauty "by gold or clothing or beautiful boys and youths" (211D3–4). To the contrary, Diotima affirms, once Socrates has learned the lessons of the previous stages and has finally come to learn of this Beauty itself, he will "know in the end what Beauty itself is" (*gnō auto teleutōn ho esti kalon:*

211C9). And once having seen Beauty itself—"unalloyed, without blemish, unmixed, and untainted" (211E1-2)—he will never mistake the mortal for the heavenly (*theion*: 211E3) beauty.

Diotima concludes by alluding to the products engendered by procreation with pure Beauty and to the manner of immortality that follows in their train. When the love of the philosopher is directed toward (5a) Beauty itself, he or she then will be able to beget (5b) "not images, but genuine virtue" (*ouk eidōla aretēs . . . alla alēthē*: 212A4-5). And along with true virtue goes (5b') friendship of the gods (*theophilei*: 212A6), which—"if indeed any human could be immortal" (212A7)—is the highest form of immortality to which any human person might aspire.

Of particular note in this final statement is Diotima's reference to the "friendship of the gods" that comes to the person who gives birth to genuine virtue and continues to nourish it. Whereas Diotima's lessons to this point have dealt with the various objects of love (*eros*) that energize the quest which is the love (*philia*) of wisdom, we now hear of the love (*philia*) of the gods by which the quest is finally rewarded. This divine love apparently is the basis for that most enduring form of immortality available to humans which Diotima cites at the very end of her discourse. An obvious comparison in this regard is with the fame and honor among humans that provided a not insignificant measure of immortality to poets like Homer and Hesiod, and to lawgivers like Lycurgus and Solon (209D). As these worthies are known with affection through the centuries for their benefits to society, so the truly virtuous person is known affectionately through the aeons by the gods. Inasmuch as the latter form of recognition alone can endure eternally, friendship with the gods provides immortality of the most lasting sort available to humankind.

4. Alcibiades' Erotic Attraction to Socrates

The final speech in praise of Eros is delivered by a late arrival who has not heard the other speeches. Here is how it comes about. Aristophanes' attempt to rebut Diotima's unsympathetic rejection of his "spherical creature" story (at 205D-E) is interrupted by a sudden (*exaiphnēs*: 212C6) commotion at the courtyard door. The suddenness with which true Beauty appears at the pinnacle of Diotima's ascent is matched by the abrupt appearance of a drunken Alcibiades, someone notorious for his exceptionally beautiful body. Why does Plato return us so quickly to the bottom of the philosopher's progression, and why is the return marked by such an outlandish commotion (the outer door rattling, a flute-girl screaming, Alcibiades bedecked like Dionysus himself)?

One obvious effect of this jarring shift of focus from Diotima to Alcibiades is to dramatize the vast disparity between the philosopher's love of Beauty and the love of power and wealth that motivated the political life of Athens during this stage in its history. At the time of Agathon's victory in tragedy which the banquet was supposed to celebrate, Athens was at the height of its military might and was in the final stages of preparation for a massive expedition against Syracuse that was intended to increase its dominance in that part of the Mediterranean.[32] The date at which the narration by Apollodorus is depicted as taking place, on the other hand, was several years after Agathon had left Athens (see 172C),[33] which places it close to the disastrous defeat of Athens that ended the Peloponnesian War. It could hardly be an accident that the time of Agathon's party itself and the time of Apollodorus' subsequent retelling of the event respectively mark off almost exactly the period during which Athens slipped from its position of cultural and military supremacy in the northern Mediterranean to that of a ruined polis on its knees before a victorious Sparta. Nor can it be an accident that the character who interrupts the party with his boisterous revelry was a recently elected young general destined to play a major part in the events that brought Athens to this ignominious position. Let us briefly review the role of Alcibiades in these events.

In a night of revelry just before the fleet set sail for Syracuse, a group of prominent Athenians allegedly "profaned the mysteries" and "mutilated the Hermae." What exactly either sacrilege amounted to we have no way of knowing.[34] The mysteries in question must have been Eleusinian rituals of some sort that were mimicked or parodied in an inappropriate setting.[35] The Hermae, in turn, were carved images of Hermes that served both as household gods and as boundary markers, consisting (as examples in contemporary museums show us) of little more than stone pillars with faces and phalli. Presumably the mutilation at point consisted in marring one of these distinctive features.[36] Alcibiades, at any rate (along with Phaedrus and Eryximachus), was accused of complicity in these events, was denied the prompt trial he requested, and embarked with the fleet under a cloud of suspicion.

As the ships under his command were being arrayed for action around the port of Syracuse some weeks later, Alcibiades received orders to return home for trial. Suspecting the worst, he jumped ship on the way back, defected to Sparta, and was condemned to death in absentia. Although he subsequently returned to Athens for several years after a shift of power in the city, Athens' fortunes at war thereafter headed steadily downward. The mighty fleet at Syracuse went down in defeat, Sparta and her allies gradually gained the upper hand and, after an extended siege during which all access by land was cut off, Athens surrendered to Lysander in 404 B.C. Alcibiades was murdered in the process by the Spartan troops he had earlier befriended.

What is to be made of this fact that the dramatic dates of the banquet itself and of its subsequent narration by Apollodorus so neatly frame Athens' fall from power into a state of subjection? A plausible answer is that Plato may have intended to associate Athen's fall with the main topic of the dialogue. In our previous discussion of Agathon's speech, to be sure, we noted indications that Plato may have considered Athen's fortunes in war to have been influenced by the practices of love in the polis.[37] This sense of an interconnection in Plato's view between the well-being of a state and the uses of love that prevail within it is reinforced by the content of Diotima's speech. One of the underlying themes of this speech, indeed, is that human nature can flourish only when the Eros by which its social interactions are driven is directed beyond the short-term gratifications featured in the opening speeches. The form of Eros that promotes individual and civic virtue, according to Diotima's discourse, is directed toward objects that transcend all particularities of place and time. When a society's erotic impulses are bound up with self-serving gratification and personal power, on the other hand—as in the case of an Athens that has just elected a hubristic leader like Alcibiades for the comparably hubristic enterprise of bringing Syracuse under its control—not only does that society fail to provide a context in which Eros can reach its highest fulfillment, but the society itself is destined for self-destruction. The fundamental flaw of Athenian society is that it has little tolerance for Eros that is directed toward wisdom—the *philosophia* addressed in Diotima's discourse, and exemplified in the person of Socrates himself. A historical connection that would be obvious to the dialogue's original audience is that Socrates was executed only a few years after the dramatic date of Apollodorus' narration.

One purpose served by the sharp juxtaposition of Alcibiades' speech with that of Socrates, in brief, is to highlight the disparity between the uses of love in an ideal social setting and those uses that may have contributed to Athen's defeat. As Alcibiades enters the banquet under the comical guise of Dionysus, the god of wine and drunken revelry, so Socrates enters Alcibiades' speech as a tragicomic personification[38] of the right uses of love. The result is an opposition of erotic natures that culminates in the failure of the attempted seduction.

This leads to what I take to be the second major point of contrast between the depictions of love provided by Alcibiades and Diotima. In Plato's dramatic representation, at least, Diotima was the teacher of Socrates; and their interaction seems to serve as an ideal model of how a young person might be instructed in the love of wisdom. In Plato's representation of the relationship between Socrates and Alcibiades, in turn, there is a sense in which Socrates was in a position to serve as the younger man's teacher as well. But something went radically wrong with the latter relationship. Bluntly put, Socrates was unable to move Alcibiades beyond his erotic attraction to physical beauty and its trappings, a flaw symptomatic of the moral decay of Athens. The second point of contrast, accordingly, is between the use of love in circumstances that are ideal for learning philosophy and its use in circumstances that are sure to thwart that purpose. Our concern at this stage is to diagnose the source of the failure. Is the fault due to the character of Alcibiades exclusively? Or does Socrates share the blame for his failure as a teacher? Let us look more closely at the interaction between Alcibiades and Socrates as depicted in the final pages of the *Symposium*.

In the opening passages of his encomium, Alcibiades compares Socrates to a statue of Silenus, a companion of Dionysus sometimes represented as the father of the satyrs.[39] The statues in question carry "pipes or flutes" (215B2)—musical instruments thought by the Greeks most strongly to arouse the emotions[40]—and come apart in halves to display miniature figures of the gods inside. Immediately thereafter, Alcibiades compares Socrates to the satyr Marsyas himself, who was known in legend for competing with Apollo in music-making. Satyrs as a class, of course, were supposed to be hybrid creatures combining the mentality of humans with the sexual appetites of beasts and were typically depicted with oversized and characteristically tumid male organs. When Alcibiades goes on to point out that Socrates cannot object to the comparison, because in fact he resembles a satyr, one is reminded of the remark to the same effect in Xenophon's *Symposium* (iv.19). Apparently Socrates actually looked like one of these mythical goat-men; and for Alcibiades, the similarity was more than skin-deep.

This already suggests that Socrates' physical appearance may not have been ideal for the role of a teacher. Not only was his physical presence unduly distracting to young men like Alcibiades and Charmides, but he actually made a point of leading them on with his banter about being attracted to handsome young men. This kind of flirting is entirely absent in the interaction between Diotima and Socrates. Were it not, then Socrates might have had difficulty himself in focusing attention on the higher beauties of Diotima's progression.

Be this as it may, a full two-thirds of Alcibiades' speech is taken up with his attraction to Socrates and with how Socrates reacted to his advances. First he mentions the erotic effect of Socrates' discourse. Just listening to Socrates speak, he confides, brings tears to his eyes, and makes his "heart throb more excitedly than in a Corybantic frenzy" (215E1–2). The effect of this enchanting discourse, he confesses, is to make him ashamed of his life, and dissatisfied with his involvement in the politics of Athens. Such is the charm of this satyr's piping, by which Alcibiades is sure "many other people are afflicted" (216C5–6) similarly.

Alcibiades' main preoccupation with Socrates in matters of Eros, however, is not with his discourse but with his physical person. Thus the body of the speech, to which this talk about shame and remorse is merely a prelude, is given over to a lengthy and detailed description of Alcibiades' unsuccessful attempt to seduce Socrates into pederastic intercourse. It seems that Alcibiades at first took seriously Socrates' lighthearted talk about being "erotically disposed toward beautiful boys" (216D2–3) and, since he considered himself to be exceptionally beautiful, he thought it only natural that Socrates might want to do something about it. So Alcibiades started meeting Socrates with no attendants present. And when nothing came of that, he invited him to the gymnasium, where they exercised and wrestled many times together—but all to no avail (*oudenos parontos*: 217C3)! Alcibiades' next move was to invite Socrates to dinner—"against the rules" (*atechnōs*: 217C8), as if he were the lover and Socrates the beloved youth—and then, on a second such occasion, to trick him into staying overnight. But even after sleeping with him through the night under the same cloak and "holding this divine person entwined in his arms" (219C1), Alcibiades reports, the encounter produced no further result than "sleeping with one's father or older brother" (219D1–2). In Alcibiades' view, this outcome was sufficiently insulting for him to accuse Socrates somewhat peevishly of insolence (*hubrisen:* 219C5) and arrogance (*huperēphanias:* 219C7), properties that notoriously characterized Alcibiades himself.

Alcibiades continues with an account of Socrates' exploits at Potidaea and Delium, which showed him not only to be extraordinarily brave, but also to be remarkably self-sufficient in matters of esteem and physical comfort.[41] The speech ends with a return to the imagery of the hollow statues of Silenus with which Socrates was compared in its opening passages. But here the analogy is applied not just to Socrates himself, but also to his verbal discourse (221D6)—the discourse to which Alcibiades had said he was attracted initially. At first hearing, Socrates' arguments appear ridiculous, clothed in words resembling the hide of some outrageous satyr. When one opens them up, however, and gets beneath their surface, one finds them to be entirely godlike (222A3) and replete with images of virtue inside. This discourse, Alcibiades acknowledges, is of utmost importance to anyone aspiring to be a truly good person (*kalō kagathō:* 222A6).

At the beginning of Alcibiades' speech, Socrates himself is likened to a Silenus statue with miniature images (*agalmata:* 215B3) of the gods inside. The same analogy is now applied to Socrates' discourse, which contains bountiful images (*agalmata:* 222A4) of virtue beneath its surface. Why just images and not the real thing itself? There is no suggestion here, surely, that Socrates lacked genuine virtue, or that what his words conveyed was somehow counterfeit. What Plato does seem to be intimating with this emphasis on imagery, however, is that the dynamics of his emotional interaction with Alcibiades prevents Socrates' true virtue from being fully displayed. In contrast with the dispassionate witness of Diotima, there is something about Socrates' erotic presence that constitutes an impediment to prospective students.

This is not the first indication in the dialogue that Plato may have harbored doubts about Socrates' ability to lead others along the path to wisdom. As part of Diotima's description of the fourth stage in her progression, she mentions quite pointedly that while Eros is a lover of wisdom (203D7), he has no share himself in "good and beautiful things" (202D4–5). Insofar as Socrates is portrayed in her speech as the personification of Eros, the notable shortcomings of Eros in this regard would seem to attach to Socrates as well. This ties in with Diotima's remark to Socrates at the beginning of that stage, saying that although she has little doubt about his ability to master the three stages preceding, she is not sure whether he is capable (*an eiēs:* 210A2) of going further.[42] But if

Socrates himself is incapable of reaching the higher beauties, this would seem to constitute a substantial liability in any attempt to lead others to this stage of accomplishment.

Nor is the *Symposium* alone in conveying a sense of this deficiency. Socrates' frequent description of himself as lacking in knowledge has been treated in previous chapters as primarily a manifestation of irony. But now, when Socrates' philosophic competencies seemingly are under question by Plato himself, it appears that beneath this cover of irony there may have been a core of truth. Although in the early stages of his writing career Plato may have been more than a little inclined to give Socrates the benefit of the doubt on this score, the time is now approaching with the *Symposium* when Plato is ready to draw attention in an unequivocal manner to Socrates' limitations as a guide in philosophy. Prior to his outright proclamation in the *Sophist* of Socratic elenchus as a form of sophistry, examined at some length in chapter 2 above, Plato has Socrates describe himself in the *Theaetetus* as a midwife of the soul who himself "is barren of wisdom" (150C4). His avowal there never to have been granted "mental offspring" (150D2) of this sort takes on added significance against the background of Diotima's discourse, where so much emphasis is laid upon reproduction by the mind in the presence of beauty. In effect, the *Symposium* anticipates the *Theaetetus* and the *Sophist* in suggesting that Socrates, although a genuine lover of wisdom, was incapable of interacting procreatively with knowledge generally. This all strongly suggests that, in Plato's view at least, Socrates was arrested at the third level of Diotima's philosophic ascent.

The apparent conclusion we are left with at this point is that Alcibiades is not solely to blame for the failure of his interaction with Socrates to yield fruitful results, and that Socrates himself falls considerably short of the standard set by Diotima as a teacher of philosophy. What is behind this seemingly negative portrayal of Socrates? And what should be made of the fact—as we have been assuming all along—that Plato himself was introduced to philosophy by the example of Socrates? These questions are addressed in the final section.

5. Socrates as the Exemplary Lover of Wisdom

The previous section ends with a seeming paradox. Whereas Diotima is represented as the ideal teacher of philosophy, Socrates is portrayed as notably deficient in the traits needed to guide a student along the pathway to wisdom. How could the person who supposedly was Plato's own teacher be represented as deficient in this respect?

The resolution of the seeming paradox is to realize that the *Symposium* does not present Socrates as a *teacher* of philosophy. Socrates is presented rather as the personification of Eros; and there is no suggestion that Eros himself is a teacher. So we are not to view Socrates in this dialogue as deficient in the role of a teacher. He is to be viewed as instead the paradigm of the love of wisdom, which inspires one to follow the path set by Diotima.

Socrates' main contribution to the topic of the evening comes in the form of a discourse describing his introduction to the art of love. The discourse begins by portraying Eros as a kind of spirit (202E1), plying the domain between the divine and the mortal. It moves on by characterizing Eros as a lover of wisdom (203D7), born from the conjunction of Resource and Need. The discourse terminates with an interchange between Socrates and Diotima in which Socrates is instructed in the pathway to the beauty of knowledge (210C7) and ultimately to the vision of Beauty itself. In this interchange, Socrates plays the role of the student, with Diotima cast clearly in the role of the teacher. There is no confusion whatsoever in Diotima' discourse between the role she occupies as Socrates' teacher and the spirit of Eros that longs for wisdom. No more should we mistake Socrates—the personification of Eros—for a teacher possessing skills like those modeled by Diotima. Eros is depicted as the son of Need, fated ever to fall short of the wisdom he longs for. How could his personification provide guidance along a pathway that Eros by nature can never complete?

There are other reasons for resisting the initial temptation to read the encounter between Alcibiades and Socrates as a defective copy of Socrates' interaction with Diotima. One dissimilarity already noted in this regard is the erotic character of the former encounter in contrast with the dispassionate interaction between Diotima and her student. The lesson suggested by this dissimilarity is that eroticism has no place in the student-teacher relationship. Another fact worth noting is that Eros himself never appears as an *object* of love in Diotima's progression. It follows that the love of Alcibiades for the person who personifies Eros is out of keeping with the sequence that leads to philosophic fulfillment. Not only is a love of Eros unproductively narcissistic, but moreover it is a reversion to the misconception of Eros that Diotima's discourse had undertaken to rectify. The problem with approaches to love like those typified in the earlier speeches, she had observed, is that they represent Eros as "being loved" rather than as "being a lover" (204C2–3). Eros subsequently was portrayed as a lover of various objects, ranging from beautiful bodies through spiritual beauty on to the Beautiful itself, but was never portrayed as being an object of love himself. Insofar as Socrates has identity as the personification of Eros, any love directed *toward* him—like the love of Alcibiades—must be understood as a departure from the path of philosophy.

Although it seemed plausible at first to interpret Alcibiades' description of his attraction to Socrates as a depiction of love's potential in the service of philosophy, along lines explored in previous sections, in retrospect this reading appears fundamentally mistaken. The amorous encounter Alcibiades describes is not an interaction with a teacher, which under other circumstances might have yielded fine fruits of philosophy. It was an interaction with the personification of Eros itself, which Alcibiades found attractive for all the wrong reasons. Socrates is not an object of love at the beginning level, from which a young learner passes to higher levels of Diotima's ascent. Nor is he a teacher of philosophy in the mold of Diotima, who is competent to lead young persons to higher forms of Beauty. The Socrates of the *Symposium* is a lover of wisdom. As such he is an exemplar of the kind of desire by which a learner is motivated to follow the path of philosophy. Thus Socrates, to repeat, is not a teacher of philosophy but rather a personification of the *philosophia* by which wisdom is pursued.

There are no automatic extrapolations to be made from the depiction of Socrates in this single dialogue to a characterization of Plato's relationship with the historical Socrates. It is conceivable that, at an early stage of this relationship, Plato did think of Socrates' physical charm as a magnet of sorts by which young men could be induced to take an interest in philosophy. Since we know practically nothing about the details of their personal interactions, whether or not this was so remains a moot issue. We do know, however, that with the *Symposium* Plato is moving into a stage of his writing career when he seems increasingly willing to express reservations about Socrates' skills in philosophy. Just as it seemed not inappropriate in the section above to associate Socrates' self-avowed barrenness at *Theaetetus* 150C with Diotima's lack of confidence in his ability to make further progress expressed at *Symposium* 210A, so too we might associate Socrates' lack of teaching ability in this dialogue with the fact that he is unceremoniously replaced by a philosopher whose skills are not limited to refutation at the outset of the conversation portrayed in the *Sophist*. And it seems unlikely, to say the least, that Plato would have expressed reservations like these if he had thought of his own relationship with Socrates as one primarily of student to mentor.

In our discussion of the interaction between Socrates and Plato thus far, to be sure, we have followed the common manner of speaking in referring to Socrates as a teacher and to Plato as his student. Inasmuch as it seems beyond question that Plato did learn various important things about philosophy from Socrates, there is no reason to discontinue this manner of speaking in casual reference to their relationship. One thing Plato surely learned from Socrates, for instance, was the importance of elenchus as a preparation for serious inquiry.[43] Another was the power of paradigmatic instances to move the mind to a grasp of general properties in things.[44] What we should avoid as a result of the considerations above, nonetheless, is the assumption that the relation between Socrates and Plato followed the pattern set in Diotima's discourse. However Plato arrived at the conception of philosophic instruction that stands behind that discourse, it probably did not come from his interaction with Socrates. The same may be said for the portrayal of philosophic training in the Seventh Letter. Although the involvement of elenchus in that process may trace back to Socrates, the rest must have come from other sources.

An important part of the philosophic discipline that Plato did *not* get from Socrates is the set of investigative procedures referred to from the middle period onwards as dialectic.[45] There are indications in the *Phaedo* and the *Republic* that Plato may have learned something about such matters from the procedures of mathematics. There are indications to be found also, notably in the *Parmenides*, that he learned a substantial amount in this regard from the Eleatics as well. It may even be the case that Plato discovered certain of these procedures himself. Whatever their origin, however, there are clear signs that Plato was shaping them and honing them through most of his career. The story of this process is sufficiently complex to require a separate chapter for its telling.

One thing about which the *Symposium* leaves no doubt, when all is said and done, is that the time he spent with Socrates provided Plato a compelling example of the love of wisdom in action. While the personal charms of Socrates may have been an extraneous factor as far as his philosophic interaction with the youth of Athens was concerned, it must be admitted that there *is* something attractive in itself about the example of someone entirely dedicated to the pursuit of wisdom. It may have been Socrates' exemplification of this love, more than anything else, that drew Plato himself to the path of philosophy. And in the case of a reader who is drawn to philosophy by an encounter with Plato's dialogues, it is the witness of Socrates provided within them that he or she initially will find most compelling. Plato had the genius to present the same influence to his readers as that primarily responsible for his own introduction to philosophy. Before the love of wisdom can mature to the point of yielding philosophic fruits, however, it must be channeled by a discipline that will give it depth and direction. This discipline is provided by dialectic, to which we turn in the following chapter.

5

DIALECTIC AND LOGOS:
TRAINING THE SHOOTS

1. The Place of Dialectic in the Curriculum for the Guardians

Plato's longest sustained discussion of dialectic occurs between 531D and 534E in Book VII of the *Republic*. Toward the beginning of this sequence, dialectic (*dialektikēn:* 532B5) is characterized as an attempt, "through *logos*"[1] (532A7), to push on to the essence of things, terminating only when "the nature of the Good itself" (*auto ho estin agathon:* 532B1) comes within the grasp of "reason alone" (*autē noēsei:* 532B1). With this result, Socrates observes, the dialectician reaches the "limit of the intelligible" (*tou noētou telei:* 532B2), just as the prisoner released from the cave, in seeing the Sun, reaches the limit of the visible realm. Glaucon then asks three questions regarding the power of dialectic:[2] first, what is the manner (*tropos:* 532D8) in which it functions?; second, into what kinds (*eidē:* 532E1) is it divided?; and third, what are the ways (*hodoi:* 532E2) by which it proceeds? Socrates declines to answer these questions directly, citing both Glaucon's inability to follow (533A2) and his own lack of certainty that he knows the answers himself (533A4–5).[3] But he nonetheless is ready to reaffirm that dialectic is the only method (*methodos:* 533B3) by which one can undertake systematically (*hodō:* 533B3) to grasp the nature of each thing as it really is.

While he has no doubts about the importance of dialectic as a method, the Socrates of the *Republic* remains uncertain about the nature of its powers and its manner of proceeding. There are numerous other passages in the middle and late dialogues, however, in which dialectic is discussed in considerable detail. The primary aim of this chapter is to formulate cogent answers to Glaucon's three questions by drawing upon the contents of these various passages. By way of anticipation, we may expect the answer to the second question to include the method of hypothesis that figures in the passages cited above, and also the method of collection and division that is called *dialektikē* at *Phaedrus* 266C8 and *Sophist* 253D3. I shall argue that the "exercise" recommended and illustrated in the second part of the *Parmenides* constitutes yet another form that dialectic might take. An answer to Glaucon's third question, in turn, comes with a description of the procedures incorporated in each of these methods. Since these procedures can be found operating in dialogues as far apart as the *Meno* and the *Philebus*, a further question to be faced is whether there is supposed to be some order of succession among these methods and why Plato gave the label *dialektikē* to procedures that are so obviously different in the first place.

Difficult as this additional question may appear to be, however, Glaucon's first question will prove more difficult to answer. As I understand it, this is the question of how the procedures of dialectic can yield philosophic knowledge. In the Seventh Letter and elsewhere, as noted previously, Plato indicates that philosophic knowledge is a state of mind and explicitly rejects *logos* (in the sense of public language) as a means for its conveyance. How then can dialectic reach the essence of things through *logos*, as claimed at *Republic* 532A? In particular, how can the Idea of the Good be "distinguished through *logos*" (534B9), and how does this enable the dialectician "to know the Good in itself" (534C4)? The main outlines of the answer to these questions will be at hand by section 5 of the present chapter, but we shall be looking for parts of the answer in chapter 6 as well.

To make a start in our examination of these issues, let us return to the conversation in Book VII of the *Republic* where Socrates is discussing the education of the Guardians. Book VII begins with the famous allegory of the Cave, which Plato introduces in conjunction with the Divided Line as an embellishment of the analogy between the sun and the Good. We shall undertake a detailed consideration of these remarkable literary images in chapter 6. For the present, it is enough to note that the allegory of the Cave is followed immediately by a discussion of the course of study needed to produce leaders for the ideal state. The topic of education for the Guardians actually was initiated toward the end of Book II, where Socrates prescribed a carefully controlled study of poetry and music, along with a rigorous course of physical conditioning. The purpose of this early training, according to Book III, is to bring "the courageous and the philosophic" (411E7) elements of the soul—i.e., ardor and reason—into "peak proportion and harmony" (*metriōtata . . . kai euarmostotaton*: 412A5–6) with each other. Music and physical training, we learn later in Book VII, will occupy candidates for guardianship up to age twenty (537B), after which they will be expected to devote a full ten years to mathematical studies.

Here is how those studies are supposed to be structured. Beginning with arithmetic and number theory, the candidates progress in sequence to plane geometry (dealing with objects in two dimensions), solid geometry (objects in three dimensions), astronomy (motion of three-dimensional objects through time), and thence to harmonic theory (motion in "auditory space and time").[4] This sequence of studies is to be pursued between ages twenty and thirty, thus occupying ten years of the candidate's life overall.

Although each of these mathematical disciplines has practical applications, they are included in the curriculum primarily for their ability to help the soul "to see the truth" (*alētheia horatai*: 527E3). Of particular interest to the Platonist is the description of the role of arithmetic (*logismos*) in this regard. The study of counting and calculation, Socrates says, not only enables one to count ships and soldiers, but when rightly pursued "is in every way an attraction toward being" (523A2–3). In order to explain how the study of numbers can attract one toward being, Socrates introduces the memorable illustration of the three fingers on a hand (the little finger, the middle, and the one in between). While there is no ambiguity about each being a finger, or being a certain shape or color, etc., our perception of their size contains latent anomalies. Appearing big in comparison with the little finger, and little in comparison with the middle finger, the finger in between appears both big and little.[5] And when a perception yields opposing impressions in this way with equal clarity, the paradox puzzles the mind and "calls for investigation" (*episkepseōs deomenai*: 524B2). In similar fashion, when we see what we take to be a pair of things, the appearance is of one and of two alike—the pair being two and each of the two being one. And when this happens, we are led to contemplate the nature of unity, and of numbers generally, which of course is the business of arithmetic. Thus the study of unity (*to hen*: 525A2) would be one that guides the soul and turns it toward a contemplation of reality. Given the character of bodily vision generally, Socrates continues, we are likely to see the same thing both as one and at the same time as "indefinitely many" (*apeira to plēthos*: 525A4–5).[6] Through the study of number, arithmetic thus "leads toward the truth" (525B1), a role which merits its inclusion in the curriculum for the Guardians.

The next study in line is plane geometry. While this discipline has obvious military uses, the application in which Socrates is interested is one that can direct "philosophic understanding toward higher things" (527B10), thereby making it "easier to behold the Idea of the Good" (526E2–3). Astronomy, in its turn, is to eschew the visible "blazonry of the heavens" (529C8), and to direct the student's attention to what can be grasped specifically "by reason and thought" (529D4–5). The study of harmonics, likewise, coming as it does at the end of the sequence, should avoid preoccupation with audible harmonies but should serve as a means "for the investigation of the Beautiful and the Good" (531C6–7). This passing reference to harmonics as an aid to investigation of the Beautiful and the Good has obvious relevance to the problematic relation between these two characters, a topic to be looked at further in chapter 6.

Candidates who pass successfully through the ten years of mathematical training, to continue the story, spend the next five years (up to age thirty-five) learning the discipline of dialectic, which is the final stage of their "formal" training. It is important to note, however, that the successful completion of this study does not bring the candidate to the point of being ready to take responsibility as a full-fledged Guardian of the state. This is because the study of dialectic does not bring him or her to a vision of the Good itself. Becoming skilled at dialectic provides a method which in later years can be used to mount an ascent to this vision. But before this method can be applied with any hope of achieving that result, the candidate must spend a full fifteen years—a trial period even longer than that devoted to mathematics—in practical service to the state. During this time, he or she is required to take command of military operations and to gain experience in other forms of civic leadership. Besides rendering service to their compatriots in such practical matters, moreover, the candidates must be tested for their "steadfastness against all temptation" (540A1). They also must prove themselves best in all kinds of action and knowledge (epistēmais: 540A6). Only when tests of this sort have been successfully met is a candidate finally ready to be brought to the goal. Only then is he or she ready to turn "the eye of the soul" (540A7) upward and to look upon "the Good itself" (540A8–9) by which all else is illuminated. Having finally achieved a vision of this highest principle, the Guardians then are to "take it as a pattern for the right ordering of the state, the common man, and themselves individually" (540A9–B1). The remainder of their lives is to be spent in philosophy (*philosophia*: 540B2), in public service, and in training other Guardians to succeed them.

Given this general role of dialectic in the curriculum for the Guardians, what specifically can be said about its nature? One practice from which it is expressly said to differ is that of disputation by way of "antilogic" (*antilogian*: 539B4), whereby young men "imitate their own confuters" (*mimoumenoi tous exelenchontas*: 539B5) and "cross-examine others" (*allous elenchousi*: 539B5) like playful puppies.[7] Contentious use of cross-examination in this fashion,[8] Socrates warns, leads to general skepticism and brings discredit upon philosophy. Repeated use of the term *elenchein* (cross-examine) in these passages should bring to mind also the practice of Socratic elenchus—described in the *Sophist* as "the sophistry of noble lineage."[9] Although this use of elenchus is never depicted by Plato as bringing discredit upon philosophy and is characterized in this later dialogue as a powerful purifier of the "conceit of wisdom" (*doxosophian*: 231B7), it is also clear by this time that cross-examination of any sort—whether "well-disposed" or otherwise—is not adequate by itself as a philosophic method. So Socratic elenchus by itself is not dialectic.[10] What exactly is this method of dialectic that Socrates is unable to pursue in the context of the *Republic*?[11]

This question is crucial for our purposes not because an answer is hard to find, but rather because several answers are at hand that seem to be at odds with each other. Three alternatives were distinguished at the beginning of this section. One is the method of hypothesis, described at the end of Book VI, by which the philosopher moves up to a "nonhypothetical first principle" (*archēn anupotheton*: 510B7). Earlier versions of this method also appear in the *Meno* and the *Phaedo*. Another alternative is the method of collection and division, which is extensively employed in several late dialogues after its initial appearance in the *Phaedrus*. Yet another is the method employed in the second part of the *Parmenides*, which also relies upon the use of hypotheses but in a manner significantly different from the method described in the *Republic*.

These three methods are examined in the three sections following. In undertaking this examination, our task is not only to see how these methods work, but also to identify the major differences among them. This should tell us something about their merits as procedures of inquiry and something also about their order in sequence of development.

2. The Method of Hypothesis from the Meno to the Republic

Although Socrates' use of hypothesis in the Meno is interesting in its own right, it does not have the appearance in that context of a distinctly philosophic procedure. It is a procedure modeled on a technique of geometrical inquiry, which is illustrated in terms of a specific problem.[12] The problem is whether a given area can be inscribed within a circle in the form of a triangle with two equal sides. Its solution proceeds from a particular hypothesis—i.e., that a certain relation is present between the triangle and a pair of similar rectangles defined along the circle's diameter. The solution is accomplished with a proof that this particular relation is both necessary and sufficient for the triangle to be inscribed in the specified manner. Following this general pattern, Socrates then hypothesizes that virtue is a kind of knowledge and purports to show that the truth of this hypothesis is both necessary and sufficient for virtue to be obtainable as the result of teaching. His next step is to put together a distinctly shaky "proof" that virtue in fact is a kind of knowledge, which seems to establish the conclusion that virtue is teachable. Both Meno and the reader are taken by surprise, however, when Socrates turns about and denies that conclusion a moment later, on the grounds that no one is capable of teaching virtue. The testy interchange with Anytus that follows clearly presages the charges that brought Socrates to trial—the charge, in particular, of his being a sophist.

There are two aspects of this exercise that turn out to be relevant to the specifically philosophic use of hypothesis discussed in the Phaedo. For one, both Socrates' argument and its geometric counterpart produced conclusions couched in terms of necessary and sufficient conditions. Being a kind of knowledge is necessary for virtue's being teachable, inasmuch as what is teachable can always be known. And being a kind of knowledge is also sufficient for this result, inasmuch as what is known (allegedly) can always be taught. This emphasis upon conditions that are both necessary and sufficient remains a mark of philosophic method through the very late dialogues.[13] The other aspect of Socrates' exercise to bear in mind for later reference is that he undertook to demonstrate that virtue is knowledge before he turned to consider whether virtue in fact can be taught. In effect, he tried to show that the hypothesis is true before making sure that it was consistent with the facts of the matter. This order of procedure is expressly rejected in Plato's next discussion of method in the context of the Phaedo.

The method of hypothesis described in the *Phaedo* is introduced as a *deuteros plous* (see 99D1)—a proverbial reference to the use of oars as a "second way of voyaging" by sea when there is insufficient wind to fill the sails.[14] Since it is called "second-best" in contrast with a way of dealing with causes attributed to Anaxagoras, with which Plato obviously is unsympathetic, this reference appears at first to be a touch of irony. As Socrates' description of the method continues, however, the sense of irony progressively dissipates. Finding himself unfulfilled in his "examination of reality" (*ta onta skopōn*: 99D6), Socrates says, he thought he should avoid harm of the sort that comes to people viewing an eclipse of the sun, who are likely to ruin their sight unless they watch its image in water or some such medium.[15] Fearing that something like that might happen in his case and that his "mind might be completely blinded" (*pantapasi tēn psuchēn tuphlōtheiēn*: 99E2) by "trying to grasp things with his senses" (99E4), Socrates thought he should take the following precaution. It seemed to him necessary "to have recourse to *logoi*" (99E5) and "through them to examine the truth of things" (99E5-6).

Since the method begins by laying down or hypothesizing the *logoi* in question, it is generally known as Plato's "method of hypothesis." Here is how the method goes. In each case, Socrates says:

> I hypothesize the *logos* which I judge to be strongest (*hupothemenos . . . logon hon an krinō errōmenestaton einai*: 100A3-4), and whatever seems to me to agree with it I set down as really so (*ha men an moi dokē toutō sumphōnein tithēmi hōs alēthē onta*: 100A4-5)—whether with regard to causes or anything else (*kai peri aitias kai peri tōn allōn hapantōn*: 100A5-6); and what does not, as not so (*ha d' an mē, hōs ouk alēthē*: 100A6-7).

Considerable effort has gone into attempts to understand this relation of agreement (*sumphōnein*), which appears at first to pose substantial logical difficulties. If agreement is tantamount to consistency among propositions, then it would be unreasonable to set down as really so whatever agrees with the initial *logos*, since many false propositions are consistent with any given true one; for this part of the method to make sense, agreement would have to have the effect of entailment instead. On the other hand, if agreement is equivalent to entailment among propositions, then it would be unreasonable to set down as *not* so whatever fails to agree with the initial *logos*, since for any true proposition initially hypothesized there will be many other true propositions not entailed by it in turn.

The best way I know to resolve this quandary is to understand *sumphonein* as a relation of mutual entailment, or what was called "convertability" in connection with the so-called "method of analysis" practiced by geometers in Plato's day.[16] Within a set of propositions dealing with equalities among specific geometrical quantities (e.g., AB + BC = 2CD and AB = 2CD − BC), any proposition consistent with another will also entail it; so convertibility with a given true proposition can be relied upon as a criterion for both truth and falsehood of other propositions within the same set. The likelihood that *some* mathematical relation of this sort was intended in Plato's statement of the method is indicated by the fact that all the characters who claim at 102A, after Socrates had stated it a second time, to find the method "wonderfully clear" (*thaumastōs . . . enargōs*: 102A4–5) are known to have been Pythagoreans and hence presumably were familiar with the mathematics of the time. One awkwardness remaining under this interpretation, of course, is that philosophy, unlike mathematics, typically does not deal with convertible propositions. Several adjustments in the method will be needed before its application to philosophy is at all perspicuous.

But there is no doubt about its relevance to philosophic issues. Directly following its initial statement—which the audience seems to have found quite puzzling (100A8–9)—Socrates illustrates the method with an account of causation based upon the existence of the Forms themselves. The account begins by "hypothesizing the existence of Beauty itself and the Good and the Large, along with all the rest" (100B5–6) of the absolute Forms. The immediate conclusion is that "if anything is beautiful other than Beauty itself" (100C4–5), then it is beautiful for no reason other than "participation in that absolute Beauty" (*metechei ekeinou tou kalou*: 100C6). Participation in the Form Beauty, that is to say, is set down as the *cause* of beauty in particular things, presumably on the basis of this account's agreement with the hypothesis that the Forms exist.

While the method itself is illustrated by this account of causation expressed in terms of participation in the absolute Forms, the account of causation also requires illustration in turn. One example focuses on participation in Beauty. A beautiful thing cannot owe its beauty just to some attractive shape or color, inasmuch as (a) there are other things that are beautiful but that lack those attributes, and (b) there are things with those attributes that do not exhibit beauty. Attractive shape and color, that is to say, are neither (a) *necessary* nor (b) *sufficient* for the presence of beauty in sensible objects. So "nothing makes the object beautiful other than the participation or presence in it of that very Beauty itself" (100D4–5)—"in whatever manner or way it comes about" (100D5–6).[17] Another example concerns the property of being two. No collection becomes dual other than by participating in Duality; so participation in that Form is *necessary* for being dual. At the same time, every collection that so participates numbers two, so participation in Duality is *sufficient* for being dual as well. The sense of cause in which he is interested, Plato is saying in effect, is the sense according to which a cause is both necessary and sufficient for bringing about the effect it produces. His account of causation by participation in the Forms is expressly tailored to meet these requirements.

After these illustrations of how the new account of causation is supposed to work, Socrates returns at 101D to the method of hypothesis itself. The major innovation in this second statement of the method has to do with the distinction between necessary and sufficient conditions revealed in the illustrations. Having hypothesized the initial *logos*, one must examine its agreement or disagreement with other *logoi* of interest. But there are two quite distinct stages involved in this examination, and they must be undertaken in the proper order. First one should consider whether its consequences "agree or disagree with one another" (*allēlois xumphōnei ē diaphōnei*: 101D5–6). When it has been determined that the consequences of the initial hypothesis are mutually consistent, one should turn next "to give a *logos* of the hypothesis itself" (101D6–7). And this second stage should proceed "in like manner" (*hōsautōs*: 101D7) to the first. That is, one should "lay down some other hypothesis" (101D7–8), whichever hypothesis "seems the best among those higher" (*tōn anōthen beltistē phainoito*: 101D8). And one should continue in this way until one "reaches some satisfactory" (*ti hikanon elthois*: 101E1) resolution. Despite the terse expression of these instructions, the procedures they specify are clearly intelligible.

It is *necessary* for the truth of any *logos* that it be consistent, which means that all its consequences "agree with one another." So the first step amounts to nothing more nor less than testing the hypothesis for self-consistency. Once it has been determined that this necessary condition of consistency has been met, the person applying the method begins to look for sufficient conditions among other hypotheses that are "higher" in the sense of "more general." It is *sufficient* for the truth of the initial hypothesis, that is to say, that it be the consequence of (be entailed by) some other *logos* that itself is true. Having found a more general hypothesis that "seems best" for this purpose, one then proceeds "in like manner" to test this higher hypothesis for consistency. And if this higher hypothesis turns out to be consistent, but itself requires further accounting, one seeks out a yet more general *logos* with which the procedure is repeated; and so forth and so on until a *logos* is reached which is "satisfactory"—i.e., which in the context of investigation requires no further accounting. In the context of geometrical analysis, this would mean a formula the truth of which had been previously established. What it means in the context of a *philosophic* investigation is left unspecified until Book VI of the *Republic*.

In laying out these instructions, Socrates emphasizes that the consistency-check should be performed before any attempt is made to establish the actual truth of the *logos* in question. The reason is simply that any effort spent trying to deduce the *logos* from some more general hypothesis would be wasted if the *logos* itself is inconsistent. In a word, one should assure that the logos in question is a *candidate* for truth before setting out to show that it actually *is* true. This requirement is considered sufficiently important, indeed, that people who ignore it are called *anti-logikoi* (101E1). It is a requirement that must be respected by anyone who "hopes to discover anything of reality" (101E3). Hence it is a requirement that will be observed by any "lover of wisdom" (*philosophōn*: 102A1).

It may be recalled that Socrates' treatment of the hypothesis that virtue is knowledge in the *Meno* follows the order here said to be typical of the *antilogikoi*. Whether this disparity between the use of hypothesis prescribed in the *Phaedo* and that actually followed in the *Meno* was intended by the author is something we have no way of knowing. My guess is that it indeed was intended and that we should think of the faulty procedure in the *Meno* as one more thing that can go wrong if someone undertakes to examine the properties of a thing (e.g., virtue and its teachability) without first knowing the nature of the thing itself (e.g., the nature of Virtue).

There are two problems with the description of the method in the *Phaedo* that by now should be apparent. One is that there is no sharp distinction drawn there between the use of hypotheses in the well-known technique of geometrical analysis and a use of hypothesis specifically adapted for philosophic purposes. Methodologically, that is to say, mathematics and philosophy are still on an equal footing. And this is a parity with which Plato cannot long remain satisfied. The other problem is that the *Phaedo* says practically nothing about what it is for a higher-level hypothesis to be "satisfactory" *(hikanon)*. Checking an hypothesis for consistency (the necessary condition for truth) seems relatively straightforward. But what might be involved, as far as *philosophy* is concerned, in locating a more general *logos* that is "satisfactory" in the sense of requiring no further accounting? Both problems are addressed in the next discussion of this method, occurring at the end of Book VI in the *Republic*.

This next discussion employs the image of a line divided in a certain geometrical proportion. In its purely formal aspect, the Divided Line is nothing more than two unequal segments of a line, each of which is further divided in the same proportion. We are told nothing about the nature of the proportion (e.g., whether it is rational or irrational), about the spatial orientation of the Line (whether vertical or horizontal), or about the distribution of its unequal segments (whether the longer goes on top or bottom, or left or right, as the case might be). Although questions of detail like these take on importance when we turn to matters of interpretation, they are irrelevant to the purely mathematical description of the Line. All the mathematics of the Line specifies is that it is divided into four distinct segments, the first in the same ratio[18] to the second as the third to the fourth, and as the first two to the last two taken pairwise. The first (assuming a vertical orientation, the bottom) section represents mirror images of three-dimensional objects, which themselves are assigned to the second section. The first and second sections together represent the visible world, or the "world of becoming," which in turn contains images of entities represented by the last two sections, together constituting the intelligible world, or the "world of being." The last two sections taken individually are related in the same manner, in that the mathematical entities represented by the third in some sense are considered to be images of the Forms, which are assigned to the fourth and final section. In brief, the first section images the second, the third images the fourth, and the first and second image the third and fourth in combination.

More will be said about the Line in relation to the Sun and the Cave when we turn to the topic of the Good in the following chapter. Our present concern is with the upper two sections—specifically, with the methods of inquiry attributed to mathematics and philosophy respectively. One feature ascribed to mathematical inquiry that seems clear from the outset is that mathematicians "avail themselves of visible

figures" (510D4) and "conduct discussions about these" (510D5), although what they have in mind are the originals which these figures
image. Geometers, for example, typically reason about "the Square or
the Diagonal as such" (510D6–8) and not the particular squares or
diagonals they have drawn by way of illustration.

The second salient feature of mathematical inquiry, as described in
this context, has to do with the mathematician's use of hypotheses.
People who engage in arithmetic, geometry, and other such studies
"hypothesize the odd and the even, various figures, and three kinds of
angle" (510C4–5), and kindred things for each such inquiry. These they
take as "known" (*eidotes*: 510C6). That is to say, "having taken these as
hypotheses" (510C6–7),[19] "they feel no obligation to give a *logos* of them
to themselves or to anyone else" (510C7–8), but take them "as clear to
everybody" (*hōs panti phanerōn*: 510C8). Taking these as starting points,
they forthwith "go through all their steps consistently until they reach
the end of what they had set out to investigate" (510D1–2).

To put it directly, mathematical deduction begins with the assumption of certain axioms or postulates which are taken as intuitively true,
or at least as not requiring further support within the context of inference. It is as if mathematical inquiry is said here to involve only the first
stage of the two-stage method outlined in the *Phaedo*. The mathematician begins with one or another hypothesis and exercises due care to
reason consistently in drawing conclusions from those hypotheses. He or
she is expert in dealing with *necessary* conditions of the *logoi* assumed.
But it is not part of the method of mathematics here described to
investigate conditions that might be found *sufficient* for the truth of its
hypotheses.

The first feature of mathematical inquiry noted in these passages is
that the mathematician employs visible illustrations of the entities being
investigated. Comparison with philosophy on this score is direct and
uncomplicated. The point, of course, is not that philosophers never use
illustrations (use of example is an integral part of the method practised in
the *Statesman*; see 278E), nor even that visible diagrams are never
helpful in philosophic discussion (recall *Meno* 82B9–10). The point is
that philosophy is not *dependent* upon sensible images, taking its illustrations from the upper rather than lower part of the Line—often, indeed,
from mathematics itself.

Comparison on the second score, however, leads directly to one of the
most difficult issues of interpretation in the entire *Republic*—what to

make of the "nonhypothetical first principle" at the top of the Line. For philosophy has its province in the uppermost segment, where the mind still "proceeds by hypothesis" (*ex hupotheseōs iousa*: 510B7), but instead of moving deductively toward conclusions, as in the case of mathematics, moves in the other direction toward a "principle that is not hypothetical" (*archēn anupotheton*: 510B7). From this vantage point the mind is enabled to "conduct its method of inquiry by means of the Forms themselves" (510B8). So philosophy and mathematics, as it were, move in different directions from their hypotheses. Mathematics moves "downward" by deductive inference, while philosophy moves "upward" to an origin (*archē*) that is not hypothetical. Philosophy moves from the hypothetical to a nonhypothetical basis, while mathematics never escapes its dependence upon hypotheses.

This description of the philosopher's upward path is repeated at 511B–C, in a passage sufficiently weighty to merit quoting at length. By the uppermost section of the intelligible, Socrates means:

> what reason by itself grasps by the power of dialectic (*touto hou autos ho logos haptetai tē tou dialegesthai dunamei*: 511B4),[20] treating its hypotheses not as first principles but just as hypotheses (*tas hupotheseis poioumenos ouk archas, alla tō onti hupotheseis*: 511B5)—as stepping-stones and springboards (*hoion epibaseis te kai hormas*: 511B6)—by which it can rise to what is nonhypothetical, the first principle of everything (*hina mechri tou anupothetou epi tēn tou pantos archēn iōn*: 511B6–7); having attained that, and holding on to its consequences, reason then turns around and descends to its final conclusion (*hapsamenos autēs, palin au echomenos tōn ekeinēs echomenōn, houtōs epi teleutēn katabainē*: 511B7–9).

This whole procedure, as noted previously, is supposed to ensue without use of sensible images, being accomplished by transitions among Forms exclusively.

Pending further discussion of the nonhypothetical first principle in relation to the Form of the Good—a major concern of the following chapter—it is enough for the present to review the points of correspondence between this method and that described in the *Phaedo*. First is the matter of checking consistency. Although there is less emphasis upon consistency in the *Republic* than in the *Phaedo*, it is safe to assume that the philosopher is no less concerned than the mathematician (see 510D1) to make sure that consistency is maintained throughout. Having attended to the necessary condition of consistent hypotheses, presumably, the philosophic inquirer next turns to seek out a more general *logos*—i.e., a conceptual basis that is sufficient for the truth of the hypothesis initially being investigated. The difference in this regard, of considerable importance in itself, is that this "upward movement" in the *Phaedo* is said to terminate with some higher-level hypothesis vaguely described as "satisfactory" (*hikanon*), whereas in the *Republic* it is characterized as a nonhypothetical first principle. In either case, it is a principle *sufficient* for the truth of the initial hypothesis. After arriving at the general principle in question, at any rate, the inquirer following either set of instructions then returns deductively to this initial hypothesis, thus anchoring it firmly to its epistemological basis.

The general outlines of the method of hypothesis at this point are sufficiently clear to warrant characterizing it in terms of successive stages. First, the philosopher following the method will (1) lay down a hypothesis or set of hypotheses to be tested. If a given hypothesis contains terms that are ambiguous or otherwise problematic, it may be necessary as the next step to (2) define whatever terms require clarification. Such definitions may then be added to the set of hypotheses under examination (cf. *Meno* 75D). The philosopher then is ready to (3) test the initial hypothesis or set of hypotheses for consistency, both (a) with respect to immediate consequences (i.e., to test for self-consistency) and (b) with respect to any other *logoi* that are accepted as true within the context of inquiry (as in the *Meno* it is accepted that there are no teachers of virtue). If found consistent, the next step is to (4) seek out some more general hypothesis from which the initial hypothesis or hypotheses can be deduced in turn. Steps (2) and (3) are then repeated for this higher-level hypothesis. And if it passes muster with respect to consistency but is found still to require support within the context in question, then step (4) is applied again in its behalf. And so forth and so on, until a level is reached where no further support is required. At this stage the method has been completed and the initial subject of inquiry has been secured to its epistemological mooring.

There are several reasons for spelling out the individual stages of this method as above. One is to enable us to see that it is entirely cogent. While a cursory reading of the passages describing it might leave the impression of a rather garbled set of procedures, the method when elaborated is sufficiently sophisticated to stand comparison with the procedures of modern experimental science. Another reason is to prepare us for a detailed examination of the structure of argument in the

Theaetetus, which occupies a key part of the agenda in the Appendix. The immediate reason for laying out the method in the detail above, however, is to prepare us for a comparison with the method of collection and division taken up in the *Sophist*. Let us turn directly to this latter method.

3. Collection and Division from the Sophist to the Philebus

The stated goal of the *Sophist* is to arrive at a "clear definition" (218C1) of the practice in question. Since this will not be an easy task, the Stranger cautions, it is best to "practice beforehand the method" (218D5) to be used for that purpose. An easier case than the sophist is the familiar angler. By working through the example (*paradeigma*: 218D9) of the angler, they can gain experience both with the type of definition (*logon*: 219A1) and with the method (*Methodon*: 219A1) they want to pursue. As one might expect with a good example, this practice definition of the angler provides a clear illustration of how the method proceeds—perhaps the clearest to be found in the corpus overall. This warrants a careful look at some of its details.

By way of beginning, we note that the definition specifies ten features which in combination delineate the angler, marking off practitioners of that skill from everyone else. In order cited, angling is (1) an art (2) of acquisition (vs. production) (3) by capture (vs. exchange) (4) involving stealth (vs. combat) (5) of living prey (vs. lifeless), specifically (6) water animals (vs. land) (7) by fishing (vs. fowling) (8) employing blows (vs. enclosures) administered (9) by day (vs. night) (10) from below (vs. above).[21] Each of these features is *necessary* to angling, in that the absence of any would put a person in another category.[22] Someone who captured waterfowl during the day by administering blows from below—e.g., by shooting ducks from a blind by bow and arrow—would be classified as a fowler instead of an angler. Moreover, these features together are *sufficient* for being an angler, in that any person with them all would fall under this category. To possess these ten features *ipso facto* is to be an angler.[23]

Whether or not a given definition is adequate depends upon its treatment of necessary and sufficient conditions. A definition might incorporate features all of which are necessary for the thing being defined, but which are not sufficient in combination to distinguish that thing from others like it. If the Stranger's definition of angling had broken off with (7) fishing, for example, the result would not be sufficient to distinguish an angler from someone who catches fish by catching them in nets or reels. Such a definition would include only necessary features, but would fall short of specifying conditions that are sufficient for angling. On the other hand, a definition could specify features which together are sufficient for being a thing of the sort in question, but not all of which are necessary in that regard. A pertinent illustration is the series of five faulty definitions of sophistry that immediately follow the definition of angling as the dialogue proceeds. Each of these five represents combinations of features that are sufficient to pick out one or another particular form of sophistry, insofar as anyone possessing all of its features by that fact alone would be a sophist. Given any one of these five characterizations, however, there will be sophists who do not possess all the features in question. So none of these sets of features is necessary for being a sophist. The upshot is that each of these preliminary definitions picks out specific types of sophistry, while none is an adequate definition of sophistry in general.

A definition of a Form or Kind is adequate, to say it again, if it specifies a set of features that together are sufficient, and that individually are necessary for being a thing of that Kind. The task of accumulating features that together are *sufficient* for being a thing of a given Kind belongs to *division*. This task is complete only when the set of features in question is sufficiently discriminating to mark off the thing that is being defined from other things of similar nature. If a division in a given case is incomplete, this is remedied by adding yet other features to the set in question. For a division to accomplish its task satisfactorily, however, it must begin with features that are necessary for being a thing of that Kind. And the task of finding *necessary* conditions falls to the process of *collection*.

The most perspicuous illustration of collection in the *Sophist* occurs where it is most needed—as the first stage of the ultimately successful definition of sophistry, beginning at 231D. The practical upshot of the five unsuccessful definitions between 221D and 226A is that each of them, by providing a set of sufficient (albeit not necessary) conditions for being a sophist, identifies a distinct paradigmatic example of the skill in question. The group of instances over which the collection for the final, and ultimately successful, definition ranges is constituted by the particular types of sophistry picked out by these five preliminary characterizations. What the Stranger helps Theaetetus see between 232B and 235B is that each of these sophists is involved in the production of images. Thus it turns out to have been a mistake to begin by trying to trace down sophistry in general under the same category of acquisitive arts that yielded the angler. Although there is something acquisitive about sophistry in all of its particular varieties, different varieties are acquisitive in different respects—a consequence of which is that no single subdivision of the *acquisitive* arts yielded a set of features shared by sophists generally. A feature all sophists do share in general, however, is that each of them is a *producer* of imitations. And it is by pointing this out, and by beginning afresh with the production of images as a common feature, that the Stranger is able to head Theaetetus into a path of division that yields an adequate definition of sophistry by the end of the dialogue. As the Stranger puts it, they must track the sophist down "through the subdivisions of the art of imitation" (235C2), "constantly dividing the part that gives him shelter, until finally he is caught" (235C3–4) in a complete description. The result is the definition of sophistry summarized in the last speech by the Stranger in the dialogue.

It is at *Phaedrus* 266B4, we recall from chapter 3, that collection and division are first identified by name as companion procedures. The first mention of collection itself, however, is at *Phaedrus* 249C, where "bringing a dispersed plurality to a single Idea" is identified with *anamnēsis* or recollection. The successor to *anamnēsis* is collection as such, as distinct from the dual method of collection and division. Let us briefly review, from our earlier discussion, the features that collection shares with *anamnēsis*.

The primary role of *anamnēsis*, in the context of the *Meno*, is to provide an ultimate source of knowledge that does not depend upon knowing other things in turn. Recollection is a process of clarification, beginning with certain items of knowledge already present in the soul. Much the same can be said of collection. In order for the process of division to get underway toward a successful definition of sophistry, for example, the parties involved have to be able to identify certain features that all sophists have in common. For that to happen, they have to bring together a set of typical instances of sophistry in which those features are exhibited. And to do this, they have to be able in turn to recognize those instances of sophistry *as such* without further cognitive preparation. Before an inquiry into the nature of sophistry in general can get underway, that is to say, the parties involved have to be able to recognize sophistry in its particular instances. This whole procedure of recognizing instances and discerning common features, of course, is what the dialogues refer to as collection or *sunagōgē*. It is because this procedure involves recognizing instances of general Kinds without further ado— i.e., as the initial stage of inquiry—that *sunagōgē* can be thought of as the successor to recollection.

This comparison of *sunagōgē* with recollection brings to the fore what appears to be an inherent weakness of collection as a dialectical procedure. The process of inquiry purports to begin with the mind or soul already capable of recognizing instances of the Kind being investigated. Not only does this capacity stand in need of explanation itself,[24] however, but it brings with it problems of a methodological nature as well. For the process of collection to get under way, it is essential that the dialectician be able to assemble a set of exemplary instances of the Kind being investigated. But Plato's description of the process nowhere provides instructions about how such a set is to be assembled. If the dialectician is fortunate enough to get a representative set together in the first place, well and good. Otherwise there is nothing to do but try again, in hopes eventually of finding a set of instances exhibiting features that will lead to a successful division.[25]

There is an interesting asymmetry in this regard between the method of collection and division and the method of hypothesis examined previously. As described in both the *Phaedo* and the *Republic*, the method of hypothesis remained vague in its reference to sufficient conditions. In the *Phaedo* the philosopher is supposed to proceed to more and more general *logoi* until one is found that is "satisfactory" or sufficient (101E1). In the *Republic*, the dialectician is to move upward to a "non-hypothetical first principle" which is sufficient to establish the truths of mathematics and the other rational disciplines. But what these sufficient conditions are supposed to amount to is left unspecified in either context. In the case of the method of collection and division, on the other hand, it is the manner of reaching necessary conditions that is left indeterminate. Sufficient conditions are taken care of by pursuing division to the point where the Kind being studied is completely isolated from similar Kinds. But the method remains vague about how the preliminary procedure of collection is supposed to get under way.

This somewhat unsatisfactory status of the procedure of collection may account in part for the fact that the other two dialogues in which this method is employed—the *Statesman* and the *Philebus*—focus on division almost exclusively. Although collection is mentioned from time to time as a relevant procedure,[26] there are no demonstrations of collection in either dialogue that even approach the clarity of that offered in the *Sophist*.

The announced purpose of the *Statesman*, like the *Sophist* before it, is to provide a definition of the skill identified in its title. And the way to be followed, as in the previous dialogue, is the "method of *logos*" (*methodō tōn logōn*: 266D7) by which definitions of the desired sort are to be found. After a hasty division of kinds of knowledge occupying less than four pages, a definition is proposed and immediately rejected. According to this initial definition, statesmanship is a theoretical form of knowledge directed toward the nurture of human flocks. The trouble with this definition, says the Stranger, is that it divides flocks too quickly between human and animal, as humanity might be divided between Greek and barbarian, or numbers between ten thousand and all the rest. As it would be better to divide numbers "according to Forms" (*kat' eidē*: 262E3) into odd or even, or humans into male and female, so flocks ought to be divided "dichotomously" (*dicha*: 262E4) into natural kinds. After adding more terms to the definition to produce a more natural set of divisions, however, the Stranger again expresses dissatisfaction. The problem this time is that the definition fails to distinguish statecraft from other skills involved in human nature, like agriculture and commerce and medicine. In order to explore alternative forms of nurture more fully, the Stranger then launches into a story about the reign of Cronos, in which the course of life runs backwards from its present order. On the basis of this illustration (*paradeigma*: 275B5) of statecraft, which shows that their previous attempts at definition had treated the statesman as a god rather than a mere mortal, the Stranger recommends to his young respondent that they set aside their previous approach and begin again.

Following a methodological digression dealing, among other things,[27] with the use of examples or paradigms discussed in chapter 3 above, the Stranger turns again to the task of defining the Statesman. Whereas previously all divisions had been dichotomous as a matter of principle (see 262E4), however, he now alerts young Socrates to the need for division into three or more parts. While divisions still are to follow natural lines of separation among the Forms, in the manner of a priest dissecting a sacrificial animal (*hoion hiereion*: 287C3), the only general rule from this point onward is that division should result in the fewest possible number of parts.

The most significant departure in what follows from the methodology of the *Sophist*, however, is that division appears to be disengaged from the exclusive task of providing definitions and turned to purposes of classification instead. As his final approach to the kingly art, the Stranger embarks on an exhaustive enumeration of the other civic skills from which statecraft must be distinguished. First come the seven general types of contributory arts, like the manufacture of tools, of containers, and of conveyances. Next is the extensive class of underlings and servants, such as merchants and moneychangers, and soothsayers and priests. The third general class, familiar from the later books of the *Republic*, comprises tyranny and other imitations of kingship, of which six kinds are singled out for reprobation. Fourth and finally come those leaders of genuine stature—generals, judges, and responsible public rhetoricians—whose skills are directed by the skill of statecraft proper. A result is that by far the greater share of the distinctions drawn within the last third of the dialogue contribute little to the elucidation of statecraft itself.[28]

This procedure of exhaustive classification introduced in the second half of the *Statesman* is heralded exuberantly in the early pages of the *Philebus*, where it is described as a "gift from the gods to men" (16C5). Like the dialogue overall in which it appears, there are several things about this godly path (*hodos*: 16B5, also 16A8) that are unusually difficult to understand.[29] It will be helpful nonetheless to look briefly at certain features of the methodology employed in this dialogue that show it to be a continuation of the techniques introduced in the later part of the *Statesman*.

Although Socrates appears once again as discussion leader in the *Philebus*, he sounds more like the Stranger of the *Sophist* and the *Statesman* than like the master of refutation and irony who dominated the early dialogues. One indication of change in dramatic character over the interim is that the Socrates of the *Philebus* claims "always" to have been "enamored" (*erastēs . . . aei*: 16B6) by this "godly method," most features of which cannot be found in any of the Socratic dialogues. To follow this divinely revealed path, he says, we ought always "to assume a single Idea and to inquire into it" (*mian idean . . . themenous zētein*: 16D1–2), and then "laying hold of that, after one to look for two, if two are there, or if not for three or some other number" (*ean oun metalabōmen, meta mian duo, ei pōs eisi, skopein, ei de mē, treis ē tina allon arithmon*: 16D3–4). Then we ought to treat "each of these ones in the same way in turn, until we see that the original one is not merely one or many or indefinite, but also how many it is" (*tōn hen ekeinōn hekaston palin hōsautōs, mechriper an to kat' archas hen mē hoti hen kai polla kai apeira esti monon idē tis, alla kai hoposa*: 16D4–7). And we ought not give up, he continues, until we "recognize the entire number" (*ton arithmon . . . panta katidē*: 16D8) between the one we started with and the "indefinite" (*apeiron*: 16E2) number of things that fall within its scope.

Following the innovations of the *Statesman*, this method thus sanctions division into "three or some other number" if the Form in question cannot naturally be partitioned dichotomously. Once a Form has been divided into two or more parts, moreover, this method calls for further division of each of these newly arrived-at unities in the same manner, resulting in a complete subdivision of all branches opened up along the way. Examples of divisions with fully developed subdivisions appearing later in the dialogue are the exhaustive classification of pleasures between 32B and 53C, and the final classification of human goods at 66A–C.

The only completely novel aspect of the "godly method" is its repeated reference to the *apeiron* ("indefinite" or "unlimited") that figures prominently in the ontology of this later dialogue. The only other dialogue in which *apeiron* plays a role of this magnitude is the *Parmenides* (the second part specifically).[30] The *Parmenides* also marks a major departure in methodology, to which we turn in the following section.

4. A New Method of Hypothesis Prescribed in the Parmenides

The mode of argument recommended and illustrated in the second part of the *Parmenides* is different from the earlier method of hypothesis in a very important respect. It handles necessary and sufficient conditions equally well.

In the first part of this earlier method, we recall, the philosopher traces out the consequences of the hypothesis in question, making sure they involve no contradiction, as well as checking the hypothesis for counterexamples. This part of the method, dealing with *necessary* conditions, seemed reasonably straightforward and manageable in practice. The weak part of the method was in its second phase of going "upward" to seek a *sufficient* condition for the truth of the hypothesis under investigation. It has never been entirely clear what seeking a "satisfactory" higher hypothesis was supposed to mean in the *Phaedo*, or what Plato had in mind in having Socrates talk about a "non-hypothetical first principle" in the *Republic*. It is hard even to imagine what a full illustration of this method might be like, lacking as we do a firm conception of the circumstances that would signify its successful completion.

While the method of collection and division deals with *sufficient* conditions in a reasonably perspicuous fashion, on the other hand, its procedure for arriving at *necessary* conditions involves the inherent obscurity discussed in the preceding section. In order to get the process of inquiry aimed at knowledge of a given Kind under way, the dialectician has to know enough about that Kind already to be able to identify its particular instances. One method is strong where the other is weak. And neither by itself appears to constitute a fully satisfactory procedure of inquiry.

What is remarkable about the new method employed in the *Parmenides*, when viewed against this background, is the way it avoids the difficulties of the other two procedures. The method in question is the one Parmenides recommends to the youthful Socrates at 135E–136C, after observing his style of argument in the first part of that dialogue. The upshot of their conversation up to this point has been that the conception of Forms advocated by Socrates—which shows every sign of being the conception of Forms at work in the *Phaedo* and the *Republic*—appears to be in deep trouble, because of difficulties raised by the elder philosopher that Socrates has been unable to answer. And yet, says Parmenides, if one "does not allow that there are Forms of things" (135B7), and "fails to distinguish a single Form in each case" (135B8–9), nor admits that "each thing has a character that is always the same" (135C1), then "one will have nothing on which to fix one's thought" (135B9). The result of not admitting Forms of this sort would be "completely to destroy the power of discourse" (*tēn tou dialegesthai dunamin pantapasi diaphtherei*: 135C2). It is in order to save philosophy (*philosophias*: 135C5) from this fate that Parmenides recommends a major change in method.

Socrates' problems, says Parmenides, stem from his "having attempted to define Beautiful and Just and Good, and the other Forms severally" (135C8–D1) before being adequately trained. If you are to avoid "the truth eluding you" (135D6), he continues, "you must draw yourself up and exercise yourself" (135D4) strenuously in what most people consider to be "idle talk" (135D5). This exercise[31] should follow the form of argument used earlier by Zeno (cf. 127C–D), but should be extended "to those objects grasped first and foremost by reason" (*malista tis an logō laboi*: 135E3) that we call Forms.

There are several things to be noted before we proceed further with Parmenides' instructions. For one, the problems Socrates has encountered with the Forms in the first part of the dialogue are diagnosed here as being due to a faulty method of inquiry. The early conception of Forms articulated by the character of Socrates in the middle dialogues (the "youthful theory") resulted from attempts to define the Forms without adequate preliminary "training" or "exercise." A more mature conception of the Forms can be attained only by a more severe "exercise" of the sort exhibited by Zeno earlier in the dialogue. A more mature conception of the Forms is very much needed, moreover, for without an adequate basis in the Forms the power of discourse itself will be destroyed. There thus appears to be a mutual dependency between an adequate conception of the Forms and an adequate philosophic method. Socrates needs a better method to define the Forms Beautiful, Just, Good, etc.; yet it is only with an adequate conception of the Forms that the method of dialectic will retain its capacity to lead the philosopher to the truth.

The method Parmenides recommends is an adaptation (to the Forms) of a style of argument already developed by Zeno. We have seen reasons in chapter 2 to believe that Zeno was the originator of the form of argument we know as the "destructive dilemma." What follows next in the dialogue looks very much like an extension of that method, which Plato manages to turn to remarkable philosophic effect.

Here is how the revised method goes. It is not enough, says Parmenides, merely to hypothesize that this or that thing exists and then "to examine the consequences of that hypothesis" (135E9–136A1). If one wishes to be trained through and through (*mallon*: 136A2) one must hypothesize as well that "the same thing does not exist" (*mē esti to auto touto*: 136A1–2).

The historical Socrates was very good at drawing out the consequences of his interlocutors' views, often to the effect of showing them inconsistent. In the earlier version of the method of hypothesis, the consistency of the *logos* initially hypothesized was supposed to be tested before the dialectician moved on to consider whether in fact it is true.

The consistency test amounted to drawing out the consequences of the *logos* in question and examining them for mutual agreement, etc. This first part of the method was concerned with making sure the *logos* met certain *necessary* conditions for truth—i.e., with determining whether it was consistent and hence a candidate for truth. This part of the earlier version is retained, with Parmenides' instruction first to consider the consequences of the hypothesis that this or that thing exists or is the case. But what of the second part of the method dealing with *sufficient* conditions for the truth of the hypothesis once it has been found consistent? It was in this regard that the hypothetical method of the *Phaedo* and the *Republic* appeared to be inapplicable, since it provided no practical guidelines by which the dialectician could arrive at sufficient conditions for the hypotheses under investigation.

What the *Parmenides* provides instead is almost startling in its power and simplicity. Sufficient conditions for the truth of the *logos* under examination are to be determined by hypothesizing the *negation* of the initial hypothesis and by drawing out the consequences of that negative hypothesis in turn. The *denial* of these consequences, by transposition ('not-p implies q' being equivalent to 'not-q implies p'), then gives the sufficient condition of the initial hypothesis. Assuming that the dialectician can circumscribe in some relevant way the consequences of the negative hypothesis, he or she can arrive at a sufficient condition for the truth of a *logos* in a manner no less direct than previously was available for dealing with the necessary conditions. A sufficient condition of p is simply the denial of the consequences of not-p. Both necessary and sufficient conditions now can be explored merely by deducing consequences from appropriately chosen hypotheses.

More detail is added as Parmenides prepares to illustrate this new method of dialectic in the last part of the dialogue. If one were dealing with Zeno's hypothesis that there is a plurality of things, he says, one must consider what consequences "follow both (1) for those many things (a) in relation to themselves and (b) in relation to the one" (*ti . . . sumbainein kai autois tois pollois pros hauta kai pros to hen*: 136A5–6), and also what consequences follow "(2) for the one (a) in relation to itself and (b) in relation to the many" (*tō heni pros te hauto kai pros ta polla*: 136A6–7). Then again, under the hypothesis that there is no plurality, one must consider the "consequences (3) for the one and (4) for the many, in relation both (3a, 4a) to themselves and (3b, 4b) to each other" (*sumbēsetai kai tō heni kai tois pollois kai pros hauta kai pros allēla*: 136A8–B1). A careful reader of the dialogues will note that there are eight distinct stages in the particular investigation Parmenides outlines. More stages might be added depending upon the number of additional alternatives one wishes to consider to the thing whose existence is first assumed and then denied. One might, for example, consider the consequences "in relation to any one thing other" (136C1–2) than the thing in question, "or several of them, or all of them together" (126C2–3). But if only two alternatives in all are considered (e.g., plurality and unity), there are exactly eight distinct stages to go through in applying the method.

This accounts for the fact that there are eight hypotheses examined in Parmenides' illustration beginning at 137C. This illustration, curiously enough, is the mirror-image of the exercise by Zeno to which Parmenides has just alluded in detailing the method. Zeno was said to have dealt with the hypothesis that *plurality* exists and its negation, tracing out the consequences in appropriate respects for plurality and unity. In his own display, Parmenides takes up the hypothesis that *unity* exists and its negation, considering the consequences as necessary for unity and for the many others (the plurality). As I have tried to establish elsewhere,[32] hypothesis I and its following argument deal with consequences for the one relative to itself of the hypothesis that the one exists thus answering to stage (1a) above (interchanging the one and the many others). The corresponding negative hypothesis is VI, answering to stage (4a) (with the same interchange), and dealing with the consequences for the one in relation to itself if it does not exist. Hypotheses II and V produce consequences for the one with respect to the others, if the one is assumed to exist and not to exist, thus answering to stage (1b) and stage (4b) respectively. Hypotheses III and VII, in turn, are examined for consequences for the others with respect to the one, if the one exists—stage (2b)—and does not exist—stage (3b). Hypotheses IV and VIII, finally, generate consequences for the others with respect to themselves, if the one does—stage (2a)—and does not exist—stage (3a).

Apparent as these features of the method are made in the text, they have frequently been overlooked by commentators bent upon trying to make sense of the very difficult second part of this dialogue. This has contributed substantially to the broad disparity of scholarly opinion that has persisted through the centuries about how Parmenides' eight hypotheses and the arguments following them should be interpreted. There is no need for present purposes to go more deeply into this controversy.[33] It will suffice to note one further consequence of the relation between the

first and the sixth hypotheses. The consequences of the first are summarized at 142A. Given that the one in question exists, "it has neither a
name nor an expression" (*Oud' ara onoma estin autō oude logos*: 142A3) by
which it can be spoken of, "nor is there knowledge nor perception nor
judgment" (*oude tis epistēmē oude aisthēsis oude doxa*: 142A3–4) concerning it. But exactly the same set of denials follow from hypothesis VI
(164B1–2), which is the hypothesis that the same one does not exist.
Whether or not this one exists, it has no name, cannot be the subject of
discourse, and can be the object of neither knowledge, perception, nor
judgment. If the arguments leading from I and VI to these conclusions
are *valid* (soundness is not a consideration, because either the affirmative
or the negative hypotheses must be true), it follows *unconditionally*[34] that
the one with which these two hypotheses deal can neither be *reasoned
about* or *known*, along with other dire consequences for what plausibly
may be understood as the exclusive one of the historical Parmenides'
"Way of Truth."[35]

Another result is the derivation of the arithmetical numbers from the
one and from the *apeiron* generated under the second hypothesis, and the
demonstration of how a wide range of characteristics might come to
attach to sensible things once these numbers have been made available.[36] In light of Aristotle's testimony in the *Metaphysics* that the
Pythagoreans thought that number proceeds from the one (986a20–21)
and that numbers provide for the existence of other things (987b24–25),
it is plausible to view this result as an endorsement on Plato's part of this
aspect of traditional Pythagorean ontology. The upshot of these two
results together appears to be a defense of Pythagoreanism against its
Eleatic opponents.

These results are only some among many of similar nature that can be
found in the second part of the *Parmenides*, when this document is
approached through the discipline of the new dialectical method. But
these are enough to show that Plato now is in possession of a method
capable of doing serious philosophic work—one well able to implement
the "power of discourse" with which Parmenides is concerned at 135C2.
The fact that the historical Parmenides apparently has been refuted by
his literary counterpart is one of the striking "ironies" of Plato's late
dialogues.

The method of the *Parmenides* represents an improvement over the
method of collection and division in its manner of dealing with necessary conditions, and an improvement over the method of hypothesis in

its treatment of sufficient conditions as well. Should this be taken as an indication that the method of the *Parmenides* replaced these other two procedures as Plato's preferred method of dialectic? The answer, I believe, is surely negative. One reason has to do with the probable sequence of the dialogues concerned. Although chronological sequence of dialogues from roughly the same period is notoriously difficult to pin down, it seems highly unlikely that the *Parmenides* was written after the *Philebus*—the latest dialogue, presumably, in which the method of collection and division appears.[37] Another reason is that the several methods concerned can be seen, upon careful reflection, to serve different purposes and that each shows at least a moderate degree of success in its appropriate applications.

Although the method of hypothesis indeed seems to fade out of sight at the end of the *Theaetetus*, it is displayed in the *Phaedo* as yielding an apparently worthy account of causation based on the existence of the Forms. And as we shall see in the appendix, it moves Theaetetus and Socrates a considerable distance toward some substantial philosophic results before it gives way to the method of collection and division at the beginning of the *Sophist*. The method of collection and division, in turn, is applied in the *Sophist* to produce definitions of Angling and of Sophistry, and to all appearances these definitions are successful. After several deliberate misapplications in the *Statesman*, moreover, it finally is put to good use in preparing the ground for credible definitions not only of statecraft but also of several other skills needed for a well-functioning state. As far as the method of the *Parmenides* is concerned, in like manner, it may be said at very least to have succeeded in isolating the underlying source of some of the problems with the account of the Forms that came under attack in the first part of that dialogue. By treating Forms as entirely exclusive unities after the manner of the unity of the historical Parmenides, for example, that account was prevented from making sense of the manner in which Forms and sensible things might possess properties in common. The manner in which this shortcoming was demonstrated—combining hypotheses I and VI in a "destructive dilemma" as indicated above—resulted in an implicit criticism of the early notion of participation based on separate Forms that is even more powerful than that of the "third man" arguments at the beginning of the dialogue.[38]

While it seems obvious that these results in the *Parmenides* could not have been produced either by the method of collection and division or by the earlier method of hypothesis, it seems equally evident that the method of the *Parmenides* itself could not have yielded either the account of causation provided in the *Phaedo* or the definition of the sophistic art provided in the *Sophist*. In like fashion, the method of collection and division seems an unlikely source for an account of causation, and the method of hypothesis seems unsuited as a procedure for arriving at definitions. In the final accounting, what we seem to have here is a set of three distinct methods of dialectic, each available to Plato for distinct philosophic purposes. None was more successful than another at the other's tasks, and none was substituted for the others at any point in the corpus. The three methods rather are complementary, in the sense of serving alternative purposes. Each method, because of the purpose it serves, has a distinct contribution to make toward philosophic inquiry generally.

With the distinction among these three methods, we have answered Glaucon's second question regarding the several kinds into which dialectic is divided (*Republic* 532E1). And by tracing out the steps involved in each of these several methods, we have responded to his third question about the ways in which dialectic proceeds (532E2). Glaucon's first question, however, remains unanswered. This question concerns the manner in which dialectic functions (532D8)—i.e., the manner in which these methods lead to philosophic knowledge. The purpose of the following section is to put that question into focus, pending a direct confrontation with the question in chapter 6.

5. Dialectic and the Achievement of Philosophic Knowledge

Each of the methods examined in previous sections consists of procedures for arriving at necessary and sufficient conditions. The method of hypothesis exhibits conditions that are necessary and sufficient for the truth of the *logoi* under consideration. The method of collection and division exhibits conditions that are necessary and sufficient for being a thing of a given Kind. And the method of the *Parmenides*, employing affirmative and negative hypotheses, shows conditions that are necessary and sufficient for a thing's existence (such things as unity, plurality, likeness, unlikeness, etc.: 136A–B). If there is a single mark of dialectic as Plato conceived it, that mark is an emphasis upon conditions that are necessary and sufficient as an avenue toward philosophic understanding.

This emphasis should sound familiar to contemporary analytic philos-ophers. According to a prominent conception of philosophic analysis, being able to articulate conditions that are sufficient and necessary for being a given thing constitutes knowledge of the thing in question. If we were to base our understanding of Plato's use of dialectic on this concep-tion, we would want to say that the results accomplished in the *Sophist* and the *Parmenides* amount in their own right to philosophic knowledge. Plato himself, we might assume, must have gained knowledge of the nature of Sophistry as part of his preparation for writing the dialogue. And we as readers can share this knowledge to the extent that we are capable of grasping his reasoning. Plato's knowledge, accordingly, is expressed in his writings and is communicated to readers who can follow his arguments.

But this is just what Plato denies in the Seventh Letter. As this document states quite explicitly (see chapter 1 above), not only did Plato himself never venture to express his philosophic knowledge in writing, but moreover such knowledge cannot be communicated by means of the perceptible symbols of public language. This is not to say, we should carefully note, that discursive arguments have nothing to do for Plato with the acquisition of philosophic knowledge. The method of the *Phaedo* that begins by hypothesizing *logoi* certainly produces arguments of one sort or another, and this is the method said there to distinguish philosophy from mere eristics. The arguments or *logoi* (286A4) pursued as part of the method in the *Statesman* are aimed at producing "better dialecticians" (*dialektikōterois*: 285D7). And the intricate arguments developed in the second part of the *Parmenides* are certainly essential to the ontological stance Plato seems to be taking in that dialogue. In the Seventh Letter itself, moreover, Plato says that a person must have a *logos* (342B2) of such entities as the Good and the Beautiful in order to arrive at knowledge of the Form itself. From the earliest to the latest of his methodological discussions, Plato's view clearly is that *logos* is essential to philosophic inquiry.

What Plato is denying, rather, is that arguments, reasons, definitions— *logoi* in whatever form we might identify them today—are *by themselves* productive of philosophic knowledge. For Plato at least, a person never gains knowledge of a topic merely by reasoning about it. On the one hand, dealing with *logoi* is an essential part of the dialectician's pro-cedure. On the other, the knowledge at which that procedure is aimed is not accomplished by *logos* alone. Thus we return to a version of

Glaucon's first question: In what manner does dialectic contribute to philosophic knowledge, and what role does *logos* (reason or argument) play in that procedure?

When we speak of collection and division, for example, as a method of dialectic, in what sense of the term 'method' should this be understood? The question is relevant at this point because of our current tendency to think of a method as a well-developed technique for accomplishing a certain end. Like a technique for designing a durable bridge, for instance, if the end is not accomplished (e.g., if the bridge collapses), then something has gone wrong with the way the technique was applied. The analogy of a mathematical algorithm comes to mind: if the results in question are not forthcoming, then either the person applying it gave up prematurely, or the algorithm itself was misapplied. In Plato's case, of course, the term in question is *methodos*. And what is important to note in this connection is that when Plato uses this term in application to dialectic (e.g., at *Republic* 533C9), the sense in question has nothing to do with an algorithmic routine.

The Greek term *methodos* comes from *hodos* (way) plus *meta* (in the sense of "according to"), so that a *methodos* literally is a path or way that one might pursue to a given goal.[39] It is not a routine procedure for cranking out certain results, like the method of long division in arithmetic; nor a process for assessing a thing's characteristics, like the method of analysis used in chemistry and geology; nor even a set of techniques for generating evidence, like the experimental method of modern science. It instead is a route for the dialectician to follow, with certain guideposts along the way.

A point to be stressed in this regard is the distinction between the goal to be reached—philosophic understanding—and the various steps to be taken in pursuit of that goal. The method in question enables one to pursue the goal effectively by pointing out the steps in sequence and by providing indications at crucial junctures of whether the steps are moving in the right direction. But achieving the goal is more than taking certain steps in the manner indicated. For while the path *enables* one to reach the state of understanding desired, it does not *guarantee* achievement merely by taking these steps.

The analogy of a trail to a mountain top might make the point more perspicuous. Following the trail is a way of gaining a view from the pinnacle. But merely following the way does not bring that goal to achievement. One also must exercise certain capacities of vision. It is

entirely possible that someone might climb all the way to the peak
without seeing anything of the surrounding region. (Perhaps one finds
the peak clouded over, or is too frightened to look, or is satisfied merely
to have made the climb and immediately heads downward.) The several
paths of inquiry delineated above, in similar fashion, are ways by which
the aspiring philosopher might be brought into a position where the
Forms are discernible. But the goal of knowing these Forms and their
various modes of relationship is not reached automatically by following
these prescriptions. Not everyone who takes the route will prove capable
of discernment.

This understanding of dialectical method helps make sense of the fact
that dialectic is always portrayed in the dialogues as a joint undertaking
between a master and someone less advanced in philosophy. Plato's term
dialektikē, after all, is a derivative of the verb *dialegomai*, meaning to
converse with another person. And the manner of conversation in
question is one in which the master philosopher directs the steps of the
relative neophyte. Dialectic, that is to say, is a stepwise procedure
through which the learner is guided by an accomplished dialectician.

This conception of dialectic also ties in nicely with the Seventh
Letter, in its emphasis upon the conversation or *sunousia* (341C7)
between teacher and student by which the latter is led to philosophic
insight. One function served by this interaction is to provide the "well-
disposed refutation" (344B6) needed to steer the apprentice away from
false opinion—in the manner of the elenchus in the early dialogues. But
there is more involved in the unbegrudging "question and answer"
(344B6-7) in which the two parties participate than merely the eradica-
tion of false opinion. The student must be guided in the direction of
eventual knowledge. And this guidance must be such not only to help
the student avoid predictable obstacles along the way, but also to help
him or her achieve genuine understanding of the matter at issue by the
time the process has been completed.

Consider the conversation of the *Sophist* by way of example. The
Eleatic Stranger, we may assume, knows what sophistry is already—he
has discussed the subject many times and has not forgotten (217B9).
He is thus prepared to lead a conversation through which Theaetetus
might be brought to a comparable state of knowledge. The style of
discourse he chooses for this purpose is that of question and answer
(217C4); and the method by which the discourse proceeds—that of
division by Kinds—is the procedure later identified as the science of

dialectic (253D3). The sequence of topics in the conversation follows the requirements of this method. Thus they begin with a simple example (*paradeigma*: 218D9) of the type of definition required (that of the Angler), and move on to a collection of particular varieties of sophistry. Having shown production to be a common feature in each of these varieties, the Stranger then begins a division of the productive arts. When the division gets hung up on the problem of making sense of false discourse at 236D, the Stranger responds by leading Theaetetus in an analysis of Being and not-Being, and then on to a definition of true and false *logoi*. They then return to the division at 264D, which continues to the end without further interruption.

But there is more to the method than a sequential ordering of topics. The form of discourse the Stranger has chosen involves posing questions to an interlocutor (217C4), requiring that the latter keep pace with the argument and respond with cogent answers. Thus the Stranger is concerned at 236D that Theaetetus is not agreeing with his perception of the problem of false appearances just "out of habit" (236D6); and Theaetetus responds by expressing his readiness to follow the argument (*logon*: 237B4) wherever it leads him. Thus also the Stranger exhorts Theaetetus at 239B to make his best effort to find an intelligible way of describing not-Being, and encourages him at 261B to take heart in the face of problems with the notion of false discourse. Given the Stranger's purpose of bringing Theaetetus to an articulate awareness of the defining properties of sophistry, to be sure, it is no mean gesture when he declines further argument (*logōn*: 265E1) for the divine origin of the natural world at 265D–E, on the grounds that Theaetetus' nature (*phusin*: 265D8) will come to realize this on its own. The upshot is that the *logos* cited at *Sophist* 218C1 as the goal of the conversation is finally achieved, and that this *logos* is in the possession of Theaetetus personally. The *logos* in which the conversation terminates, that is to say, consists not in the words Plato inscribed in his manuscript, nor in the words we read on the printed page. It consists in Theaetetus' *own* understanding of the nature of sophistry that he has achieved under the Stranger's guidance.[40]

The reason the dialectical methods figuring in Plato's dialogues all involve the question-and-answer format is that philosophic training is not just a matter of leading a student in the desired direction and of putting him or her through certain exercises along the way. No less importantly, it is a matter of shaping the student's progress in a manner consistent with eventual understanding. In a matter of speaking, the master dialectician trains the growth of an able student in much the manner that a master gardener trains a plant growing along a garden wall. The training of a young philosopher is the shaping of a growing soul with the help of the disciplines provided by dialectical procedure.

Our discussion of the function of dialectic is incomplete without a careful consideration of nature of the philosophic understanding at which it is aimed. In terms of the horticultural model adapted from the *Phaedrus*, what we need to undertake next is an examination of the nature of philosophic understanding that constitutes the fruit of dialectical training. This need sets the topic of the following chapter.

6

THE GOOD AND THE BEAUTIFUL: REAPING THE FRUITS

1. The Sun as the Image of the Good

There is a widespread conception among professional philosophers today that philosophy is concerned primarily with philosophic theories and that fulfillment in the enterprise of doing philosophy is a matter of producing theories (typically in written form) that are interesting enough to gain sustained attention from one's colleagues and students. This view of philosophic fulfillment is explicitly rejected by Plato in the Seventh Letter when he says (341C) that philosophic knowledge cannot be expressed discursively like other subjects and that he personally had never ventured to compose any written works in this regard. Fulfillment in the philosophic quest, he says, comes rather with a mental vision that is "generated suddenly in the soul" (341D2), in the manner of a torch ignited by a leaping flame. These and related passages have been examined at length in previous chapters. But we have yet to pursue in any degree of detail the various issues associated with the nature of this mental vision. The purpose of the present chapter is to address the more salient of these issues.

One outstanding problem has to do with the influence of the Good upon the mind of the dialectician. In his comparison of the Good with the sun in Book VI of the *Republic*, Socrates remarks that the Good not only gives truth to the objects of knowledge, but also renders the knower capable of knowing, whereby it is the cause (*aitian*: 508E3) of both truth and knowledge. While the influence of the Good is puzzling in either case, it might be expected that any insight we can gain into one of these roles will help us understand the other as well. A particular task of the discussion below is to gain some sense of how the philosopher's grasp of the Forms might be enabled by the Good.

Another problem concerns the relation between the Form of the Good and the nonhypothetical *archē* of the Divided Line. The primary role assigned to the latter principle in this context is that of supporting a "downward" (*katabainē:* 511B9) inference to conclusions proceeding through Forms alone. Although it is commonly assumed that Plato intended the Good and the nonhypothetical *archē* to be identical, however, it is not at all clear how the Form of the Good could serve as the basis—nonhypothetical or otherwise—of any form of logical inference. At the same time, it is equally unclear how the nonhypothetical *archē* could render the mind of the philosopher capable of knowledge. These considerations are examined in detail below, as part of an argument that the Good and the nonhypothetical *archē* are in fact entirely different principles.

Yet another problem is the relation between the Good and the Beautiful. Even though both the *Republic* and the *Symposium* contain several passages in which these two superlative entities seem to be treated as one and the same, it is hard to understand how the Beautiful of the *Symposium* could so much as begin to fill the august role of the Good in the *Republic*. The relation between these two Forms is further complicated by the discussion of the Good in the *Philebus*, terminating with the remark that the Good is a unique combination of Truth, Beauty, and Proportion. A further goal of the chapter is to put together a coherent picture of what Plato had to say about the Good in these three different dialogues.

Since all of these problems involve the Form of the Good, our first task must be to pin down as best we can the role played by this principle in its several contexts. Let us begin by recapitulating the line of discussion that leads to Plato's comparison of the Good with the sun toward the end of Book VI in the *Republic*.

Responding to the challenge by Glaucon at the beginning of Book II to show that justice is a good we welcome for its own sake alone, as well as for its advantageous consequences, Socrates has adopted the strategy (368E ff.) of studying justice first in the large-scale model of the state and then applying the results by analogy to the individual soul. The state has been portrayed as composed of a commercial class, a class of soldiers or "auxiliaries," and a class of counselors or "guardians proper," corresponding to the appetitive, the spirited, and the rational parts of the soul respectively; and justice has been defined, on the levels of the state and of the soul alike, as a manner of organization in which each part serves its own proper function (441D). When the rational element rules wisely, when the spirited element defends courageously, and when all three elements work together in harmony and temperance, then justice prevails within the polity overall. And when temperance, courage, and wisdom reign in justice within the individual person, the result is a "kind of health and beauty and vigor of the soul" (444D13–E1) which, like bodily well-being, is desirable as an end in itself.

In Book V, Socrates has confronted three "waves of paradox" (cf. 472A), dealing with the equality of men and women in the polis, the abolition of the family unit, and the need for philosophers to serve as kings in the well-ordered state. Philosophers were characterized as "those who love the sight of truth" (475E5) and who are capable of knowing "the Good and the Bad and all such Forms" (476A5–6). Particular stress was put on the ability of philosophers to see or discern[1] Beauty itself, in a manner yielding knowledge as distinct from mere opinion.

Book VI begins with a list of character-traits that mark a person as suitable for philosophic training, including good memory, quick apprehension, magnanimity, graciousness, and both "friendship and kinship" (487A4–5) with truth, justice, courage and temperance. Discussion of the topic of philosophic education gets underway at 504B with the admonition that what Socrates will have to say on the matter can be no more exact than his preceding account of justice in the soul.[2] In order to gain a really clear view of such things, he warns, one would have to take the "longer way about" (504B3) described earlier as not only more lengthy but "more laborious" (435D4). The goal of this "longer way," Socrates says, is a knowledge of the Good itself, without which no other knowledge would be of any value (505A6–7). The reason given for this dependency is that reference to the Idea of the Good renders justice and such things advantageous and useful (505A5). Since Socrates and his present company are incapable of the longer path, however, their discussion cannot aspire to the nature of the Good itself (506D8). What Socrates offers instead is a series of evocative images, beginning with the Sun[3] providing an analogy for the Good.

Here is how the analogy is introduced. What he is capable of speaking of instead, says Socrates, is "the offspring of the Good" (506E3)—namely the visible sun, which the Good begot to stand in proportion (*analogon*: 508C1) to itself. What the Good is in the intelligible domain "to intelligence and its objects" (508C2–3), he continues, the sun is in the visible domain "to sight and the objects of vision" (508C3–4). This proportionality between the sun and the Good is then spelled out in several specific respects.

For one, the sun provides for the generation (*genesin*: 509B3) of visible things and also brings them "growth and nurture" (509B4). Analogously, objects of knowledge (509B6) receive "existence and being" (*to einai te kai tēn ousian*: 509B7–8) from the Good. But as the sun "itself is not generation" (209B4), so "the Good is not the same as being" (509B8–9) but rather exceeds being "in dignity and power" (509B9–10). For another respect, just as the sun "provides their capacity for being seen" (509B2–3) to the objects of vision, so objects of knowledge receive their power of being known (*gignōskesthai*: 509B6) from the Good. A similar parallelism holds for the faculties of vision and knowing. Just as the Good renders "the power of knowing" (508E2) to the mind, so the sun analogously is the cause (*aitios*: 508B9) of vision in the eye. And as sight is the most sunlike (*hēlioeidē*: 509A2) of the faculties of sense, so the faculty of knowledge is like the Good itself (*agathoeidē*: 509A3).

In what sense is the faculty of vision sunlike, and how might the faculty of knowledge be like the Good? An indication of what stands behind this pair of comparisons comes at 508B, where Socrates first refers to the eye as especially sunlike (*hēlioeidestaton*: 508B3) and elaborates by remarking that it receives its power through an infusion dispersed from the sun. This mention of an infusion received from the sun brings to bear the conception of vision found in the *Timaeus*, according to which the eye emits a stream of "pure fire" (*pur eilikrines*: 45B7) which coalesces, in light of day, with a corresponding stream of fire emitted from the object of vision (described in some detail at 67C ff.) The importance of daylight for this intermingling of fluxes is made evident at 45D, where Timaeus describes how the stream of vision is shut off by encountering an element unlike itself—i.e., the nighttime air, which lacks the fire that sustains vision by the light of day.[4] The general idea seems to be that the sun not only provides the sole medium in which fire from the eye can coalesce with fire from the visible object, but also is the source of the "inner fire" by which the eye is enabled to see in the first place. In order to gain full advantage of the analogy between the sun and the Good, accordingly, we will have to make out some sense in which the Good not only empowers the faculty of knowledge but also provides a context or "medium" in which the mind can "intermingle" with its appropriate objects. As matters stand, however, there is an apparent gap in the analogy with respect to the medium through which this enabling effect is accomplished. Whereas light is explicitly identified as a bond or yoke (*zugō*: 508A1) that links together "the faculty of sight" (507E7) and "the power of being visible" (507E7), there is no unequivocal mention in the text of a corresponding medium linking the faculty of knowing with the capacity for being known.[5] Although this apparent disanalogy may be due to inadvertence on Plato's part, there is reason to believe that it was probably intentional. We shall return to this topic as part of the discussion of the nature of the Good in section 3 below.

A fourth point of comparison between the sun and the Good that seems entirely straightforward is that each can be apprehended by the faculty it energizes. While the sun is the cause (*aitios*: 508B9) of vision, it is also seen by the very vision it causes. Similarly, while the Good is the "cause of knowledge" (*aitian d' epistēmēs*: 508E3)—standing behind "the power of knowing" (508E2) as it does—we read in a later passage that the Good also can be "grasped by thought itself" (532B1). As we learn further from the discussions of the Line and Cave, however, neither the sun nor the Good it symbolizes can be apprehended easily or without preparation. Only after beginning with shadows and objects illuminated by the sun and then moving on to the moon and stars at nighttime will the viewer finally be able to look upon the sun and "to contemplate what it is" (516B6–7) in itself. In a comparable manner, the dialectician is able to apprehend the Good only when reaching "the final goal of the intelligible" (532B2), parallel to "the goal of the visible" (532B3) finally reached in the ascent from the depths of the cave.

A fifth point of comparison, accordingly, is that the sun and the Good alike can be apprehended only through a stagewise progression involving care and discipline as well as orderly sequence. A figurative account of the ascent to a vision of the sun is provided in the allegory of the Cave. The corresponding account of the ascent to the Good, it appears, takes the form of the mathematical symbolism of the Divided Line. So it appears, at least, if we can assume a sufficiently close relation between the Good and the nonhypothetical *archē* in which the latter ascent culminates. While our examination of the relation between these two superlative principles must wait for the following section, the relevant characteristics of the Line itself have already been discussed in chapter 5. Let us therefore turn directly to a consideration of the imagery of the Cave.

Plato's allegory of the Cave is perhaps the most widely recognized feature of his entire written corpus and has attracted commentary of an extent that would be literally impossible to document. Even beginning readers of Plato are likely to have a vivid impression of the setting in mind, making it superfluous to recount more of the story than bears directly upon our present interests. One thing about the Cave that is easy to overlook, however, is that it is an extension of the analogy of the Good with the sun and that accordingly it should be interpreted with that previous image in mind. Although the Cave comes directly after the Line in textual sequence, it is only in the context of this initial analogy that the relation between the Line and the Cave can be adequately appreciated.[6]

There is one respect in which the imagery of the Cave constitutes an obvious improvement over that of the Line as an elucidation of the analogy between the Good and the sun. Although the Line is explicitly introduced at 509C as an elaboration of this analogy, neither the sun nor the Good is assigned an explicit place within its symbolism. Insofar as the sun itself is visible, it might be thought of as fitting indiscriminately along with other visible objects into level B of the Line.[7] But the sun is importantly unlike other visible objects, being the source of their generation and of their being visible in the first place, and it seems inappropriate to lump the cause of visibility along with the objects it renders visible. In like fashion, insofar as the Good itself is a Form, it could find a place with the other intelligible objects on level D. But the Good not only is intelligible itself, but is the cause of the intelligibility of the other Forms. So it seems likewise inappropriate to relegate it indiscriminately to the upper level of the Line. A more appropriate diagrammatic representation would provide a location for these entities that indicates their superiority within their respective domains while at the same time showing the dependency of the sun upon the Good.[8] Inasmuch as no such expedient is provided by the mathematics of the Line as it stands, this image remains incomplete in its representation of the ontological relations involved.

The allegory of the Cave repairs this deficiency by integrating the symbolism of the Sun and the Line into one comprehensive system of images. Within the cave itself there is the fire projecting shadows upon the wall facing the prisoners of the various artifacts being carried along the parapet behind them. As 517B makes explicit, the artificial figures represent the visible objects on level B of the Line, while their shadows are the reflections of level A. The fire that projects these shadows, in turn, represents the sun as it figures in the earlier analogy. Insofar as the artificial forms of men and animals presumably would be fashioned with the help of metal tools, there is a clear sense in which fire (in the blacksmith's forge) would be the cause of their coming into being. Within the confines of the cave proper, accordingly, the fire—like the sun in the earlier image—is the source both of the visibility of objects seen and of the eye's capacity to see these objects. As the prisoner finds upon being released from his bonds, moreover, the fire itself is capable of being seen, although not without pain to the eyes initially (515E2). While including every major feature of the two previous images in this regard, the image of the Cave thus makes clear that the fire—and the sun it symbolizes—is distinct from other visible objects in power and position.

In the world outside the cave, similarly, there is the sun projecting shadows on one or another surface of human beings and other three-dimensional objects. As in the initial analogy of the series, the sun here is a symbol of the Form of the Good. But the symbolism of the upper world extends beyond that of the sun itself. The former prisoner's ascent to this upper world, Socrates points out at 517B, stands for "the soul's upward journey into the intelligible region" (517B5)—i.e., into the region symbolized by levels C and D together of the Divided Line (509D2). A consequence is that we are not only to treat the sun as a symbol of the Good but moreover are to think of the solid objects in this domain and the shadows they cast as corresponding to the contents of the upper two levels of that earlier image. Within the image-system of the allegory, that is to say, the sun represents the Good, the human figures and other three-dimensional objects represent the Forms, and the shadows of these objects represent the entities studied by mathematics.[9] In other respects, the imagery of the Sun-analogy remains intact. As the sun is the cause of the generation of visible objects, so the Good is the cause of the being of the Forms; as the sun is the source of visibility and vision, so the Good is the source of intelligibility and intelligence, etc. Although the sun itself is visible as well—albeit not easily (516B)—it is clearly distinguished from other visible objects as the source of the light by which they are made visible. And so it is, *mutatis mutandis*, with the Good itself. The allegory of the Cave thus not only includes most of the important symbolism of its two preceding images,[10] but indicates clearly as well how these earlier images are to be related.

Another notable aspect of the relation between the Line and the Cave is that the multileveled imagery of the latter fits entirely within the lower two levels of the Line itself. In something akin to the manner in which the series of natural numbers can be projected onto a subseries of itself, the imagery of the Cave projects the entire Line (A + B + C + D) onto its visible subsection (A + B). The effect, as already noted, is that the underground cave itself comes to represent lower levels A and B of the Line, while the visible outer world is made to represent the upper levels C and D. Within the context of the allegory of the Cave, accordingly, the imagery of the Divided Line becomes even more complex. Not only is the Line a (i) mathematical image of a system of increasingly abstract (ii) imaging relationships, all of which serves the author's purpose as a (iii) literary image, but now we see further that it has (iv) self-imaging capacities as well, insofar as the entire Line can be mirrored into a subset of itself.[11] By collapsing the Line upon itself in this fashion, Plato is able to show not only how the sun fits into its visible section as the entity uniquely responsible for there being a visible realm in the first place, but also how the Good occupies a parallel role in the domain of the intelligible. It is nothing short of remarkable that a projection of the entire Line upon itself can be used in this fashion to produce a set of images substantially richer than the original Line itself.

There is one notable respect, nonetheless, in which the parallelism between the Cave and the Line might be misleading. In the discussion of the Line, we hear that the dialectician moves upward in the domain of the intelligible to a nonhypothetical *archē*. In the story of the Cave, the freed prisoner moves upward until he reaches the world outside, where eventually he arrives at a vision of the sun. But in each case, there is movement in the other direction as well. Having reached the first principle, the dialectician turns around and descends (*katabainē*: 511B9) to its conclusions. Likewise, having achieved his vision of the sun (equivalently, of the Good) the former prisoner goes back down (*katabas*: 516E4) into the cave to inform the inhabitants of what might be found above. But the return of the sometime prisoner to the cave seems quite disparate from the downward movement of the dialectician.[12] If the standard interpretation of the dialectician's downward turn is anywhere near correct, this exercise has something to do with drawing conclusions by reason from the self-supporting *archē*. The return journey of the liberated prisoner, however, is not a matter of reasoning, but clearly a matter of politics instead. In developing his story about the aftermath of the vision of the Good in this later image, Plato is concerned with the vicissitudes of philosophy in the public arena, rather than with the establishment of a body of knowledge free from unexamined supposition.

If one views the Cave primarily as an extension of the Divided Line, this lack of parallelism might be taken to indicate a deeply seated problem of some sort in Plato's conception of the philosopher.[13] In a proper conception of these images, however, both the Line and the Cave are extensions of the analogy of the Sun instead, and each is addressed to its own set of issues. With this proper relation among the images firmly in view, no tension appears in the divergent orientations of the Line and the Cave. For a problem of this sort to threaten in the first place, moreover, we must assume that the nonhypothetical *archē* of the Line and the Good of the other two images were intended by Plato to be equivalent entities. And this assumption is one that should not be made incautiously. Before pursuing these matters further, let us look more carefully at the relation between these two superlative principles.

2. Why the Good Is Not the Same as the Nonhypothetical archē

Although commentators commonly take for granted that the Good as it figures in the Sun and the Cave is identical with the nonhypothetical *archē* of the Divided Line,[14] formidable difficulties appear when this assumption is examined critically. One obvious problem is that it lacks clear support by anything said in the text. While there are several passages in both the *Republic* and the *Symposium* suggesting a direct link between the Good and the Beautiful (a matter for detailed consideration below), Socrates more than once alludes to the Good and to the non-hypothetical *archē* in neighboring passages with no indication that these entities are even related.

One might argue, to be sure, that the relation between them is supposed to be obvious, inasmuch as Plato would not have introduced *two* such basic principles at this point in the dialogue without intending the reader to think of them as identical. The fact that nothing is said about how they are related, in effect, might be interpreted as implicit evidence that the two entities in question are one and the same. Quite apart from its highly speculative character, however, an argument for identity along such lines is far from convincing. Inasmuch as the two entities play quite different roles in their respective contexts, indeed, it is not clear that an identification of the Good with the nonhypothetical *archē* even makes sense.

Let us recall the respective roles of these principles in general outline. As characterized in comparison with the sun, the Good is the source of the "existence and being" of the Ideas, as well as of their power of being known. The Good also provides the mind its "power of knowing"—not actual knowledge, we have noted, but the capacity to know, analogous to the sun's providing the eye its capacity for vision. In the context of the Divided Line, on the other hand, the nonhypothetical *archē* stands in contrast to the hypotheses of mathematics. While the mathematicians leave their hypotheses unexamined and take them to be obvious, the dialectician treats such hypotheses as "stepping-stones and spring-boards" along the way to a nonhypothetical starting place. The starting place at which the dialectician finally arrives, if successful, is "the first principle of everything" (*epi tēn tou pantos archēn:* 511B7), which sustains "dependencies" (*echomenōn:* 511B8) or "implications"[15] to be traced out in the further development of dialectical knowledge. In short, the nonhypothetical *archē* is a principle with a distinctive role to play in the generation of knowledge, and in its immediate context serves primarily to distinguish the methods of mathematics from those of dialectic.

Although the respective roles played by these two entities may not be strictly incommensurable, they certainly do not appear to be inter-changeable. Difficult as it may be in itself to conceive how the Good might be the ontological source of the "existence and being" of the Ideas, it seems next to unintelligible to attribute that ontological role to an apparently *epistemological* principle like the nonhypothetical *archē*. In like fashion, there is no immediately evident sense in which a principle of this sort—nonhypothetical or otherwise—could be thought either to make the Ideas knowable or to render the mind capable of knowing them. While there may be some intelligible respect in which the dialectician's first principle could enable the mind *actually* to know the Ideas, this is quite a different matter from making the Ideas *knowable* (i.e., giving the Ideas this property) and making the mind capable of *knowing* them (i.e., giving the mind this capacity).

By reverse token, it is not at all clear how an ontological principle like that characterized in the analogy of the Sun could serve in the epis-temological role called for in the context of the Divided Line. For one thing, the Good is a Form—a "super Form" to be sure, but a Form nonetheless. And there is no clear sense in which a Form by itself might sustain implications of the sort involved in the dialectical production of knowledge described at 511B–C. There is also the problem of how the

Good could be involved in any kind of dialectical inference in the first place. Given our tendency today to think of inference as a matter of manipulating formal symbols, at any rate, a principle sustaining implications of the sort with which the dialectician is concerned would reasonably be presumed to have an overtly symbolic status. Inasmuch as the Good is said explicitly in the Seventh Letter to be beyond representation in any kind of sensible symbols, this would seem to make it unavailable for service in inference generally.

While considerations such as these strongly suggest that the Good and the nonhypothetical *archē* are not identical principles, however, they contribute little to our understanding of the nature of these principles themselves. And we are going to have to understand something of the nature of these principles in order to understand how, if at all, Plato intended them to be related. Let us begin with the nonhypothetical *archē*, saving the Good for the following section.

One obstacle to a proper understanding of what Plato meant by the expression *archē anhupotheton*, it may well be, is the ready assumption that any principle that could play the role indicated at 510B and 511B must have the form of a logical *premise*.[16] While both mathematician and dialectician reason from premises, we tend to read these passages as saying, the premises concerned have different statuses. The premises of mathematics remain hypothetical, while the basic premises of dialectic somehow transcend hypothesis—having the alleged status perhaps of Descartes' *cogito ergo sum* or of Kant's synthetic *a priori* judgments. We tend to assume, in brief, that the nonhypothetical *archē* of the Divided Line is some kind of "super proposition," thought by Plato to be capable of establishing mathematics and the other sciences on an unimpeachable logical basis.[17]

One thing to note at the outset in this regard is that if the term *archē* at 510B and 511B was intended to convey the sense of "logical premise," then this would be one of very few contexts in Plato's writing where the term carries that meaning.[18] Apart from *Republic* 533C, which recapitulates these earlier passages, the only other use of the term that suggests such a reading occurs in the second statement of the method of hypothesis at *Phaedo* 101E, where Socrates warns against mixing up "the principle and its consequences" (*tēs archēs . . . kai tōn ex ekeinēs hōrmēmenōn:* 101E2–3). Since the *archē* in question is clearly the hypothesis with which the method begins, to be sure, it is not implausible to think of this use of the term in the *Phaedo* as a precedent for a similar reading in the context of the Divided Line, where a more sophisticated version of the same method is being discussed.

The major problem with this reading of *archē* in either of the passages indicated, however, is that it is not supported by the examples Plato chooses to illustrate the methodological descriptions in question. For all the talk about the laying down of *logoi* and agreement among hypotheses that we find at *Phaedo* 100A and 101D, the illustration Socrates actually offers of this kind of reasoning involves what he calls his "well known way of beginning" (100B4) in such matters—namely, by "hypothesizing the existence" of such entities as Beauty and the Good themselves (100B5), and so forth. As far as this particular illustration goes, at least, what is hypothesized as part of the method in question are not logical premises from which certain conclusions are deduced but rather the Forms themselves that stand behind the reasoning.

In the context of the Divided Line, even more distinctly, the hypotheses that the mathematician is said to leave unexamined are not axioms or postulates or other propositional entities. The hypotheses in question rather are "the odd and the even, and various figures, and three kinds of angle" (510C4–5), and similar things. Because of our deep-seated understanding of mathematics as employing an axiomatic method, we find it natural to read this passage as referring to the postulation of axioms *about* the odd and the even, *about* various geometrical figures, and so forth. But this is not what the passage says. What the arithmeticians and geometers "lay down" (*hupothemenoi*: 510C4) as a beginning, according to this description, are not propositions of some sort about their subject matter but rather the odd and the even themselves, the three kinds of angles, and various similar things about which they then proceed to reason. What mathematicians hypothesize, in short, are not propositions about their subject matter but their subject matter itself. This is what they take "as known" (*hōs eidotes*: 510C6), what they consider "as clear to everyone" (*hos panti phanerōn*: 510C8), and what they characteristically consider not to need an account (*logon*: 510C7).

The basic difference between the mathematician and the dialectician in this respect, of course, is that the latter treats such hypotheses "not as first principles, but just as hypotheses" (*ouk archas, alla tō onti hupotheseis*: 511B5). For the dialectician these hypotheses serve instead as "stepping-stones and springboards" (511B6) from which to rise to the nonhypothetical *archē*. The contrast intended here between mathematics and dialectic surely is not a matter of the former being satisfied by laying

down its *subject matter*—the odd and the even, the various angles, etc.—
as known, whereas the latter proceeds to some kind of super *premise* that
has unconditional status. The contrast lies in the mathematician treating as known what is merely hypothetical, whereas the dialectician seeks
to ground what is hypothesized by the mathematician in an *archē* that is
not hypothetical. What the dialectician seeks, in brief, is a starting point
which relieves the subject matter of mathematics of its hypothetical
character. And whatever this might amount to, it seems to have no
direct involvement with axioms or premises that have some special
propositional status.

But if the nonhypothetical *archē* of the *Republic* is not some sort of
"super proposition," then what is it? The answer I want to put forward is
found at 531D, when Socrates returns to the topic of dialectic as the
capstone of his curriculum for the Guardians. Having completed his
discussion of the several branches of mathematics and of the parts they
should play in the education of the Guardians, Socrates introduces his
remarks on dialectic with the following observation. All of the studies
we have been considering, he says, will have the desired effect only if
they carry us to the point of realizing "their kinship and community with
one another" (*tēn allēlōn koinōnian . . . kai xungeneian*: 531D1–2), and
"bring together in our minds their mutual relationships" (*xullogisthē tauta
hē estin allēlois oikeia*: 531D2–3). Glaucon immediately observes that
seeing the various subject matters of mathematics as interconnected in
this way is a large undertaking that goes beyond mathematics itself; and
Socrates confirms that it is the task of dialectic instead. With regard to
the topics of mathematics at least, the business of dialectic is served by
an investigation of the *interrelations* among the odd and the even, the
three angles, the various kinds of figures, and so forth. Instead of taking
these entities as simply given, which is characteristic of mathematical
method, dialectic seeks to bring them together in a synoptic vision that
displays their kinships and interconnections in the nature of things.

This theme of the comprehensive view of dialectic is pursued further
in the final pages of Book VII, where Socrates sums up by saying that the
"disorganized studies" (*chudēn mathēmata*: 537C1) in the early stages of
the curriculum must be brought together "in a synoptic view of their
connections with one another" (*eis sunopsin oikeiotētos allēlōn*: 537C2)
and their connections also with "the nature of reality" (*tēs tou ontos
phuseōs*: 537C3). Whereas at 531C–D it was left unclear whether the
comprehensive vision of dialectic was to extend beyond the subject

matters of the mathematical disciplines themselves, here at 537C the dialectician-to-be is made responsible for seeing the relationships among the various studies and reality itself. Socrates then concludes his discussion of dialectic with the summary remark that dialectic just *is* the ability to see things as interconnected—specifically, that "someone capable of seeing the whole together is a dialectician" (*hō men gar sunoptikos dialektikos:* 537C7)[19] and "otherwise not" (*hō de mē ou:* 537C7).

In the context of the Divided Line, dialectic is characterized as a discipline that makes no use of images and that proceeds upwards from hypotheses to a nonhypothetical starting point. At the opening of his more detailed discussion of dialectic's role in the curriculum for the Guardians, Socrates observes that the aim of dialectic is pursued by investigating the interconnections among the various subject matters of mathematics. The person who seeks the nonhypothetical *archē*, in effect, is also the person who aims at seeing such interconnections. And in summing up the curriculum, Socrates says in so many words that the dialectician is none other than the person capable of seeing how things fit together. Once again, the person capable of grasping the nonhypothetical *archē* is just the person capable of this synoptic vision. The sense of these several passages together is that the *archē* or starting point at which dialectic aims in some manner provides the basis for the mental vision in question.

The conclusion I draw from these considerations is that the nonhypothetical *archē* of dialectic is none other than the interconnected field of eternal Forms—i.e., the totality of Forms in their natural relationships. What this amounts to in detail, presumably, is more than anyone save perhaps Plato himself (or one of his fully seasoned Guardians) would be prepared to say, and Plato gives clear notice in the Seventh Letter that he never would attempt to say himself. As a rough estimate, however, we might expect to find included within the *archē* interconnections like that between the Form Odd and the odd numbers cited at *Phaedo* 104A, and like the relations among Forms and the various figures and angles required to do geometry in the manner of *Republic* 511B. Moving beyond the subject matter of mathematics to that of dialectic proper, we would also find the interdependencies that enable the downward movement "through Forms from one to another" mentioned at 511C1, which may well include relations like those among Existence, Motion, and Rest explored in the *Sophist*. In general, the interconnections in question must include the relations of consonance and incompatibility discussed in connection with the dialectician's "voyage of discourse" (*Sophist* 253B11)—the very "blending of Forms" (259E5–6) said subsequently to bring discourse into being.

If this view of the matter is correct, indeed, then the field of blending Forms upon which discourse is said to depend in this passage from the *Sophist* is just the nonhypothetical *archē* at which dialectic is said to aim in the *Republic*. Viewed in this light, these key passages from the *Sophist* call to mind the oft neglected passage in the *Meno* accompanying the initial articulation of the notion of *anamnēsis*. Inasmuch as "all nature is alike in kind" (*tēs phuseōs hapasēs sungenous ousēs*: 81D1),[20] Socrates there observed, when the soul "recollects a single thing, nothing prevents it from discovering all the rest" (*ouden kōluei hen monon anamnēsthenta . . . talla panta auton aneurein*: 81D2–3) if only it shows perseverance. Although Plato's views about the preconditions of knowledge have changed during the interval between these two dialogues, his sense of the interconnectedness of reality has remained basically the same. All existence by nature is interrelated, and philosophic knowledge is obtained by tracing out its interrelationships.

Yet another context to recall in this regard is the description of dialectic following the palinode in the *Phaedrus*, where the dialectician is identified as someone capable of "dividing according to Forms," following their "natural articulation" (265E1–2). This is parallel to the remark at *Sophist* 257A9 that "the Kinds are of a nature to share with one another" (*echei koinōnian allēlois hē tōn genōn phusis*). Other passages stressing natural relations among the Forms are *Statesman* 262B–E, *Philebus* 17D as well as 18C–D, and of course *Sophist* 256E ff. In each of these passages Plato is talking about the knowledge of dialectic or philosophy, and in each case this knowledge is to be achieved by discerning some Form or set of Forms in its natural setting within the field of related Forms. Although the method of division figuring in these later contexts differs significantly from the method dominating the discussion of the Divided Line (see chapter 5), whatever the particulars of the dialectical procedures involved it seems reasonably clear that the *epistēmē* or knowledge represented by the top section of the Divided Line comes when "the vision of the soul" (519B3, also 533D2 and 540A7) is directed toward relevant sectors of the interconnected field of Forms.

The sense in which an interconnected field of being like this could serve as an *archē* for dialectic is reasonably perspicuous. But in what sense might it be considered nonhypothetical? As used in the context of the

Divided Line, the term *hupothesis* means a supposition laid down as a basis for rational inquiry. Thus the mathematicians posit the various kinds of figures, for example, as a basis for reasoning about the properties of figures. In what manner might the *archē* of dialectic avoid postulation of this sort?

As noted repeatedly in the course of this study, the knowledge of the philosopher or dialectician was conceived by Plato as a manner of mental vision.[21] The language of mental vision figures explicitly in the discussions of dialectic in both the *Sophist* (254A10) and the *Republic* (533D2, 540A7). And as already noted, the dialectician is characterized expressly at *Republic* 537C7 as someone capable of viewing the interconnections among things. What we should be looking for at this point, accordingly, is a sense in which the mind might avoid supposition in its view of reality. Helpful analogies may be found in Gestalt psychology. When we see a pedestrian enter a tunnel to pass beneath a busy street and then emerge from the opposite side a few moments later, we *surmise* that the person has walked the distance in between. But we do not actually observe the passage from entry to exit. Our commonplace perception of the pedestrian's passage from one side to the other thus involves hypothesis as well as actual observation; we augment what we actually see by supposition about what happened while the pedestrian is hidden from view. In order to avoid hypothesis in this manner, we would have to accompany the person through the tunnel ourselves, or at least take up a vantage point from which the passage could be viewed without interruption. Another relevant perceptual situation is when we see one common object located behind another in such a fashion that the former is partially blocked from view. The lower portion of my copy of the *Theaetetus*, for example, is currently obscured by a copy of the *Republic* resting upon it. Although it would be perfectly in order to say that I see the copy of the *Theaetetus* on the desk before me, I only surmise that the portion currently blocked from view is there on my desk with the rest of the book. A presentation of these objects that was nonhypothetical in the relevant sense would enable me to see the book in its entirety without need for conjecture.

One way of describing perceptual situations like these is to say we "complete" our view of the object in question by fleshing out missing portions by an activity of imagination. Thus, for example, we do not actually see the pedestrian moving through the underpass but rather imagine the passage between entry and exit by way of providing continuity between visible sequences of motion. In such cases, our imagination gives form to the hypotheses we find ourselves positing in order to bring coherence to the experience overall. This description of hypothesis as a sort of mental imagery should bring to mind the characterization of the method of hypothesis at *Phaedo* 99D ff. In order not to "blind his soul" (99E2), said Socrates, he adopted a way of proceeding that involved hypothesizing the *logos* he judged strongest and on that basis set about trying to look for the truth of things. While disclaiming its uniqueness in this respect, Socrates remarks explicitly that a feature of this procedure is its employment of images (*eikosi*: 100A2). The hazard against which he is guarding, presumably, is a direct (hence potentially "blinding") mental view of the Forms themselves, in which no imagination—i.e., no surmise—is involved whatever.

The sense in which Socrates' approach to the Forms through *logos* is hypothetical, in brief, is that the apprehension it offers of its intended objects to some extent relies upon supposition. In like fashion, the procedures of mathematics in the context of the Divided Line are hypothetical in the sense that they provide a grasp of their subject matter in a manner that falls short of full comprehension. The sense in which the *archē* of dialectic is nonhypothetical, by contrast, is that nothing is left to the mind's surmise when the field of Forms is finally grasped in its full interconnectedness. What the absence of hypotheses in this case amounts to is not a matter of propositional entities, like axioms and postulates, but has to do rather with the unrestricted completeness of the field of view that the dialectician achieves when the *archē* is reached.

If this characterization of the nonhypothetical *archē* is generally on target, then there is yet a further reason why this principle cannot be identical to the Good itself. Insofar as the field of Forms consists of individual entities that owe their status (their "existence and being": 509B7–8) to the Form of the Good, the very field of being that constitutes the dialectician's nonhypothetical *archē* is dependent for what it is upon this highest of Forms. Since the Good surely is not dependent in this particular fashion upon itself, this in itself is enough to show that the two principles in question are not identical.

3. The Nature of the Good

Although the Form of the Good is explicitly mentioned as early as 476A in the *Republic*, the unique role of this particular principle becomes evident only at 505A, when Socrates identifies it as that by which things that are just and otherwise virtuous "come to be useful and beneficial" (505A4). What Socrates says immediately thereafter is that "we have no adequate knowledge of it" (*autēn ouch hikanōs ismen:* 505A5–6), a disclaimer vigorously repeated in the first person at 506D7–8. But if Socrates (as Plato represents him) did not know the nature of the Good, there appears to be little hope in that regard for the present-day commentator. Given what the Seventh Letter says about the incommunicability of philosophic understanding, moreover, even if someone at some point *were* to gain knowledge of the Good, there is no chance of this knowledge being conveyed in either speech or writing. Plato himself did not try; nor should any other sober author.

Nonetheless, it may still be possible to say something useful about what the Good must be like in order to play its assigned roles in Books VI and VII of the *Republic*. Of particular concern are the several features of the Good stressed in the analogy of the Sun. What might it be for the Good to be (1) the cause of the "power of knowing" (508E2) on the one hand, and (2) the cause of the "capacity for being known " (509B6) on the other? And what might it mean for the objects of knowledge (3) to receive their "existence and being" (509B7–8) from the Form of the Good? A further desideratum is to come to terms with the remark at 505A that (4) it is with reference to the Good that just things and the like come to be useful and beneficial. These four features impose a basic requirement of intelligibility for the success of any attempt to make sense of the Good.

One of the more persistent attempts in recent years is an illuminating study by Gerasimos Santas.[22] Santas' treatment of feature (4) is relatively straightforward.[23] Inasmuch as all action is undertaken for the sake of the Good, as Socrates observes at 505E1–2, the usefulness or beneficialness of any action in promoting its purpose (including actions that are just or otherwise virtuous) can be grasped only with reference to that Form itself. His account of features (2) and (3), however, is rather more complicated, and relies upon a distinction between ideal and proper attributes pertaining to the Forms themselves. An *ideal* attribute is one belonging to a Form by virtue merely of being a Form, without regard to the specific Form it is—e.g., its changelessness and eternal existence. A *proper* attribute is one that belongs to a Form because of the specific Form it is and hence distinguishes it from other Forms—e.g., the beauty of the Form Beauty and the circularity of the Form Circle.[24] In Santas' way of thinking, the Forms other than the Good owe their ideal attributes to participation[25] in the Good. It is because of their ideal attributes (being always what they are, and in no way otherwise, etc.), moreover, that the Forms other than the Good "are the best objects of their kind (or, have superlative goodness of kind)."[26] The upshot, as Santas puts it, is that these other Forms are the best objects of their kind by "virtue of participating in the Form of the Good, and . . . are the most real objects of their kind for the same reason."[27] The other Forms are superlative because of their relation to the Good, while the Good is superlative just "by virtue of itself."[28]

Couched in these terms, Santas' explanation of feature (2) is (a) that the Good is the cause of the knowability of the other Forms precisely in that the other Forms owe their ideal attributes to the Good and (b) that it is their ideal attributes (especially their changelessness) which makes the Forms knowable.[29] His explanation of feature (3), in turn, is that the *ousia* (which I have translated 'being' and he translates 'reality') of a Form consists in its being the best of its kind, and that since the Forms owe their superlative characters to their ideal attributes, they owe them ultimately to participation in the Form of the Good.[30] Santas' account of feature (1) is little more than a restatement of the above, the sense being that dialectic enables reason to reach an understanding of what it is that makes the Forms knowable.[31]

Although Santas' account appears to be headed in the right direction, there are several respects in which it seems strained. One concerns the origin of what he calls the Forms' ideal attributes—such as changelessness, eternal existence and always being the same. Insofar as such attributes require explanation at all,[32] there are other Forms at hand that seem well suited for the task. Among the "very important Kinds" of *Sophist* 254D, in particular, there is Existence to account for the Forms' existence, Rest to account for their resistance to change, and Sameness to account for their being the same. It might be urged that another Form is needed to contribute *eternalness* to the possession of these attributes.[33] But if so, the Good is not an obvious candidate for this role; it would seem more natural to assign it to some Form like *to aidion* or *to aiōnion* instead. Another problem of this sort is how a Form corresponding to "good" (a *noncomparative* grammatical form) could be responsible for the other Forms being the *best* objects of their kind, as Santas claims. On a grammatical basis alone, it would seem more plausible to make the Good responsible for the status of being good instances merely—e.g., a particular person as a good example of virtue—and to assign responsibility for the Forms' unique status of excellence to some Form in a "grammatically superlative mode" like *to beltiston* or *to ariston*.[34]

A deeper problem lies with the understanding of participation that underlies Santas' account. Not only is an explanation required of how participation in the Good makes the individual Form the best of its kind, but he needs an explanation as well of why sensible things become *less* than perfect instantiations by the same participation. The expedient Santas adopts is that of "degrees of participation,"[35] the general idea being that sensible instances are precluded from *full* participation in the Goodness that the Forms other than Goodness enjoy. The problem with this expedient is that it finds no backing in Plato's texts and that it arises only as a requirement of Santas' particular account. A major source of dissatisfaction with the account generally, one might think, is that the distinction between ideal and proper attributes upon which it rests is one borrowed from Aristotle, and one for which no support is found in Plato. Although any attempt to make sense of Plato's Form of the Good is bound to involve a certain amount of conjecture, it would be preferable to hold out for an alternative approach that avoids remaking Plato in the image of Aristotle. I undertake to suggest such an approach in the remaining pages of this section.

From the early period in his writing (e.g., *Euthyphro* 6E6) up to the rather late (e.g., *Timaeus* 49A1), Plato had the concept of ideal paradigms or standards by which the properties of sensible things could be measured and identified. The term *paradigma* was used throughout in reference to these standards.[36] In the middle and later dialogues, moreover, these standards were assigned a number of additional attributes and came to be known as well under the labels *eidos* (Form), *idea* (Idea), and *genos* (Kind). Paramount among the attributes added in the *Phaedo* and the *Republic* were being changeless (*Phaedo* 78D4), being autonomous (*Phaedo* 80B1-2), being the cause of sensible things (*Phaedo* 100B ff.), and being knowable in themselves (*Republic* 511B–C). While all of these attributes have distinct roles to play in Plato's mature conception of the Forms, the attribute that contributes most to the practical significance of the Forms remains that of providing fixed standards by which other things could be assessed and identified.[37]

One respect in which Santas' account succeeds, I believe, is its singling out the role of the Forms as fixed standards as our most promising clue to the nature of the Good. In order to grasp the basic significance of this role, however, it is not necessary to take a stand on the issue of whether or not the Forms exemplify the properties for which they provide standards.[38] There are other ways of providing standards than by perfect exemplification.[39] And the sober truth of the matter would seem to be that some Forms (e.g., Rest) are self-predicative, while others (e.g., Motion) are not. As far as Circularity (one of Santas' main examples) is concerned, it seems better to think of this Form as a precise norm with reference to which a figure is circular rather than as an *entity* (perforce nonsensible) that is perfectly circular itself. The point is that self-predication is not essential for a Form to serve as a standard.

But if being a perfect instance of its kind is not essential for a Form to serve as a standard, then what is? Otherwise put, what is required for a Form to be a standard that might be elucidated with reference to an absolute Good? The answer, it seems to me, is that there must be values of a fixed sort for these standards to measure in the first place. Put in the simplest terms available, what is required for the Forms to operate as fixed standards is the world's being so disposed that there is such a thing as objectively *being right*.

Think for a moment about the term 'right' in English. The term in normal use has dozens of synonyms, most of which are relevant to the point at hand. There is 'right' in the sense of correct or satisfactory, 'right' in the sense of due, meet, or proper, 'right' in the sense of auspicious or worthy, 'right' in the sense of deserving or befitting, likewise in the sense of veracious or factual, of faithful or sound, of authentic or genuine, etc. In Greek, senses within this general range are conveyed by a comparably broad range of terms, including notably *alēthēs*, *axios*, *dikaios*, *kalos*, *orthos*, *summetros*, *chairos*, and of course *agathos* itself. All of these terms are used by Plato at one point or another in connection with the Form he calls the Good. What is particularly interesting about these respective listings is that, of all the Greek terms conveying one or another sense of our highly versatile term 'right', *agathos* stands out as most closely approximating this English term in degree of versatility. Thus actions are rightly done, there are right answers to questions, rightful claims have right responses, etc.—all of which can be expressed in terms of *agathos* (adjective) or *agathōs* (adverb).[40]

Put in terms of this Greek counterpart to the English 'right', the answer I propose to the question above is that the basic requirement for Forms to serve as fixed standards is that the world be so disposed that there is such a thing as being *agathos*. And the role of the Good, in overview, is to dispose the world in this general manner. The role of the Good, that is to say, is to establish what might be called a "field of being" in which there are objective distinctions between things shaped accurately and only approximately, between things done well and things done poorly, between things seen correctly and things seen otherwise, etc. In any given sector of this "field of being," moreover—ethical, epistemological, ontological, etc.—there are standards by which these objective values can be measured. These standards, as a matter of definition, are what Plato calls Forms. But these standards, by and large, are not "perfect instances" of their kind, and whatever excellences they have are not owed to the Good.[41] What they owe to the Good is a world in which there are values to be measured—i.e., a world in which standards of the sort they represent have a legitimate application.

If this proposal is basically correct, then our response to the intelligibility requirement above can be more direct than might otherwise be expected. With regard to feature (4), we can abide with Santas' account—which, after all, is drawn from the adjacent text (505E) without demand for interpretive embellishment. Given the conception of action as oriented naturally with respect to the Good, that is to say, there is an obvious sense in which just and other virtuous actions serve their purposes (i.e., become "useful") in relation to that superlative Form. An elucidation of feature (3) following that of Santas is also available without drawing on his distinction between ideal and proper attributes. The feature in question, as Socrates puts it, is that of "existence and being" (to einai te kai tēn ousian: 509B7–8) being added (proseinai: 509B8)[42] to other Forms because of the Good. Contrary to the interpretation of Santas, this passage as I read it does not say that the other Forms themselves are caused by the Good.[43] Its sense rather is that the other Forms would not be what they are apart from the presence of this superlative Form. But what the Forms are, first and foremost, are objective norms by which things are identified and come to exhibit discernible attributes with varying degrees of excellence. What the passage says, accordingly, is that the other Forms owe their being (ousia) what they are (einai)—i.e., their being objective norms—to the presence of the Form of the Good. What they receive from the Good is not their being itself, but rather their being objective norms.

Features (1) and (2), on the other hand, have to do with a pair of capacities that are said explicitly (508E3–4) to be caused by the Good. One is the capacity to be known on the part of the Forms, the other the power of knowing on the part of the knower. What makes the Forms knowable is their being true.[44] The sense of truth in question, clearly enough, does not pertain to propositions, but could intelligibly be glossed as "genuine" or "real," in opposition to mere appearance. In their role as objective norms, the Forms serve as genuine measures to which the mind can appeal in judging the true worth of other things. The Forms, that is to say, not only measure what is right—taking 'right' in the sense above roughly equivalent to 'good'—but also are the right measures for that particular purpose, and what it is to be right in that latter respect is to be accessible to mind and applicable in inquiry.

What now can be said in this light about feature (1), which is the mind's capacity to know these measures? In our earlier discussion of the visual side of the analogy, it seemed helpful to bring in the "flux theory" of vision spelled out in the *Timaeus*. The basic idea was that a stream of "fire" is emitted from the object of vision which, in the presence of an enabling medium of light, coalesces with another stream of "fire" in the opposite direction that emanates from the organ of sight. Since the opposing fluxes and the medium in which they meet all are forms of fire or light, there is an intelligible sense in which the sun might be thought to be responsible for the capacities both of vision and of visibility. Turning in the paragraphs above to the other side of the analogy, we have identified a sense in which the Good may be thought responsible for the knowability of the Forms—it renders them measures suitably applicable by the inquiring mind. Is there a corresponding sense in which the Form of the Good might be considered the cause of the mind's capacity to know? There is a sense close at hand that is disarmingly straightforward. It is this. Whatever else knowledge might amount to, it is at least a correct grasp of its proper object. And since everything correct or right owes its being so to the Good, this superlative Form sustains the rightness of the knower's grasp as well as the rightness of the object known. As the sun contributes to vision through both object and faculty, the Good's normative contribution both to Form and to intellect makes it the ultimate cause of the philosopher's knowledge. Although it would be a mistake to convert this manner of speaking into a "flux theory" of knowing, there appears to be a more extensive parallel between seeing and knowing than commentators on these passages have generally realized.

There remains the matter of the connecting medium. When first examining the various provisions of the analogy of the Sun, we noted an apparent disparity in the fact that there is no medium linking the faculty of knowing with its object, corresponding to light in the case of vision. What we should be prepared to see now is that, while indeed there is no medium between the mind and the Forms (a medium being some sort of physical connection), there nonetheless is a *bond* (*zugō*: 508A1) by which these things are yoked together. The bond in question is the dimension of rightness that both mind and the Forms owe to the master Form of the Good. It is by virtue of their joint sharing in this selfsame principle that the mind can mingle[45] with the intelligible Forms.

What we have with these remarks, it must be stressed, is far from a complete "theory" of the Good in relation to the factors involved in knowing.[46] What we have here at best is an indication of the general direction in which a person should look who wants to inquire further into the nature of this principle. But perhaps enough has been said already for a profitable comparison of the Good and the Beautiful. For this, we must look again at the *Symposium* and the *Philebus*, the other two dialogues in which these two Forms are featured.

4. The Good and the Beautiful

There are reasons for thinking that the Good and the Beautiful were understood by Plato to be the same Form. There are stronger reasons, I believe, for thinking that he considered them distinct. But there is no doubt that he considered them to be closely related. Let us review the evidence that links them together.

For one thing, the Good and the Beautiful are mentioned in direct conjunction far more frequently than any other two Forms. In the *Phaedo* we find reference to "Beauty itself, and Good and Great" (100B5-6), in the *Philebus* to "man and Ox and Beauty and Good" (15A4-6), and in the Seventh Letter to "Good and Beauty and Justice" (342D4) along with Forms of various shapes. Other texts in which these Forms are directly paired include *Lysis* 216D4, *Cratylus* 439C8, *Phaedrus* 276C3, 278A4, and *Parmenides* 130B8. But it is in the *Symposium* and the *Republic* that their association appears most intimate.

By way of a further look at passages previously considered, we may note first the seemingly perfunctory exchange of *agathos* for *kalos* at *Symposium* 204E, in a manner suggesting that the two terms are equivalent. There is also the description of Eros at 203D5 as being a schemer after the beautiful and the good indifferently, and the parallel descriptions of the lover as seeking the beautiful at 204D and as seeking the good at 206A. In addition, there is the admission of Agathon at 201C that good things are beautiful, the Greek expression of which (*ta de agatha kala*: 201C3) has been rendered by some translators as saying that what is good and what is beautiful are the same.[47]

Turning next to the *Republic*, we find "Good itself and Beauty itself" (507B5) mentioned specifically at the beginning of the analogy of the Sun as among the things that we say exist. A few pages on, the Good itself is said to possess an "inconceivable degree of beauty" (509A6), surpassing that to be found in either knowledge or truth. Since beauty in this degree might be thought to belong to the Form of Beauty exclusively, this passage suggests more than an incidental link between the Good and the Beautiful. The two Forms seem to be paired on more than a coincidental basis also at 531C, where the mathematical part of the curriculum is said to be particularly "useful for the investigation of the Beautiful and the Good" (531C6–7).

The most compelling indication of Plato's intent to link the Beautiful of the *Symposium* with the Good of the *Republic*, however, is the fact that each Form in its context stands at the apex of an elaborately described philosophic progression. Enough has been said already about the parallelism between Diotima's ascent in the *Symposium* and the Divided Line in the *Republic* to make it evident that their several stages are in close correspondence. The correspondence on the upper levels is particularly striking.[48] In Diotima's ascent, the initiate is introduced to the higher mysteries of love with an attraction to the practices and customs of a well-ordered polis (stage 3 in the ordering of chapter 4). The political discourse there encountered in the form of laws and ordinances corresponds nicely (for Plato) with the *dianoia* of mathematical thought in the context of the *Republic*. At the next stage, the initiate becomes enamored with the beauties of knowledge, a direct parallel with the *epistēmē* achieved at the top of the Line. Having "grown and been strengthened" (210D7) there for an extended period, the lover of wisdom (so identified at 210D6) finally reaches the peak of the ascent and gains fulfillment with a vision of the very Form of Beauty. With this achievement comes "genuine virtue" (212A4–5), along with "love of the gods" (212A6) and "immortality" insofar as humanly possible. This theme of divine blessedness is echoed at the end of Book VII of the *Republic* with the remark that the philosopher, after successful tenure as a Guardian, will be recognized as "godlike and spiritually blessed" (540C2–3).

In the *Symposium* fulfillment of the philosopher's quest is characterized as a mental vision of the Beautiful. In the *Republic* it is characterized as a mental grasp of the Good. This argues that the Good and the Beautiful are very intimately associated indeed and perhaps even (in certain contexts, at least) that one cannot be grasped without the other. But it does not indicate that the two Forms are the same. If what was said about the nature of the Good in the previous section is approximately correct, moreover, there are conclusive reasons why they cannot be identical. What these reasons boil down to, by way of common denominator, is that the Beautiful is not a plausible candidate for the roles assigned the Good in the analogy of the Sun.

One role assigned the Good in the analogy of the Sun is that of affording the mind its power of knowing. The way this provision was interpreted in the section above is that the Good enables the mind to "get things right" in its apprehension of what exists in the world. Inasmuch as an apprehension that is *kalos* (beautiful, fair, morally noble, etc.) is not for that reason invariably right, *to agathon* in that connection is not replaceable by *to kalon*.[49] Similar considerations prevent our thinking of Beauty as a plausible cause of truth in the objects of knowledge. For an object to possess beauty in any of its forms seems quite distinct from that object's being authentic or true.

The basic impediment to thinking of the Beautiful and the Good as interchangeable in this connection, however, is that Beauty by itself seems inadequate as a putative source of "existence and being" (509B7–8) on the part of the other Forms. The sense suggested for this role in the preceding section is that the Good establishes a "field of being" in which there is an objective distinction between being *right* and being otherwise. And this is a role which Beauty by itself cannot fill. The reason is just that, while being beautiful or fair is one way of being right, there are some ways of being right that require more than being *kalos*. Examples are rightness in dialectical discourse (vs. the charms of rhetoric), and rightness in reasoning generally (vs. the elegance of sophistical argument). The fact that rightness of this epistemological sort is stressed in the passages from the *Republic* we have been examining is reason enough why the Beautiful cannot replace the Good in that general context. One manner of expressing this disparity between the two Forms in question is to say that the relation between them is asymmetrical. Another is to say that the Good can be conceived as the cause of Beauty but that Beauty is not conceivable as a cause of the Good.

As part of the argument above to the effect that the Good (*to agathon*) for Plato covers the broad range of senses commonly associated with the English word 'right', it was observed that a substantial portion of these senses are conveyed in Greek by a group of more specific value terms including *alēthēs, kalos, summetros,* etc. With this in mind it may be useful to think of Beauty and Truth each as a limited aspect of Plato's Good. In a context giving preeminence to the subset of positive values typified by beauty and comeliness, like the *Symposium,* terms for beauty and for good might be used interchangeably. In such a context it would be understood that beauty is the specific aspect of the Good that is relevant to the discussion at hand. For *agathos* and *kalos* to be interchangeable in a particular context of this sort, however, is no indication that the Good and the Beautiful are generally equivalent.[50] All it indicates is the specific range of positive values in question.

A similar point can be made about the relation between *agathos* and *alēthēs* in the context of the Divided Line. Inasmuch as the Line is explicitly introduced as an elaboration of the analogy of the Good with the sun, it appears peculiar at first that no mention of the Good appears with it. What we find instead is a characterization of the Line's proportion with respect to the truth (*alētheia*, as at 510A10 and 511E4) associated with the objects it represents. Given that the Line is concerned primarily with the conditions of knowing, however, and given that truth (as argued above) is the feature that makes the objects of knowledge knowable, it appears to be a natural terminological shift for Socrates to stop talking about *agathos* generally and to direct the discussion toward *alēthēs* in particular. Truth is the specific aspect of the Good with which the Line is concerned,[51] and Plato's choice of terminology helps make that apparent.

Beyond the *Symposium* and the *Republic,* the *Philebus* is the only other Platonic dialogue in which the Good is assigned a major role. This dialogue opens by joining a conversation already underway in which Philebus has been maintaining that good consists in pleasure, and Socrates has been defending intelligence as a better state for humankind. Protarchus ("in defense of principle") takes over the defense of pleasure, and the conversation proceeds at a rapid pace through a resolution of the One-Many Problem (17D) with the help of the "godly method" (16C ff.) to an agreement on the criteria by which the Good can be identified. It is the lot of the Good, as Socrates puts it, to be adequate (*hikanos*), complete (*teleos*) and universally desirable (*pasi hairetos*).[52] With these criteria at hand, it is quickly determined that neither pleasure nor intelligence can be identical with the Good. Pleasure by itself cannot be complete, because it is better when someone is intelligently aware of it. And intelligence in turn is more desirable in the case of a person capable of enjoying its fruits. On this basis, Socrates and Protarchus agree that what is good must be a mixture including both pleasure and intelligence. The question then arises of which component is more worthy.

By the end of the dialogue, the Good has been pinned down as a unified trio of "beauty, proportion, and truth" (*kallei kai summetria kai alētheia*: 65A2), which is said to be responsible for what is good in any mixture. The final business, before we leave the continuing conversation, is a ranking of what is good among human possessions. In order, we have (1) measure, moderation, and appropriateness, (2) proportion, beauty, completeness, and adequacy, (3) thought and intelligence, (4) knowledge, skill, and right opinion, and (5) a set of "purified" pleasures attending knowledge and perception. As Socrates observes in a parting sally, the pleasures initially advocated by Philebus have no place in this list of goods. Let us pass over the problems posed by this listing and focus on what Socrates says about the makeup of the Good.

The Good itself has turned out to be a mixture, albeit a mixture whose unity merits special emphasis.[53] At first glance, the fact that the Good here turns out to be composite seems to put it at a far reach from the Good of the *Symposium* and the *Republic*, since the Forms of the middle dialogues are said explicitly to be incomposite (*axuntheta* at *Phaedo* 78C6; *monoeidei* at *Phaedo* 80B1, also *Symposium* 211B2). It is unavoidable that one's reading of 65A will be influenced by what one makes of the *Philebus* overall; and any reader who is convinced that Plato's conception of the Forms remained unchanged from the *Phaedo* through the *Philebus* will take the composite character of the Good described at 65A as disqualifying it from being a Form in the first place. My own view, defended at length in *Plato's Late Ontology*, is that Plato's conception of the Forms has been substantially altered by the time of the *Philebus* and that in fact all Forms are understood there as being composed of the Great and the Small and Unity in the manner alluded to by Aristotle in Book I of the *Metaphysics*. If this view is right, then the Good is composite as a matter of course, and we are free to concentrate on the particular makeup described in the text. To get on with the matter, let us assume that this view is right.

What leaps to mind immediately, with this assumption in place, is that two of the three components assigned the Good at 65A are beauty and truth—the very aspects of the Good given precedence in Diotima's ascent and in the Divided Line respectively. Inasmuch as the *Symposium* is concerned primarily with the love of wisdom and with the various forms of comeliness toward which love might be directed, it is natural that Good under the aspect of Beauty be the dominant factor in that discussion. Inasmuch as the discussion of the Divided Line, likewise, is concerned primarily with knowledge, it is fitting that Good under the aspect of Truth play a dominant role in that context. As if to single out these familiar aspects of the Good for special attention, Plato has itemized them specifically at this point in the *Philebus* as notable Forms through which the Good might influence human affairs.

But what of the third component, Proportion (*summetria*), which receives little exposure in the early and middle dialogues?[54] For this, we must return to the fourfold classification of "everything in the universe" (23C4), which Socrates introduces as a first step in the investigation of the relative merits of intelligence and pleasure. Two of these basic classes are the Unlimited (*apeiron*: 23C9) and Limit (*peras*: 23C10), previously mentioned in connection with the "godly method" (cf. 16C10). Third is the Mixture (*meikton*: 25B5) of Limit and the Unlimited, and fourth the Cause (*aitia*, cf. 27B2) by which mixture is accomplished. The distinctive mark of the Unlimited, as Socrates describes it, is the admission of qualities characterized by "more and less" (24E7) but lacking determinate relations among themselves. The role of Limit, in turn, is to bring determinacy to the Unlimited, by the introduction of proportionate numbers and measures (25B1). When the cause operates in a particular case to accomplish a "correct blend" (*orthē koinōnia*: 25E7) of these factors, the result is the production of health or strength, or of any number of other things that are "wholly comely" (*pankala*: 26B7).

It is in connection with the factor of Limit that Proportion finds a place in this ontological framework. For as Socrates says in summing up his description of Limit, the effect of the introduction of number to the Unlimited is the production of features that are "proportionate and harmonious" (*summetra . . . kai sumphōna*: 25E1–2). Proportion, that is to say, is the result of a mixture in which Limit and the Unlimited are "correctly blended" together. What Truth is to knowledge and Beauty to affection, Proportion is to the existence of things that are comely. Proportion, in brief, is the specific aspect of the Good that most directly pertains to the ontology of the *Philebus*.

By way of recapitulation, there are three dialogues in which the Good receives top billing, each featuring a different aspect of this superlative Form. Of particular concern in the *Symposium* is the aspect of Beauty, which nourishes the philosopher's quest for wisdom. The Divided Line is concerned primarily with the aspect of Truth, which sets the goal in the *Republic* for the education of the Guardians. And in the *Philebus* it is Good under the aspect of Proportion that provides the structure through which comely things are brought into being. Plato's final discussion of the Good occurs at the end of this dialogue, where it is characterized as a tripartite Unity of Truth, Proportion, and Beauty. Far from being out of touch with the *Symposium* and the *Republic*, the discussion in the *Philebus* stands rather as a summary statement of what was said of the Good in these earlier contexts.

5. Overview

A thesis guiding this study from the start is that philosophic knowledge is a state of mind, as distinct from a discursive theory that can be expressed in written or spoken language. This thesis is clearly articulated in the Seventh Letter and is indicated in less direct ways in dialogues ranging from the *Meno* to the *Statesman*. It is not part of this thesis, however, to deny that public language has a great deal to do with the process by which knowledge of this sort can be achieved. Language not only is the medium of refutation by which the ground of the intellect is made receptive, but also is the vehicle of the verbal paradigms that function as "seeds of knowledge" with which that ground is sown (*Phaedrus* 276E7). The beauty of Socrates' language is symbolic of the eroticism by which the growth of knowledge is nurtured (*Symposium* 215D–E). And the dialectical process by which that growth is channeled consists of discursive procedures from beginning to end.

Thus we should be not at all surprised to find Socrates saying in the *Republic* that the dialectician can distinguish the Good in *logos* (534B9), or that the essence of each thing, including the Good, can be apprehended by means of discourse (532A7). The sense of these passages, however, is not that dialectical knowledge takes the form of propositionally based theories but rather that discourse plays an essential role in the dialectical disciplines by which that knowledge is achieved. Knowledge, for Plato, remains a state of intellect. And if there is a sense in which that state might be characterized as linguistic, it is that of the *logos* in the mind of the learner of which Socrates speaks at *Phaedrus* 276A.

In a way, perhaps, it would be convenient if Plato had seen fit to go back on his word and to give us something approaching an explicit description of what the mental vision of dialectic is like.[55] We can infer from conclusions reached earlier in this chapter that its objects are the Forms in their natural relationships, and that this vision is due ultimately to the Form of the Good. From the considerations of the preceding chapter, we know that this vision is shaped by the procedures of dialectic, whether the method of hypothesis in the middle dialogues or the method of collection and division that became prominent later. And we know from the account of the Seventh Letter that this vision is reached, if at all, only by hard work and strict discipline, undertaken in conversation with a master philosopher. But we are left with hints and guesses at best about the nature of this vision when it finally appears. Very likely this was deliberate on Plato's part, inasmuch as an attempt to write on such a topic would violate the prohibition laid down in the Seventh Letter.

The fact that Plato did not include a full treatment of this topic in any of his writings, however, does not mean that he has left us without resources to pursue the topic on our own. If the central thesis of this study is correct, indeed, then he has done something better than tell us his own views on the topic. What he has done is provide us an opportunity ourselves to experience the path toward understanding. For if the central thesis of this study is correct, then the dialogues themselves are capable of serving the role assigned to *sunousia* with a master philosopher in the Seventh Letter. This is not to say that the mere act of reading a dialogue by itself establishes a conversation between author and reader. It is to say, rather, that the dialogues are capable of being read in this fashion, and that they probably were written with this role in mind. In order to appreciate more fully what such a reading amounts to, it will be helpful to work our way through the conversation of a typical dialogue as if it were intended also to be a conversation between ourselves and Plato. This is the business of the appendix following. If the *sunousia* provided by this exercise is successful in the case of the reader, then the understanding he or she will have achieved itself will bring the present study to a fitting conclusion.

Appendix

HOW TO READ A PLATONIC DIALOGUE: SUNOUSIA IN THE THEAETETUS

1. Guidelines for Engaging the Conversation

An underlying theme of this study is that the Platonic dialogues, by and large,[1] were written as teaching instruments through which author and reader might engage in conversation. The sense of 'conversation' at point is that of *sunousia*, cited by Plato in the Seventh Letter as a necessary part of the discipline aimed at the achievement of philosophic knowledge. Quite apart from the brief description in the Seventh Letter, it is clear that instructional conversation of this sort played a major role in Plato's own philosophic career. Not only was his own introduction to philosophy probably due to interactions of this general character with the historical Socrates, but moreover the genre of the Socratic conversation provided the format for most of his written dialogues. This much, of course, is obvious. What is adventuresome about the underlying theme mentioned above is the suggestion that the relationship into which we enter with Plato, in undertaking a serious study of one of his dialogues, constitutes an interaction similar to that in which Plato engaged with Socrates himself. This suggestion was elaborated and defended in chapter 1, and some of its ramifications were explored in subsequent chapters.

If the Platonic dialogues were written as conversations to engage the attentive reader, however, this clearly has consequences regarding how they ought to be read. The purpose of the present exercise is to articulate a few of these consequences in detail and to illustrate them with reference to a specific dialogue. Several considerations recommend the *Theaetetus* as a natural choice for this role. For one, it is the only dialogue dedicated specifically to an examination of the nature of knowledge. For another, the interaction depicted within it between Socrates and Theaetetus probably comes as close as any within the corpus to matching the relationship Plato shared with the historical Socrates. A further reason, not unrelated to those above, is that the dialogue includes a discussion by the character Socrates of the type of *sunousia* he engages in with young persons seeking knowledge. The specific purpose of this appendix, accordingly, is to show how the *Theaetetus* might be read as a *sunousia* between author and reader not unlike the conversation Socrates shares with Theaetetus. The reader is asked to keep this limited purpose in view and to bear in mind that this discussion is not intended as a contribution to contemporary scholarship on the dialogue.[2]

The first and most obvious guideline for reading a Platonic dialogue is that it be read *as* a conversation. What does this mean? For one thing, reading a dialogue as a conversation is to read it as an interchange of vocal utterances. In the case of the early and middle dialogues particularly, it is often helpful actually to read the printed words out loud, as one typically should read a piece of poetry. The point is not so much to hear the sound of the words (one likely will be reading a translation anyway), but rather to feel the pace of the conversation and to get some sense of how the characters are interacting personally. To this end, it is sometimes illuminating to have each of the main parts read by a different "actor," if readers are available (as in a typical classroom) who are able to imagine themselves transported to the precincts of ancient Athens. Actually "performing" the dialogue in some such way is the best assurance against missing the arrogant discourtesy of Meno's abrupt question that begins his dialogue with Socrates ("Are you able to tell me—[you] Socrates—if virtue can be taught, and if not whether . . . ?"), and dripping irony with which Socrates took control of the conversation immediately thereafter ("Well now, Meno, the Thessalians used to be renowned among the Greeks for their wealth and horsemanship"—like a university today being renowned for its athletics—"but now, it seems, they are known for wisdom as well . . ."). Although the personal dynamics of this opening exchange contribute nothing to the arguments with which Socrates "stings" Meno later in the conversation, they are essential for understanding the young officer's change in attitude that makes him such a subdued respondent toward the end of the dialogue. "Performing" relevant parts of the *Protagoras*, likewise, is the best way of noting the booming voice of Prodicus (337A–C, 331A–D, 357E–358B) and of appreciating his role in setting the elaborate trap in which Socrates managed to catch Protagoras at the end of their encounter.

Now it obviously would be impractical on most occasions to read an entire dialogue out loud in this fashion, and in most circumstances the purpose could be served well enough by a careful oral reading of a few select passages. There are a certain few dialogues from the late period, moreover—notably the *Timaeus*, the *Critias*, and the *Laws*—for which an oral reading of any portion would seem extraneous. By the time of his later works generally, Plato was writing dialogues less as conversations between notable historical characters and more as dramatic interchanges between notable philosophic viewpoints. But even for most of these later writings, the dramatic ambience contributes importantly to the dialogue's overall effect; and there is no better way to get a sense of a dialogue's dramatic setting than by reading parts of its conversations out loud. One of the most poignant sequences in the entire Platonic corpus is the closing scene of the relatively late *Theaetetus*, where Socrates departs with the offhand remark that he must go to the stoa of the King-Archon to be indicted, from which he returns the next day to yield his leadership in the on-going conversation to the Eleatic Stranger. This interchange of main characters is obviously relevant to the different accomplishments of the *Theaetetus* and the *Sophist*. And there is no better way to direct attention to the differences than to juxtapose oral readings of Socrates' lament that he lacks the knowledge possessed by great men of recent times (*Theaetetus* 210C5–6) and of the glowing recommendation of the Stranger from Elea with which Theodorus opens the subsequent dialogue.

Not only are the dialogues conversations; for the most part, as noted above, they are conversations among well-known personages. Plato's first generation of readers would recognize most of his characters by name and would have some general sense of how the personalities in question would be likely to influence the course of any conversations in which they might become involved. A fourth-century B.C. reader of the *Symposium*, for example, would not have to be told that Alcibiades was an unprincipled leader of the great expedition to Syracuse who defected to the Spartans rather than returning to Athens to stand trial for religious profanation. But most contemporary readers who pick up the *Symposium* for the first time will not know about Alcibiades and should find out who he was before spending much time on the dialogue. They should also learn a thing or two about each of the other participants in order to become sensitive to the subtle interactions among persons that provides the dialogue its interest and dramatic depth.

The second general guideline is that the reader should acquire a basic familiarity with the historical figures upon which the characters of the dialogue are based.[3] Inasmuch as we will be concerned primarily with the *Theaetetus* in subsequent sections of this appendix, it will be useful to illustrate this rule with a few reminders about the characters and major circumstances of this particular dialogue. Theaetetus is a young mathematician who later will gain great prominence as a member of Plato's Academy and who often is listed with Archytas and Eudoxus as one the most outstanding mathematicians of his century. He was noted especially for his work in completing the mathematics of the five regular solids and for his contributions to the study of the irrational numbers, a preview of which is given in the opening pages of the dialogue. Due notice of Theaetetus' present promise and subsequent achievement is very much relevant to our interpretation of the *Theaetetus*, if for no other reason than that we thereby come to realize that Plato here has paired Socrates with his most capable respondent of any of the dialogues. Theaetetus is no less brilliant and pliable and inherently humble than Meno was arrogant and uncooperative and mentally sluggish. If Socrates cannot bring Theaetetus to a grasp of the nature of knowledge—which by the end appears to be the case—then the failure cannot be attributed to lack of intellect in his respondent. When Theaetetus is paired with the Stranger from Elea in the sequel dialogue, indeed, the result is not only achievement of the definition of Sophistry they had set out to accomplish, but also at least a provisional resolution of most of the problems left over from his earlier conversation with Socrates.

The occasion of the outer dialogue is an interchange between Euclides and Terpsion in which the former remarks that he has just accompanied the severely wounded Theaetetus—now in his mid to late 40s—on his way back to Athens to die and offers to share with Terpsion a written version of a conversation that Theaetetus as a youth once had with Socrates. Euclides and Terpsion were also paired in the *Phaedo*, where they were mentioned among the friends of Socrates who were present at his execution. There they were identified as natives of Megara, where Plato was said to have visited them for a while after Socrates' death. By the time of this later dialogue, they must have been about fifty years old.

The two characters besides Theaetetus with speaking parts in the inner dialogue are Socrates and Theodorus. Theodorus is a widely known mathematician from Cyrene who has been instructing Theaetetus and some of his young companions (including a youth also named Socrates) in arithmetic and geometry. Although Theodorus was a friend and frequent companion of the (now deceased) sophist Protagoras, he considers discussions on topics like the nature of knowledge too abstract for his liking. Despite being roughly the same age as Socrates, he seems already to have reached senility. Of Socrates' powers, at this point, we need no further reminder.

A third general guideline for reading a Platonic dialogue is that if one hopes to accomplish more than merely scratching its surface, one must be prepared to read it again and again. The reason for this is not simply that the dialogue is likely to prove hard to read and that several passes through will probably be required for a grasp of all the details. While some dialogues (e.g., the *Sophist*, the second half of the *Protagoras*, and most notably the second part of the *Parmenides*) are indeed quite hard to read, there are numerous other dialogues that read quite easily and yet are such that one will feel the need to read them repeatedly. In the early period there is the *Gorgias*, the *Meno*, and the *Euthyphro*; in the middle most distinctly the *Symposium* and the *Phaedrus* along with the (perhaps overly long) *Republic*. In the later period this is particularly true of the *Theaetetus*; and other commentators will have other dialogues to add to this list.

The reason dialogues like this must be read several times through by anyone who wants to mine their philosophic content is that this content is structured to be approached in layers. Preparing to extract the contents of a mature Platonic dialogue is similar in some respects to preparing for an athletic contest. While three or four hundred hours of training overall may be enough to bring a runner into shape for competition, these practice hours must be spread over a period of several months. The athlete must build up basic skills during early periods of exercise in order even to begin later stages of preparation. Time is required between sessions for the body to regenerate and to consolidate its resources for coping with more advanced training. In like fashion, a reader generally is not prepared to plumb the depths of a Platonic dialogue by one or two initial readings, however methodical and careful. One must be prepared to consolidate insights gained from earlier readings of a dialogue in order even to begin a search for its richer layers of content.

As we should be able to see shortly, the *Theaetetus* provides a particularly apt illustration of this multilayered structure. The dialogue begins with a definition of power (*dunamis*) in a mathematical sense, proceeds on to a definition of power pertaining to the perception of physical objects, and ends by bringing the adequately prepared reader to a position of being able to realize that an extension of this conception of power into the domain of the Forms (with the "combining Kinds" of *Sophist* 259E) could provide the account of knowledge still missing by the end of the dialogue. By considering carefully the significance of *dunamis* in the mathematical sense, the reader is enabled to understand aspects of *dunamis* in the case of perception that were previously inaccessible; and by reflecting on the powers that are engaged in perception, he or she is brought to a position of beginning to see what powers are required of the Forms to make knowledge possible. Other examples of layered content will emerge when we look at the dialogue more closely.

Something should be said finally about particular approaches one might rely upon in extracting the layered contents of a Platonic dialogue.[4] There probably are as many different strategies for entering a dialogue as there are individual readers who have successfully gained entry. One method that might generally prove useful for readers undertaking a serious study of Plato for the first time, however, is to approach the dialogue through a series of perspectives corresponding to the several stages of the horticultural model employed in the body of this study.

The *Theaetetus* is a dialogue dealing with the nature of knowledge. Let us take for granted that the typical reader would like to gain from the dialogue some understanding of what knowledge is (as Plato conceived it, at least) and of what is required for knowledge to be possible. To arrive at such insight into the nature of knowledge is the state of fruition (the topic of chapter 6) that one would like to reach by the end of one's study. The initial step toward this end will be one of clearing the ground (chapter 2), in which the reader considers the effect of the various arguments by which Socrates removes erroneous opinions about the nature of knowledge. Next, one might pay particular attention to the images and paradigms provided in the dialogue by which "seeds of knowledge" about knowledge might be sown in receptive minds (chapter 3). Following that, it is time to turn to matters of productivity and nourishment by which the inquiring mind is stimulated to sustain its growth (chapter 4). One then might focus on the dialectical structure of the conversation (chapter 5), by which the awareness of Theaetetus and of the reader alike is channeled in a direction that leads to knowledge.

The final stage, mentioned above, should bring fresh insight into knowledge, as one reaps the fruits of inquiry assiduously cultivated in earlier stages. These several stages will be illustrated in the next five sections. Although the necessarily abbreviated discussion of the contents of the *Theaetetus* that follows certainly is no substitute for a careful study of the dialogue itself, it might at least provide a preview of the fruits there to be reaped.

2. The Structure of Socrates' Elenchic Argument

The main body of the *Theaetetus* divides neatly into three sections, each beginning with an hypothesis proposed (or "brought to birth") by Theaetetus and continuing with a series of arguments by which Socrates clarifies the hypothesis and examines it for "viability." The first hypothesis identifies knowledge with sense perception (151E) and is finally "exposed" as a "false birth" for being self-contradictory or inconsistent. Second is the proposal that knowledge is the same thing as true judgment (187C). While this hypothesis shows no signs of inconsistency, it is easily defeated by a counterexample—but not until Socrates has initiated and then rejected several attempts to explain the distinction between true and false judgment. The third hypothesis results from an effort to repair the defects of the second by requiring that true judgment be accompanied by an account or reason (*logos*) in order to count as knowledge (201C–D). This final hypothesis is never refuted, either by counterexample or by proof of inconsistency, but instead is perfunctorily set aside after failure of a halfhearted attempt to find a sense of *logos* that would fill the bill. After nearly seventy pages of conversation the day is growing late and Socrates has still to meet his indictment before the stoa of the King-Archon closes.

All arguments of interest in the dialogue are associated with one or another of these hypotheses and all have the form of refutations. Only a few of these arguments, nonetheless, are refutations of one of the three hypotheses as such. It may be useful to indicate the main arguments associated with each hypothesis in turn.

Following the initial identification of knowledge with perception, there is a series of brief and somewhat trifling arguments that serve to rule out of consideration certain common senses of both perception and knowledge. Knowing a foreign language, for example, clearly is not merely perceiving its characters (163B), nor can knowing something by memory be a matter of perceiving it (163D–164B). Nor is the perceiving in question merely a matter of properly functioning sense organs, such that a person might both see and not see with one eye open and one covered (165B–C).

Another set of arguments is associated specifically with the Protagorean thesis that "man is the measure of all things" (152A), introduced by Socrates as closely akin to Theaetetus' proposal that knowledge is perception. The gist of these arguments (161C–E, 170A–171C, 178B–179B) is that Protagoras is caught in some kind of self-defeating posture when he maintains both (a) that each person individually is an arbiter of truth and (b) that he himself, as a paid sophist, is wiser than other people. These arguments are developed in dialectical interaction, with an apparently serious attempt by Socrates to make sense of Protagoras' position, and hence become more sophisticated as the dialectic progresses. The final argument (178B–179B) traps Protagoras into having to admit that he is a better judge than other people regarding the truth of judgments about what arguments would prove effective in courts of law, which is flatly in contradiction with his famous thesis that each man is a measure of the truth himself.

This sustained attack against Protagoras is relevant because of the involvement of the Protagorean thesis in the complex definition of perception articulated at 156A–157C. Also involved in this definition is the equally famous saying of Heraclitus that all things are forever in a process of change. This Heraclitean doctrine in turn is subjected to refutation at 182C–E, with the observation that if everything is in change then words cannot have constant meanings. The clear implication is that the doctrine of universal change cannot even be expressed in meaningful language—an unmistakable case of a thesis contradicting itself. By independently refuting the Protagorean and Heraclitean components of the account of perception in this manner, Socrates shows that these two theses are distinct, not only from each other but also from the hypothesis of Theaetetus that knowledge is perception. If knowledge and perception in fact were always the same thing, it would be no bar to this fact that all things are forever in change; the consequence of this latter would be only that knowledge and perception are always changing identically. In order to disprove the hypothesis of Theaetetus itself, yet another argument is needed.

The argument refuting Theaetetus' hypothesis is given between 184B and 186E, and harks back to the account of perception at 156A–157C to which both Heraclitus and Protagoras contributed. This account was developed expressly as an attempt to meet the necessary conditions, laid down at 152C, for the truth of the hypothesis identifying knowledge and perception. The conditions themselves are quite straightforward. Given that knowledge is both infallible and has something that exists (*ontos*: 152C5) as its object—assumptions that are never explicitly questioned in the dialogue—it follows directly from the identification of knowledge with perception that perception also is infallible and takes things that have being as its objects. The conditions (1) of infallibility and (2) of objects with being must be met simultaneously for Theaetetus' hypothesis to be true. And the final refutation of this hypothesis at the end of the first section consists basically of pointing out that the circumstances under which the first requirement would be met preclude the second's being met as well.

The condition (1) of infallibility is satisfied by the account of perception in the following manner. Drawing upon the Heraclitean doctrine of perpetual change, the account represents the world of perception as consisting entirely of motions. These motions are of two sorts—"parent" motions and "offspring" motions—each characterized as having the power (*dunamis*) either to act or to be acted upon. The "parent" motions interact to produce the "offspring," which are always generated in exclusive pairs. In each pair of generated motions, one is always an act of perception and the other is always its unshared object. This means that any given act of perception serves as sole access to its associated object. In Protagorean terms, each act is the sole "measure" of the object perceived, a consequence of which is that each act is infallible in what it makes of its object. If the perpetual world is such as this account depicts it, perception meets the necessary condition (1) of infallibility.

Another consequence of the Heraclitean character of perception, however, is that the objects of perception are never fixed. Being forever in change, the perpetual world is always in a state of becoming, which as Socrates observes "rules out being altogether" (157A–B). The objects of perception thus are precluded from being. In effect, the very circumstances that enable condition (1) to be met render it impossible that condition (2) should be met simultaneously. It follows that necessary conditions (1) and (2) cannot both be met, which shows the hypothesis identifying knowledge and perception to be inconsistent (under the given account of perception).

The untoward consequences of this account of perception are laid out explicitly in the final refutation of Theaetetus' first hypothesis at

184B–186E. In knowing, the mind grasps the existence (*ousian*: 186C3) of things; and among things the mind knows are that color and sound are *different* from each other, that they are *two* distinct things (185A–B), etc. But not only is sense perception incapable of grasping existence; moreover, because of the unique access each perception has to its object, there is no single sense modality—sight, hearing, or any other—that can grasp *both* color and sound in order to determine that the two are different. On both counts, it follows that knowledge cannot be identical to sense perception. The mind's knowledge must come instead from some kind of reasoning (*sullogismō*: 186D3), an observation that leads directly to Theaetetus' second hypothesis.

In evaluating this purported refutation, it should be noted that the first hypothesis is defeated only under the assumption that knowledge is always of what exists (requirement (2) above), as distinct from things in a state of becoming. A strict Heraclitean—i.e., someone who accepted the account of the perceptual world given at 156A–157C as a complete ontology—clearly would not accept this assumption and hence would not consider the thesis that knowledge is perception to have been refuted by Socrates' argument. Such a person could maintain, for example, that knowledge is a grasp of the sequence of individual sensory objects to which perception has access, something in the manner of the prisoners in the Cave who gave prizes to those who could best account for the association and sequence of shadows passing on the wall before them. Plato returns to this conception of knowledge with the "dream theory" at the end of the dialogue, where it is shown inconsistent without recourse to assumptions that the strict Heraclitean could conveniently deny.

The second hypothesis, identifying knowledge with true judgment (*alēthēs doxa*: 187B5–6), is shown untenable by the counterexample at 201A–C of the jurymen who arrive at a true judgment of guilt without actually knowing the facts of a case. This counterexample could have been raised immediately after the statement of the hypothesis at 187B, making the entire second section of the dialogue scarcely more than a page in length. For reasons that become clear only when we look at the dialectical structure of the dialogue overall (section 5, below), Plato instead has Socrates and Theaetetus address the task of accounting for the distinction between true and false judgment. The most interesting arguments of this section are associated with the last two of the five attempts to explain this distinction—i.e., with the accounts employing the models of the wax block and the aviary. Let us briefly review the first three attempts.

The first attempt relies entirely upon the distinction between knowing and not knowing some object or another, in a sense of 'knowing' (*eidenai:* 188A2) that amounts to "seeing with the eye of the mind." But the difference between true and false judgment cannot be one merely of knowing or not knowing in this sense, for that would require false judgment to be about something of which the mind making the judgment is not aware, a consequence that is unintelligible. The second attempt shifts to a distinction with respect to objects of judgment, with the proposal that a true judgment is about some object that exists (i.e., about what is) while a false judgment is about what is not. Since thinking (by way of judging) *what is not* is equivalent to thinking *no* thing, which is the same as thinking nothing (189A), however, this makes false judgment turn out to be no thought (hence no judgment) at all. The third attempt employs an initially vague distinction between judgment and some other way of being present to mind (unspecified, perhaps just thinking of something), and proposes that true and false judgment differ in being correct and incorrect identifications, respectively, of existent objects of thought—as one might judge, for instance, that what is really beautiful is ugly (189C). But this has the absurd consequence that someone might think of an ox and at the same time judge it to be a horse (190C), etc. More apt distinctions are needed than these attempts provide to account for the difference between true and false judgment.

The account featuring the wax block begins with a much sharper distinction between two ways of being present to mind. Existing things might be present to mind either as objects of perception or as memory images of previously perceived objects. This account also establishes a number of typical cases in which sense and memory images thus present could be correctly or incorrectly identified.[5] One might already have memory images of both Theodorus and Theaetetus, for example, and then upon seeing the two persons together correctly pair the fresh sensory images with the old images of memory. On the other hand, one might misidentify both persons on a subsequent encounter (seeing them from a distance, for example), by matching the sensory image of Theaetetus with the memory image of Theodorus, and vice versa. According to this fourth attempt, true judgment is a correct match between sensory and memory images, while false judgment is a mismatch between sense and memory.

Although this account is obviously limited in application, it has several merits in its immediate context that should be noted. For one thing, it is fully cogent as far as it goes. While one might have reservations about this rather mechanical way of describing things, we often do misidentify objects in some such manner. Another important virtue is that the wax-block model provides a clear *criterion* by which correct and incorrect judgments can be distinguished. An identification of sense and memory image is correct if and only if both are images of the same original object. It is precisely the lack of a criterion of this sort that causes the following account based on the aviary to founder. Yet another point in favor of the wax-block account is that it seems to provide the basis for making sense of the truth or falsehood of any judgment regarding the identity of perceptual objects. While such an account is powerless to deal with objects of judgment that cannot be perceived, as Socrates is quick to point out by way of rebuttal (195E–196B), it seems to apply at least to all forms of judgment yet to be treated in this particular dialogue.

The account likening the mind to an aviary is aimed specifically at accommodating judgments about abstract objects of the sort that the wax block could not handle. This fifth and final attempt is based on a distinction between two sorts of mental possession not unlike that between "long-term" memory and immediate recall. Items of knowledge are passed into the mind like birds are passed into an aviary, whereupon they become present in the mind's stock of persistent memories. In order to become available for any specific cognitive purpose, however, these "birds of knowledge" must be recalled to immediate possession. The "repossession" of the right item of knowledge (e.g., the number 12) under the right circumstances (e.g., the mind's search for the sum of 5 and 7), according to this account, amounts to true judgment, while its grasp of the wrong item (e.g., the number 11) under those circumstances yields a judgment that is false.

One awkwardness of this account to which attention is drawn imme-diately is that it makes false judgment or ignorance (grasp of the wrong item of knowledge) a consequence of knowing (199C–D). As Socrates says, one might as well make blindness a consequence of vision. Theaetetus' spontaneous response is the suggestion that the aviary should contain "birds of ignorance" as well (199E), so that false judgment could be explained as repossession of ignorance. It is the difficulty introduced by this suggestion, however, that finally shows why the account cannot be made to work.

Not only does the aviary account make possession of items of knowledge the source of ignorance; in view of the prevailing hypothesis that true judgment is knowledge, it labors under the additional burden of making knowledge (in the sense of "long-term" possession) a precondition of knowledge (in the sense of immediate possession). This predicament is reminiscent of the "paradox of the learner" in the *Meno*, according to which one could come to know something only by knowing something already. As the careful reader in fact will have noted, this very paradox has already entered the discussion at 198C, which should alert us to an impending infinite regress. If there are to be both items of knowledge and items of ignorance in the aviary, recovery of which constitutes true and false judgment respectively, then some criterion is needed to distinguish one from the other. Whereas the so-called "theory of recollection" came to the rescue in the *Meno*, however, the best Socrates can come up with in the present context is yet *another* aviary containing knowledge about the knowledge and the ignorance of the first, which poses the same problem all over again; and so on *ad infinitum*. The wax-block account had a ready-made criterion for distinguishing true and false judgment, but could not accommodate judgments about abstract objects. Now it appears that the aviary account, expressly formulated to handle abstract judgments, cannot provide a basis for distinguishing truth from falsehood. At this point the counterexample of the jurymen is introduced, and Theaetetus relinquishes his second hypothesis.

A considerable body of literature has built up around the "dream theory" introduced by Socrates in immediate response to the third hypotheses that knowledge is true belief accompanied by *logos*.[6] One of the central problems addressed by this literature is why this theory was brought into the *Theaetetus* in the first place.[7] We need not settle the question of its role in the dialogue, however, in order to see why the theory is untenable.

The "dream theory" suggests one sense of the elusive term *logos* in which *logos* might be thought to make the difference between mere true judgment and knowledge. According to this theory, everything is composed of perceptible elements (202B) which admit names but no descriptions or *logoi*. *Logoi* can be given of these composite things, however, consisting of a combination of the names of their constituent elements. True judgment about a composite object occurs when the mind thinks correctly of the object's composition. And this true judgment becomes knowledge when augmented by the *logos* containing the names of the object's constituents. Thus knowledge is possible of composite objects, but not of their elements of which no *logoi* can be formulated.

Although the argument refuting this theory is somewhat complex,[8] in structure it is similar to the argument used to defeat Parmenides' conception of a single being in the *Sophist* (244B–245E). The theory treats composite objects as composed of parts. In any given case, the whole object is either (1) the same as the sum of its parts or (2) different from the sum if its parts. If (1), given that the whole can be known, it follows that the parts can be known also, since there is no difference between the whole and all its parts.[9] This is contrary to that component of the theory which says that the parts cannot be known. If (2), however, the whole, being without parts, must itself be incomposite, from which it follows that this whole cannot be known, since it admits no *logos* formulated from names of constituents. This is contrary to that component of the theory which says that the wholes can be known. If either (1) or (2) is the case, then the "dream theory" is wrong; yet either (1) or (2) must be the case, for they exhaust all alternatives.

Arguments disqualifying the remaining three senses of *logos* may be briefly noted. *Logos* in the sense merely of vocal utterance (206D) obviously cannot turn true judgment into knowledge, since all persons who are not dumb can give voice to their judgments, whether knowledgeable or ignorant of what they are talking about. *Logos* in the sense of an enumeration of parts also will not do, for reasons quite distinct from the logical problems of the abstruse "dream theory." The counterexample used to disqualify this proposal trades upon the fact that the names of both Theodorus and Theaetetus begin with the same syllable, T-H-E. Someone might be able to enumerate the parts of the first syllable in Theaetetus' name without thereby knowing the syllable, as shown by failure in an attempt to spell the first syllable in Theodorus' name. Hence having true judgment about the spelling of this syllable in Theaetetus' name is not converted into knowledge of this syllable by an enumeration of its parts, since the syllable is not known when it occurs in the name of Theodorus.

The final sense of *logos* considered before the dialogue ends is that of distinguishing mark, as the sun is distinguished by being the brightest of the heavenly bodies (208D). If someone had arrived at a true judgment about Theaetetus, this account suggests, then that judgment would be converted into knowledge by a *logos* distinguishing Theaetetus from other persons. The problem with this proposal, however, as Socrates points out, is that in order to arrive at a judgment *about* Theaetetus in the first place, the mind would need to have grasped his distinguishing features already; for otherwise the judgment would be no more about *him* than about some other person. So the addition of a *logos* giving distinguishing features would be redundant and could not make the difference between true judgment and knowledge.

This completes our summary of the arguments of the *Theaetetus*. Without exception, the arguments are aimed at refuting views or proposals introduced by some participant in the conversation. As such, they correspond to the elenchic style of argument so prominent in the early Socratic dialogues, with the difference that they are directed more toward ideas than toward the persons holding them. (Apart from the arguments against Protagoras and Heraclitus, the arguments of the *Theaetetus* are not *ad hominem*). One reason for beginning a study of the dialogue by examining its arguments, accordingly, is to enable us to experience firsthand some of the difficulties associated with common notions about the nature of knowledge—some of which (e.g., that the addition of a justifying account makes knowledge out of true judgment) are as prevalent today as they apparently were during Plato's lifetime.

Another reason for beginning in this way, however, is to enable us to see how little has been accomplished of philosophic interest by focusing on the arguments in isolation from the rest of the dialogue. So far, very little has been extracted from the conversation between Socrates and Theaetetus that could not be written up more effectively in the form of an essay or journal article. And so far nothing has been noted that would explain why the *Theaetetus* merits its reputation as one of the greatest contributions to theory of knowledge in the entire Western philosophic tradition. Some of the arguments are interesting for the challenges they pose in coming to understand them. Some are mildly interesting for the conclusions they support. And some (e.g., those of the "dream theory") are even sufficiently germane to issues of the twentieth century to have generated spirited responses from contemporary philosophers. But these arguments by themselves do not make the dialogue great. And it is quite certain that Plato did not write the dialogue primarily as a vehicle to present these arguments to his readers.

For someone more than casually acquainted with the middle books of the *Republic*, one of the most interesting things about the way the *Theaetetus* ends is the mention of the sun as the brightest of the heavenly bodies. Here at the very end of a lengthy, and apparently unsuccessful, discussion of the nature of knowledge is the image of the object of the highest form of knowledge. For the Good not only is an object of knowledge itself, but is the source of our knowledge of everything else. Let us turn, as a natural next step, to a consideration of the imagery in the *Theaetetus*.

3. Analogies, Symbols, and the Use of Paradigms

In a manner linking it with the earlier Socratic dialogues, the *Theaetetus* is replete with analogies and similes drawn from the common crafts and trades. When Theodorus, himself an outstanding mathematician, praises Theaetetus' qualities of mind at the beginning of the dialogue, he is likened by Socrates to a portrait painter especially qualified to describe someone's physical appearance. In the course of this verbal byplay, we learn that Theaetetus very much resembles Socrates in facial characteristics (snub-nose, bulging eyes, not handsome physically). At the beginning of his arguments against Protagoras, Socrates likens Theodorus to an onlooker at a wrestling school who refuses to display his own physique, which gives Theodorus another opportunity to stress his advanced age (about the same as Socrates', who is leading the present demonstration of "mental sparring"). Later in the same sequence, Socrates likens the superior ability of Protagoras to anticipate the effect of an argument in a court of law to the ability of a pastry cook to anticipate the taste of a confection, which shows the inadequacy of Protagoras' thesis that each man is his own measure. Analogies like these are plain in their purpose and make obvious contributions to the vitality of the dialogue.

Another group of analogies bear more directly on the philosophic import of the conversation. Approximately in the middle of the dialogue, just before the final refutation of Protagoras, Socrates leads Theodorus into an interlude contrasting the life of philosophy with the life of the rhetorician in the law court or public assembly. This midway break serves several purposes in the dramatic makeup of the dialogue. It separates the more diffuse arguments between 161C and 172B from the serious refutations about to begin at 178B (the refutations, in order, of Protagoras, of extreme Heracliteanism, and of the first hypothesis of Theaetetus), and gives the reader a rest before moving into these more difficult arguments. It also invokes aspects of the imagery of the Cave in the *Republic*, along with the theme of philosophy as a preparation for afterlife in the *Phaedo*, thus establishing continuity with those two previous dialogues. For purposes of contrast within the digression itself, the philosopher is likened to a "free man" (172D) who always has time at his disposal for conversation about things that really matter in human existence, while the lawyer or politician is compared with a slave who must speak by the clock (172E) and who is concerned constantly to serve his masters by flattery and cunning (a role Socrates pointedly refuses in his upcoming trial). The image of the political rhetorician as a slave connects this passage with the portrait of the despot in Book VIII of the *Republic*, a man driven into all manner of unjust and desperate acts in order to preserve his life in a lawless society. The characterization of the philosopher as a free man anticipates the disclosure of the "free man's knowledge" at *Sophist* 253C, where the account of knowledge that eludes Socrates and Theaetetus in the present conversation finally emerges in dialogue with the Eleatic Stranger.

The most important analogy of this sort in the *Theaetetus*, however, is the comparison of Socrates, in his teaching role, with the midwife who assists women in physical birth. There are two aspects of this analogy that are particularly significant for the interpretation of the dialogue, which may be briefly described by way of summary of the more detailed discussion in earlier chapters. The first has to do with the effect of Socrates' maieutic practice upon the young men whom he assists in "delivery." Socrates is not teacher to these students in the sense that sophists like Protagoras and Gorgias were teachers—masters of rhetoric and eristic, willing to instruct wealthy youths in these technical subjects for a fee. He was not a teacher, perhaps like Anaxagoras, who had certain theoretical doctrines to pass on to students with inclination and patience to commit them to memory. Nor did he teach, apparently in the manner of Aristotle, by presenting arguments for his pupils to master on topics of diverse philosophic interest. Socrates' manner of teaching, instead, was an attempt to help his students arrive at important truths by their *own* reflection and insight.[10] This explains why all Socrates' arguments in the dialogue are negative—i.e., why there are no *positive* arguments for one or another philosophic thesis.[11] His aim is to get Theaetetus to see things for himself, not to "coerce" him into acceptance by irresistible arguments. A related point of interest is that this also is the way in which we *as readers* may may expect to learn the important lessons contained in the dialogue. As readers beyond numbering have seen before now, the *Theaetetus* has remarkable powers to induce philosophic insight. But the way in which it does this is not by use of compelling arguments. Among the various ways in which it does this instead is a skillful use of analogies and other images of the sort we are now examining.

The second aspect of the midwife-analogy to be noted at this point is Socrates' claim to be barren himself. Not only is he not disposed to teach by passing on bits of knowledge to his pupils; he himself, in some important sense, is ignorant of the very things he would help them come to know. As he puts it rather wistfully at 150C, he is not capable himself of giving birth to wisdom. There is a note of sublime pathos in his final speech at 210C where he remarks once again that he himself has none of the knowledge that belongs to "great and admirable men" of the past and present. This, of course, is his final speech (not counting the *Euthyphro*) before returning on the following day to be replaced by a Stranger, one of whose first acts is to identify Socrates' art of mental purification as a "noble kind" of sophistry.

Another kind of image employed to good purpose in the *Theaetetus* is what might be referred to as symbols, the purpose of which is to high-light some particularly significant feature of the conversation underway. The most conspicuous symbol in the dialogue is that of the sun, which figures in the final characterization of *logos* (208D) offered by Socrates before the dialogue closes. Inasmuch as the sun represents the Good in Book VI of the *Republic*, and inasmuch as the Good is identified there as the source of knowledge (508E3), its appearance at the end of the *Theaetetus* may be a sign that the source of knowledge is now close at hand.[12] The sense in which this is so will be examined presently; but it is not irrelevant to note the "chance discovery" of the "free man's" (i.e., the philosopher's) knowledge at 253C of the next day's conversation.

A second symbol relevant to the interpretation of the *Theaetetus* is the manner in which we, as readers, gain access to the main conversation: we overhear the conversation between Socrates and Theaetetus as read from a written version by a slave of Euclides (143B3, C8). The pointed criticism of writing as unsuitable for a medium of philosophic under-standing in the *Phaedrus* and the Seventh Letter makes it natural to look upon the fact that the conversation between Socrates and Theaetetus is being *read* as an indication that it is fated to fall short of its announced goal of arriving at knowledge about knowledge. The further fact that it is read by someone who, quite literally, is not a "free man" (recall 253C of the *Sophist* noted above) can only heighten our anticipation of failure. On the other hand, Euclides' manuscript allegedly has been checked time and again for accuracy with Socrates himself (143A). So while nothing *better* than true opinion is likely to be conveyed by a slave reading a written report, there is a good chance that this opinion *at least* will be reliable.

It may be instructive to put this observation in terms borrowed from the Divided Line of the *Republic*. After an illustrative definition giving necessary and sufficient conditions for being a power or surd in mathematics—an achievement by definition falling on the penultimate level of the Divided Line (*dianoia*)—the attempt to define knowledge slips to the lowest level of all (*eikasia*) with the hypothesis that knowledge is nothing but sense perception. The next hypothesis, identifying knowledge with true judgment, moves the discussion up one level to that of belief (*pistis*), at which level it remains stalled for the remainder of the dialogue. If an adequate sense of *logos* were forthcoming in the final pages—one that would make the difference between true judgment and knowledge—then this might have been enough at least to move the discussion up again to the level of *dianoia* on which it began. As matters stand, however, the entire discussion of knowledge takes place on the underside of the main division of the Divided Line. If we as readers are going to gain much insight into the positive nature of knowledge from the conversation in the dialogue, this result will depend largely upon our own powers of discernment.

The account of roots or powers (*dunameis*) provided by Theaetetus at the beginning of the conversation is an important example of a third kind of image employed in this dialogue, namely that of models or paradigms. In his initial response to Socrates' request for a definition of knowledge, Theaetetus had merely itemized various examples—knowledge of geometry, knowledge of shoemaking, etc. This is the sort of response that led Socrates in earlier dialogues, the *Meno* for instance, into long discussions about why a list of examples does not constitute a definition. Theaetetus, however, not only sees the difference immediately, but moreover is able to provide his own example of the kind of definition Socrates was looking for. The Pythagoreans had already distinguished between "square" numbers (representable by tokens arranged in a square), equal to products of an integer multiplied by itself, and "oblong" numbers like three, five, etc., the square roots (as we would say) of which cannot be measured by the unit of the integers. It was Theaetetus' proposal to call the square roots of numbers of these two classes "lengths" (*mekoi*) and "powers" (*dunameis*) respectively, and then to define the powers as square roots incommensurable with any of the lengths. Obvious as such a definition may seem to a mathematician today, at the time of the conversation it was something of a breakthrough. Early Pythagorean mathematics had foundered on the problem of integrating the irrational numbers (like the square root of two in the *Meno*) into the system of integers; and here Theaetetus has come up with a completely general definition of the former in terms of the latter. The definition is general in providing conditions for being a root that are both necessary and sufficient. While all lengths (integers) are commensurable with any other, all roots and only roots are incommensurable with any length. This is a model (*mimoumenos*: 148D4) of the kind of definition, Socrates says, that he would like to have of knowledge itself.

Use of the term *dunamis* in this sense of "root" or "surd" was not standard in Greek mathematics before Euclid. Surds like the square roots of three, five, and six, obviously enough, have the *power* to become commensurable with the integers when squared, so this use of the term *dunamis* is not inappropriate. But one might still wonder why Plato chose to use the term in this seemingly unusual sense. Part of the answer surely has to do with the fact that *dunamis* receives a remarkably similar use in the account of perception given at 156A–157C. The similarities between the *dunamei* of Theaetetus' definition and those of the account of perception are sufficiently strong, indeed, to warrant our taking the former powers to be symbols of the latter.[13]

As the powers in the mathematical definition are incommensurable with any of the lengths, so the powers (156A6) of acting and being acted upon in the account of perception are exercised in the production of offspring in twin sets that admit no common measure from pair to pair. The two members of each pair, as we have noted, are related as act of perception to its object, with the result that the two are so inextricably associated that no object of one pair can be measured by the act of another. Objects of perception, as a consequence, admit no shared measure, and hence are incommensurable like the surds of mathematics. Furthermore, as the powers of mathematics become commensurable with the lengths on a higher level—the level of their squares (148B)—so there is a higher level on which the objects of perception become commensurable with respect to each other. This higher level in the case of perception is that of reflection (*sullogismō*: 186D3) or judgment, as that form of mental activity is depicted in connection with the second hypothesis which identifies true judgment with knowledge. While perceptions, that is to say, cannot be compared on the level of perception itself, they are commensurable on some more abstract level of awareness on which the mind reflects upon them and "compares one with another" (186B8). A proposal about the mechanics of this comparison is made with the help of the model of the wax block, in which the mind is able to retain images from past sensory encounters for comparison with images from current perception. As we recall, the gist of this account is that true judgment results when the mind identifies a past and a present image which both stem from the same object, whereas if the images identified have different origins then the judgment is false.

Another symbol that plays a key role in the dialogue is that of the elements composing a phonetic syllable. The image first appears in this dialogue in the discussion of the "dream theory," where it is employed in criticism of the thesis that complexes can be known but not their components, and then is applied again in disqualifying the penultimate sense of *logos* as an enumeration of elements. The significance of Plato's use of this model at this particular point in the *Theaetetus* should be assessed in light of its frequent occurrence in other late dialogues where Plato is wrestling with issues concerning the nature of knowledge. In the *Sophist* it is the parallel case of the grammarian who knows which letters combine and which do not that ostensibly leads Theaetetus and the Eleatic Stranger to their "chance discovery" (253C) of the "free man's knowledge." In the *Statesman* the learning of letters that go into syllables is offered as an example of the kind of example or paradigm (278B-E) that the Stranger here thinks is an important aid to the acquisition of knowledge. At *Philebus* 18C–D, moreover, knowledge of the art of letters serves as a prime illustration of what can be achieved by the method extravagantly described there (16C) as "a gift of the gods." Yet other uses of this model for similar purposes can be found in earlier dialogues, notably at *Republic* 402A–B and *Cratylus* 423E–425D, 433A–C.

Like the appearance of the sun in the final proposal regarding *logos*, the use of this symbol in these two passages of the *Theaetetus* was probably not fortuitous. Plato was too much of an artist to let powerful images like these slip in unintended. Inasmuch as this symbolism of syllables and letters occurs so frequently in contexts concerning the ways of achieving knowledge, its use here may signal that the conversation of the *Theaetetus* has brought us close to a point where a definition of knowledge is within our grasp. The image of the syllables thus joins that of the sun in leading us to expect substantial achievements regarding the acquisition of knowledge in the conversation of the following day with the Eleatic Stranger.

4. Socrates and the Imagery of Procreation

In Theodorus' initial remarks at 143E he makes a point of comparing Theaetetus to Socrates in facial appearance, drawing attention to the snub-nose and protruding eyes of the latter. This characterization should be enough to remind the reader of Meno's description of Socrates at *Meno* 80A as like a flat torpedo fish, not only in appearance but in his effect upon others. Meno's reference here to the torpifying effect of the Socratic elenchus is part of the story told in that dialogue about learning as a form of recollection. At birth, according to this story, the knowledge possessed innately by the soul is clouded by the onrush of sensation and rash opinion, and the process of regaining this innate knowledge is abetted by clearing the mind of false opinion in the manner accomplished so effectively by Socratic refutation.

Another dialogue in which even more is made of Socrates' unusual appearance is the *Symposium*. Chapter 4 above provided occasion to examine in some detail the symbolic role played by the person of Socrates in this dialogue, both in the story of his instruction by Diotima in the mysteries of Eros and in the seemingly anticlimactic eulogy by the drunken Alcibiades. In the story of Diotima, Eros is a daemon who serves as intermediary between gods and men, and who inspires the lover toward ever more lofty forms of beauty in his or her search for the immortality that procreation in the presence of beauty provides. Eros is characterized by Diotima as unkempt and shoeless, lacking in physical beauty, and both austere and in constant need, but at the same time as enterprising in pursuit of beauty and goodness, and as a lover of wisdom (*philosophōn*: 203D7) his whole life through. Inasmuch as this description fits Socrates word by word as we find him in most of the early and middle dialogues, it is plausible to assume that Plato intended the reader to think of Eros as modeled after Socrates personally. The effect is to make the person of Socrates himself into a symbol for the longing after beauty that leads the genuine philosopher ultimately to the beauties of wisdom. In Diotima's story, Socrates is more than a laboring pupil who may or may not prove capable of grasping the higher mysteries of love (210A); in his presence before the company as teller of the story, he is also a personification of the spirit of Eros that inspires mortal lovers in their restless search for beauty.

The Meno draws attention to Socrates' appearance in terms of the image of a numbing stingray. The focus of this imagery is on Socratic elenchus, which is capable of blocking out the effects of false opinion to assist his interlocutors in the recovery of knowledge. In the Symposium, Socrates' appearance stands behind Diotima's mythical account of Eros, the dramatic effect of which is to make Socrates himself a personification of the love of wisdom. The imagery of the Meno, in brief, stresses refutation, while that of the Symposium stresses procreation. Both patterns of imagery reappear in the Theaetetus, with Socrates' description of himself as a midwife assisting the minds of young men in labor. In this latter context, however, Socratic refutation is recast as a process of examining the offspring of young minds for viability—a "veritable circling around in argument" (160E8)[14] by which the newborn is "inspected" and (if found acceptable) admitted as a legitimate member of the family of discourse. And the imagery of procreation, in turn, is realigned to focus upon the delivery of offspring, as distinct from their conception as in the Symposium.

Something not to be overlooked in this connection, nonetheless, is that the skill of the midwife, as Socrates describes it, goes hand in hand with that of the matchmaker. Interestingly enough, the connection between the two skills is characterized explicitly in terms of the horticultural metaphor that we find operating in the Phaedrus and that has provided the thematic structure of the present study. There is an art, Socrates says, that has to do with the tending and harvesting of crops, and one as well of knowing what plants to set and what seeds to sow in a given type of soil (149E1–4). At base, these respective skills are part of the same horticultural art. And so it is too with the art of midwifery, where the skill of sowing is inseparable from the skill of harvesting. In midwifery dealing with women, this joint technē comprises knowing what couplings (sunousan: 149D7) will produce the best offspring, as well as knowing how to aid in bringing these offspring to birth. Although such persons are loath to practise their matchmaking skills openly for fear of being known as procurers, Socrates points out, the genuine midwife is the only one prepared to make proper matches for other people.[15]

In similar fashion, the midwifery practiced by Socrates in the birth of thoughts carries with it the skill of making matches for young men whose minds have yet to conceive. Many such people he claims to have referred to Prodicus (151B4–5), and many as well to other similarly "wise and inspired persons." An ambiguity arises at this point, however, regarding whether by his use of the midwife metaphor Socrates intends to represent himself not only as a matchmaker in this regard, but also as a contributor to the conception of some of the beautiful things (kala: 150D8) he helps young men bring to light. It is true, of course, that these beautiful things are described as having been discovered and brought to birth entirely within the minds of these young persons themselves (150D7–8).[16] The same may be said for the offspring of women delivered by midwives like Socrates' mother (149A1–2). But it is compatible with this description in either case that the offspring in question admit dual parentage. Although Socrates makes a point of saying that the young men in question never learned anything from him personally (150D6–7), what he had in mind presumably is full-fledged truths of the sort mentioned at 150C3; and this does not preclude Socrates himself serving as the source of seeds (e.g., examples and paradigms) from which these mature truths eventually grow.

There are several features of the midwife metaphor as it functions in the *Theaetetus* that suggest Socrates may have had a part in the insemination of mental offspring as well. One is the prominent appearance of the term *sunousia* in the description of Socrates' interaction with his young associates.[17] Although the term in this context seems best translated as "conversation" or "association," it also was commonly used to convey the sense of sexual intercourse. The fact that the cognate term *sunousa* is used in this latter sense explicitly in the same context (at 149D7) suggests that Socrates' association with his comrades may have been for purposes beyond those of a mental midwife. To be sure, we have seen reason to think that some of the "beautiful truths" that germinated in Plato's own mind may have been seeded originally by the historical Socrates, and it is not farfetched to conjecture that intimations of this personal experience on Plato's part might have found their way into his characterization of Socrates in the dialogue.

Another indication is the fact that associations with Socrates apparently extended over a considerable period of time (cf. 150E2–3)—certainly longer than would have been necessary for the mere delivery of mental offspring. When young men like Aristides came back to Socrates after time spent in other company, after all, presumably more was at stake than resumption of an interrupted process of delivery. Moreover, when Socrates refers certain barren young men to Prodicus for help in conception, presumably the reason would be that they had remained infertile during their time in his presence. The sense once again is that in his interaction with talented young men like Theaetetus, at least, Socrates contributed not insignificantly to the parentage of the offspring he subsequently delivered. As far as Theaetetus himself was concerned, perhaps we should take literally his remark at the end of the dialogue that Socrates has led him to give utterance to more than he had in him originally (210B6–7). This is not the sort of remark one would make to a mere obstetrician.

A further complication arising within the midwife metaphor is that, strictly speaking, Socrates' confession that he has never given birth to wisdom himself (150C8–D2) should disqualify him from serving as a midwife to other people. It was in light of the principle that human nature acquires skill only in areas where it has had experience, Socrates affirms at 149C1–2, that Artemis assigned the role of midwife to women who, although past bearing, had once given birth to children themselves. If the same principle applies to midwives of the mind, as presumably it should, then Socrates' self-professed failure ever to have given birth to anything like wisdom would preclude his being competent to assist other people in births of that sort.[18] In point of fact, Theaetetus does fail to produce knowledge of the sort in question by the end of the dialogue, and we may not go far astray in suspecting that this result was foreshadowed in Socrates' own failures of knowing.[19]

The result of these considerations is that the metaphor of Socrates as a midwife in the *Theaetetus* turns out to be a rather more fertile image than it appears at first. On the one hand, Socrates is seen to be implicated in all stages in the production of mental progeny—in matchmaking and seeding, as well as in delivery. On the other hand, he is seen as incapable of assisting young people in either the conception or the delivery of the kind of knowledge specifically to which the enquiry of the dialogue was directed. In this respect, the portrayal of Socrates in the *Theaetetus* remains consonant with his portrayal as the personification of Eros in the *Symposium*. Inasmuch as Eros is desire for something not actually possessed, the love of wisdom by nature falls short of its goal. If Socrates were portrayed as being fully competent in the ways of wisdom, then he could not at the same time serve as a personification of Eros.

As matters stand, Socrates is a paradigmatic instance of philosophic eroticism. He is intimately involved in the mental procreancy of the young men with whom he holds regular *sunousia*. Because he has never experienced the birth of wisdom himself, however, whatever love of wisdom these young persons may have within them cannot be brought to fruition by his ministrations alone. As the personification of Eros, Socrates is able to inspire his associates to the calling of philosophy. But the love of wisdom they acquire in his presence can never be satisfied under the guidance of someone who has never reached philosophic fulfillment himself. Socrates is fated always to remain a lover of wisdom only, and never its possessor.

In order for philosophy to be moved from desire to fulfillment, the erotic impulse by which it is driven must be channeled in the direction of genuine knowledge. For the Plato of the middle period onward, the guidance of this impulse falls within the province of dialectic. Let us turn to the role of dialectic in the *Theaetetus*.

5. Procreancy Channeled through Dialectic

A summary of the major arguments in the *Theaetetus* was given in section 2 above. All of these arguments, as noted there, take the form of refutations and are associated in one way or another with the three hypotheses regarding the nature of knowledge. What was not noted in this previous discussion is that these arguments all fit neatly within the structure of the method of hypothesis. Although this seems to have escaped the notice of most commentators on the *Theaetetus*, every major turn in the conversation between Socrates and Theaetetus can be identified with an appropriate step in the sequence of procedures delineating that method in the *Phaedo* and the *Republic*. In effect, the *Theaetetus* represents the most extensive application of the method of hypothesis to be found in the dialogues, which is also the last application before Plato takes up the method of collection and division in the dialogues following.

Although the method of hypothesis has already been examined in chapter 5, it will be helpful to reiterate its major features. In following this method, the philosopher or dialectician first (step 1) posits the hypothesis to be tested. The next step (2) is to define or otherwise to explicate any terms in the hypothesis that require clarification. This accomplished, the hypothesis is ready for (3) a test of consistency both (a) with respect to its logical consequences and (b) with respect to assumptions of the context in which the discussion takes place. If inconsistent in either respect, the hypothesis is rejected and the process starts over again. If the hypothesis proves consistent, however, the next step (4) is to seek out some more general hypothesis from which it can be deduced in turn. Steps (2) and (3) then are repeated in sequence for this more general hypothesis. When a more general hypothesis is found that proves consistent, the dialectician must assess its status within the context of discussion. If it requires further support to count as true within that context, then step (4) is repeated for it in sequence; and the process is continued until a hypothesis is found that requires no further accounting. In application to the *Theaetetus*, as we shall see, the method is not pursued past the consistency test of step (3). The effect is to restrict the discussion of knowledge in this dialogue to the underpart of the Divided Line. Before turning to consider Plato's self-imposed restriction in this regard, we should specify the dialogue's accomplishments in terms of the method.

Theaetetus' first hypothesis (step(1)) identifies knowledge and perception. The sense in which perception is to be understood is defined (step (2)) primarily by the account of perception,[20] formulated between 152A and 160E with the help of well-known theses attributed to Protagoras and Heraclitus. Clarification of Theaetetus' hypothesis continues with the independent refutation of these other two theses, showing them to be distinct from the hypothesis specifically under examination. Two consequences of Theaetetus' hypothesis noted at 152C are (1) that perception is infallible and (2) that perception takes things that have being for its objects. Given the sense of perception defined just previously, these two consequences are tested for consistency (step (3a)) and found wanting, requiring the rejection of the first hypothesis. The only major portion of the discussion between 151D and 186E not accommodated thus far is the digression at 172C–177C contrasting philosophy and rhetoric. Although the primary purpose of this digression, as already suggested, is probably to provide "breathing space" for the reader (or "audience"),[21] its clear allusions to the Cave of the *Republic* also serve to establish the context in which Theaetetus' hypotheses should be evaluated. The concern of the conversation underway is the knowledge of philosophy, as distinct from the "technical" know-how of the rhetorician.

Theaetetus' second hypothesis identifying knowledge with true judgment constitutes a new beginning with step (1) of the method. In terms of the method strictly interpreted, the only reason this hypothesis should not be refuted immediately (by the counterexample of step (3b)) is that it contains terms that require definition (step (2)). The definition of *doxa* (judgment) itself is handled in a rather perfunctory fashion at 189E–190A (the mind agreeing with itself in its silent discourse),[22] but the definition of truth and falsehood pertaining to judgment poses a whole series of problems. By the end of the fifth attempt (the aviary) to pin down the distinction between true and false judgment, the required meaning of truth still remains elusive. A consequence is that the second hypothesis cannot be subjected to the consistency test of step (3A). The counter-example of the juryman, however, quickly shows the identification of knowledge and true judgment to be inconsistent with the undoubted fact of the matter—i.e., the fact that true judgment can be reached in the absence of knowledge. Theaetetus' second hypothesis thus fails at step (3b), requiring yet another return to the beginning with a new hypothesis.

Discussion of the third hypothesis (step (1)), proposing that knowledge is true judgment accompanied by *logos*, is limited to an examination of four attempts to clarify a sense of *logos* (step(2)) that would make that proposal plausible. The first is bound up with a theory of logical atomism (the "dream theory") in such a fashion as to put the whole theory on trial, beyond the account of *logos* that it contains. This may be why Socrates returns to a very similar sense of *logos* in the second of the three remaining attempts, but this time without the atomistic trappings. The first of the remaining attempts, of course, proposes that *logos* is simply the sounds of vocal speech, while the third suggests that *logos* be thought of in the sense of a distinguishing mark. Inasmuch as none of these four purported definitions of *logos* proves adequate, the final hypothesis never proceeds beyond step (2) of the method. As a consequence it is never tested for consistency, and certainly cannot be said to have been refuted.[23]

While the *Theaetetus* clearly ends on a note of failure, accordingly, its argument does not establish that knowledge is *not* true judgment accompanied by *logos*. Nor, by the same token, should the failure of the dialogue to arrive at a satisfactory definition of knowledge be taken in itself as an indication of some deep-seated defect in the method of hypothesis. If Plato had seen fit, he could have structured parts of the conversation in the *Sophist* after this method as well.[24] As far as those parts of the *Sophist* dealing with the nature of knowledge are concerned, indeed, something rather close to this seems to have happened. By 264B of this later dialogue, an apparently satisfactory account of true and false judgment has been provided; and an apparently adequate sense of *logos* accompanying the "free man's knowledge" has been isolated by 253E. These, of course, are the two components the absence of which stalled further progress by the method of hypothesis at the end of the *Theaetetus*. And with these components at hand, Plato had the option of moving on to a consistency check (step(3)) of the third hypothesis that knowledge is true judgment accompanied by *logos*.

One reason Plato chose against this option, nonetheless, may have been his awareness that the "voyage of logos" (*Sophist* 253B11) that produces the "free man's knowledge" was departing in subtle ways from the composite conception of knowledge articulated in that third hypothesis. The sense of philosophic knowledge one gets from these passages in the *Sophist* is not such that it is synthesized by adding *logos* to judgment that happens to be true. The sense rather is that the *logos* in question itself constitutes knowledge. More specifically, the sense is that the *logos* in question is the mind's grasp of reality "through reason" (*dia logismōn*: 254A8)—something beyond the powers of the "vulgar mind's eye" (*tōn pollōn psuchēs ommata*: 254A10). The conception of the relation between true judgment and knowledge that Plato seems to be working with at this point, accordingly, is not such that knowledge is the same thing as true judgment with *logos* added, but rather such that true judgment plus *logos* is *compresent* with knowledge. The sense, in brief, is that when one knows by virtue of having the requisite *logos*, then with the backing of that *logos* one's judgments will be true. As a consequence, one who knows has true judgment along with that *logos*, and one who judges truly with that *logos* at the same time knows. We will return to this topic in the final section.

When the company reconvenes on the following day for a conversation about sophistry, at any rate, a different approach to knowledge is in the works, along with a new discussion-leader who is experienced in a different dialectical method. But the accomplishments gained on the previous day through the method of hypothesis are not left behind. It is time now to stand back for an overview of how these accomplishments prepare us for this new approach to knowledge.

6. Dunamis *in the Conversation of the* Theaetetus

By the end of the conversation between Socrates and Theaetetus, no satisfactory account has been reached of the nature of knowledge. Most commentators interpret this lack as a failure, and there are various conjectures about why Plato wrote the dialogue to end in this fashion. One prominent view is that of F. M. Cornford, who interpreted this apparent failure as an indication on Plato's part that knowledge cannot be defined without reference to the Forms.[25] Cornford's sense seemed to be that Plato had a satisfactory definition of knowledge at hand, but withheld it by way of demonstrating that knowledge requires as its objects entities that do not "change in any respect."[26] Other more recent commentators take the view that Plato was uncertain how knowledge should be defined while writing the *Theaetetus* and hence that the apparent failure should be understood as genuine.[27] There is another perspective to be taken on the apparent failure of the dialogue, however, that may give us a more sympathetic view of Plato's own thinking on the matter. This perspective takes us back to the theme of both the *Phaedrus* and the Seventh Letter that philosophic knowledge cannot be communicated through writing.

The *Theaetetus* is a dialogue doubly bound to the written word. Its featured conversation between Theaetetus and Socrates is read by Euclides' slave from a written copy. This featured conversation, in turn, is contained within an introductory dialogue, involving Terpsion, Euclides, and (implicitly) the slave boy, that was written by Plato for our subsequent reading. If the theme from the *Phaedrus* and the Seventh Letter noted above is to be taken at face value, as we have seen reason in chapter 1 to believe it should be, then *of course* the conversation between Socrates and Theaetetus had to be represented as falling short of its goal. To represent it as successful would be to represent Socrates as eliciting genuine knowledge from Theaetetus through his maieutic activity, which in turn would involve purporting to express philosophic knowledge (about knowledge) in written form. Since this is something Plato expressly said could not be done—not even by him (Seventh Letter 341D)—it should be taken as a foregone conclusion that nothing Plato wrote as part of the conversation between the two main characters would constitute knowledge of the sort being sought within the dialogue.

What this means, however, is that the fact that neither Socrates nor Theaetetus is depicted as possessing knowledge of the sort in question at the end of the dialogue cannot correctly be taken to constitute failure on the part of the dialogue itself. The dialogue fails only if what its author intended to achieve in writing it is not accomplished. And since we have

quite definite reasons for thinking that Plato did not intend the conversation of the written dialogue to end with a representation of philosophic knowledge, it cannot count as a failure of the dialogue that it ends
without such a representation. Given what he said elsewhere about the
suitability of writing for the communication of knowledge, how could
Plato *write* a scene in which a *slave boy* reads words from a *manuscript*
(attributed to Socrates or anyone else) purporting to convey *knowledge* of
the nature of knowledge?

As a product of Plato's dramatic art, the written conversation between
Socrates and Theaetetus cannot be expected to conclude with either
character speaking words conveying knowledge about knowledge. But
the dialogue between Socrates and Theaetetus (or that between Euclides
and Terpsion, by the same token) is not the only conversation Plato was
dealing with in writing the *Theaetetus*. The underlying theme of the
present study is that Plato wrote most of his major dialogues as teaching
instruments to guide the attentive reader to the kind of insight of which
he spoke in the Seventh Letter. If this is true of any dialogue, it certainly
is true of the *Theaetetus*, with its explicitly dialectical structure (following the method of hypothesis point by point) as well as its explicit
concern with the nature of knowledge. In keeping with its central image
of *dunamis*, or power, the *Theaetetus* has the capacity to impel the
attentive reader into a series of conjectures that themselves might move
the mind beyond the unsatisfactory state of *aporia* in which Theaetetus
was left at the end of the dialogue.[28]

From this perspective, the question of the success or failure of the
written dialogue hangs upon what can be learned from it by sustained
attentive reading. And the question of what an attentive reader is able
actually to learn from the dialogue, in turn, is equivalent to the question of
what genuine knowledge he or she can gain through the conversation it
enables the reader to have with the author. Without becoming unduly
preoccupied with the apparent oddity of referring to an interchange of this
sort as a conversation (a matter discussed in chapter 1 above), let us turn to
reflect upon what someone might be able to learn about the nature of
knowledge from repeated encounters with this particular dialogue.

One thing to reiterate by way of preparation is that what one learns
about knowledge from the dialogue—learns in the sense of genuinely
coming to know—is not likely to coincide very closely with anything
written as comments by either of the main characters. This is so not only
because all the substantive proposals about the nature of knowledge put

forth in the discussion between Socrates and Theaetetus are shown to be inadequate; it is so more importantly because of Plato's conviction that philosophic knowledge cannot be put into writing. Nonetheless, what one stands to learn by careful and sustained reading of the dialogue is likely to be in keeping with the dialectical thrust of the *sunousia* already underway in the dialogue, which means that it is likely to concern the relation between knowledge and *logos*. What might one learn about knowledge in relation to *logos* from the line of dialectic underway in the *Theaetetus*?

One pertinent reflection to reiterate in this regard is that the final hypothesis identifying knowledge as true judgment accompanied by *logos* is not actually refuted, as were the previous two hypotheses. The grounds on which this third hypothesis is ostensibly given up at 210B amount to nothing more than the failure of three or four relatively implausible proposals about the sense of *logos* that might serve as the distinguishing factor between true judgment and knowledge. There is no question whatever that several far more promising senses of the term were available to Plato had he chosen to explore them.[29] The entirely commonplace inference from this is that Plato chose deliberately not to explore these senses. A further inference is that his reasons for doing so had to do with a dialectical interchange he was hoping to set up with future readers that would go beyond the interchange in the recorded conversation between Socrates and Theaetetus. Whatever Plato's reasons in this regard, we naturally enough might come to think that perhaps one of these more promising senses of *logos* will fill the bill, and that knowledge will turn out to be true judgment accompanied by *logos* after all.

Among available senses of *logos* that seem to merit consideration here are those of *explanation* and *reason*. If one had an explanation of a certain matter—say the nature of knowledge—then this explanation, in combination with true judgment, would certainly appear to be a reasonable candidate for knowledge. Likewise, if one were aware of the reason why a certain mental state amounts to knowledge, then one's awareness of that reason might well appear to amount to knowledge of the matter. Why did Plato not have Socrates examine these additional senses of *logos* in connection with the third hypothesis before ending the dialogue in apparent failure?[30]

There is another sense of *logos*, indeed, that seems even more promising. This is the sense of account or *definition*—a sense that plays

a prominent role at the beginning of the dialogue and that has associations with knowledge made apparent by Socrates himself. After
Theaetetus had produced his own example of an account giving an
entirely general characterization of the mathematical surds or *dunamei*,
we recall, Socrates asks him if he can come up with a similar definition (*logon:* 148D2) of knowledge. What he wants, Socrates goes on the
say, is a "single account" (*heni logō:* 148D7) that applies to the many kinds
of knowledge. The account of the surds provided by Theaetetus is
entirely general in that it gives conditions that are both necessary and
sufficient for being a quantity of that particular sort.[31] So what Socrates is
looking for in the case of knowledge, we may confidently surmise, is a
logos giving conditions that are both necessary and sufficient for a
person's being in that mental state. The knowledge about knowledge
that would constitute success in the maieutic interchange between
Socrates and Theaetetus, in brief, would be an account of knowledge in
terms of its necessary and sufficient conditions. Why does Plato refrain
from bringing this specific sense of *logos* back into consideration when he
depicts Socrates as looking for a *logos* that would convert true judgment
into knowledge?

Part of the answer to this question may be that Plato wanted his
readers to think of this particular sense of *logos* on their own, which is
not too much to expect given its prominence at the beginning of the
dialogue. Once we start thinking carefully about how the term in this
sense would fit into the formula identifying knowledge as true judgment
with *logos*, however, we become aware of certain anomalies that are
instructive in their own right. Another part of the answer, accordingly,
may be that Plato wanted his readers to discover the truth that follows on
the heels of these anomalies from "within themselves" (*par' hautōn:*
150D7) alone. If these difficulties had been brought to the attention of
his readers in the manner of birds introduced into aviaries—i.e., by
explicit arguments put into the mouths of his characters—then the
medium of language might have impeded any knowledge that comes
with them. A better course, in Plato's view, would be to help his readers
discover these things themselves. What anomalies accompany a definition of this sort?

There indeed is a *logos*—that of necessary and sufficient conditions—
possession of which is tantamount to possession of knowledge of a given
thing (e.g., of knowledge itself). The interchange between Socrates and
Theaetetus at 148D makes this clear. On reflection, however, we see that

this is not a sense of the term we should want to propose as the *logos* that produces knowledge when it accompanies true judgment. There are several reasons why this is so. One reason is familiar from recent commentary on the issue[32]—namely, that purporting to complete a definition of knowledge as true judgment plus *logos* by specifying a sense of *logos* that is itself equivalent to knowledge would simply be circular. The "other alternative" to which the discussants allude at 209E–210A seems to pick out the shortcoming of this proposal quite nicely. Inasmuch as we are inquiring after the nature of knowledge, and inasmuch as *logos* in this sense amounts to knowledge already, it is "altogether silly" (*pantapasi . . . euēthes:* 210A7), as Socrates put it, to suggest that knowledge is correct judgment "together with a *knowledge* of differentness or of anything whatever" (210A8–9). There is no advance to be made toward understanding knowledge by thinking of knowledge as true judgment with knowledge added.

But the problem with this proposal cuts deeper than that. Given that *logos* of a certain sort (that giving necessary and sufficient conditions) is acknowledged at the beginning of the dialogue to be equivalent to knowledge, the definition of knowledge for which Theaetetus is seeking should serve as a definition of this kind of *logos* as well. And the attempt to define this *logos* as true judgment accompanied by *logos* of *any* sort seems misguided in the first place. The problem on this deeper level is not exactly one of circularity, for there is no reason why a term in one sense should not be defined with the help of a homonymous term carrying a distinctly different sense.[33] The problem lies rather with purporting to define *logos* in the sense of knowledge as a combination of true judgment plus *logos* in a "weaker" sense that falls short of knowledge. If A (*logos* in the sense of knowledge) can be produced by adding B (a weaker *logos*) to C (true judgment), then A presumably could be produced by adding C to B as well. And if a person is in possession of *logos* about a certain matter that falls short of knowledge, it is hard to see how the addition of true judgment could convert that initial *logos* into a *logos* in a "stronger" sense tantamount to knowledge. Starting with *logos* in any one of the final three senses considered at the end of the dialogue (speech, enumeration of parts, characteristic mark), for instance, there seems to be no conceivable way in which it could be converted into the *logos* equivalent to knowledge by the addition of true judgment. If a given *logos* falls short of knowledge by reason of failing to give necessary and sufficient conditions, this deficiency will not be remedied by the addition of judgment of any sort whatever. Assuming that the judgment remains distinct from the *logos* itself, as seemingly required by the form of the third hypothesis, the deficiency will not be remedied even by true judgment about such conditions. The difference between one of these "weaker" senses of *logos* and the *logos* that is tantamount to knowledge, in brief, seems to have nothing to do with judgment at all.

What this all suggests is that a fruitful approach to an understanding of the *logos* exemplified by Theaetetus' account of the surds—to an understanding, that is, of the *logos* equivalent to knowledge—would not proceed by way of judgment at all, true, false, or indeterminate. If someone is in possession of a *logos* about a certain topic that amounts to knowledge, then whether or not that person makes a judgment in language about the topic is quite irrelevant. If a person, on the other hand, has a *logos* only that falls short of knowledge, then that *logos* is not converted to knowledge by any transaction involving language. The reason in either case is that knowledge is a state of mind that, as Plato sees it, cannot be expressed in language. And insofar as judgment is a transaction conducted in language—the language of public symbolism (even though "spoken silently" to oneself; *Theaetetus* 190A) which is excluded from true knowledge—it contributes nothing to the state of mind in question.

What can be learned from reflection along these lines, I suggest, is that knowledge (as a state of mind) and judgment (as a transaction in language) are quite different forms of mental involvement and are directed toward objects of quite different sorts. Knowledge, for Plato, takes Forms as its objects, while judgment is directed toward linguistic entities of the sort we call propositions. Because of this essential difference in proper object, the latter cannot be converted into the former by the addition of any other component whatever. It is relevant to note, in this connection, that the characterization of the "free man's knowledge" at *Sophist* 253C–E makes no mention of judgment. Although true and false judgment are finally defined a few pages before this dialogue's end (263B–D), this definition serves only in the final account of Sophistry, and contributes nothing to the description of the philosopher's knowledge.[34]

The upshot, if this reading is anywhere near correct, is that the third hypothesis, equating knowledge with true judgment along with *logos*, is slated for rejection after all. Since knowledge on the one hand is a mental state, and judgment on the other is a linguistic act, there is no manner of *logos*—indeed, nothing else whatever—that could augment true judgment to produce a state of knowledge. The best that can be made of Theaetetus' final hypothesis is that knowledge is *compresent* with true judgment expressing *logos*. When one knows by virtue of having the requisite kind of *logos*—namely, a *logos* articulating necessary and sufficient conditions—that is to say, then one's judgments expressing that *logos* are bound to be true. In effect, to be in a state of knowledge is equivalent to being in possession of the kind of *logos* that guarantees truth to judgments made on the topic in question. So in a manner of speaking, one might still maintain the general equation of knowledge with true judgment in the presence of *logos*; but the sense quite pointedly is not that true judgment becomes knowledge when *logos* is added. The sense is that *logos* itself might constitute knowledge and that a *logos* amounting to knowledge guarantees truth in judgment.

A more fruitful approach to the nature of knowledge than the approach followed in the *Theaetetus* would be to leave judgment out of the picture entirely and would aim instead at a general characterization of the sort of *logos* illustrated in Theaetetus' account of the surds. This, of course, is what happens in the *Sophist*. And, as already noted, the view of the relation between knowledge and *logos* that we find adumbrated in this later dialogue corresponds point by point with the view we have arrived at from a careful reading of the *Theaetetus*. My guess, accordingly, is that Plato shaped the *Theaetetus* as an apparent failure, not because he lacked resources to end it otherwise, but because he conceived it as a dialectical exercise to prepare the reader for further reflection of the nature of knowledge. Thus the *Theaetetus* prepares us for the *sunousia* of the *Sophist*.

NOTES

Introduction

1. A. N. Whitehead, *Process and Reality: An Essay in Cosmology*, chapter 1, section 1.

2. The terms *sunousia* and *dialogos* are used interchangeably at *Protagoras* 338C7–8, for instance. Other uses in this sense occur in the *Alcibiades* (114D1), the *Theaetetus* (150D4, 150E4, 151A2), the *Sophist* (217D9), and elsewhere in the *Protagoras* (310A2, 335B3, 5, 335C1,4).

3. I will follow the convention of phonetic transliteration for words containing gamma before kappa, chi, xi, or another gamma.

4. See the Budé edition of the Letters, translated and annotated by Joseph Souilhé (Collection des Universités de France, Paris, 1949), p. 49.

5. I am indebted to Glenn Morrow's *Plato's Epistles* for this and other historical material in the discussion following.

6. There is evidence of some doubt about the Twelfth Letter from the time of Thrasyllus, and Proclus was said to have rejected all thirteen. See Morrow, *Plato's Epistles*, p. 6.

7. Ibid.

8. This generalization is based primarily on the survey by Brisson in *Platon: Lettres*.

9. Despite Morrow, *Plato's Epistles*, p. 14. Also see Guthrie, *A History of Greek Philosophy*, vol. V, 401n., in this regard.

10. In Brisson's *Platon: Lettres*, dealing with thirty-two authors, the Seventh Letter is rejected only by scholars who reject all the others as well. The picture is less clear according to Guthrie (1978), which lists only scholars who reject some Letters other than the first but do not reject all, and which gives an acceptance rate of five to two for the Seventh Letter.

11. See Guthrie, *A History of Greek Philosophy*, vol. V, p. 401n.

12. Gulley also rejects the entire set in his "The authenticity of the Platonic Epistles."

13. As Solmsen points out in his review, Edelstein's arguments would work against the *Philebus* and the *Laws* as well as the Seventh Letter.

14. The words are those of Friedrich Solmsen, in his review of Edelstein's book.

15. See, for example, the remark of Richard Robinson quoted in Guthrie's *A History of Greek Philosophy*, vol. V, 402n.: "Until the Seventh Letter is demolished with arguments considerably superior to those put forward by the late Professor Edelstein . . . most scholars will quite properly remain unconvinced."

16. Morrow, *Plato's Epistles*, p. 14.

17. As Solmsen puts it, such a forger would stand at a "huge distance . . . (from the) rank and file of Greek epistolographi" (review of Edelstein, p. 34). See also Morrow, *Plato's Epistles*, p. 57, in this regard.

18. This apparent discrepancy is nicely summarized in Brisson's *Platon: Lettres*, p. 142.

19. Detailed discussions of Plato's likely motives in this undertaking found in Morrow's *Plato's Epistles*, pp. 44ff., and in Gaiser's "Plato's Enigmatic Lecture 'On the Good'."

20. The amount of attention given this alleged difficulty is somewhat surprising in light of the fact that the term occurs only five times in Plato's writing overall, the above four in addition to *Menexenus* 239A3.

21. See Brisson's *Platon: Lettres*, p. 143, and Solmsen's review of Edelstein, p. 163. Vlastos' article "*Isonomia politike*" is also very helpful, despite the fact that he sees fit (without argument) to reject the Seventh Letter.

22. A relatively superficial problem is that the Forms are not mentioned as such in these passages, as observed by Morrow in *Plato's Epistles*, p. 75. In addition to Morrow's rebuttal with reference to the distinction between the *ti* and the *poion ti* (as at 342E), it should be noted that the Good, the Beautiful, and the Just are explicitly cited at 342D4.

23. Edelstein, *Plato's Seventh Letter*, p. 167. Another specialized problem is raised in Tarrant's "Middle Platonism and the *Seventh Epistle*," to the effect that Plutarch would have referred to these passages if they had been available to him with the rest of the letter. This problem is too conjectural to count against authenticity on its own.

24. See the review of Edelstein's book by Solmsen. In this regard, also see Morrow's *Plato's Epistles*, pp. 66ff.

25. Edelstein, in *Plato's Seventh Letter*, p. 167, among others.

26. One of the earliest studies dealing with the style of Plato's writing was Campbell's *The Sophistes and Politicus of Plato*, published in 1867. See the summary of Campbell's work employing relevant measures in chapter 2 of Brandwood's *The Chronology of Plato's Dialogues*.

27. See Morrow's *Plato's Epistles*, p. 10, and Brisson's *Platon: Lettres*, p. 72.

28. For Raeder and Wilamowitz-Moellendorff, see the citations in Morrow, *Plato's Epistles*, p. 11n.

29. Ledger, *Re-counting Plato*, p. 25.

1. Why Plato Wrote Dialogues

1. The *Dissoi Logoi* is a document by an unknown author from the end of the fifth century B.C. Its Doric dialectic and eristic character suggest Megara as its source. In this regard, see John Burnet, *Greek Philosophy*, Part I, p. 231.

2. Xenophon gives his own version of Socrates' public defense (also called *Apologia*), based on the presumably eyewitness account of Hermogenes (mentioned at *Phaedo* 59B), which differs substantially from Plato's story. According to the opening statement of Xenophon's account, there were other written versions of Socrates' defense as well. The point is that both Xenophon's and Plato's accounts should be read more as reflections on the significance of this historical event than as verbatim reports of the event itself. Given the emotionally charged atmosphere of the occasion, how can we imagine an actual eyewitness—Hermogenes or anyone else—calmly sitting there taking notes on the details of the proceedings?

3. A good place to start in checking the dramatic dates of the various dialogues is A. E. Taylor's *Plato: The Man and His Work*.

4. Additional arguments to the effect that the dialogues were not written as representations of actual Socratic conversations may be found in Charles Kahn's "Did Plato Write Socratic Dialogues?" pp. 305–20.

5. F. M. Cornford, *Plato and Parmenides*, p. 109.

6. K. M. Sayre, "A Maieutic View of Five Late Dialogues," p. 227.

7. A recent twist on this theme appears in Gregory Vlastos' *Socrates, Ironist and Moral Philosopher*. In both the early and middle dialogues, Vlastos argues, the words Plato assigns his character Socrates express Plato's own current conception of philosophic truth. The main difference between the two groups in this respect, Vlastos argues, is that the views articulated in the early dialogues correspond with those of the historical Socrates, while those expressed in the middle dialogues represent Plato's own improvement upon this earlier (Socratic) philosophy.

8. For a discussion of Plato's changing conception of the Good, see K. M. Sayre, *Plato's Late Ontology: A Riddle Resolved*, chapter 3, section 4.

9. For an analysis of this trap, see K. M. Sayre, "Propositional Logic in Plato's *Protagoras*."

10. See the judicious footnote in this regard on p. 4 of Gerasimos Santas' "Plato's *Protagoras* and Explanations of Weakness."

11. This claim is defended at length in my "Why Plato Never Had a Theory of Forms."

12. A useful study in this regard is R. K. Sprague's *Plato's Use of Fallacy: A Study of the Euthydemus and Some Other Dialogues.*

13. Gilbert Ryle, *Plato's Progress*, ch. II.

14. Mitchell Miller, *Plato's Parmenides: The Conversion of the Soul.*

15. Ibid., p. 8.

16. The reader may be aware of other accounts of Plato's dramatic form than the three I have found occasion to discuss in this section. Among the more important is that of Stanley Rosen, displayed most admirably in his *Plato's Symposium*. Rosen's account, it should be noted, gives prominent place to the testimony of the Seventh Letter.

17. The text is not entirely clear on what exactly the *pragma* in question is supposed to be. Part of the sense of paradox generated by this passage comes from assuming that the matter at hand is simply *philosophy*, as distinct from professed *knowledge* thereof.

18. The reference to "unwritten teachings" (*agrophois dogmasin*) in Aristotle's *Physics* 209b15, upon which this view relies in part, does not obviously pertain to "teachings" by Plato.

19. A bibliography listing many thousands of pages of learned conjecture on the topic of Plato's "unwritten teachings" may be found in Hans Joachim Krämer's recently translated *Plato and the Foundations of Metaphysics*. A critical review of this book by the present author appears in *Ancient Philosophy* 13, no. 1 (1993): 1–18.

20. A tangent to a circle at a given point is a straight line sharing that point alone with the circumference.

21. See Miles Burnyeat's "Socratic Midwifery, Platonic Inspiration," for considerations showing that the midwife imagery probably was not associated with the historical Socrates.

22. The relevance of this analogy was pointed out to me by David O'Connor.

23. What Socrates says literally is that the serious farmer will not plant his seeds in a "garden of Adonis" (*Adōnidos kēpous:* 276B3), expecting good results within eight days. I owe to Charles Griswold (*Self-Knowledge in Plato's Phaedrus*, p. 285) the explanation that "Adonis' gardens grew and died in a short span of time, in commemoration of Aphrodite's brief affair with her beloved, Adonis."

24. Immediately before mention of conversation "for the sake of teaching and learning" at 278A2, there is reference to written discourse that "at its best" (278A1) can become a "reminder to those who know" (*eidotōn hupomnēsin:* 278A1). If "those who know" include the learner in whose soul the discourse in question is being "written," there may be an allusion here to the account of recollection (*anamnēsis:* 249C2) in the palinode some thirty pages earlier.

25. At 266B, interestingly enough, Socrates describes himself as eager to follow in the footsteps of any dialectician he should encounter, which would be to cast himself in the role of a learner.

26. There are indications, most notably in the *Theaetetus* and the *Sophist*, that Plato's association with Socrates did not carry him all the way to the state of illumination described in the Seventh Letter. In some way or another Plato may have had to go the final distance on his own. This is compatible with the likely fact that *sunousia* with Socrates provided guidance to Plato at the early stages of the journey at least.

27. Reference is to the "performance" view generally, but to Miller's version in particular.

28. Given the many allusions to Plato's views in the writings of Aristotle, we have reason to surmise that the *Symposium*, the *Theaetetus*, the *Sophist*, and the *Parmenides*, among others, were familiar to him at least. Yet it is noteworthy that Aristotle only occasionally refers to particular dialogues by name, as the *Timaeus*, for example, is cited in the *De Anima* and the *Physics*, as the *Prior Analytics* cites the *Meno*, and as the *Politics* mentions the *Republic* and the *Laws*.

2. Refutation and Irony: Preparing the Ground

1. See W. K. C. Guthrie, *Socrates*, p.11.

2. Such is Strepsiades' opinion at least; see line 98.

3. The charge of corrupting the youth is made against Socrates at *Apology* 24B.

4. The most informative of these is *Metaphysics* 1078b, which says nothing about refutation but will be relevant to our discussion at a later point. In this passage, Socrates is said to have been interested (among other things) in "universal definitions" (*horizesthai katholou*: 1078b18–19, 29) and in "inductive arguments" (*epaktikous logous*: 1078b28). This was appropriate, says Aristotle, because Socrates was trying to "syllogize" (*sullogizesthai*: 1078b24), and "seeking the essence" (*ezētei to ti estin*: 1078b23–24) is appropriate to such activity.

5. Given that Plato in other contexts was so persistent in displaying sophistry in an unfavorable light, it is sometimes perceived as eccentric, if not downright perverse, to associate Socrates with the likes of Protagoras and Gorgias. On the other hand, it is not uncommon for historians of ancient Greece to list Socrates among the sophists as a matter of course (see, for example, J. B. Bury's *History of Greece*); and G. B. Kerford's judicious study *The Sophistic Movement* arrives at the guarded conclusion that "Socrates should be treated as having a part to play *within* the sophistic movement" (p. 57, his emphasis). The first thing to be noted, by way of antidote to the sense of outrage one might feel toward the thought of Socrates as a sophist, is that the term *sophistēs*—meaning "wise man"—had a highly favorable meaning before the fifth century. The Seven Sages (Solon, Thales, etc., see *Protagoras* 343A for a full list) were known by that title, as were various other presocratic poets and

philosophers. By the beginning of the Peloponnesian War, however, the term had taken on a more restricted meaning, referring to the more or less professional teachers of oratory and other political skills who made their services available to young persons of political ambition. As with professionalism of any sort, the services of the sophists were offered in exchange for money; and where money is involved inevitably there are conflicts of interest.

6. G. B. Kerford, *The Sophistic Movement*. Gregory Vlastos, in "The Socratic Elenchus," finds fault with "the assimilation of the elenchus to Zeno's dialectic," which he attributes to Kerford, Robinson, and others, for the reason that "Zeno's refutations are unasserted counterfactuals," whereas (allegedly) "Socrates . . . will not debate unasserted premises—only those asserted categorically by his interlocutor, who is not allowed to answer 'contrary to his real opinion' " (p. 29). In support of this supposed proscription on Socrates' part, Vlastos quotes a few passages from the earlier dialogues in which Socrates rather imperiously instructs his interlocutors to put their own opinions up for cross-examination. One thing Vlastos fails to note in this regard is that most of these passages (one in the *Crito* excepted) Socrates is trying to outmaneuver an impatient and sometimes downright hostile opponent (e.g., Callicles and Thrasymachus)— not at all the type of situation in which the elenchus could realistically be used to "test one's seriousness in pursuit of truth" (p. 36) or any of the other highminded purposes to which Vlastos thinks the elenchus was put by Socrates. In one of these passages, for example (*Protagoras* 331C), Socrates has just tripped up Protagoras with a rather silly argument to the effect that Justice and Holiness are the same; and when Protagoras in exasperation dismisses the argument by saying "have it your own way," Socrates rubs his nose in it further by saying he wants Protagoras to stop being evasive and to say what he really thinks. A few lines after this, Socrates drops this line of argument and takes up another which Protagoras finds equally annoying in its superficiality. This is not the way someone argues as "a challenge to his fellows to change their life," as Vlastos describes it (p. 36), but rather a way to make someone angry for tactical effect.

Another thing Vlastos overlooks is a number of passages in which Socrates actually *urges* his opponent to debate positions which the latter expressly rejects. Two passages of this sort which Vlastos does note are *Protagoras* 333B–C and 352D–E, which he describes quite erroneously as occasions on which "Socrates is willing to waive the rule" in a gesture to spare the "battered ego" of his opponent from further "mauling" (p. 37). In the first of these, Socrates asks Protagoras to respond to questions directed against a position the latter refuses to accept, by way of setting him up for yet another captious argument which— far from sheltering Protagoras' "battered ego"—makes him so angry that he refuses to answer further questions along that line and breaks out into a bit of oratory that soon has the audience applauding. In the second of these instances,

Protagoras is induced to answer for the "common man" on a view he personally finds shameful at first, but later (358A–B) is tricked into accepting through some verbal byplay between Socrates and Prodicus. What Vlastos never saw is that these maneuvers were necessary to set Protagoras up for the final refutation (see my "Propositional Logic in Plato's Protagoras" for an analysis of the argument). Two other relevant passages that Vlastos simply overlooks are *Meno* 87B, where Socrates recommends to Meno an explicitly hypothetical mode of argument as a preface to further elenchus, and *Parmenides* 135E–136A, where Parmenides recommends to Socrates a mode of argument exactly matching that presumably used by Zeno. For these reasons, I cannot credit Vlastos' view that Socrates has a "rule" (p. 37) of debating only premises his interlocutors categorically assert; accordingly I cannot accept Vlastos' censure of Kerford, and others for likening Socratic elenchus to the dialectic of Zeno.

7. Kerford, *The Sophistic Movement*, p. 62. The term Kerford glosses as 'antilogic' is *antilogikē* (p. 61).

8. Ibid., p. 63.

9. The discussion in question occurs in Cornford's *Plato and Parmenides*, where he cites the use of the term at *Phaedrus* 261D and identifies Zeno as the "Eleatic Palamedes" who "can make the same things appear to his hearers to be both like and unlike, one and many, at rest and in motion" (pp. 67–68).

10. *The Sophistic Movement*, p. 66.

11. Pericles, Plutarch said, was a student of Zeno the Eleatic, who developed a powerful technique of examining opponents; and what this amounted to was bringing them to a state of *aporia* through *antilogias*. See Kerford, *The Sophistic Movement*, p. 85, for a translation.

12. Although Kerford does not maintain a sharp distinction between the historical Socrates and the Socrates of the dialogues, it is clear from ibid., pp. 55–57, that his concern is with the former primarily.

13. For an analysis of this argument, see K. M. Sayre, *Plato's Analytic Method*, pp. 130–32.

14. The historical status of this account is highly dubious; but this is irrelevant to Plato's dramatic purposes.

15. Although Socrates is not mentioned by name in this context, there is near consensus among commentators that the allusion here is to Socratic refutation.

16. This "method of argument" so-described at 227A8 and 230B6, it might be noted, is *not* dialectic, contrary to the tendentious translation by Jowett found in some English editions of the *Sophist*.

17. The reader may be reminded at this point of Socrates' claim in the *Apology* (30E–31C) to be godsent as a gadfly to the people of Athens, that they may be aroused to pay heed to matters of virtue.

18. In the *Apology*, Socrates explains his public activity as a gadfly—for which he quite pointedly denies ever accepting a fee (31B–C)—as due to a

mission stemming from a revelation to Chaerephon by the oracle at Delphi (21A). Whether or not this explanation is to be taken at face value (the Chaerephon in question is called a madman at *Charmides* 153B2), it seems clear that refusal to take a fee was a matter of principle bound up with his conception of his personal mission.

19. A case in point occurs at *Meno* 71B2–3. While I would not go so far as Robinson to say that "Socrates seems prepared to employ any kind of deception" in order to entice his interlocutors into elenchus (see R. Robinson, *Plato's Earlier Dialectic*, p. 9), I cannot believe that his frequent professions of ignorance are to be taken entirely at face value without regard for their roles in the ongoing conversations.

20. Protagoras' *sunousia* (*Protagoras* 316D1) led his students from city to city (315A), causing resentment as he distracted them from *sunousia* with other sophists (316C7). The *Apology* mentions the *sunousia* of Gorgias, Hippias, and Prodicus (20A), citing their ability to entice young men to leave the companionship of their fellow citizens. And Socrates' art of midwifery, of course, is said in the *Theaetetus* (150D4, 151A2) to be applied in *sunousia* with the persons he assists in birth.

21. Vlastos comes close to making elenchus a technique for imparting virtue in his proposed solution to what he terms "*the* problem of the Socratic elenchus" ("The Socratic Elenchus," p. 30, author's italics). The problem, in brief, is how Socrates can purport (as Vlastos says he does) to have proved the falsehood of a given interlocutor's faulty assertion p, when all he does is show the inconsistency of p with a set of premises upon which he and the interlocutor agree but which have not been established as part of the argument. This is important for Vlastos because he believes that (the early) Socrates "uses the elenchus exclusively in the pursuit of moral truth" (p. 14 of a later writing discussing the same issue, namely *Socrates, Ironist and Moral Philosopher*), and because he believed furthermore that Socrates was convinced that he could actually "discover moral truth by means of his elenctic arguments" (p. 15). Vlastos' solution is that Socrates considered that moral truth "was already *in* each of his interlocutors in the form of true beliefs" (ibid.), and that Socrates counted on these inherent beliefs as premises from which the negation of the interlocutor's false moral beliefs could be derived by elenchus. In a word, Socrates assumed that the premises needed to disprove a given false assertion p are in the mind from the beginning, a notion that inspired Plato later on to that "wildest of . . . metaphysical flights" (p. 56 of "The Socratic Elenchus")—the theory of learning as recollection. One thing that makes this account hard to accept is the unlikelihood that Plato would have taken Vlastos' problem seriously in the first place, inasmuch as it rests upon the assumption that Socrates was trying to establish moral truths by logical demonstration. Another is that, by Vlastos' account, *any* application of elenchus could have served in the demonstration of these moral

truths, which means that Protagoras and Gorgias might have served as moral teachers in the same manner as Socrates if only they had chosen. A more credible treatment of this "problem" can be found in Charles Kahn's careful study "Drama and Dialectic in Plato's *Gorgias*," in *Oxford Studies in Ancient Philosophy*, vol. I, pp. 75–121. Kahn's response avoids treating the problem as a purely formal matter, and stresses the powerful impact upon the interlocutor (and subsequent reader) of Socrates' person as a "paradigm lover of the good" (p. 120).

22. This stop in Athens would have been part of a series of events the later stages of which were recorded in Xenophon's *Anabasis*.

23. This characterization of virtue in terms of its particular manifestations is just what would be expected from someone with a "classical education" based on the Homeric poems; see Alasdair MacIntyre, *After Virtue*, ch. 10.

24. Overt reference to religious Mysteries about to be enacted in Athens presumably was intended to draw attention indirectly to the mysteries of philosophy as well; see *Symposium* 210A1.

25. *Webster's Collegiate Dictionary* (1963) lists Socratic irony as a primary sense of 'irony' per se.

26. I owe to David O'Connor the observations that being *haplous* is one of the chief marks of Aristotle's magnanimous man, and that the ironical man was viewed as hiding something while the true gentleman speaks his mind (rightly or wrongly) without deceit.

27. Gregory Vlastos, *Socrates, Ironist, and Moral Philosopher*.

28. This and the quotations immediately following are from ibid., p. 31.

29. These cases are discussed in ibid., pp. 236 ff.

30. See ibid., pp. 28–29. While this altered meaning may not have been in place by the time of Aristotle, Vlastos documents its presence in the writings of Cicero.

31. As part of the initial stage-setting, the reader should visualize Socrates standing aside, talking with some other group of people, and Meno riding up on horseback and unceremoniously demanding his attention. The abrupt onset of this dialogue is in stark contrast with the generally leisurely and socially graceful introductions of the other major Socratic dialogues.

32. According to Xenophon, some 1500 men were included in his retinue, a number of which were probably hanging around the Agora (or other public place in Athens) where the encounter took place. These presumably joined Meno, along with the "many attendants" of which we hear at 82A8, in gazing expectantly at Socrates as the conversation begins.

33. See W. K. C. Guthrie, *The Sophists*, p. 25.

34. Socrates' most conspicuous irony in this interchange is in his defense of the sophists as professional teachers of virtue (92D), which clearly is calculated to rouse Anytus' ire. Here is a use of irony that clearly is not part of an elenchus conducted "without indulgence of ill-will" as specified in the Seventh Letter.

35. If these pronouncements were ironically intended, the irony must be aimed at the audience rather than Meno himself; and their irony pales in contrast with the *major* irony cited in n. 34 above.

36. Xenophon records a case like this in *Memorabila* IV, in which Socrates sets up a conversation with unnamed companions in order to engage the attention of Euthydemus (see ii.2 of that book specifically).

37. Meno's first general definition of virtue as the capacity to govern men (73C) would have sounded initially plausible to some of Plato's first readers, as would the poetically inspired definition at 77B.

3. Recollection and Example: Sowing the Seeds

1. Other versions of this argument appear at *Euthydemus* 276D and at *Theaetetus* 198C.

2. The paradox of *Meno* 80E appears in another form to epitomize the quandary that besets the attempt in the *Theaetetus* to account for false belief by likening the mind to an aviary.

3. See *The Presocratic Philosophers*, by Kirk, Raven, and Schofield, pp. 21, 219–20, passim, for the doctrine of reincarnation in the Orphic and Pythagorean traditions. A rather complex account of cyclic reincarnation appears in the eschatological writings of Empedocles as well.

4. Aristotle actually speaks of a plurality of persons as originators of the theory of Forms, presumably (for reasons revealed earlier in the First Book of the *Metaphysics*, section 6) including the Pythagoreans as well as Plato.

5. The upshot is that refutation is not sufficient for bringing the mind to a state of knowledge, as noted in my *Plato's Late Ontology*, p. 191. Another problem noted there is one of coherence. The realm of truth for Plato presumably is *atemporal*. How could the mind confront truth in that realm *before* entering the body?

6. The term *eidos* is used several times at 72C–E in the sense of general character. Whether or not these characters are to be considered Forms (as in Grube's translation), they play no role in the discussion of recollection later in the dialogue.

7. Recalling merely that one knew perfect Equality previously would not enable comparison of Equality itself with its imperfect instances.

8. Although Socrates employs several examples to make the point that dissimilarity as well as similarity can prompt recall, these examples all involve being reminded of *another* sensible object—a picture of Simmias reminding one of Cebes, a lyre reminding one of its owner, etc. His only example of a sensible instance reminding one of a Form is that of imperfectly equal sticks and stones (74A8–9) being similar to the Form Equality itself.

9. The absence of terminology for Forms in the *Meno* and its presence in the *Phaedo* is only one among several reasons behind the majority view that these two dialogues were written in that order. When my discussion relies on judgments of chronological sequence that depart from the majority view in any critical respect, this departure will be noted and, when possible, defended in context.

10. The capacity of intelligibility (*noēton*) is listed at 80B1 among other features of the absolute Forms, including immortality, indissolubility, and self-identity. This capacity of the Forms for being known plays a major part in the refutation of the "Friends of the Forms" in the *Sophist* (cf. 248E in light of 247E).

11. Imitation through similarity is treated as the basis of participation at *Parmenides* 132D, where Parmenides is criticizing the theory of Forms represented by the character Socrates of the middle dialogues.

12. The term *anamnēsis* and its cognates occur several dozens of times outside the *Meno*, the *Phaedo*, and the *Phaedrus*, mostly in late dialogues ranging from the *Theaetetus* to the *Laws*. A survey of these other occurrences reveals that none of them has any apparent relevance to the notion of recollection introduced in the *Meno*. Interestingly enough, there are several occurrences in the early pages of the *Meno* itself that have nothing to do with the maxim introduced at 81B–D (i.e., 71C10, 73C7, 76B1).

13. In this, I am assuming that the *Phaedrus* was made public before the *Sophist*, the *Statesman*, and the *Philebus*, the only other dialogues in which collection and division play an explicit role. This assumption is not problematic in the context of current studies of the chronology of Plato's writings.

14. Despite reference at 265C9 to two procedures in the palinode, only the first appears there explicitly. Socrates' sense may be that both procedures are illustrated in his preceding discourses on the madness of love (the palinode and the speech it recants, as mentioned at 266B).

15. The sense in which Beauty reveals itself in its instances is only that the instances are recognizable as beautiful, not that the Form itself is seen in beautiful things. There is no tension between this passage in the *Phaedrus* and the account in the *Symposium* of the stagewise ascent to a vision of Beauty itself.

16. If the *Phaedrus* was made public within a few years of the *Symposium* and the *Republic*, as many scholars believe, it would have been written roughly two decades after Socrates' death.

17. The fact that Socrates himself considered such examples to be essential to his public role is indicated by an anecdote recounted in Book I of the *Memorabilia*. During the reign of the Thirty, as Xenophon tells it, Socrates had made a disparaging remark about the amorous relation between Critias and Euthydemus "the handsome" (IV.ii.1). Word got back to Critias who, by way of retaliation, passed a law forbidding the teaching of "the art of words" (*logōn technēn*: I.ii.31), and expressly ordered Socrates not to hold conversations with

anyone under thirty. Socrates had a number of questions about what the law meant, to which Critias responded by saying that Socrates would have to refrain from speaking about "cobblers and carpenters and blacksmiths" (I.ii.37); for in his opinion, said Critias, they "are already worn out and cut to pieces by your treatment" (ibid.). Socrates then asked whether he was to forswear the *lessons* he drew from these artisans—lessons "of justice and holiness and other such matters" (ibid.). The answer was affirmative. But soon thereafter the Thirty fell.

18. What Plato has a well-known public figure say *about* Socrates in his dialogues seems *prima facie* to have a greater claim to historical accuracy than the words he puts in the mouth of his character Socrates, on the ground that any palpable inaccuracies in the former would misrepresent *two* widely known persons instead of only one as in the latter case.

19. A lesson taught early in the *Sophist* is that a successful division must be preceded by a collection of instances. This matter is discussed in chapter 5.

20. Grammatical paradigms are employed by Plato time and again in contexts where epistemological issues are under discussion. Other notable examples are *Theaetetus* 202E ff., *Sophist* 253A ff., and *Philebus* 17B, 18B–D.

21. The sense is that a well understood instance of a given thing might be compared with a less well understood instance of the same thing, enabling both to be characterized by the same true statement. It is not irrelevant to note the similarity of this general characterization of the use of example to the general characterization of recollection at *Phaedo* 73C7–8, as discussed in section 2 above.

22. It is relatively unproblematic that the *Phaedrus* was made public before the major dialogues of the late period in which the Forms play a role. There is no suggestion here that the *Phaedrus* was the first dialogue in which the Forms appear.

23. The problem is that, according to the first thesis, one can know a name only if already knowing what it stands for, but that, according to the second, one must know the name in order to know the thing it stands for. This appears to make coming to know a name impossible for someone who cannot learn it from another person. The relatively unsubtle character of this paradox, and its similarities to the "paradox of the learner" in the *Meno*, suggests (but does not establish) a relatively early composition date for the *Cratylus*.

24. I stress the 'might' here, and do not mean to suggest that Plato has the *Theaetetus* end in failure merely to illustrate the inadequacies of an approach to knowledge featuring *logos* over images. Nonetheless, the approach of the *Sophist* following, which features collection based on images in the sense of paradigmatic instances, notably succeeds where the *Theaetetus* fails.

25. The claim that the five "faulty" definitions of sophistry at the beginning of the dialogue provide the collection which enables the final definition to succeed is defended in my *Plato's Analytic Method*.

26. I am uneasy with Charles Griswold's judgment (in *Self–Knowledge in Plato's Phaedrus*, p. 219) that "Plato's decision to write shows that he does not agree with Socrates' position (as presented in the *Phaedrus*) on the matter." Plato's written dialogues constituted what Socrates here refers to as a "literary garden," one role of which is to seed the minds of those who follow in his (Plato's) footsteps.

4. Love and Philosophy: Nourishing the Growth

1. *Greek-English Lexicon*, Liddell and Scott, 1883.
2. From Herodotus, via Guthrie's *The Sophists*, p. 29.
3. *Symposium* iv.62.
4. It must be acknowledged from the outset that this stress upon the affective dimension of philosophy is somewhat at odds with the way professional philosophers often view their calling today. For us, as for contemporaries of Socrates like Isocrates and Xenophon, there often is no effective distinction to be made between the *love* of wisdom and the more or less disinterested life of the mind as such. Thus we feel at ease in speaking about the standard group of early thinkers as the "presocratic philosophers," while fully aware that Thales was no more a philosopher than an astronomer or geometer, that Empedocles and Anaxagoras count also as the first biologists, and that Democritus is perhaps better classified as a physical theorist than as a philosopher per se. What warrants our grouping these figures under the common title "philosopher" is their reliance upon modes of inquiry and understanding that are recognizably rational, as distinct from what we are prone to call mythological and superstitious. We list them as philosophers primarily on the basis of how their inquiry was conducted, with little regard for the interests which motivated it. This contemporary conception of philosophy as a search for knowledge based on rational argument seems to have stemmed in large part from Aristotle, who in the *Metaphysics* defined wisdom as "knowledge concerning principles and causes" (982a2) and who referred to his predecessors as "lovers of wisdom"—i.e., as philosophers—insofar as they pursued such knowledge for its own sake alone (cf. 982b11–28). It was this broad conception equating philosophy with the rational pursuit of knowledge as an end in itself that enabled Aristotle to classify both mathematics and physics as "theoretical philosophies" (*philosophiai theōrētikai*: 1026a18–19), a classification Plato would have rejected for reasons made clear in the *Republic* and elsewhere.

5. A partial list of Socrates' companions (not all young) is given in the opening paragraphs of the *Phaedo*. Others are listed by Xenophon at *Memorabilia* I.ii.48, and elsewhere.

6. Plato's Socrates actually declares himself to be in love with Alcibiades at *Gorgias* 481D, making the latter's complaint of *Symposium* 222B somewhat

understandable. For other Socratic talk about loving beautiful boys, see *Charmides* 154B–C, *Meno* 76C, and *Protagoras* 309A.

7. *Protagoras* 315D–E. See also Xenophon's *Symposium* viii.32, where Pausanias is said by Socrates to defend his relationship in terms reminiscent of those used by Phaedrus in the previous speech.

8. This distinction between a "Common" and a "Heavenly" Aphrodite is acknowledged by Socrates, somewhat skeptically, in Xenophon's *Symposium* viii.9.

9. Pausanias here refers to a practice apparently prevalent in Athens during his time. See Kenneth Dover, *Greek Homosexuality*, pp. 81–84.

10. The name *Eruximachus* means "belch-fighter," appropriate for the character who "cures" Aristophanes of his hiccups in the manner of 185D–E. We note that Eryximachus' speech must have been delivered in accompaniment with the ridiculous distraction of Aristophanes trying to stop his hiccups in the background, quite out of keeping with the pedantic nature of the speech.

11. The association here between the Heavenly Love and good harvests is relevant to the theme of this chapter, which is the role of love in bringing to fruition the "seeds of *logos*" planted by the dialectician in the soul of the learner (cf. *Phaedrus* 276D).

12. See Stanley Rosen's insightful commentary on Aristophanes' speech in his *Plato's Symposium.*

13. One might be tempted to read this first set of speeches as the beginning of a veiled criticism of the homosexuality prevalent in Athens at the time, which is continued in the pointedly heterosexual interaction between Socrates and Diotima. We have reason to believe that Plato strongly disapproved of pederasty, in his later years at least, on the ground that it is unnatural, encourages intemperance, and constitutes "deliberate murder of the human race" (*Laws* 838E7–8). While questions regarding the relative merits of homosexuality are not irrelevant to what is going on in the *Symposium*, it would probably be a mistake to base our reading of the dialogue on conjectures about Plato's attitudes toward this sexual practice. For one thing, the language of the *Symposium* is homosexual in orientation throughout, and if Plato had found this language distasteful he probably would not have been able to handle it with the taste and skill evident in the execution of the dialogue. So well suited is this language to his purposes, indeed, that Plato makes Socrates a master of homosexual innuendo—not only in the *Symposium* and the *Phaedrus*, but quite notably in other basically nonerotic dialogues such as the *Protagoras* and the *Gorgias*. (Note that this is not to make Socrates out to be homosexual himself; in this regard see the remarks attributed to Socrates in Xenophon's *Symposium* ii.10, viii.3, which are decidedly favorable to heterosexuality.) Another thing to note in this regard is that, while the *Symposium* includes some mildly unfavorable allusions to possible political side-effects of pederasty, it says very little in

favor of heterosexuality. The only distinctly positive reference in this regard is Aristophanes' remark that the gods count on heterosexual intercourse to perpetuate the species, after which he nonetheless finds an opportunity (191D–E) to second Pausanias' observation (181A, E) that heterosexual love tends to encourage promiscuity. Once again, however, the inference to be drawn from this is not that Plato himself thought poorly of heterosexuality, but that it was not among his purposes in the dialogue to take a stand on any particular sexual practice.

14. Although Mantinea was an actual Greek city, and 'Diotima' was known as a feminine name during the classical period (see Kenneth Dover, ed., *Plato: Symposium*, p. 137), scholars often suspect wordplay in Plato's text at this point. David Halperin, for instance, notes that "Diotima of Mantinea means, literally, something like 'Zeus-honor from Prophet-ville' " (D. M. Halperin, *One Hundred Years of Homosexuality*, pp. 120–21). Other authors with views on the matter are cited in James A. Arieti, *Interpreting Plato: The Dialogues as Drama*, p. 115n.

15. The brief passage between 199E and 201C contains the only elenchus in the dialogue. This in itself indicates that a different aspect of the Socratic character is being developed in the *Symposium* than comes to the fore in other Socratic dialogues.

16. Agathon's chagrin at being so easily refuted may have been alleviated somewhat by Socrates' remark that Eros *tōn agathōn endeēs eiē* (201C4)—which he could hear as "Love wants Agathon."

17. See A. E. Taylor, *Plato: The Man and His Works*, p. 224.

18. A more speculative consideration is that Diotima represents a counter-force to certain civic tendencies in Athens—e.g., the self-centeredness manifested in all of the previous speeches—that Plato viewed as contributing to the rapid decline of that city's military and political fortunes beginning shortly after the dramatic date of the dialogue. For more details, see section 5 below.

19. It is not irrelevant to recall that Socrates is depicted as having another female instructor in the *Menexenus*—in this case Aspasia, the mistress of Pericles. In the *Menexenus* Socrates repeats a funeral oration he attributes to Aspasia for the Athenian dead (in contrast with the oration of Pericles himself?) and claims that Aspasia had been his teacher in rhetoric (235E, 236C). Inasmuch as the oration in question is obviously ahistorical, referring as it does to several events that occur after the death of the actual Aspasia, and inasmuch as Socrates' claim to be her pupil plays no other apparent role in the dialogue, the point of the claim may be to dramatize the fact that Socrates did not learn rhetoric from male-oriented teachers like Protagoras and Gorgias—a point consonant with Menexenus' remark that Socrates is always "making fun of" (235C6) the rhetoricians.

20. The most exhaustive treatment of this topic I know is that found in David Halperin's "Why Is Diotima a Woman?" included in his *One Hundred Years of Homosexuality*.

21. The fact that Diotima is represented as being not only a woman of exceptional wisdom who enabled Athens to delay a great plague, but also as a philosopher of outstanding abilities, serves to reinforce one of the main contentions of the *Republic*—namely, that selection and training of the Guardians of the state should have nothing to do with a candidate's sex.

22. This angle is suggested in Thomas Gould, *Platonic Love*, p. 193n34.

23. Our position as readers is one of fifth remove from Diotima's discourse, mediated by the discourses of Apollodorus (fourth remove), of Aristodemus (third remove), and of Socrates (second remove) in between. It may be relevant to compare this five-tiered hierarchy with that of Diotima's ascent, where the love of Beauty itself appears at the pinnacle. This comparison locates Socrates at the penultimate level of the love of knowledge, suggesting he may never have reached the peak of the ascent.

24. For the typically passive role of the youth in Greek homosexuality, see Dover's *Greek Homosexuality*, p. 16, passim.

25. 204E2 is only one of several passages in Diotima's speech suggesting a close association between beauty and goodness. In her account of Eros' lineage, she describes him as a schemer for "the beautiful and the good" (203D5) alike. And at 206A1 she claims that the object of everyone's love is the good, paralleling the earlier remark at 204D3 that it is the nature of Eros to love beautiful things. There is also the admission of Agathon immediately preceding Diotima's address that "good things are beautiful" (*ta de agatha kala*: 201C3), meaning either that what is good is also beautiful (with Nehamas and Woodruff) or that the good and the beautiful are just the same (with Robin, Jowett, and Joyce). The significance of this near-identification of the good and the beautiful will come into focus when we return in chapter 6 to the Good of the *Republic*.

26. Socrates continues his beguiling pun on the name of Agathon by having Diotima ask what *ho erōn tōn agathōn* (the lover of good things: 204D5) desires.

27. Happiness has been defined as the possession of good and beautiful things at 202C7–D1.

28. A nuanced discussion of this ambiguity may be found in David Halperin, *One Hundred Years of Homosexuality*, pp. 140ff.

29. Notable for its absence here is any mention of the immortality to be achieved through the production of such offspring. The "beautiful discourse and thought " of the philosopher may be presumed to bring recognition to their progenitor that is no less enduring than the fame brought to Lycurgus and Solon by the beautiful laws they engendered. Plato may have elected to omit any reference to the renown that might be gained by a lover of wisdom in order to allow Socrates to avoid the appearance of self-congratulation that had marked the speeches of the other symposiasts.

30. Use of the term *exaiphnēs* at 210E4 has drawn attention from several commentators. Robin (in a footnote to his translation of this passage; Budé

edition, Paris, 1949) contrasts the suddenness of the revelation with the gradual character of the preceding initiation. Rosen (*Plato's Symposium*, p. 269n148), following Robin, notes seemingly parallel uses (*Republic* 515C7, 516E5) in the context of the allegory of the Cave and also suggests (less plausibly) a connection with the definition of the instant at *Parmenides* 156D3 ff. More significant than any of these is the parallel (noted also by Rosen, loc. cit., and by Bury, in his translation of the Seventh Letter, Loeb Classical Library, 1929) with the use of the term at 341D1 of the Seventh Letter. There the philosopher's hard work and discipline is said to be rewarded by a flash of insight "suddenly (*exaiphnēs*) generated in the soul like a torch light kindled by a leaping flame." The sense that these parallel uses are more than coincidental is reinforced with the remark at 342D of the Seventh Letter that the Beautiful itself—along with the Good and the Just—is one of those entities the philosopher aspires to grasp by this characteristic flash of insight.

31. This judgment is based on the features of the Forms listed in the introduction of my *Plato's Late Ontology*.

32. Approximate dates of the relevant events are given in Taylor, *Plato: The Man and His Works*, p. 519.

33. See Taylor, ibid., pp. 210, 520.

34. Our primary source of information on these mysteries is the brief account by Thucydides in Book VI of *The History of the Peloponnesian War*.

35. Thucydides described the "profanation" as a mock celebration of the mysteries in a private house, ibid., ch. 28.

36. Thucydides (ch. 27) says that the faces (*prosōpa*) were mutilated; but it is hard to imagine a group of drunken revelers not attending to the lower appendages as well.

37. It is not irrelevant to note that each major speech in the *Symposium* has something to say about the uses of love in civic affairs. The theme of the political consequences of love is explored by John Brentlinger in his introduction to *The Symposium of Plato*, translated by S. Q. Groden.

38. The personification is comic in its comparison of Socrates with the satyr-figures, yet tragic in the foreshadowed failure of Socrates to sway Alcibiades from his path of civic and personal self-destruction. There may be some connection here with the final sequence of the dialogue (223D), where Socrates is trying to persuade Aristophanes that a playwright should be able to write both comedy and tragedy. The point about the personification of Dionysus by Alcibiades is due to Rosen, *Plato's Symposium*, p. 287.

39. See Liddell and Scott, eds., *Greek-English Lexicon*.

40. See n. 100, p. 65, in Nehamas' and Woodruff's translation of the *Symposium*.

41. The contributions of Socratic self-sufficiency to his erotic presence are examined in David O'Connor's "The Erotic Self-Sufficiency of Socrates: A Reading of Xenophon's *Memorabilia*."

42. It is not uncommon for commentators to read this passage, fictional as it is, as reflecting Plato's evaluation of the achievements of the historical Socrates. See, for example, F. M. Cornford, "The Doctrine of Eros in Plato's *Symposium*," p. 125.

43. This is among the topics treated in chapter 2. The discussion of elenchus in connection with the "sophist of noble lineage" in the *Sophist* has the effect of giving Socrates credit for perfecting this skill.

44. In this regard, recall the discussion of chapter 3. While Socrates did not "make the universals stand apart," as Aristotle puts it at *Metaphysics* 1078b30, his treatment of definitions nonetheless was said to have contributed to Plato's conception of the Ideas (1078b31–32).

45. Aristotle testifies to Socrates' lack of dialectical power at *Metaphysics* 1078b25.

5. Dialectic and Logos: Training the Shoots

1. Given its wide range of possible meanings, the term *logos* in this discussion will remain untranslated, save in contexts where the meaning it conveys is relatively unproblematic.

2. The expression *dialegesthai dunamis* first appears in the *Republic* at 511B4. In addition to this occurrence at 532E1, it also appears at 533A8 and 537D6. Other notable occurrences are at *Parmenides* 135C2 and *Philebus* 57E7. It should be noted that the term *dialegesthai* is commonly used before the *Republic* in various senses having to do with conversation generally. In both the *Gorgias* and the *Theaetetus*, however, it is used in reference to philosophic discussion in particular (e.g., *Gorgias* 471D5 and *Theaetetus* 161E6). And in the *Republic* it is used specifically in reference to dialectic (see 532A6 and 532B5). After the *Republic*, the term is used only occasionally, while use of *dialektikē* remains conspicuous (in the *Sophist*, the *Statesman* and the *Philebus*, notably).

3. Other indications that the conversation of the *Republic* is foreordained to fall short of the truth in matters of ultimate philosophic importance appear at 435D, 504B, 506E, 517B, and 534A.

4. A point of some interest regarding this list is that study of the geometry of solids is represented as being in no more than a rudimentary state (528E) at the dramatic date of the dialogue, so that Plato's including it in his ideal curriculum was more a challenge to contemporary mathematicians than a contribution to educational theory. For a nuanced description of the state of this study at the time, see Myles Burnyeat's "Platonism and Mathematics: A Prelude to Discussion," p. 218.

5. Socrates' remarks at this point continue as follows. Having been confronted by "big and little" in such a manner, the mind is led to question what

"really is the nature of the great and the small" (*ti oun pot' esti to mega au kai to smikron*: 524C11), thereby bringing it to address an "object of intelligence" (*noēton*: 524C13) as distinct from an object of vision. The description of the philosophic value of arithmetic should be particularly intriguing to a student of Plato's metaphysics for its inclusion of several phrases and themes that play key roles in the exposition of the mathematically inspired ontology in the *Parmenides* and the *Philebus*. Among the key themes of this numerically based ontology, as Aristotle reports at length in Book A of the *Metaphysics*, are that Forms are composed of "the Great and the Small" (or "Indefinite Dyad") and Unity, and that sensible things are constituted by "the Great and the Small" and the Forms in turn. One expression Aristotle often used to designate this dual principle of Plato's is *to mega kai to mikron* (e.g., *Metaphysics* 987b20, 988a13–14). Essentially the same expression is used at 524C11, when Plato has Socrates raise the question concerning the "real nature" of the great and the small. This appearance of the expression *to mega kai to smikron* in the *Republic* is all the more interesting in view of the fact that the expression is found in this specific (and rather peculiar) grammatical form nowhere else in the Platonic corpus.

6. This is the earliest occurrence of the term *apeiron plēthos* in the Platonic corpus. In the second part of the *Parmenides* the term is used (e.g., at 143A2, 158C7–8, and 164D1) in reference to the Great and the Small reported in Aristotle's *Metaphysics* (arguments for this are given in my forthcoming commentary on the *Parmenides*). Unity, in turn, is the subject of the eight hypotheses in the second part of the *Parmenides*, which with their consequences mark the watershed between Plato's earlier Eleatic proclivities and the Pythagorean orientation of his late ontology. The significance carried by these several expressions in Plato's later writings is discussed at length in my *Plato's Late Ontology*. It is by no means clear that their brief appearance in the *Republic* has any connection at all with their later (more or less technical) usage. The possibility of some such connection, however, raises the provocative question of the extent to which Plato's very late metaphysical thinking might have been anticipated in the writings of the middle period. It is also possible that some of these passages at 524–25 may have been interpolated into the *Republic* at some later date. Insofar as any such connection would be extremely hard to pin down, however, it is better for the present to pass on without further speculation.

7. The contrast between antilogic and dialectic is even more explicit at 454A. *Philebus* 15D–E also might be read in this connection.

8. Not all uses of cross-examination are contentious; compare *Seventh Letter* 344B6.

9. Socratic elenchus as a form of sophistry is discussed in chapter 2.

10. Jowett's translation of *tois logois* at *Sophist* 230B6 as "the dialectical process" is misleading in its suggestion that Socratic elenchus itself constitutes

dialectic. In point of fact, there is nowhere in the dialogues where elenchus by itself is identified as a form of dialectic. Jowett's translation may have been abetted by the entry under *dialektikos* in Liddell and Scott's *Greek-English Lexicon* (1883) saying that dialectic was invented by Zeno and perfected by Socrates. In this, Liddell and Scott inauspiciously follow Grote (*Plato, and the Other Companions of Sokrates*, p. 241 ff., p. 256 ff.; see also p. 95 ff.). Grote's use of the term 'dialectic' in this connection is obviously much broader than the sense attached to the term in Plato's writings.

11. This shortcoming may not be due to the philosophic inadequacies of his interlocutors alone, as some commentators have suggested (see, e.g., Mitchell Miller, *Plato's Parmenides*, p. 19). We should not forget Diotima's doubts about Socrates' abilities as a lover of wisdom at *Symposium* 210A.

12. The problem is described in relevant detail by Ivor Thomas, in *Greek Mathematical Works*, pp. 396–97.

13. The distinction between necessary and sufficient conditionality can be directly indicated in terms of the implication relation. If p implies q, then the truth of p is sufficient for the truth of q, and the truth of q is necessary for the truth of p.

14. Use of this proverbial expression for "the next best way" may be noted also at *Statesman* 300C1, where it characterizes government by law as second-best to rule by a truly knowledgeable statesman, and at *Philebus* 19C2–3, where not being ignorant of oneself is said to be the next-best thing to knowing everything. The precise respect in which Socrates labels the method "second best" is a matter of considerable scholarly disagreement, on which no stand is taken in the text above. For a recent discussion of the issue, see "Plato's Unnatural Teleology," by James G. Lennox.

15. The imagery of this passage seems to anticipate that of the Sun and the Cave in Books VI and VII of the *Republic*. The sense is that the "eye of the mind" would be damaged by a premature attempt to examine *ta onta* directly and that an initial approach through the images of things in *logoi* is a necessary precaution.

16. For references and further discussion, see my *Plato's Analytic Method*, ch. 1, sec. 2. For a more recent approach that makes no effort to tie Plato's method in with current mathematics, see Jyl Gentzler "*Sumphōnein* in Plato's *Phaedo*."

17. This expression of uncertainty about what the relation of participation amounts to should remind us of Aristotle's remark in *Metaphysics* A that Plato and the Pythagoreans "jointly neglected to inquire" (*apheisan en koinō zētein*: 987b14) into the nature of participation. Despite the vigor with which this account of causation is pursued in the *Phaedo* and the *Republic*, the fact remains that little is said in these dialogues about how the relation of participation itself is to be understood. By the time Plato comes face to face with some of the problems of participation in the first part of the *Parmenides*, he seems ready to

give up major aspects of his early theory of Forms. But at this early stage in the development of the theory, he seems content to have Socrates say just that participation comes about "some way or another."

18. John Paul Dreher, in "The Driving Ratio in Plato's Divided Line," offers an interpretation of the Line according to which the ratio of the first section to the second is only approximately the same as that of the third to the fourth. Although I have sympathy with Dreher's interpretation (applying the golden section to the line), it seems unlikely that Plato would have employed *ana ton auton logon* in any other than a strict sense in a mathematical context.

19. There is no clear sense in which one could "lay down" as a *logos* the odd and the even, etc., themselves. The explanation may be either that the mathematicians hypothesize *definitions* of these entities to get their inquiries started or that the manner of hypothesizing here in question is not identical to that described at *Phaedo* 100A3–4.

20. There is near-unanimity among the major translators in rendering *logos* here by 'reason' and *dialegesthai* by 'dialectic.'

21. If the reader is curious why it is necessary to strike from below by day, he or she may wish to consult *Ion* 538D. Apparently the Stranger is dealing with an archaic form of angling in which a sharp prong is lowered to the bottom on a sinker and yanked upward when a fish passes over it. Daylight would be required so that the angler could tell when fish are in the right position to be impaled.

22. While all ten features cited are required for angling, it is not required that all ten be explicitly included within the definition. Since fish by nature are living water animals, items (5) and (6) are necessary features as well. Although the definition is perfectly adequate as it stands, it would be no less adequate— and perhaps more elegant—if (5) and (6) were not explicitly mentioned. The requirement is that all features included in the definition be necessary, not that all necessary features (of which there may be countless) be explicitly mentioned. Moreover, while acquisition by capture is necessary to angling, this does not preclude the angler from being productive in other respects, or even from acquiring other things by exchange. A given angler might produce an income by the acquisition of fish, or may exchange part of that income to acquire lodging and clothing. The point is that angling is only *incidentally* productive, or involved in exchange, etc. It is not essential to angling that the art be used to produce an income, or to produce anything else; hence that feature is only incidental. But it is essential that the angler acquire fish by catching them, whereby acquisition and capture are necessary features.

23. Another thing to note about this definition is that the features defining the angler are not listed in any particular order with respect to generality. Commentators persist in assuming that Plato's mode of definition based on division is an early version of Aristotle's definition by genus and species (for a recent case, see Constance Meinwald's interesting *Plato's Parmenides*,

pp. 67–69, *passim*.), conveniently modeled by a series of increasingly smaller concentric circles. A more accurate model for a definition like this one of the angler is a series of circles that overlap in the manner of Venn diagrams, with the thing being defined represented by the area of overlap. Problems with the Aristotelian reading of Plato's procedure here are discussed in my *Plato's Analytic Method*, ch. 3, sec. 7.

24. The notion of innate knowledge operating in the *Meno* is provided explanation of sorts with the story of prenatal existence borrowed from the poets and religious teachers. The only hint of an explanation of the mind's preformed ability to recognize instances of Forms for what they are, however, comes in the *Phaedrus* with the allusion at 250A–B to certain Forms that have the capacity to manifest themselves in their instances. While there is sparse textual evidence beyond this passage, Plato seems to be operating here with a notion of the Forms as self-revealing that would at least partially account for an ability of the properly conditioned mind to recognize them in their instances. This is discussed further in section 4 of chapter 3.

25. For one attempt to see how the "search" for an adequate collection might proceed, the reader may wish to see chapter 4 of my *Plato's Analytic Method*.

26. Uses of the term *sunagō* in reference to collection may be found at *Statesman* 267B7, and at *Philebus* 23E5 and 25A3, D7, 8.

27. Another matter of importance treated in this set of passages is the measurement of excess and defect, both relatively and by a mean, which correlates with the treatment of Limit and the Unlimited in the *Philebus*.

28. An associated anomaly is that the final touches in the elucidation of statecraft consist in a series of further comparisons with the paradigm (*paradeigma*: 287B2, 305E8) of weaving, to which the process of division makes no further contribution.

29. A sustained attempt to make sense of some of the more puzzling aspects of the *Philebus* at large, and the "godly method" in particular, may be found in chapter 3 of my *Plato's Late Ontology*. See also "The *Philebus* and the Good: the Unity of the Dialogue in which the Good is Unity," which contains a more detailed look at some of these issues.

30. The interested reader might refer to chapter 1, section 4, of my *Plato's Late Ontology*.

31. The sense of *gumnasia* here is that of training or discipline, not of mere "mental gymnastics;" see 135C8, 135D4, 135D7, 136A2, and 136C5.

32. See my *Plato's Late Ontology*, ch. 1, sec. 2.

33. Further explanation and defense of this way of dealing with the eight hypotheses is undertaken in my forthcoming commentary on the *Parmenides*.

34. This follows unconditionally in the manner that q follows unconditionally from 'p implies q' and 'not-p implies q,' in conjunction with 'either p or not-p.' It is in this respect that the method resembles Zeno's destructive dilemma.

35. See *Plato's Late Ontology*, pp. 46–48. Only these two hypotheses deal with the one of the historical Parmenides. An account of the subjects of the remaining hypotheses is offered in my commentary on the *Parmenides* (forthcoming, University of Notre Dame Press), along with an explanation of why Parmenides' instruction at 136A2 is not violated by the several hypotheses concerning unity in several different senses.

36. See my *Plato's Late Ontology*, pp. 54–60.

37. Appendix B of my *Plato's Late Ontology* points out considerations favoring a later dating for the second than for the first part of the Parmenides. This at least partially relieves the tension stemming from the stylometric studies (e.g., Ledger's *Recounting Plato*) placing the *Parmenides* as a whole in the early part of the late period. But I see no evidence that even the second part of the *Parmenides* was written after the *Philebus*.

38. It is argued in my forthcoming commentary that hypotheses IV and VIII yield results directly critical of the early theory of separate Forms.

39. The term *hodos* is often used by Plato in a sense equivalent to method itself. It is in response to Glaucon's request that Socrates explain to him "the ways" (*hodoi*: 532E2) of the power of dialectical reasoning that dialectic is described in the *Republic* as the "method of grasping" (*methodos . . . lambanein*: 533B3) what each thing is. Timaeus expresses confidence that his listeners will be able to follow his discourse because of their experience with "scholarly methods" (*tōn kata paideusin hodōn*: *Timaeus* 53C2–3). In the *Philebus*, the extravagantly praised "godly method" is referred to as a *hodos* (16A8 and 16B5) rather than a *methodos*. And in the Seventh Letter Plato, speaking in his own voice, describes philosophy as a "wondrous pathway" (*hodon . . . thaumastēn*: 340C3) to which a man worthy of the calling will devote his whole life.

40. It is easy to imagine a similar conversation with another person—e.g., Meno or Euthyphro—in which basically the same dialectical progression would produce no improvement in the cognitive state of the respondent. That the conversation of the *Sophist* succeeds is due to the capacities of both discussants—to the skills of the Stranger as a dialectician but also to the talent of Theaetetus as a ready student.

6. *The Good and the Beautiful: Reaping the Fruits*

1. See the terms *idein* at 476B7, *kathoran* at 476D1, and *horōntas* at 479E2. Use of the terminology of mental vision for the philosopher's grasp of the Forms continues through Book VII and becomes quite pointed with reference to *tēs psuchēs opsin* at 519B3, to *tēs psuchēs omma* at 533D2, and to *tēs psuchēs augēn* at 540A7.

2. Explicit notice that Socrates is not conveying a full view of matters at hand to his listeners is given also at 506E, at 533A, and at 534A, with a further

hint to that effect at 517B. Some commentators have conjectured that the reason Socrates is made to speak inexactly in these passages has to do with the philosophic immaturity of his interlocutors and indirectly with the immaturity of the students in the Academy for whom the *Republic* may have been written (e.g., Mitchell Miller in *Plato's Parmenides*, ch. 1). Another conjecture, suggested in chapter 4 by our assessment of Socrates' less than perfect philosophic accomplishments, is that Socrates (in Plato's version at least) may not have been capable of a more exact account himself (cf. 533A). A less speculative answer, however, is that the "longer and harder way" corresponds to the philosopher's creative activity at the higher two stages of Diotima's ascent, the results of which cannot be put into words by Socrates, by Plato, or by anyone else. Socrates' repeated disclaimers of full accuracy in Books VI and VII may be just Plato's way of warning the reader that the contents of this discussion should not be taken as even purporting to be a philosophic *theory* capable of discursive formulation.

3. The term 'Sun' hereafter will be capitalized when used in reference to Plato's image; similarly for 'Line' and 'Cave'.

4. Cornford neatly summarizes what he calls "Plato's theory of vision" in a note to 507B7 (*The Republic of Plato*, p. 219n. 1). According to Cornford:

> Plato's theory of vision involves three kinds of fire or light: (1) daylight, a body of pure fire diffused in the air by the Sun; (2) the visual current or 'vision,' a pure fire similar to daylight, contained in the eye-ball and capable of issuing out in a stream directed towards the object seen; (3) the colour of the external object, 'a flame streaming off from every body, having particles proportioned to those of the visual current, so as to yield sensation' when the two streams meet and coalesce. (*Timaeus*, 45 B, 67 C)

5. There is a remark at 508D about the soul gaining understanding and knowledge when fixed upon an object "irradiated by truth and reality" (*katalampei alētheia te kai to on*: 508D5), as if "truth and reality" were to knowledge what light is to vision. There are three problems, however, with this apparent correspondence. One is that "truth and reality" here link *actual* knowledge with its object, rather than the *capacities* of knowing and being known. (In the case of vision, we should note, the presence of light between the faculty and the object does not always result in the object actually being seen—inasmuch as the eye might be closed, for example, or looking in some other direction.) The second problem is that "reality" (*to on*) here sounds very much like the "existence and being" (*to einai te kai tēn ousian*) said at 509B to be received from the Good, parallel to the generation visible objects receive from the sun, and that "being" or "reality" cannot very well correspond both to light at 508B and to generation at 509B. The third is that truth is also attributed to the objects of knowledge (508E1), resulting in the incongruity of a property of these objects serving also as an alleged medium between themselves and the Good.

6. All three images—Sun, Line, and Cave—deal with the nature and the pursuit of philosophy. Someone comfortable with the Aristotelian doctrine of causes might think of the Sun as a portrayal of the *final* cause of philosophy—the final goal, that is to say, toward which the pursuit of philosophy is directed—and of the Line and the Cave as treating the *formal* and the *efficient* causes respectively. As the Line depicts the structure of the philosopher's progress toward the Good, that is to say, so the Cave depicts the process by which this goal might be achieved. If this much seems plausible, one might complete the picture—without undue solemnity—by including the first half of Book VI as a characterization of the *material* cause. The philosophic character (*phusis*), that is to say, is the matrix within which the fruits of the philosophic pursuit take shape.

7. This discussion continues the practice of chapter 5, following Cornford, of labeling individual sections of the Line, in ascending order, 'A' (for *eikasia*), 'B' (for *pistis*), 'C' (for *dianoia*) and 'D' (for *noēsis*).

8. One possibility would be to add a third subdivision to each of the two major sections of the Line, locating the sun and the Good "above" the other objects of their respective domains. Another way, involving less structural change to the Line itself, would be to locate the sun to the *side* of the visible section of the Line (as the drill sergeant marches alongside his or her troops), with lateral distance toward that section a mark of dependency, and to handle the Good in similar fashion. The superiority of the Good to the sun then would be indicated in the same manner as that of Forms to visible objects—by elevated position along the Line.

9. A problem of interpretation to which various commentators have drawn attention (see, e.g., J. Annas, *An Introduction to Plato's Republic*, p. 251) concerns the sense in which the objects studied in mathematics (e.g., numbers and geometrical figures) might be thought of as *images* of Forms, as distinct from Forms themselves. One available answer, as Annas notes, comes with the notion of "intermediate mathematicals" attributed to Plato by Aristotle in *Metaphysics* 987b16–18. A discussion of what these "mathematicals" amount to, and of their appearance in the *Philebus*, may be found in chapter 2 of my *Plato's Late Ontology*. Unlike Annas, I do not take it as obvious that the "square itself" and the "diagonal itself" about which mathematicians are said to reason at *Republic* 510D are Forms (each uniquely one) rather than "mathematicals" of this sort (eternal and unchanging, but many of them alike). When Socrates reasons with Meno about the area of a square based on the diagonal of a given square (note that two squares are under consideration), for instance, he is not reasoning about either the *unique* Form of Square or that of Diagonal.

10. Among important features *not* included are those depending on the mathematical characteristics of the Line, as for example the fact that sections B and C are equal.

11. Although it is undoubtedly possible that there are subtleties here beyond anything intended by the author, reflections of this sort are interesting nonetheless in view of Plato's sustained attempt in the *Timaeus* to elucidate participation in terms of the imaging relationship. For discussion, see my *Plato's Late Ontology*, pp. 238–55.

12. The opening term of the *Republic* is a form of *katabainō*, which is also the term for descent appearing at 511B9 and 516E4. While there is no apparent respect in which the ensuing discussion with Glaucon, Polemarchus, and the rest can be said to correspond to the downward movement of dialectic, there may be a plausible parallel with the return of the philosopher (Socrates) to the cave (the precinct of the Piraeus). The possibility of a connection here with the descent of Odysseus into the precinct of Hades has been pointed out to me by David O'Connor.

13. A case in point is provided by the above-cited discussion of Annas in *An Introduction to Plato's Republic*.

14. E.g., G. Santas in "The Form of the Good in Plato's *Republic*," p. 232; A. MacIntyre in "The Form of the Good, Tradition and Enquiry," p. 251; and Henry Teloh, *The Development of Plato's Metaphysics*, p. 144. The assumption is sanctioned, after very brief argument, by Richard Robinson in *Plato's Earlier Dialectic*, pp. 159–60, and is questioned but not rejected by Annas in *An Introduction to Plato's Republic*, p. 250.

15. The term *echomenōn* in this context is difficult to translate. While it is reasonably clear that the dialectician here is said to be concerned with what is *supported* by the nonhypothetical *archē*, or what *depends* upon it, it is not obvious from the language that these dependencies are to be thought of as *logical* consequences in any straightforward sense.

16. See, for example, Richard Robinson, *Plato's Earlier Dialectic*, p. 200, and Nicholas White, *Plato on Knowledge and Reality*, p. 96.

17. A reading of the nonhypothetical *archē* that makes it explicitly propositional is found in W. D. Ross's "The Sun and the Idea of the Good," p. 100.

18. In almost every other passage where Plato uses *archē* in connection with argument or reasoning, the sense is that of a beginning point of a discussion. It is relevant to note in this regard that Liddell, Scott, and Jones, *A Greek-English Lexicon* (1968 edition) contains no entries under *archē* that correspond to logical principle or premise of an argument.

19. What the passage says literally is that such a person is dialectical, the sense being that someone who can see interconnections of this sort has a "dialectical nature" (537C6).

20. The same term for "likeness in kind" is used at *Meno* 81D1 and at *Republic* 531D2.

21. I recant my previous rejection of this point, e.g., in *Plato's Late Ontology*, p. 304n. 19.

22. Santas, "The Form of the Good in Plato's *Republic*." Another attempt worth special notice is M. Miller's "Platonic Provocations: Reflections on the Soul and the Good in the *Republic*." Other worthy attempts through the last hundred years or so are listed in Santas' article, p. 257n. 2.

23. Santas' account actually stresses the importance of our knowledge of the Good rather than that of the Good itself, but the results are transferable to the latter topic.

24. Santas' account in this respect relies on Forms "as ideal exemplars complete with non-Pauline self-predication" (p. 243), for which description he refers the reader to Gregory Vlastos' "A Note on 'Pauline Predications' in Plato." Santas' sense is that the property of which a given Form is an ideal exemplar is properly predictable of the Form itself—e.g., the Form Justice itself is just.

25. A. MacIntyre, in his "The Form of the Good, Tradition and Enquiry," points out that the passage on which Santas relies in this regard (505A) contains nothing of the vocabulary of participation but says only that the Good is "that by reference to which" (*hē*: 505A3) just things and the rest become useful and beneficial. The vocabulary of participation is so fluid in the middle and late dialogues, however, that it is not clear how much Santas' case is damaged by having to retract on this point. No matter what the relation is labeled, it seems cogent to join Santas in thinking that it is because of this relationship with the Good that other Forms receive the kind of excellence that enables them to serve as paradigms.

26. Santas' "The Form of the Good in Plato's *Republic*," p. 240.

27. Ibid., p. 252.

28. Ibid. Another objection raised by MacIntyre against Santas' account is that while sensible things possess properties in a way that depends upon Forms, the perfection of a Form belongs to it *auto kath' hauto*, and need not "be explained by appeal to a higher order form" (p. 249). MacIntyre in certainly right in stressing that things are what they are in a way that depends upon the Forms, while Forms are what they are independently of sensible things. For Forms to be *auto kath' hauto* as far as sensible things are concerned, however, does not preclude their properties being derivative in important ways from their relations with other Forms. The *Sophist* stresses that "the Kinds are of a nature to share with one another" (257A9), which means that they depend upon each other for what they are. Thus motion is said in the *Sophist* to be the same as itself "through participation in the Same" (256B1) and also not the same as other things "through sharing with Difference" (256B2–3). The *Republic* itself picks up on this theme at 476B when Socrates says that all the Forms not only share properties with actions and physical things, but also "share with one another" (*allēlōn koinōnia*: 476A8) in their many different aspects. On balance, it seems not to count as a forceful objection against a view that it makes Forms depend on other Forms for some of their attributes. MacIntyre may well be right,

nonetheless, in insisting (see "The Form of the Good, Tradition and Enquiry," p. 249) that the other Forms do not depend for their perfection upon a higher-order Form.

29. If he had chosen, Santas could have cited the authority of *Metaphysics* 1078b15–17 in this regard.

30. The exception, according to Santas ("The Form of the Good in Plato's *Republic*," p. 238), is the Good itself, which has as proper attributes those characteristics that count as ideal in the other Forms.

31. Santas' discussion of feature (1) is notably perfunctory, occurring as it does within the final few sentences of a lengthy and otherwise carefully argued article.

32. Which MacIntyre, for one, denies. See MacIntyre "The Form of the Good . . . ," p. 249.

33. It might also be suggested that the "very important Kinds" of the *Sophist* were not available to Plato when the *Republic* was being written. Be this as it may, if Plato had felt the need for such Forms in the *Republic*, he could have brought them to bear without obvious difficulty. What is not apparent in any case is why the Good should have been conceived as the source of properties like eternal existence which *in themselves* do not appear to be unqualifiedly good (consider, e.g., the eternal existence of a superlatively evil being).

34. Mitchell Miller seems to show awareness of this problem in proposing that the Good should be thought of as ' "the perfect" *as such*' ("Platonic Provocations," p. 182, author's emphasis). But this in turn gives rise to the question why Plato assigned this role to a Form corresponding to the *noncomparative* "good" only, rather than to a Form *to teleion* ("the Perfect") or such like.

35. Santas, "The Form of the Good in Plato's *Republic*," pp. 247, 251.

36. As noted in chapter 3, the term *paradigma* was commonly used in other senses as well.

37. These are standard features of the Forms, recognized under one or another set of descriptions by most commentators on Plato. A fuller description on my part may be found in the introduction to my *Plato's Late Ontology*. It may be noted that Aristotle fixed upon the knowability of the Forms as their most important feature (see *Metaphysics* 1078b12–17), but also that if the Forms were divested of their role as standards there would be no practical reason for anyone to want to know them.

38. As noted above, Santas' account requires the assumption of "non-Pauline self-predication" ("The Form of the Good in Plato's *Republic*," p. 239). To make this assumption for all Forms across the board is sufficiently problematic by itself to cast doubt upon this account.

39. Consider, for example, the fact that the standards for measuring the intensity of earthquakes provided by the Richter scale are not themselves earthquakes of paradigmatic magnitudes.

40. An occurrence of this unusual form may be found in Aristotle's *Rhetoric* 1388b6. There are no occurrences in Plato.

41. Their properties as Forms, I should think, ought to be due exclusively to their own natures. In this, I am inclined to side with MacIntyre against Santas (see MacIntyre, "The Form of the Good, Tradition and Enquiry," p. 249).

42. The term *proseinai* occurs infrequently in Plato, related occurrences being at *Republic* 347C1, *Meno* 78D10 and *Phaedo* 96E3. The sense is distinctly that of something being added to the other Forms rather than of the other Forms being produced by or derivative from the Good (as in the translations of Cornford, Shorey, Jowett, et al.).

43. See Santas, "The Form of the Good in Plato's *Republic*," p. 237. In support of his use of the term 'cause' in this connection, Santas refers to 517C. What this later passage says, however, is that the Good is the cause of all right and beautiful things, not that it is the cause of the other Forms generally.

44. This reading of *alētheia* in its several occurrences at 508E–509A preserves parallelism with the power of visibility (*tēn tou horasthai dunamin:* 509B2–3) provided by the sun. Although Santas is right in singling out eternality and changelessness as the attributes that make the Forms *proper* objects of knowledge, in these passages Plato is concerned with what makes them *available* to the knower. The Forms are available not because they are changeless; the attribute that makes them available, rather, is explicitly identified as their truth.

45. It is a matter of interest that the term *koinōnein* is used for the relation between the knowing mind and its object at *Sophist* 248A10 and 248B2, suggesting a parallel with the "single body" (*hen sōma:* 45C5) said in the *Timaeus* to be formed by the mingling of the two fluxes involved in vision.

46. If the approach of this chapter is on the right track, it is simply a mistake to attempt to fabricate a general theory of the Good in Plato's behalf, in the manner, e.g., of Santas' account. But this should not discourage someone from pursuing on his or her own a fuller understanding of the role this principle plays in Plato's thought. A useful list of questions to consider along the way is included in White's *Plato on Knowledge and Reality*, pp. 99–103. While some of these questions are premised on mistaken assumptions (e.g., that the non-hypothetical *archē* is a proposition or set of propositions about the Good), the reader may wish to take it as an exercise to see how many of the remaining questions are answered, at least in part, by the discussion of the present chapter.

47. Benjamin Jowett and Michael Joyce, for example. Jowett gives a similar translation to *Lysis* 216D4.

48. The correspondence is less obvious on the lower two levels. There is a sense, nonetheless, in which bodily beauty (in one person or all persons alike) is a reflection—i.e., a visible image—of the beauty of soul to which the lover progresses at the second level.

49. Socrates explicitly distinguishes *to agathon* from things that are *kalos* at *Republic* 505D. See also *Gorgias* 474C–D in this regard.

50. Because of this lack of general equivalence, it would be incorrect to think of the Good and the Beautiful as aspects of one another. The view here being advocated must be distinguished from the "dual-aspect" conception of Good and Beauty found in A. J. Festugiére, *Contemplation et vie contemplative selon Platon*, p. 206, according to which the same general principle would be called the Good in one context and the Beautiful in another.

51. It is noteworthy that the lack of identity between the nonhypothetical *archē* and the Good does not mean that the latter is absent from the Line; it is present under the aspect of Truth specifically.

52. These criteria are first stated at 20D, repeated at 22B, and reiterated in part at 60C, 61A, and 67A.

53. In *Plato's Late Ontology*, pp. 168 ff., I argue that this description may help illuminate Plato's claim that the Good is Unity, reportedly (by Aristotle, through Simplicius) made by Plato on the occasion of his Lecture on the Good. The interested reader may want to note the exchange between Phillip Mitsis and myself on the terminology of this passage in John Cleary, ed., *Proceedings of the Boston Area Colloquium in Ancient Philosophy*, vol. 2, pp. 69, 74.

54. Apart from technical applications at *Meno* 76D4 and *Republic* 330A1, A7, the term *summetria* appears only twice before the *Theaetetus*—at *Gorgias* 525A5 and *Symposium* 196A4.

55. A brief discussion of the "visual model" of knowledge may be found in chapter 3 of Henry Teloh, *The Development of Plato's Metaphysics*. Teloh's discussion goes astray, I think, in opposing this model to the "discursive model" of dialectic (p. 145) and in suggesting that the development of Plato's thought leads him from the former to the latter (p. 100). Teloh overlooks key uses of the terminology of mental vision at *Sophist* 254A10–B1 and *Philebus* 16D8. The metaphor associating philosophic understanding with fire or bright light, it may be noted, is found throughout the middle and later writings—e.g., *Phaedo* 99D, *Republic* 508D ff., *Sophist* 254A, *Philebus* 16D, and Seventh Letter 341D, 344B.

Appendix: How to Read a Platonic Dialogue: Sunousia in the Theaetetus

1. It must be acknowledged that a few dialogues, notably the *Timaeus* and the *Laws*, do not lend themselves naturally to this characterization.

2. Notable recent contributions to scholarship on the *Theaetetus* include John McDowell's *Plato: Theaetetus*, David Bostock's *Plato's Theaetetus*, and Myles Burnyeat's *The Theaetetus of Plato*. While the present discussion is

indebted to each of these books in numerous respects, it is much too confined to engage more than a small number of the issues treated within them.

3. Along with this inevitably will come some knowledge of the major events in which these figures participated. In case the action of the dialogue engages circumstances that are not common knowledge in the history of the period, moreover, the reader should try to find out a bit about those circumstances as well. Any comprehensive history of Ancient Greece might be useful for this purpose (my favorite is J. B. Bury's *A History of Greece*). For most of the dialogues, A. E. Taylor's *Plato: The Man and His Work* is also very helpful in this regard.

4. So far nothing has been said about reading the dialogues in translation. Provided a reader is equipped with a reasonably faithful rendition of the Greek, there is no reason why he or she should not be well served by that translation through several successive readings. The translation I have chosen for the discussion below is that of Cornford, which is both highly readable and relatively literal. As one's study of a given dialogue continues, however, there comes a point where further insight into its contents requires working with the original language. When a previously Greekless reader reaches this point, his or her appetite for Plato's fare may be sufficiently whetted to provide a strong incentive for learning the language.

5. McDowell's notes on 191A–195B in *Plato: Theaetetus* are helpful in this respect. See also my *Plato's Analytic Method*, pp. 111–14.

6. Recent attempts to come to terms with this episode in the dialogue are traced in David Bostock's *Plato's Theaetetus*.

7. My own view, developed in *Plato's Analytic Method*, is that the "dream theory" is an ontological extension of the theory of perception in the first part of the dialogue, refutation of which finally defeats the strict Heraclitean without question-begging assumptions. For details, see ibid., pp. 123–30.

8. For a detailed analysis, see *Plato's Analytic Method*, pp. 130–32.

9. McDowell's *Plato: Theaetetus*, is useful in criticizing this part of the argument.

10. Chapter 1 above examines at length the parallels between Socrates' description of his midwifery at 149A–151D in the *Theaetetus* and Plato's own description of the process of arriving at philosophic knowledge in the Seventh Letter. Both contexts contain mention of the need for conversation (*sunousia*: cf. 150D4, 151A2) with a master, for hard work and dedication to the topic, and for critical examination to eliminate obstructive false opinion. And both give central importance to the fact that when philosophic truth is finally brought to light, it comes directly from within the learner's own mind (150D). No point is made in either context about prior states of mental existence in which these truths might have found their way into the learner's mind. The explanatory story about recollection in the *Meno* and the *Phaedo* is a

thing of the past. What Plato is concerned with in this regard from the *Theaetetus* onward is how knowledge can be *elicited* from the potentially knowledgeable mind.

11. By "positive argument" here I mean something more highly structured in terms of premises and conclusions than the series of considerations underlying the theory of perception at 156A–157C.

12. Although the extensive use of this symbolism in Books VI and VII of the *Republic* does not mean that mention of the sun should be understood as having the same significance in every subsequent occurrence (*Timaeus* 38D is a clear counterinstance), it would be obtuse not to keep its imagery in mind while dealing with later contexts that share concerns with this earlier context.

13. There are disanalogies between the two accounts, of course. In the mathematical definition, the powers themselves are incommensurable, whereas in the account of perception it is the offspring of the powers that lack a common measure. In the mathematical case, moreover, some surds are commensurable with other surds; the square root of 8, for instance, shares a measure with the square root of 2—namely, the square root of 2 itself. But the relationship of interest between these two accounts is not one of mere analogy. It is a matter rather of the powers in the mathematical definition symbolizing certain things about the treatment of power in the later context.

14. My paraphrase. See McDowell's commentary on this passage in his *Plato: Theaetetus.*

15. In Xenophon's *Symposium* iii. 10, Socrates claims he could make a lot of money as a procurer (*mastropos*) if he cared to do so.

16. This emphasis on the internal origin of knowledge is one feature of the midwife passage that ties it to the account of the onset of knowledge in the Seventh Letter.

17. The term, as already noted, appears at 150D4, 150E4, and 151A2. Use of this term is another feature of the midwife passage shared with the account of philosophic instruction in the Seventh Letter.

18. This anomaly has been pointed out by R. G. Wengert in his "The Paradox of the Midwife."

19. One possible way of reconciling Socrates' midwifery with his lack of wisdom is to allow him powers to assist at the "birth of true opinion" only, on the grounds that he surely has had the requisite experience in that regard. A problem with this way out is that Socrates could scarcely distinguish true opinion from knowledge before delivery, so that he might find himself delivering knowledge inadvertently. It would be grotesque to consider his throwing out such offspring along with the "wind eggs" (210B9) just because he was not "qualified" to bring them to light.

20. Various common senses of *aisthēsis* and *epistēmē* are ruled out by the other arguments between 163A and 165B; see section 2 above in this regard.

21. Repeated reference to the court of law as the venue where rhetoricians hold forth may furthermore remind the reader of Socrates' impending trial.

22. Definitions along the same line are given also at *Sophist* 264A and *Philebus* 38D–E.

23. Cornford's translation of Socrates' final assessment of the results of the conversation at 210A9–B2, it might be noted, is unduly assertive, in having him say that neither perception, nor true belief (judgment), nor an account (*logos*) added to true belief "can be" (*an eiē:* 210B2) knowledge. A more accurate rendition of *an eiē* under the circumstances would replace 'can' with 'might', after the spirit of McDowell's 'it would seem'. The sense, in brief, is that it *appears* at this point that knowledge is not true judgment, a sense reinforced by Theaetetus' response "*Ouk eoiken*"—"apparently not."

24. Not only is there place for extension of the method of hypothesis into the *Sophist*, but moreover the method of collection and division has already made its appearance in the *Theaetetus*. Anyone who takes the small amount of time and trouble needed to diagram the five attempts to define true and false judgment following the second hypothesis (illustrated on pp. 107–15 of my *Plato's Analytic Method*) will see distinct similarities with the definitions of Angling and of Sophistry in the *Sophist* following. Although the *Theaetetus* is structured overall according to the method of hypothesis, it appears that both hypothesis and division are allowed to fail in the conversation between Theaetetus and Socrates.

25. See *Plato's Theory of Knowledge*, pp. 162–63. Cornford's interpretation has been challenged by a number of prominent commentators, including R. I. Robinson (in "Forms and Error in Plato's *Theaetetus*,"), W. G. Runciman (in *Plato's Later Epistemology*, p. 28), and John McDowell, (in *Plato: Theaetetus*, pp. 257–59). A useful recent survey of the issue can be found in the essay accompanying R. A. H. Waterfield's translation of the *Theaetetus*, pp. 241 ff.

26. Cornford, *Plato's Theory of Knowledge*, pp. 162–63. The main problem with Cornford's interpretation, I take it, is that nothing about the *Theaetetus* indicates clearly that the alleged failure results from knowledge not being provided permanent objects in that particular context, or that a satisfactory definition would have resulted had the Forms been available.

27. Nicholas White, for instance, suggests in his *Plato: On Knowledge and Reality* that the problem with the final sense of *logos* brings Plato back to the paradox of inquiry in the *Meno* (p. 181), for which at this point he has no ready answer (p. 183). The view of David Bostock, in his *Plato's Theaetetus*, for another example, is that Plato is driven by his own arguments to admit some knowledge that amounts to nothing more than true belief (p. 267), which effectively provides a counterexample to the final definition of knowledge as true belief with the addition of *logos*. Other philosophers taking similar tacks are noted by Burnyeat in *The Theaetetus of Plato*, p. 235n. 125.

28. There is nothing novel in the thought that the *Theaetetus* has the capacity to lead the reader to results beyond those achieved by the members of the immediate conversation. Gail Fine, for instance, has offered an interpretation of the "dream theory" according to which *logos* as an enumeration of elements is replaced by a manner of accounting for elements by "locating them within a systematic framework, interconnecting and interrelating them" ("Knowledge and *Logos* in the *Theaetetus*," p. 386). Her view is that this "interrelational model of knowledge" (p. 394) provides relief from the apparent circularity coming with the final sense of *logos* as knowledge of a thing's distinguishing mark.

29. In the final pages of his introduction in *The Theaetetus of Plato*, Burnyeat mentions several alternative senses of *logos*, but goes on to argue that none of them avoids regress, suggesting that several senses of the term might be required to provide an adequate account of knowledge in its various circumstances.

30. There might indeed be problems with these senses of *logos* as well, such as those explored by White in his *Plato on Knowledge and Reality* (pp. 180 ff.). But this in itself does not explain Plato's not having even brought these senses up for consideration.

31. This is explained in section 3 above.

32. The work of Burnyeat, Bostock, Waterfield, and White, among others, deserves mention in this regard.

33. As already noted, Burnyeat draws attention, in *The Theaetetus of Plato*, p. 240, to the possibility that several senses of *logos* might be needed for a definition of knowledge.

34. Further evidence that knowledge, in Plato's view, does not contain judgment as a component can be found at *Timaeus* 37B–C, where judgment is traced back to the "circle of the Different" (37B7), while knowledge is said to find its origin in the "circle of the Same" (37C2) instead. Since these two "circles" move on different planes entirely, there is no question of knowledge being produced from judgment by the addition of some other element.

BIBLIOGRAPHY

Annas, J. *An Introduction to Plato's Republic*. Oxford: Clarendon Press, 1981.

Arieti, James A. *Interpreting Plato: The Dialogues as Drama*. Savage, Md.: Rowman & Littlefield, 1991.

Bostock, David. *Plato's Theaetetus*. Oxford: Clarendon Press, 1988.

Brandwood, Leonard. *The Chronology of Plato's Dialogues*. Cambridge: University Press, 1990.

Brentlinger, John, ed. *The Symposium of Plato*, trans. S. Q. Groden. Amherst: University of Massachusetts Press, 1970.

Brisson, Luc. *Platon: Lettres*. Paris: Flammarion, 1987.

Burnet, John. *Greek Philosophy*. Part I. London: Macmillan, 1920.

Burnyeat, Myles. "Platonism and Mathematics: A Prelude to Discussion." In *Mathematics and Metaphysics in Aristotle*, ed. Andreas Graeser. Bern: P. Haupt, 1987.

———. "Socratic Midwifery, Platonic Inspiration." *Bulletin of the Institute of Classical Studies* 24 (1977): 7–16.

———. *The Theaetetus of Plato*, trans. M. J. Levett. Indianapolis: Hackett Publishing Company, 1990.

Bury, J. B. *A History of Greece*. New York: Modern Library, 1937 (with frequent subsequent editions).

Campbell, Lewis. *The Sophistes and Politicus of Plato*. Oxford: Clarendon Press, 1867.

Cleary, John J., ed. *Proceedings of the Boston Area Colloquium in Ancient Philosophy* 2 (1987).

Cleary, John J., and W. Wians, eds. *Proceedings of the Boston Area Colloquium in Ancient Philosophy* 9 (1993).

Cornford, F. M. "The Doctrine of Eros in Plato's *Symposium*." Reprinted in Gregory Vlastos, ed., *Plato*, vol. 2: 119–31.

———. *Plato and Parmenides*. London: Routledge & Kegan Paul, 1939.

———. *Plato's Theory of Knowledge*. London: Routledge & Kegan Paul, 1935.

———. trans. *The Republic of Plato*. Oxford: University Press, 1941.

Dover, Kenneth. *Greek Homosexuality*. London: Duckworth, 1978.

——, ed. *Plato: Symposium*. Cambridge Greek and Latin Classics, 1980.

Dreyer, John Paul. "The Driving Ratio in Plato's Divided Line." *Ancient Philosophy* 10, (1990): 159–72.

Edelstein, Ludwig. *Plato's Seventh Letter*. Leiden: E. J. Brill, 1966.

Festugiére, A.-J. *Contemplation et vie contemplative selon Platon*. Paris: Libraire Philosophique J. Vrin, 1967.

Fine, Gail. "Knowledge and *Logos* in the *Theaetetus*." *The Philosophical Review* 88 (1979): 366–97.

Gaiser, K. "Plato's Enigmatic Lecture 'On the Good.'" *Phronesis* 25 (1980): 5–37.

Gentzler, Jyl. "*Sumphōnein* in Plato's *Phaedo*." *Phronesis* 36, no. 3 (1991): 265–76.

Gould, Thomas. *Platonic Love*. New York: Free Press of Glencoe, 1963.

Griswold, Charles. *Self-Knowledge in Plato's Phaedrus*. New Haven: Yale University Press, 1986.

Groden, S. Q., trans. *The Symposium of Plato*, ed. John Brentlinger. Amherst: University of Massachusetts Press, 1970.

Grote, George. *Plato and Other Companions of Socrates*. London: John Murray, 1865.

Gulley, N. "The authenticity of the Platonic Epistles." In *Pseudepigrapha*, vol. 18, K. von Fritz, ed. Entretiens Hardt. Vandoeuves Geneva, 1971.

Guthrie, W. K. C. *A History of Greek Philosophy*. vol. 5. Cambridge: University Press, 1978.

——. *Socrates*. Cambridge: University Press, 1971.

——. *The Sophists*. Cambridge: University Press, 1971.

Halperin, David. *One Hundred Years of Homosexuality*. London: Routledge, 1990.

Kahn, Charles. "Did Plato Write Socratic Dialogues?" *Classical Quarterly* 31 (1981): 305–20.

——. "Drama and Dialectic in Plato's *Gorgias*." In *Oxford Studies in Ancient Philosophy*, vol. 1, pp. 75–121. Oxford: Clarendon Press, 1983.

Karsten, H. T. *Commentatio Critica de Platonis quae ferunter Epistolis*. Utrecht, 1864.

Kerford, G. B. *The Sophistic Movement*. Cambridge: University Press, 1981.

Kirk, G. S., J. E. Raven, and M. Schofield. *The Presocratic Philosophers*. 2nd ed. Cambridge: University Press, 1983.

Klagge, James C., and Nicholas D. Smith, eds. *Oxford Studies in Ancient Philosophy*, Supplementary Volume. Oxford: Clarendon Press, 1992.

Krämer, Hans Joachim. *Plato and the Foundations of Metaphysics*. Ed. and trans. John R. Caton. Albany: State University of New York Press, 1990.

Ledger, Gerard R. *Re-counting Plato: A Computer Analysis of Plato's Style*. Oxford: Clarendon Press, 1989.

Lennox, James G. "Plato's Unnatural Teleology." In *Platonic Investigations*, ed. Dominic J. O'Meara. Washington, D.C.: Catholic University of America Press, 1985.

Liddell, Henry G., and Robert Scott, eds. *A Greek-English Lexicon*. Oxford: Oxford University Press, 1883. *A Greek-English Lexicon*. Revised and augmented by H. S. Jones. Oxford: Oxford University Press, 1968.

MacIntyre, Alasdair. *After Virtue*. Notre Dame, Ind.: University of Notre Dame Press, 1981.

——. "The Form of the Good, Tradition and Enquiry." Chapter 12 in *Value and Understanding: Essays for Peter Winch*, ed. R. Gaita. London: Routledge, 1990.

McDowell, John. *Plato: Theaetetus*. Oxford: Clarendon Press, 1973.

Meinwald, Constance. *Plato's Parmenides*. New York: Oxford University Press, 1991.

Miller, Mitchell. "Platonic Provocations: Reflections on the Soul and the Good in the *Republic*." In *Platonic Investigations*, D. J. O'Meara, ed. Washington, D.C.: Catholic University Press, 1985.

——. *Plato's Parmenides: The Conversion of the Soul*. Princeton: University Press, 1986.

Morrow, Glenn. *Plato's Epistles*. Indianapolis: Bobbs-Merrill, 1962.

O'Connor, David. "The Erotic Self-Sufficiency of Socrates: A Reading of Xenophon's *Memorabilia*." In *The Socratic Movement*, ed. Paul A. Vander Waerdt, pp. 151–80. Ithaca: Cornell University Press, 1994.

Robinson, R. I. "Forms and Error in Plato's *Theaetetus*." *Philosophical Review* 59 (1950): 3–30.

——. *Plato's Earlier Dialectic*. Oxford: Clarendon Press, 1953.

Rosen, Stanley. *Plato's Symposium*. New Haven: Yale University Press, 1968.

Ross, W. D. "The Sun and the Good." In Sesonske, Alexander, ed., *Plato's Republic*.

Runciman, W. G. *Plato's Later Epistemology*. Cambridge: University Press, 1962.

Ryle, Gilbert. *Plato's Progress*. Cambridge: University Press, 1966.

Santas, Gerasimos. "The Form of the Good in Plato's *Republic*." In *Essays in Ancient Greek Philosophy*, ed. J. P. Anton and A. Preus. Albany: SUNY Press, 1983.

——. "Plato's *Protagoras* and Explanations of Weakness." *Philosophical Review* 75, no. 1, (1966): 3–33.

Sayre, K. M. "A Maieutic View of Five Late Dialogues." In Klagge and Smith, eds., *Oxford Studies in Ancient Philosophy*, Supplementary Volume (1992), pp. 221–43.

——. "The *Philebus* and the Good: The Unity of the Dialogue in which the Good Is Unity." In Cleary, ed., *Proceedings of the Boston Area Colloquium in Ancient Philosophy* 2 (1987), pp. 45–71.

——. *Plato's Analytic Method*. Chicago: University of Chicago Press, 1969.

——. *Plato's Late Ontology: A Riddle Resolved*. Princeton: University Press, 1983.

——. "Propositional Logic in Plato's *Protagoras*." *Notre Dame Journal of Formal Logic* 4, no. 4 (1963): 306–12.

——. "Why Plato Never Had a Theory of Forms." In Cleary and Wians, eds., *Proceedings of the Boston Colloquium in Ancient Philosophy* 9 (1993), 167–93.

——. Review of H. J. Krämer, *Plato and the Foundations of Metaphysics*. *Ancient Philosophy* 13, no. 1, (1993): 167–84.

Sesonske, Alexander, ed. *Plato's Republic: Interpretation and Criticism*. Belmont, Calif.: Wadsworth, 1966.

Solmsen, Friedrich. Review of Edelstein's *Plato's Seventh Letter* in *Gnomon* 41 (1969): 29–34.

Sprague, R. K. *Plato's Use of Fallacy: A Study of the Euthydemus and Some Other Dialogues*. London: Routledge & Kegan Paul, 1962.

Tarrant, Harold. "Middle Platonism and the *Seventh Epistle*." *Phronesis* 28 (1983): 75–103.

Taylor, A. E. *Plato: The Man and His Work*. London: Methuen & Co., 1926.

Teloh, Henry. *The Development of Plato's Metaphsyics*. University Park: Pennsylvania State University Press, 1981.

Thomas, Ivor. *Greek Mathematical Works*, vol. 1. Loeb edition, Cambridge, Mass.: Harvard University Press, 1941.

Vlastos, Gregory. "*Isonomia politike*." In his *Platonic Studies*. Princeton: University Press, 1973.

——. "A Note on 'Pauline Predications' in Plato." *Phronesis* 19, no. 2 (1974).

——. *Plato*, vol. 2. Garden City: Doubleday, 1971.

——. *Socrates, Ironist and Moral Philosopher*. Ithaca: Cornell University Press, 1991.

——. "The Socratic Elenchus." In *Oxford Studies in Ancient Philosophy*, vol. 1, pp. 27–58. Oxford: Clarendon Press, 1983.

Waterfield, R. A. H. Essay accompanying his translation of the *Theaetetus*, pp. 132–246. Penguin Books, 1987.

Wengert, R. G. "The Paradox of the Midwife." *History of Philosophy Quarterly* 5 (1988): 3–10.

White, Nicholas P. *Plato on Knowledge and Reality*. Indianapolis: Hackett Publishing Company, 1976.

Whitehead, Alfred North. *Process and Reality: An Essay in Cosmology*. New York: Macmillan, 1929.

INDEX OF PASSAGES CITED

INDEX OF NAMES

GENERAL INDEX

Academy, xxi, 8–11, 256n.2
Agora, 241n.32
Alexandria, xx
Aporia, 9, 16, 43
Argument
    contentious (eristic), 16, 36, 56, 57,
      65, 97, 159
    dialectical, 36
    destructive dilemma, 38f., 50, 65, 153,
      157
Art. *See Technē*
Antilogic (*antilogikē*), 37–40, 44–47, 59,
    135, 140
Athens, 1, 2, 22, 26, 34, 37, 42, 47, 57,
    99, 107, 109, 120–23, 128, 198,
    239n.17, 241n.22, 241n.24, 241n.32,
    246n.13, 247n.18, 248n.21
Aviary, model of, 19, 66, 207, 208, 209,
    224, 229

Belief (*pistis*), 29, 215
    and false opinion, 21, 41, 51, 58, 61,
      62, 63
Benevolent cross-examination. *See*
    Elenchus

Cave, allegory of, 131f., 141, 169–73, 206,
    213, 223
Collection and division, 17, 51, 79f.,
    81ff., 85f., 87f., 91, 93f., 132, 135,
    145ff., 157f., 160, 179, 195, 222,
    265n.24

Delium, 124
Delphi, 240n.18
Dialectic, method of, xiv, xv, xvii, 1, 21,
    36, 68, 80ff., 82, 86ff., 88, 91, 93f.,
    128, 129, 131f., 134f., 143, 154, 157ff.,
    172, 175–80, 194, 195, 222, 225, 227,
    228, 262n.55
Divided Line, 29f., 114f., 132, 141,
    169–81, 189, 191, 193, 194, 215, 223,
    257n.6, 257n.9
Dream theory, 38, 206, 209ff., 217, 224,
    263n.7, 266n.28

Eudaimonia, xvii, xviii, 113
Eleatic Palamedes, 239n.9
Elenchus, xvi, xvii, 21, 23, 33–52, 56,
    58–64, 67, 70–72, 75f., 83f., 94, 125,
    128, 135, 161, 203, 211, 240n.21
    benevolent cross-examination, 14,
      16f., 23f., 33, 60f., 64, 101, 161
Eleatics, 27, 128, 156
Example. *See* Paradigm

Flux theory of vision, 187
Form
    of Beauty, 14, 78–79, 81f., 89, 92, 100,
      108, 114–20, 138f., 152f., 159,
      166, 167, 176, 182, 189ff., 193,
      243n.15
    of Good, xvi, xviii, 5, 7, 21, 85, 92,
      114, 131, 134, 138, 141, 143,
      152f., 159, 165–76, 181–91,

289